ACADEMIC SERVICE-LEARNING ACROSS DISCIPLINES

MODELS, OUTCOMES, AND ASSESSMENT

EDITED BY:
JONATHAN H. WESTOVER, PH.D.

ACADEMIC SERVICE-LEARNING ACROSS DISCIPLINES

MODELS, OUTCOMES, AND ASSESSMENT

EDITED BY:
JONATHAN H. WESTOVER, PH.D.

Common Ground

First published in Champaign, Illinois in 2012
by Common Ground Publishing LLC
as part of The Learner series

Selections and editorial matter copyright © Jonathan H. Westover 2012;
Individual chapters copyright © individual contributors 2012

Library of Congress Cataloging-in-Publication Data

Academic service-learning across disciplines : models, outcomes, and assessment / edited by
Jonathan H. Westover.

    p. cm.

Includes bibliographical references.
ISBN 978-1-86335-984-9 (pbk : alk. paper) -- ISBN 978-1-86335-985-6 (pdf)
1. Service learning. I. Westover, Jonathan H. II. Title.

LC220.5.A33 2012
361.3'7--dc23

2011034512

Table of Contents

Part VII : Examples of Service-Learning across the Disciplines

Acknowledgments

I want to thank Common Ground Publishing for providing me with a venue for publishing this edited compilation. Additionally, I would like to thank the many individuals who contributed their own research to this edited work. Of course, this book would not be possible without each of their important contributions. Most of all, I would like to publically thank my beloved wife, Jacque, and my five wonderful children (Sara, Amber, Lia, Kaylie, and David) for all of their love and support!

Contributor Information
(In Order of Contribution Appearance)

Jonathan H. Westover, Ph.D.

Jonathan H. Westover is an Assistant Professor of Business at Utah Valley University, specializing in international human resource management, organizational behavior, and adult learning. He received a Master's of Public Administration with an emphasis in Human Resource Management and Organizational Behavior from the Marriott School of Management at Brigham Young University. As a doctoral student at the University of Utah, his research interests combined comparative international sociology and the sociology of work and organizations. His ongoing research examines adult learning, social entrepreneurship, and issues of globalization, labor transformation, work-quality characteristics, and the determinants of job satisfaction cross-nationally.

Dr. Lea Ramsdell

Lea Ramsdell is Associate Professor of Spanish and Director of Latin American and Latino/a Studies at Towson University. She has published articles on Latin American women writers, cultural production in Cuba, and the Latino diaspora. She has incorporated service in the local Latino community into several of her language, literature, and culture classes and currently serves on the Civic Engagement / Service Learning Subcommittee at Towson University. In 2003, she received the State of Maryland Regents' Award for Excellence in Teaching for her efforts to motivate students to improve their language skills and cultural competency through service activities.

Jo Ann O'Quin, Ph.D.

Jo Ann O'Quin, Ph.D., Professor of Social Work, University of Mississippi She is a Clinical Psychologist that has worked in the field of gerontology for over 25 years. She incorporated service-learning in all of her classes starting in the mid 1980's before we knew the term. She continues to teach intergenerational service-learning in gerontology, even in her on-line classes.

Adriaanna Pearce

Adriaanna has been in education since 1992. She started her teaching career at a school which was followed by 12 years of College teaching in Business English and Communication. She has also been involved in developing learning material for a private training company. She completed her BEd in 1996 through Unisa and has been at Monash South Africa since February 2005 teaching Academic English to the foundation level. In 2006 she volunteered to be part of the SL pilot programme.

Regan Harwell Schaffer

Regan Harwell Schaffer is an associate professor of management and the director of academic-based service-learning and the nonprofit leadership program at Pepperdine University. She teaches community based research and a capstone course on servant leadership and continues to do research on service-learning pedagogy in management and leadership education. While at Pepperdine, Professor Schaffer has been honored with the Center for Teaching Excellence Innovative Teaching Award and the highly selective Howard A. White Award for Teaching Excellence.

C. Sheldon Woods

C. Sheldon Woods, PhD (aka Mutua Mati') is a science educator dedicated to community service and development as part of a broader understanding of scientific literacy. His research areas included, but are not limited to evolution education, HIV/AIDS education and multicultural education and increasing pre-service teacher's efficacy in teaching science. Dr. Woods is passionate about the preparation of elementary educators and the need for diversity, (which includes males) in the work force.

Dr. Esther Yogev

Esther Yogev Ph.D, is the Rector of the School of Education at the Kibbutzim College of Education at Tel Aviv. Dr. Yogev has majored in economic history and lectured at the History Departments of Tel-Aviv University and the Kibbutzim College of Education. At present, Dr. Yogev is conducting researches on the dilemmas facing history education in regions beset by a protracted, and as yet unresolved ethno-political conflict. In addition to various articles on her subjects, Dr. Yogev has published three books: *Histories, Towards a Dialogue with the Israeli Past*, (2002), Tel-Aviv, Babel Publishers (with Eyal Naveh), (in Hebrew); *General Knowledge and Culture Infrastructure: Challenges and Objectives in Teacher Training and Higher Education* (Jan. 2008), Tel Aviv, Mofet Institute (with Nimrod Aloni, Dorit Hop, and Ilana Avisar), (in Hebrew); *Designed Supervision* (with Ruth Zozovski).

Dr. Nir Michaeli

Nir Michaeli Ph.D, is the Head of the Education Department, and member of the Progressive Education Institute at the Kibbutzim College of Education in Tel Aviv, Israel. Dr. Michaeli has majored in the history and philosophy of education and interested in progressive and non-formal pedagogy, education policy and civic education. His PH.D thesis: "People for tomorrow: The New Israeli Communal Groups-Intentional Communities or Signs of Labor Movement revival" conducted at Tel Aviv University. In the past was the general manager of an Israeli Youth Movement and graduated at The Mandel Institute for Educational Leadership. Published various articles focusing on social actual and theoretical aspects of education, educational privatization and teacher's training. Dr. Michaeli has published a book: *"Change and Improvement in Educational Systems: An Anthology"* (2011), Jerusalem, The Branco Weiss Institute and Avney Rosha. (with Gal Fisher).

Dr. Barbara Sposet

Dr. Barbara Sposet is Professor ofEducation at Baldwin-Wallace College in Berea, Ohio. She is the author of two scholarly books by The Edwin Mellen Press on the topic of second language acquisition. She is one of two full-time instructors of *Education in A Diverse Society* at BW. Dr Sposet taught Spanish at the 7-12 and college levels for 30 plus years. Her research interests include diversity, culture learning and culturally-relevant pedagogy. Dr. Sposet is also the creator of a unique one-hour elective for BW education majors entitled "Communicating with Spanish Speakers in Educational Settings."

Dr. Loshini Naidoo

Dr Loshini Naidoo is a senior lecturer in sociology in the School of Education at the University of Western Sydney, Australia. Her academic areas of interest include social justice education, cultural diversity and difference and transnationalism. Her current research is related to internationalization of higher education, refugee and indigenous issues particularly literacy amongst newly arrived refugees in Greater Western Sydney secondary schools and literacy needs of Aboriginal students in Tennant Creek High, Northern Territory. She was a recipient of the Vice Chancellor's Award for Excellence in Community Engagement. She also received a citation from the Australian Teaching Learning Council for her outstanding contribution to student learning and an ALTC team winner for a program that enhances learning.

Dr. Jodie Parys

Jodie Parys is an Assistant Professor of Spanish at the University of Wisconsin-Whitewater. She teaches courses in Spanish language and Latin American literature in the Department of Languages and Literatures. Her research interests focus primarily on the intersection of disease and narrative in Latin American literature, centered specifically on the AIDS epidemic. She is also interested in literary and cultural productions from post-dictatorial Southern Cone countries, as well as the use of service learning as a pedagogical tool in Spanish language classrooms.

Dr. Carroll Tyminski

Dr. Tyminski received her doctorate in education from Temple University in 1995 and bachelor's and master's degrees from the University of North Carolina at Chapel Hill. She developed a certification program in special education, as well as a concentration in special needs. Although she has taught a wide variety of courses, her primary areas of teaching focus on the areas of inclusion and cognitive, behavioral, physical, and health impairments. Prior to joining the Elizabethtown College faculty, she taught at York College of Pennsylvania, coordinated and supervised a full inclusion program in Maryland, and taught special education students in the public schools of both Maryland and Pennsylvania.

Sharon Kossack, Ph.D.

Sharon Kossack, Ph.D., Professor of Reading, Department of Curriculum and Instruction, College of Education, University Park Campus, Florida International University Dr. Kossack coordinates school-based Professional Development Academies which deliver at-risk-student-embedded, on-site Reading M.S. degrees. Stateside coordinator of the Abaco, Bahamas, Every Child Counts literacy and special education project and cooperates with the University of the West Indies and Trinidad/Tobago Reading Association to develop a B.Ed. with specialization in Reading and M.S. degree. Serves on the Interntational Reading Association Publications Committee and reviews publications for IRA and American Reading Forum. Has been column editor for IRA.

Eric Dwyer, Ph.D.

Eric Dwyer, Ph.D., Assistant Professor of Modern Language Education, Department of Curriculum and Instruction, College of Education, University Park Campus, Florida International University

Dr. Dwyer, Assistant Professor, Modern Language Education, is associated with the TESOL (Teaching English to Speakers of Other Languages) program. Serves on Board of Directors for TESOL International. He's interested in vocabulary development of bilingual students.

Hilary Landorf, Ph.D.

Dr. Hilary Landorf is the Director of the Office of Global Learning Initiatives and an Associate Professor in the College of Education at Florida International University. She has a Ph.D. in International Education from New York University and a B.A. from Stanford University. Dr. Landorf's current research interests include integrative global learning in higher education and the connection between global learning and human capability development. She has published widely in national and international journals, and is regularly consulted for her expertise in globalizing K-20 curricula across the curriculum. Her recent publications include "Toward a philosophy of global education" in *Visions in Global Education*, and "Education for sustainable human development" in *Theory and Research in Education*.

Dr. Virginia Jagla

Dr. Virginia Jagla received her PhD from the University of Illinois at Chicago in Curriculum and Instruction, her MS from the University of Chicago, and her BS from DePaul University. She has been a teacher and administrator in urban schools, museums and arts organizations. She has taught for various colleges and universities. Currently Dr. Jagla is an Associate Professor at National Louis University in the Chicago area. She is co-editor of the online journal *i.e.: Inquiry in Education*. She leads the university Service-Learning Team. Dr. Jagla has a published book, *Teachers' Everyday Use of Imagination and Intuition: In Pursuit of the Elusive Image*, and numerous published chapters and articles in various juried journals. She is a frequent presenter at local, national, and international conferences and symposia. Her research interests include imagination and intuition in education, the use of the visual and creative arts in education, with particular emphasis on creative drama; and service-learning, particularly as it applies to middle level education.

Assist.Prof. Pinar Girmen

Eskisehir Osmangazi University, Turkey

Dr.Leisa Martin

I am currently working as an Assistant Professor in Middle Level Education at The University of Akron in Akron, Ohio, United States. My background includes previous work as a middle school social studies teacher, a tutor, and a university Assistant Professor. My work deals with students' and teachers' perceptions about domestic and international citizenship behavior.

Dr.Lynn Smolen

I am currently working as a Professor of Literacy and Teaching English as a Second Language at The University of Akron in Akron, Ohio, United States. My background includes work as an elementary school teacher and reading teacher. My research focus is on multicultural and global literature as well as second language teaching and learning and diversity issues.

Dr. Doreen S. Geddes,

Associate Professor of Communication Studies, Department of Communication Studies, Clemson University

Dr. Doreen Geddes teaches courses in gender, nonverbal and small group communication in the Department of Communication Studies at Clemson University. She includes service learning in her classes and has worked with two African service learning projects that were communication-intensive. Her areas of research interest are gender communication, international service learning, and global perspectives on communication in families with an alcoholic.

Dr. Duncan MacLellan

Duncan MacLellan is an Associate Professor in the Department of Politics and Public Administration at Ryerson University, and his teaching and research interests include educational politics and policy making at the local and provincial levels, state and teacher relations, and local and urban governance issues. Duncan has published articles and book chapters on teacher unionism and school board leadership, and he is one of the authors of the book, Teachers' Unions in Canada.

Dr. Claudia Pragman

Dr. Claudia H. Pragman is a Professor in the Management Department at Minnesota State University, Mankato. She earned her Ph.D. in the management disciplines from the University of Nebraska-Lincoln. At the undergraduate level she has taught principles of management and operations management regularly, as well as statistics at the graduate level. Her recent research interests include service learning, teamwork, evaluating team performance, and teaching business ethics and corporate social responsibility.

Dr. Brenda Flannery

Dr. Flannery is an Associate Professor of Management in the College of Business at Minnesota State University, Mankato. Her teaching assignment includes Principles of Management as well as undergraduate and graduate classes in Leadership. She is currently serving as Assistant Vice President for Undergraduate Studies and International Education.

Donna L. Cowan
Rachel Faber Machacha
Cheryl Hausafus
Margaret Torrie

Karen Videtic

Professor Videtic has taught retail buying, fashion merchandising, product development, management, and fashion branding in VCU 's Department of Fashion Design and Merchandising since 1984. She is the co-author of *Perry's Department Store: A Buying Simulation 3rd Edition, 2009*, and *Perry's Department Store: A Product Development Simulation*, 2006. Both textbooks are published by Fairchild Books. Professor Videtic's academic experience includes the use of simulation and action learning in courses such as buyer behavior, buying, retail store development, and line development. Ms. Videtic spent 5 months at the University of Ballarat, Australia as lecturer for the School of Business. She taught Buyer Behaviour, Management, and Human Resource Development using action learning principles. Professor Videtic's retail and wholesale fashion experience includes management, promotions, merchandise planning, product development and forecasting. She attends the NYC and Las Vegas markets on a regular basis. Professor Videtic's research interests include the expatriation of faculty teaching abroad, and alternative learning experiences such as action learning. She has developed and conducted seminars for VCU faculty and the Virginia Port Authority, Marketing Representatives on cross-cultural topics.

Dr. Allison Krogstad

Allison D. Krogstad is an Associate Professor of Spanish at Central College, Pella, Iowa, where she also chairs the Modern Languages Department and the Latin American Studies major. She earned her Ph.D. in Hispanic and Luso-Brazilian Literatures and Linguistics in 1999 from the University of Minnesota, Minneapolis. Her areas of interest include service-learning, human rights and social development (particularly in Guatemala), colonial literature and culture, and pre-Columbian cultures. Outside of work, she stays busy with her 3 little boys and husband.

Dr. Bridget Connor

Associate Professor at the College of Notre Dame for the past eight years.

Dr. Dosinda Garcia-Alvite

Dosinda Garcia-Alvite is an Associate Professor of Spanish at Denison University. She has taught several service learning courses that combined foreign language and cultures learning with service to the community. Her research interests and publications focus on: critical consciousness pedagogy, border studies, cross-cultural identities and bilingualism in the areas of both Mexico-USA and Africa-Spain.

Dr. Sharlett Gillard

University of Southern Indiana, USA

Michael W. Smith

Michael W. Smith, Ph.D., J.D. is a Full Professor in Sociology at Saint Anselm College (Manchester, N.H.). He teaches terrorism and genocide, criminology, law & society, and race & ethnicity. Dr. Smith's published research has been on terrorism, genocide, plea bargaining, official deviance, immigration and wrongful convictions. He has been a criminal defense and civil rights attorney in Massachusetts since 1993.

Byoung Sug Kim

Dr. Kim earned his Bachelor's and Master's Degree in Science Education in South Korea and Doctor of Philosophy in science education from Illinois Institute of Technology in Chicago. He is currently in the Elementary Education Program in the Department of Curricular Studies at Roosevelt University. He has taught courses in elementary science teaching methods, early childhood teaching methods, inquiry in classroom and a student teaching seminar. His main research interest is related to the nature of science, scientific inquiry, and transformative learning. He has been actively involved in a professional development project which was designed to enhance K-12 science teachers' pedagogical knowledge and skills in relation to the nature of science and scientific inquiry. In addition, he has integrated service-learning experiences into his science teaching methods courses and into an introductory chemistry course in collaboration with the science department.

Dr. Audrey Cohen

Audrey J. Cohen is an Associate Professor of Business at Kingsborough Community College in Brooklyn, NY. Dr. Cohen earned her master's and doctoral degrees at Harvard University Graduate School of Business Administration. She is on the Editorial Board of the *International Journal of Case Method Research & Application*. Recently she taught in China at the University of Shanghai for Science and Technology. As a result of those experiences, her recent papers focus on the impact of culture on the undergraduate classroom and the alleviation of poverty.

Dr. Dennis S. Gouws

Dr. Dennis Gouws is an Associate Professor at Springfield College and a Lecturer at the University of Connecticut, Storrs. His research and teaching interests include masculinities, the manhood question in Victorian literature, and the male-positive education of men and boys. He has published essays on men's issues and is writing a book on masculinities in George Eliot's novels.

Dr. Steven Newmaster

Author of more than 30 publications including the new released Flora Ontario, several botanical field Guides such as Wetland plants of Ontario, several book chapters, more than a dozen Journal articles on biodiversity and several government reports on ecosystem management and conservation. He is currently working on over 20 generic treatments and 4 family treatments for the Flora of North America (FNA) Project, with the Missouri Botanical Gardens, and writing books on bryophytes and ethnobotany. His research program, the "Floristic Diversity Research Group" (FDRG) has generated over $3 million dollars in biodiversity research. The FDRG is well situated within the Biodiversity Institute of Ontario (BIO) OAC Herbarium here they conduct research in patterning of floristic diversity, anthropogenic impacts on biodiversity, taxonomy, invasive species biology and ethnobotany. Accomplishments of the FDRG include the development of the Flora Ontario Integrated Botanical Information Service (FOIBIS), The Ontario Invasive Plant Information Service (OIPIS), a digital identification system for plants Polyclavis© (Newmaster & Ragupathy 2004), a new sampling methodology for biodiversity studies "Floristic Habitat Sampling" (Newmaster et al. 2005) and front-line research on a molecular identification system for plants with the internationally recognized Barcode of Life Network.

Introduction

While service-learning is not a new phenomenon, this "civically-engaged" experiential learning pedagogy has increased in popularity and usage in educational settings in recent years. As we live in an increasingly hyper-competitive and interconnected globalized world, where consumers and citizens are demanding greater levels of corporate social responsibility and civic engagement from organizational leaders within their local community, service-learning is being utilized more and more to provide meaningful community service opportunities that simultaneously teach civic responsibility and encourage life-long civic engagement, while also providing opportunities for significant real-life, hands-on learning of important skills and vital social understanding for students.

This edited collection will help you answer the following questions:

- What is service-learning and how do I know if service-learning activities are right for my curriculum?
- What are the common service-learning models and how can they be adapted to be effectively utilized in my specific course?
- What are the educational, professional development, and other student outcomes of using service-learning activities in my course?
- How can the successes of my service-learning efforts be effectively assessed?
- What are some examples of effective service-learning efforts across different academic disciplines?

These are just some of the pressing questions facing the educational and community leaders of today.

Overview of the Format of the Book

This edited collection provides a comprehensive introduction to service-learning, its outcomes, and approaches to effective assessment of service-learning activities, presenting a wide range of cross-disciplinary research in an organized, clear, and accessible manner. It will be informative to both K-12 and higher education teaching professionals, administrators, students, and community leaders seeking to understand proven practices and methods for effective Service-Learning implementation across academic disciplines.

This book is comprised of 18 core chapters and 10 service-learning examples, divided into seven parts: (1) An Overview of Service-Learning, (2) Service-Learning Models, (3) Service-Learning and Diversity Education Outcomes, (4) Service-Learning and Teacher Education Outcomes, (5) Service-Learning and other Student Outcomes, (6) Assessment of Service-Learning, and (7) Examples of Service-Learning across the Disciplines. Each part starts with a brief overview, outlining the overall theme of the section and specific chapters that it contains.

Chapters 1-3 make up Part 1 of the book, which provides a general overview to service-learning. Chapter 1 looks at the role of reciprocity in the service-learning pedagogy. Chapter 2 explores how one can implement service-learning in a higher educational setting. Chapter 3 looks at the pros and cons of adopting a service-learning approach in your courses.

Chapters 4-6 make up Part 2 of the book, which focuses on models of service-learning. Chapter 4 looks at an effective service-learning model in higher education. Chapter 5 explores community-based learning as a core component to service-learning. Chapter 6 provides a look at a democratic civic education model.

Chapters 7-10 make up Part 3 of the book, which focuses on service-learning and diversity education outcomes. Chapter 7 explores the need for diversity education in an increasingly diverse society, from a sociological perspective. Chapter 8 looks at the role of service-learning in transnational learning. Chapter 9 explores usung service learning as a means to broad one's worldview and understand diverse cultural perspectives. Finally, Chapter 10 explores using service-learning to promote a sense of belonging.

Chapters 11-13 make of Part 4 of the book, which focuses on service-learning and teacher education outcomes. Chapter 11 explores service-learnings role in "authentic academics." Chapter 12 looks at how service-learning increases a teacher's capacity to meet the needs of diverse learners. Chapter 13 looks at the role of service-learning in teacher preparation and professional development.

Chapters 14 and 15 make up Part 5 of the book, which focuses on service-learning and other student outcomes not previously discussed. Chapter 14 looks at using service-learning as a learning mechanism to promote citizenship education and promote social justice. Chapter 15 explores service-learning's role in preparing students for the global workplace.

Chapters 16-18 make up Part 6 of the book, which focuses on service-learning assessment. Chapter 16 first addresses the need for effective service-learning assessment strategies. Chapter 17 explores different service-learning assessment methods. Chapter 18 looks at the importance of student reflection in service-learning.

Part 7 of the book is made up of 10 different examples of service-learning courses taught across a wide variety of disciplines, including: (1) fashion design, (2) Spanish, (3) math, (4) foreign language, (5) information systems, (6) sociology, (7) science, (8) management, (9) literature, and (10) biology.

Part I
An Overview of Service-Learning

Overview

Chapters 1-3 make up Part 1 of the book, which provides a general overview to service-learning. Chapter 1 looks at the role of reciprocity in the service-learning pedagogy. Chapter 2 explores how one can implement service-learning in a higher educational setting. Chapter 3 looks at the pros and cons of adopting a service-learning approach in your courses.

Chapter 1

The Heart of Service-Learning

Reciprocity

The Heart of Service-Learning

Lea Ramsdell, Assistant Professor of Spanish, Department of Modern Languages, Towson University, USA

Abstract: Service-learning is a pedagogy deeply grounded in John Dewey's conceptualization of civic engagement and Paulo Freire's model of transformative education (Deans 15). In recent years, the value of such a pedagogy to institutions, students, and the community has been heralded in countless studies that have proven its effectiveness (Vogelgesang and Astin 25). Yet, as Lori Varlotta observes, few people on university campuses are able to articulate what is meant by service-learning (83). Indeed, they often conflate the term with other related approaches to student involvement outside the classroom, such as community service, civic engagement or experiential learning. A probe of the distinctive character of service-learning necessitates an examination of the theory and practice of reciprocity. The following discussion of the theoretical importance of reciprocity is accompanied by practical guidelines for designing a service-learning course.

In recent years, the value of service-learning as a pedagogy has been heralded in countless studies that have proven its effectiveness (Vogelgesang and Astin 25). Yet, as Lori Varlotta observes, few people on university campuses are able to articulate what is meant by service-learning (83). Indeed, they often conflate the term with other approaches to student involvement outside the classroom, such as community service, civic engagement or experiential learning. Yet service-learning is a pedagogy deeply grounded in John Dewey's conceptualization of education as a democratizing force and Paulo Freire's model of transformative education, both of which underline the importance of the dialectic of reflection with action, theory with praxis (Deans 15). What sets service-learning apart from other modes of experiential education is the reciprocity between the learning and the service, the interaction between the academic course content and the practical experience as well as between the student and the community agency being served. The following discussion of the theoretical importance of reciprocity is accompanied by practical guidelines for designing a service-learning course. Specific examples are drawn from my experience in facilitating service-learning courses for composition and literature courses in Spanish.

Because of the general lack of understanding regarding the role of reciprocity in service-learning, "faculty are reluctant to invest the extra time that teaching service-learning courses entails, and many are skeptical of the educational value of service-learning" (Gray 103). Faculty must be convinced that the methodology is more than simply student volunteerism. As Varlotta emphasizes, in order for a service-learning course to be successful, the "learning," or academic component must be equally important as the "service" (83). The implications of this are far-reaching because the volunteer work must be directly tied to the course curriculum and integrated into class activities and assignments. According to G. Markus, J. Howard and D. King, "The kinds of service activities in which students participate should be selected so that they will illustrate, affirm, extend and challenge material presented in readings and lectures" (417). If the student serves in the community, but cannot make the connection between that service and the course content, then reciprocity has not been achieved, regardless of how positive the learner may be about the experience. An example is cited by Pierrette Hondagneu-Sotelo and Sally Raskoff, who made the following observation in relation to sociology courses with no activities that incorporated the service experience: "students typically approached the end of the semester and the required paper with the response 'I enjoyed my work in the community, but what did it have to do with sociology?'" (250).

Integration thus becomes the principal feature distinguishing service-learning from community service. It also represents a great challenge to the instructor for it requires a course design in which the service experience is analyzed, discussed, and compared to other texts in the course. While integration is key to maintaining reciprocity between the service and the learning, it is often problematic for instructors accustomed to more traditional approaches to teaching. On university campuses, "the thinking has been that the place for service is outside the classroom – done on a student's 'own time'" (Vogelgesang and Astin 25). Changing this mindset so that integration becomes possible requires a paradigm that instructors and students alike can readily understand.

Varlotta's conceptualization of the service experience as one of the "texts" that is studied in a service-learning course is extremely useful for facilitating the integration of the community work into the course. She emphasizes that, because the service text is more fluid than written "academic" texts, a degree of flexibility must be built into the course so that sufficient time is allowed for this nontraditional text to be addressed. She outlines three basic types of service-learning courses based on the degree to which the service text is integrated into the course. Though all three are legitimate forms of service-learning, each comes with its own set of advantages and disadvantages.

In the multitextual course, the service text is recommended to students, but not required. With its status as "recommended reading," the number of students who choose to participate varies greatly. This limits the extent to which the service-text can be integrated into the course. A case in point is a Spanish Composition and Conversation course that I was teaching in which only three of the eighteen students enrolled chose to work with Spanish-speaking middle schoolers in an English as a Second Language (ESOL) program. The integration of the experience was limited to two presentations that the participants made to the rest of the class regarding their service. However, in a Contemporary Latin American Narrative class that I taught, students had the option of working in the community or reading a novel and then writing a research paper on it. In this case, sixteen of the nineteen students enrolled opted for volunteering as interpreters at a local clinic or in an ESOL program. Because of the higher level of participation, the service-text was referred to repeatedly in small group and class discussions and became the theme of a final paper for all but three of the students. Despite the limitations on integration, the multicultural course is especially appropriate for instructors who are inexperienced at designing a service-learning course and would like to test the waters. This type of course also gives them the opportunity to foment relationships with the community in order to understand how students may best work to meet their needs.

A step up from the multicultural course is the "crosstextual course," in which service is a required text, but its integration is unidirectional. For example, a course that requires that academic texts be used to analyze the service-text sets up the unidirectional relationship of theory practice. Most service-learning courses being taught today fall under this category. The Latin American Women Writers course that I teach is such a course because the students read theoretical material about coding in women's cultures and then are asked to find examples of this coding in the oral expression of the Latino immigrant women with whom they are working. But not all crosstextual courses work in the same direction. There are some in which the reverse occurs so that the service-text becomes the springboard for probing traditional texts, transforming the relationship to practice theory. Both types of crosstextual courses augment student learning by increasing their motivation and comprehension of the course material. However, the learning outcomes are limited due to the lack of complete reciprocity between the traditional texts and the service-text.

On the far end of the integration continuum, there is the intertextual course, in which "the service text (as a form of practice) and the academic texts (as forms of theory) mutually inform each other so that neither habitually occupies a privileged position in the course" (Varlotta 79). Clearly, the more highly integrated intertextual course links abstract theory and concrete practice more fully and achieves the highest degree of reciprocity. Because of this potential, Varlotta states that "intertextual integration is arguably the model to which service-learning instructors should aspire" (82). Indeed, this type of course becomes the ideal that yields the best learning outcomes, though it is not always realistic given time and administrative constraints.

Keeping the service-as-text metaphor in mind also facilitates the creation of activities designed to integrate the text into the course. Discussions in class, in small groups, online or in panels are essential for effective integration because students working in the community are in a situation where their knowledge, skills, perceptions, and values are challenged on a regular basis. They need a venue in which to talk about both the gratifying and disturbing observations that they make while on site. Small group discussions that are guided by thought-provoking questions prepared by the instructor provide the students with the opportunity to share and process what they are experiencing. They are also an excellent catalyst for class discussions and lectures that draw the connection between the material in traditional texts and the service text.

Writing assignments based on the volunteer experience may also be used to achieve integration and therefore reciprocity between the service and the learning. Journal writing is a staple for service-learning courses because it allows both students and the instructor to track the learning that occurs in relation to the service. However, in order to avoid journal entries that are nothing more than lists of activities performed rather than true reflection, each entry should be written in response to questions carefully prepared by the instructor: "Without the guidance of these questions, many students could not apply academic concepts to their community service settings" (Hondagneu-Sotelo and Raskoff 250). Fiction writing based on the community experience is another effective exercise because it prods students to imagine what life must be like for some of the individuals that they serve. In Latin American literature classes that I have taught, I have assigned the students to write short stories in which the people with whom they work in the community become the characters. The results have shown a depth of insight that the students were not always able to express in other class activities because the assignment allowed the students to see things from the perspective of the individuals being served.

Multimedia projects designed to benefit the agency are also a compelling way of integrating the service into the course. Projects put service into a package that is more manageable for the instructor and more satisfying for the students because they limit the parameters of the service and the end-product is concrete. In the Advanced Spanish Composition course that I teach, students are charged with creating an informational brochure in Spanish by the end of the semester that will be distributed not only at the agency where they have worked, but among other agencies serving Latinos as well. However, they must be active in the community and carry out substantial research in order to arrive at the thorough understanding that they need in order to produce such a brochure. Students are eager to combine their knowledge of theory and their experience in the community into a tangible form that is of use to many.

While integration of the service text in the course is essential to achieving reciprocity between the traditional texts and the service text, we academics especially must avoid the temptation to keep our focus on the learning in service-learning. Reciprocity means that the community also benefits from the relationship, which requires that the needs and limitations of the community partner be identified and respected. The fact that the proportion of scholarly articles with a focus on the community perspective of service-learning is small compared to the number of publications exhorting the benefits of service to the learner may be indicative of an overall lack of reciprocity in the practice of service-learning. Joseph Ferrari and Laurie Worrall point out that: "little research exists that focuses on the agency's views of the student service provider" (35). Indeed, monitoring student performance on site and soliciting feedback from the community agency is a time-consuming endeavor and, for that reason, is often neglected.

Precisely because many public agencies operate with limited resources, they could benefit from "community service providers" who have an expertise that they are willing to share free of charge (Ferrari and Worrall 35). Conversely, if students are ill-prepared for or resentful of the experience, they in fact represent a burden to the agencies. Many organizations are understaffed and cannot afford to devote the time necessary to train volunteer workers, especially if the return on their time investment is only an hour of work a week during one semester. In order to minimize the possibilities of such a counter-productive relationship, the public agencies must be carefully selected, class time must be devoted to preparing students for their work in the community, and evaluations of the contribution of the students must take place on a regular basis.

It is important for the instructor to develop a rapport with each organization in order for open lines of communication to be maintained. Such a rapport begins with a site visit. It is virtually impossible for the instructor to understand the agency's needs, and thus to prepare student volunteers, without being physically present to witness the surroundings in which the students will be working. During the site visit, the instructor will be able to ascertain several important aspects of the agency, including the volume and nature of its clientele, its management style, and its preparedness for volunteers. For example, organizations that have a volunteer coordinator or a volunteer program already in place will be poised to reap greater benefit from the students' expertise than will organizations that are not set up for volunteers. It is also important to determine whether the investment that the agency will have to make in the student volunteers in terms of training and monitoring will render sufficient benefit from students who work only one to two hours a week during the course of the semester.

In order to increase the probability of a fruitful partnership with the community, class time must be devoted to preparing the students to serve. The first step in this preparation phase is the identification of the needs and interests of each student so that an appropriate placement may be made. As much as possible, options should be presented to the students so that they may place themselves. In my case, I have required students to work in ESOL programs, but have given them the option to work either with children or adults. Self-placement leads to a more positive attitude regarding the volunteer work.

However, in order for the students to make an informed choice about where they want to work in the community, they need to become familiar with the mission of each of the community partners. Literature and web sites produced by the agencies should be included among the assigned readings and discussed in class. A representative from the agency, either a staff member or a client, should be made available to answer student questions. An initial orientation meeting should be scheduled at the site during class time so that students may feel comfortable about their choice or be given the opportunity to change it.

In addition to proper placement, students must be intellectually prepared to gain the most from their experience in the community. Texts that explain the basics of a service-learning methodology should be assigned and discussed so as to eliminate confusion about how community work is related to course content. I have used Zlotowski's 18-volume series on the role of service learning across a variety of disciplines because it contains excellent essays that introduce the methodology within the context of specific disciplines. In addition, Varlotta's conceptualization of service-as-text is a helpful metaphor to remind students of the academic value of the service experience. In fact, the inclusion of the service text in the syllabus as one of the texts that will be covered during the course highlights its integral role in the class. During discussions of the theory and praxis of service-learning, students need to be alerted to the "white knight syndrome" which "occurs when students position themselves as saviors" in the community (Hondagneu-Sotelo and Raskoff 251). Classwork should continually reinforce to the students the reciprocal nature and mutual benefit of their relationship with members of the community. They need to be made aware that, in exchange for providing a service, they are acquiring invaluable skills and understanding from the community.

Once the preparation phase is completed and the students begin their service, evaluation of the benefit to the agency must occur regularly and issues need to be resolved in a timely manner. Consistent, simple, and quick written or oral evaluations conducted throughout the semester are an efficient means of eliciting feedback from the community. Ferrari and Worhall, in their article "Assessments by Community Agencies: How 'the Other Side' Sees Service-Learning," outline the questions asked of community based organizations in an unpublished survey created for assessing the contribution of college students to the agencies that they served. Claudette Williams, the professor who designed the survey instrument, states that the survey was easy to administer, the community partners could complete it quickly, and the students found the questions nonthreatening (37). Any such evaluation instrument must take into account these three factors in order to be valuable.

However, one must always keep in mind that the agency is not at the service of the students or instructor. An evaluation system that does not tax the already overburdened staff must be agreed upon. Very often the personnel in organizations recoil at the thought of more paperwork in the form of written evaluations. For this reason, I have opted for informal oral evaluations from the agencies.

Feedback can be attained simply by periodic check-in calls. It was through such an exchange that I discovered that the director of the ESOL program wanted the students to bring their dictionaries to the site since quite often they were not familiar with some of the vocabulary being used in class. Though such oral exchanges allow the instructor to monitor community satisfaction with the student volunteers, ultimately the most obvious way for evaluating the benefit that the students provide to the agency is if the staff continues to request that students return semester after semester.

But the personnel of public organizations are not the only ones who can gauge the needs of the community. Student volunteers who work directly with clients also become aware of ways to better serve the community and their feedback should also be heeded. For example, a student who was working with Latino immigrants at a local clinic witnessed a frustrated mother whose daughter was denied entrance into school because she had never visited a dentist. In order to address this need, she proposed the idea that we create a brochure in Spanish explaining the medical documentation that children must have in order to be able to attend public schools. With the involvement of the student, the community, and the instructor, the evaluation process becomes reciprocal in three-directions, with the instructor playing an important role as mediator.

Reciprocity truly is at the heart of service-learning on many levels. As Vogelgesang and Astin have shown, the greater the integration of the service experience into the classroom, the greater the learning that takes place. Varlotta has made a convincing case that this integration is facilitated by the reciprocity of theory and practice, where academic texts do not take precedence over the service text. Moreover, service-learning courses must aim for reciprocity between the community and the students so that community needs and expectations are placed on an even ground with those of students. With reciprocity as the guiding principle, the service-learning experience is bound to meet with success.

References

Deans, Thomas. "Service-Learning in Two Keys: Paulo Freire's Critical Pedagogy in Relation to John Dewey's Pragmatism." *Michigan Journal of Community Service Learning* 6 (Fall 1999): 15-27.

Ferrari, Joseph R. and Laurie Worrall. "Assessments by Community Agencies: How 'the Other Side' Sees Service-Learning." *Michigan Journal of Community Service Learning* 7 (Fall 2000): 35-40.

Gray, M. J., et al. *Combining Service and Learning in Higher Education: Evaluation of the Learn and Serve America, Higher Education Program.* Santa Monica, CA: RAND, 1999.

Hondagneu-Sotelo, Pierrette and Sally Raskoff. "Community Service-Learning: Promises and Problems." *Teaching Sociology* 22 (July 1994): 248-254.

Markus, G.B., J. Howard and D.C. King. "Integrating community Service and Classroom Instruction Enhances Learning: Results from an Experiment." *Educational Evaluation and Policy Analysis* 15 (1993): 410-419.

Varlotta, Lori. "Service as Text: Making the Metaphor Meaningful." *Michigan Journal of Community Service Learning* 7 (Fall 2000): 76-84. Vogelgesang, Lori J. and Alexander W. Astin. "Comparing the Effects of Community Service and Service-Learning." *Michigan Journal of Community Service Learning* 7 (Fall 2000): 25-34. Zlotowski, Edward, ed. *Service Learning in the Disciplines* [an 18 volume series]. American Association of Higher Education, 1997-2000.

Chapter 2
Serve to Learn, Learn to Serve

Serve to Learn, Learn to Serve

Implementing Service-Learning in Higher Education

Jo Ann O'Quin

Gaining widespread attention in higher education in the United States since the early 1990s, the concept of service-learning has been implemented in a variety of educational settings from K-12 to higher education. The Corporation for National and Community Service and Campus Compact are two important entities in this movement that have provided funding and technical assistance to support the tremendous growth especially in higher education settings nationwide (Bringle & Hatcher, 2002, p.117). There is a proliferation of material on service-learning that describes and delineates the range of ideas and outcomes of this teaching process. Service-learning is implemented at many levels of the educational process and in a variety of settings where service and learning intersect. This paper will focus on introducing service-learning concepts in the higher education settings at both undergraduate and graduate levels by presenting an overview of common definitions and goals, examples of implementation in specific disciplines and courses, and suggest resources for successful integration of service-learning in a university setting.

Defining Service-Learning

A variety of definitions of service-learning exist. According to the National and Community Trust Act of 1993, service-learning "is a method whereby students learn and develop through active participation in thoughtfully organized service that is conducted in and meets the needs of communities "(Corporation for National & Community Service, 2002, p. 12). We conceptualize service-learning as a teaching method that directs students to apply critical thinking skills and academic knowledge to meet genuine community needs through service. The goal is to integrate service with the academic enterprise so that the service experience reinforces and strengthens the learning and the learning reinforces and strengthens the service. Simply put, one of the primary goals is "serve to learn, learn to serve" (O'Quin, 2002).

Furco (2000) recites a list of over ten different definitions of service-learning each varying around the theme of experiential education. Given that the scope of what is described as service-learning may actually vary and a single model is not available, presenting a concise model and conducting evaluation research is a challenge. Most models are more or less consistent with the 1993 Act in addressing the following key service learning goals: coordinate schools and community efforts; foster civic responsibility; enhance the curriculum and education components; and provide for structured time for reflection (Corporation for National & Community Service, 2002, p.12). Ideally, service activities enhance academic knowledge through real world experiences and, additionally, foster civic responsibility and professional or career development by exposing students to real-world experiences with potential employers in community agencies in real-world settings. Nonetheless, as noted by Eyler (2002), "the actual experiences of students range from intensive community experiences with close integration into academic study to brief 'add on' service activities largely unconnected to classroom discourse" (p. 518).

Reflection as a Prime Ingredient

Integrating the service activities and the academic enterprise is essential to the service-learning process. A hallmark of this integration is the use of reflection in order to understand the content of the course and to connect the experiences in a broader civic context. (Bringle & Hatcher, 2000; Cooper, 2000; Eyler, 2002; Kottkamp, 2000; Mills, 2001; Reed & Koliba, 2003). This component is instrumental in distinguishing fully implemented service-learning from other service or experiential based activities such as volunteerism, practicum, internships or other practice-based experiences and may serve to identify problems that hinder learning, reveal attitudes, or challenge concepts within a larger social context (Bringle & Hatcher, 1999; Cone & Harris, 1996).

One of the challenges in evaluation is the lack of standards for measuring and cataloging meaningful outcomes. Even with these limitations, there are studies that point to the positive outcomes of many service-learning activities.

How to incorporate classroom reflections of experiences in a meaningful way is a key issue and should continue to be an important focus of the service-learning research. Eyler (2002) notes the mixed results of the research on the service-learning, although there is "evidence to suggest that service-learning programs which thoroughly integrate service and academic learning through continuous reflection promote development of the knowledge, skills and cognitive capacities necessary for students to deal effectively with the complex social issues that challenge citizens" (p. 517). In order to provide some guidance in this area, there are resources that can assist faculty in designing the reflection component of a course. One must consider the course goals and objectives when designing reflection and outcome activities that will help connect the community service activities with the academic content of the course.

There is no one "right" way for students to process and assimilate the learning that takes place through their service experiences. Faculty must choose the methods of assessment and reflections that meet their time constraints, course goals, and learning objectives. One innovative trend is to utilize electronic journaling with the increased accessibility of web-based resources on campus. Mills (2001), using the *Blackboard* technology–a popular course management system on many campuses, instituted various types of electronic journaling in his service-learning classes. His experience provides guidance on implementing this method of reflection. He found that students liked his electronic alternative to traditional journaling. In utilizing a group and individual forum for reflection, Mills makes the case for a "...Web-based approach to student journaling that simultaneously maximizes the benefits of journaling and responds to practical burdens of service-learning endeavor" (p. 34). This method of journaling and reflection affords the added benefit of a group interactive experience not available with a more traditional individual written journal.

Community Partners in the Mix

Another important facet of the service-learning process is the meaningful communication and open relationships with community partners that are essential in maximizing the academic experience for students in promoting social responsibility and change. Research on building community-university partnerships points to the need to nurture these relationships and the need to promote a true partnership in order to facilitate mutual learning (Gelmon, et al. 1998, Vernon & Ward, 1999). Problems can develop when the community relationship part of the equation is neglected. Vernon and Ward note that: "By inviting the community service agency to have a voice and become an active partner in the academic service-learning process, higher education can more fully realize its public service and outreach mission, actualize a social change model for service-learning, and achieve the ideals of the engaged campus" (p. 36). They provide recommendations that emphasize open communication among faculty administrators and community agency coordinators. Campuses should utilize innovative ways to increase community visibility on campus and increase awareness of community partners about ways to connect with course curriculum. Further recommendations point to the need to clearly communicate about joint issues of recruitment, training, and retention with the service providers; and that campuses should develop guidelines for purpose and expectations of the students in the service initiatives especially when there is a need to distinguish roles of students from interns or other academic training relationships (pp. 35-36).

Examples of Service-Learning Courses

Many academic areas of study and specific courses are conducive to the concept of service-learning. Since there were both graduate and undergraduate involved in the courses, with many of the projects, the graduate students served as team leaders with the undergraduate students. The use of these teams led by the more advanced students allowed for a more effective group experience with the community partners.

In our university, we were able to introduce service-learning in the following courses:

Gerontology

Since service had been a long standing commitment in these classes, the university faculty relationships with community agencies and partners were well-established. The students were encouraged to participate in service that allowed them to experience more than one population of older adults. Given the interdisciplinary nature of the courses and the enrollment of students from different disciplines, faculty and community partners worked to match students with activities that were compatible with their professional interests. Activities and projects addressed needs identified by the community partners. Intergenerational activities included: an 'Old Time" Radio Show hour for residents of a facility; creating Memory Books for early stage dementia residents; leading an aerobics class for older adults; socialization and exercise with older developmentally delayed individuals; working with a social service agency and elementary schools to initiate programs for grandparents raising grandchildren; and delivering home-delivered meals to home-bound older adults..

Social Work, Education, and Psychology

An after-school program in the local middle-and high school had 150 students in need of one- on -one tutoring and mentoring. Graduate students in Developmental Psychology participated in the tutoring in order to learn about issues in stages of developmental, cognition and behavior. Undergraduate social work students also studying human development benefited by a relationship with students and exposure to some of the social-environmental issues in dealing with high risk students. Undergraduate pre-service education majors gained experience with students and teachers in the setting in which they plan to work.

Research Methods

Since service-learning activities ideally involve an evaluation component, one innovative way to accomplish this evaluation on campus is to find a research methodology class that requires a "service" component to actually design and conduct a research project. The faculty member of the research class was asked to assist by the staff of a funded service-learning project on campus that did not have the time or expertise to implement the research process required of the external funding agency. The research methodology course for social work majors involved design and implementation of a research project by students during the semester. The course met both the academic objectives of the social work faculty by providing students a beneficial hands- on research experience while meeting a valuable need of the community partner that needed the service-learning project evaluation.

Civic Journalism

The local newspaper editors appealed to the Journalism department faculty to produce a special supplement focused on the issues of aging in the community. The staff did not have the time or expertise to produce the special addition and approached the university to see if they could assist with this identified need from the community readership. A graduate seminar on Civic Journalism was being offered and proved to be a mutually beneficial match to meeting the students needs to learn about the process of civic journalism and producing this supplement. The supplement "Faces and Facets of Aging" was a compilation of articles and photos by the students working with faculty and the local newspaper staff. The students not only accomplished the academic knowledge of working on civic issues, but they were able to all have one or more published articles about real issues and real people in the paper. The addition was so well received that there is an ongoing effort to continue the special "Faces and Facets of Aging" as a regular addition to the paper.

Reflection and Student Evaluation of Experiences

Shumer (2002), in his evaluation of the impact of a statewide school partnership grant with higher education, reported that the most frequent areas of student impact were in the areas of personal development. Students reported improvements in self-confidence, patience, and responsibility. Their professional development was enhanced by greater awareness of and career options, and an appreciation for the importance of civic responsibility, volunteering, and "giving back.". Comments provide revealing testimony to the variety of experiences, mostly overwhelmingly positive, as expressed through written reflections. This sample is provided to illustrate real student voices and to, hopefully, encourage faculty to implement service components in the learning process.

> "What I learned from this group of 19 beautiful people is attributes most don't have, especially a college student. I learned patience, flexibility, and genuine compassion. This group...showed me that I was not there to teach them, I was there so they could teach me. How humbling this was...I was the one that had the rewarding experience, so rewarding that I stayed past my fifteen hours; I more than doubled it. I also came out with something even more incredible, a job offer. Now I was going to get paid for doing something so rewarding. How great is this?"

> "Burt is an amazing person. At 93, he appeared to have maintained a love for life...I felt a bond between us through the conversation we had. Perhaps he was seeing himself in the past. I hope I was seeing a reflection of me in the future."

> "In the field of exercise science we so often interact with people that we almost have to force to workout and here were these older adults that were ecstatic about their new exercise program...I realized for the first time that maybe I would like working with older adult, instead of young healthy people. How many other clients do you know that will eagerly await your arrival and send you home with a smile and a few laughs at the end of the day."

> "My understanding of civic responsibility has been changed by my experience.... I have to care about what's going on in the environment, and I have to be involved as if I didn't have to be there. I feel like I'm purposefully inclusive now, and not just involved."

> "Questions on ageism and sexism made me more observant. I wasn't aware of any of this until I started to look around."

> "Reflective questions really made you think. They help ground you, connecting you with the class and the outside experience."

> "This class has taught me that working with the elderly is where I want to be."

> "Working at After School has shown me that I definitely want to teach. I was challenged every day to find ways to help my After School student learn."

> "I learned a lot about myself. This has been the most rewarding experience of my life!"

> "I have gotten more out of this class that I have any other class that I have taken here for many reasons. Throughout our discussions, visits, volunteer work for and about the elderly, I have taken with me a lot of knowledge and life lessons....I get a sense of appreciation and personal growth. For this reason, I will continue doing volunteer work with the elderly and I might even end

up having a career working with them…I think that taking this class as one of my last at Ole Miss leaves me with a sense of learning something other than facts and numbers. I learned a lot about life and growing up."

Resources for Faculty

General Resources

Two national organizations that provide excellent resources such as toolkits for faculty, syllabi and curricula, and links to additional higher education resources are the National Clearinghouse for Service-Learning at www.servicelearning.org and Campus Compact at www.compact.org. A listing of university courses by disciplines called "101 Ideas of Combining Service and Learning" can be found at www.fiu.edu/`time4chg/Library/ideas. In addition, a brief videotape on service-learning can provide a good introduction for faculty, administrators and students in providing an overview of the components of serving, learning, and reflecting (see O'Quin, 2002).

Resources on Reflection

Excellent readings are available from the Campus Compact publication *"Introduction to Service-Learning Toolkit: Readings and Resources for Faculty". In this publication,* Bringle and Hatcher (2000) provide a description of reflection activities for the classroom that include: reflective journals (e.g., "Key Phase, Double-Entry, Critical Incident, and Three Part Journals"); experiential research papers, ethical case studies, directed readings, class presentations, and electronic reflections (p. 115-6). Kottkamp (1990) provides an excellent "how to piece" for reflection used in professional practice that highlights the meaning and use of reflection. Cooper (1998) offers suggestions on why and how faculty should accommodate student learning styles and differences by offering a variety of reflection activities (p. 125). Reed and Koliba compiled a manual, *Facilitating Reflection: A Manual for Leaders and Educators, as a useful suppl*ement to educators and leaders of community and service organizations and it offers a variety of exercises and practical examples of reflective activities (available at www.uvm.edu/-dewey/reflection_manual/index.html).

Conclusion

Service-learning is an academic concept that is gaining widespread attention across university campuses. It integrates the academic coursework and outside service activities with the intent of promoting civic responsibility and meeting community needs. Students can benefit in several ways depending on the structure of the activities, the community partnerships and relationships, and the effectiveness of bridging the experiences with the classroom process. Not all of these goals are easily achieved, and faculty members are challenged to create meaningful service experiences with partners in the community. Of utmost importance, however, is an institutional appreciation for and commitment to the ideals of service-learning because it is a labor intensive enterprise for faculty. "Teachers and professors need technical assistance to develop skills at design and implementation of reflective programs; they need support in the form of community liaisons or service-learning centers to help create and sustain community relationships; they need practical resources, including transportation for projects. College professors need to find professional reward in commitment to students, community, and high quality instruction" (Eyler, 2002, p. 531).

Integral to the true service-learning process is the ability to distinguish this experience from purely volunteer activities that do not fully promote civic responsibility and build on the academic course content through reflection on and evaluation of the learning experiences. When successfully implemented, all constituents should benefit and the university can further its missions of promoting academic excellence in teaching while serving the broader community. Under these circumstances, service-learning offers a valuable pedagogy in higher education for all constituents—students, faculty, administrators and community members.

Bibliography

Bringle, R.G. & Hatcher, J.A. (2002). Campus-community partnerships: The terms of engagement. *Journal of Social Issues*, 58, 3, 503-516.

Bringle, R.G. & Hatcher, J.A. (2000). Reflection in service learning: Making meaning of experience. Reprinted in Campus Compact (2000). *Introduction to Service-Learning Toolkit: Readings and Resources for Faculty*, Campus Compact, Brown University, R.I., 113-119.

Cone, D. & Harris, S. (1996). Service-learning practice: Developing a theoretical framework. Reprinted in Campus Compact (2000). *Introduction to Service-Learning Toolkit: Readings and Resources for Faculty*, Campus Compact, Brown University, R.I., 43-59.

Cooper, D. D, (1998). Reading, writing, and reflection. Reprinted in Campus Compact (2000). *Introduction to Service-Learning Toolkit: Readings and Resources for Faculty*, Campus Compact, Brown University, R.I., 121-126.

Corporation for National and Community Service (2002). *Students in Service to America*, Washington, D.C. Eyler, J. (2002). Reflection: Linking service and learning–linking students and communities. *Journal of Social Issues*, 58, 3, 517-534.

Furco, A. (2000). Service-Learning: A balanced approach to experiential education. In Campus Compact (2000). *Introduction to Service-Learning Toolkit: Readings and Resources for Faculty*, Campus Compact, Brown University, R.I. www.campuscontact.org.

Gelmon, S.B. Holland, B.A., Seifer, S.D., Shinnamom, A., & Connors, K. (1998). Community-university partnerships for mutual learning. *Michigan Journal of Community Service Learning*, Fall, 97-107.

Kottkamp, R. (1990). Means for facilitating reflection. Reprinted in Campus Compact (2000). *Introduction to Service-Learning Toolkit: Readings and Resources for Faculty*, Campus Compact, Brown University, R.I., 127-140.

Mills, S. D. (2001). Electronic journaling: Using the web-based group journal for service-learning reflection. *Michigan Journal of Community Service Learning*, Fall, 27-35. O'Quin, J.A. (Producer and Director). (2002). "Intergenerational service-learning: Crossing new paths." [Video recording] University of Mississippi, Oxford, MS. Reed, J. & Koliba, C. (2003). Facilitating reflection: A manual for leaders and educators. www.uvm.edu/-dewey/reflection_manual/index.html. Shumer, R. (2002). Mississippi Lighthouse Project Evaluation Report. Unpublished manuscript.

Vernon, A. & Ward, K. (1999). Campus and community partnerships: Assessing impacts & strengthening connections. *Michigan Journal of Community Service Learning*, Fall, 30-37.

Chapter 3
Is Service-Learning Right for You?

Finding your Place in the World of Service Learning. Is the Journey Worth the Effort?

Adriaanna Pearce, Monash South Africa, Gauteng, SOUTH AFRICA

Abstract: There is a need for institutions to realise that Service Learning is becoming necessary because of the reality that education is becoming more isolated from real life. Past Service Learning research shows that involvement in Service Learning has personal and academic benefits. It is because of this reality and the passing of a law (The White Paper) that encouraged Higher Institutions in South Africa to be involved with community projects, that we initiated a Service Learning Pilot project. This journey (the actual pilot of a Service Learning programme) reflects on the problems that were encountered, the experiences of the students and volunteers as well as the mistakes that were made with regards to the timing of the project, the setting of outcomes and the selection of community partners. The reflections clearly show that you need more than enthusiasm and passion for Service Learning to succeed. You need willing institutions that will prioritise Service Learning by offering support in the form of training and resources.

Background

Over the past 20 – 25 years, Service Learning has been given many definitions, but is generally defined as "... as the integration of community service into the academic content of coursework" (Pryor, 2005:1). I believe that Bringle and Hatcher (1995:112) have the most embracing definition which defines Service Learning as a "credit-bearing educational experience in which students participate in an organised service activity that meets identified community needs".

General aims for Service Learning are to help students increase community awareness by applying their academic learning, knowledge and skills to a pre-identified community need. This links with the generally accepted requirement, that for Service Learning to be considered a viable pedagogic approach, the service has to link with the specific academic content being delivered.

Community involvement has always been part of Higher Institutions' mission and vision. In defence of Higher Education management it has been noted that many have begun to "...embrace a scholarship of engagement" (Butin, 2006:473) although research does not clearly identify the actual level of this embrace (Boyer: 1990; Shulman: 2004 cited in Butin, 2006:473). It seems that Higher Educational Institutions have involved themselves with a form of Service Learning, yet on the surface it appears to be nothing more than a focus on community engagement. The exact extent and level of involvement would have to be investigated further in order to offer a qualified opinion.

In spite of these efforts it is a sad reality that education as we know it leaves a gap in the holistic education of students. The HEQC (Higher Education Quality Committee) in South Africa has also observed this tendency and has reported that graduating students do not relate to their surrounding communities. The HEQC found that: "Higher Education has not succeeded in laying the foundations of a critical civil society with a culture of tolerance, public debate and accommodation of differences and competing interests, nor has it contributed significantly to a democratic ethos and a sense of citizenship..." (CHE, 2006: 3). This is the gap that Service Learning aims to fill.

The new democratic direction and the 'new' South Africa (mid 1990's), and subsequent transition in many spheres, provided many new challenges to address the past imbalances of prejudiced laws in South Africa. In addition to these mentioned challenges a growing emphasis was placed on the need for universities to become more relevant to the socio-economic realities of South Africa (Marais & Botes, 2005: 179). Concern over the widening gap (between formal education and 'real life') and the objective of moving towards a more holistic approach to education became a major challenge within Higher Education. Research conducted by Butin (2006) stated that Service Learning has became more evident within Higher Education (in the USA) with over 950 colleges associating themselves with Campus Compact and participating in Service Learning activities. No doubt this was an attempt to close the gap between formal education and the needs of communities and to make education more meaningful. But how does this compare to the reality in South Africa?

Unfortunately, not as favourably. When the concept of Service Learning was first introduced in South Africa in 2001, there were only five universities that were involved in the implementation of the CHESP[1] initiative which was funded by JET[2] (Fourie, 2003:35). Currently, limited numbers of institutions in South Africa have shown major involvement within Service Learning. Major involvement implies a dedicated department with full time staff, involved with, not only the development but also the promotion and maintenance of Service Learning programmes and activities. Only a few of the larger South African public universities, who initiated Service Learning, actually established dedicated offices and departments for the development and maintenance of Service Learning projects. Much to our dismay, most of these institutions have recently dissolved or reduced their departments and have withdrawn or reduced their projects. Fortunately some individual Service Learning champions (who have been re-deployed into other departments) are still responsible for the Service Learning courses. Most institutions cited budget constraints as the reason for this rather harsh move, but it is probable that the root cause of these perceived drawbacks was due to a lack of institutionalisation (Mitchell: 2005) of Service Learning.

The HEQC has embarked upon an urgent search for solutions to the challenges mentioned earlier and has come to expect that Higher Institutions become involved in some form of Service Learning. In addition, the White Paper (1997) has also laid the foundation for "...making community service an integral and core part of Higher Education in South Africa" (CHE, 2006: 7).

With the initial call for community engagement, as stated in previous paragraphs, there were a total of five institutions (Fourie:2003) which took up this challenge and piloted Service Learning projects. MSA also embarked upon this unique challenge.

The Journey Starts

"It is said that if you want to know reality, you must try to change it" (Uphoff, 2005: 60)

This is a very significant quote and one that I believe is very relevant to describe the real struggles and attempts to implement and institutionalise Service Learning in a truly academic environment, not only in South Africa, but internationally.

---

1. CHESP – Community Higher Education Service Partnership Programme. The Goals of CHESP is to contribute to the reconstruction and development of South Africa

2. JET – Joint Education Trust

MSA piloted a Service Learning programme. This paper will describe the pilot and the experiences of the participants. It will discuss the activities that took place from the introduction to the pilot, as well as the problems and barriers faced by the volunteers. It will also review the actual implementation of the programme. The paper will focus on the feedback received from the students and staff involved and offer reflections for future use and studies.

The data was collected through three focus group interviews, even though four groups of students participated in the programme. The three group interviews were held with the students who were part of the Academic English, the Maths and the Computer Studies units.

Of the four lecturers who participated, two were formally interviewed. The third lecturer's views were obtained anecdotally through an informal conversation. An informal information session was also held with the community engagement officer.

I would just like to add that as I was also involved in the pilot, I have reacted with some bias as the journey has been experienced more personally. The conclusions are more anecdotal reflecting my perceptions, interpretations and opinions about the feedback that was received.

Why Service Learning?

Even before embarking upon this unique and interesting pedagogy, we had to be sure that this approach was going to be beneficial to our students, so the question was posed: "Why Service Learning?"

> *"I can honestly say that I've learned more in the last year in (service-learning) than I probably have learned in all four years of college. I have learned so much, maybe because I found something that I'm really passionate about, and it makes you care more to learn about it – and get involved and do more. You're not just studying to take a test and forget about it. You're learning and the experiences we have are staying with us"* (Eyler & Dwight, 1999: 1)

Reflections and feedback like this quote from Eyler & Dwight in addition to many other examples from past research helped to clarify the reasons for Service Learning. According to Fourie (2003:31), "Western Universities have traditionally had a strong teaching function while at the same time being filled with a strong sense of public responsibility which takes on different forms". He expanded on the idea that universities have not always succeeded in their three-fold responsibility of teaching, research and community service. In addition to pedagogical benefits it seems that Service Learning is the ideal pedagogy to link the following three functions that should be embraced by all Institutions of Higher Learning:

- a teaching method that delivers many positive and lasting results;
- a methodology that ensures that community needs are met and
- a path that can open doors to many different research possibilities.

From numerous conversations, it became evident that in many cases community service programmes 'practiced' by institutions are only a shallow representation of what could have been a meaningful impact. In advocating for the inclusion of Service Learning in the curriculum, Higher Education has emphasised the benefits of this pedagogy for both social and academic development. In addition, past research has shown that the majority of students who have participated in a Service Learning programme, have benefited both personally and academically. This is also emphasised by the Monroe report (Pryor, 2005: iii) that found that: "Students who take Service Learning classes respond differently to pre- and post test measure of factors including the following: an increased awareness of community needs; an increased awareness of community resources and an investment in community involvement".

The review of the literature resulted in MSA realising the pressing need for the introduction of a Service Learning programme. It was decided to institute the programme at the Foundation level because of the flexibility of the Foundation Programme curriculum.

The Foundation Programme initiated the implementation of the pilot programme for Service Learning. Four volunteers were willing to look into Service Learning and adapt course content to link with Service Learning outcomes. After informal meetings, workshops and some extensive reading, the pilot was launched.

The "mired" Journey

Even before the pilot was attempted, several challenges emerged. Of these, three main problems were evident:

- The first was that some members of senior management had not bought into the Service Learning pedagogy. We were, however, not prepared for the resistance that followed after the initial enthusiasm. In spite of this resistance, we pushed ahead. Initially the resistance was perceived to be lack of confidence in our abilities to pilot this project as senior management were not convinced that we should be running the pilot for two reasons:
  - Firstly, the Foundation Programme staff had not as yet embarked upon much research and
  - Secondly, the Foundation Programme students were the junior intake at the institution. The hesitance could also have been due to a lack of understanding by management about what Service Learning actually was.

In spite of these objections and our own personal lack of training, we were unwavering in our commitment with regards to implementing this pilot, and to respond to the call from the HEQC[3].

- The second problem was that there was no formal policy, related to the procedures relevant to Service Learning, in place and the draft policy was still being finalised and in the process of being approved.

The third problem was the disjointed link between Service Learning programmes and academic achievement. Due to lack of training, staff lacked the necessary skills and expertise to effectively integrate Service Learning activities into their current academic curriculum.

Although the volunteers did not have a broad knowledge of Service Learning, they were drawn by the potential enhancement of their students' learning. Their enthusiasm could be seen in comments such as: *"the moment I heard about Service Learning, I knew it was the right thing to do". "The philosophy sounded sound and I believed that both student and staff would benefit from this"*.

Part of the journey included the student volunteers. In one particular subject, participation was expected from all the students, whereas the other three courses were on a volunteer basis. The students had their own individual reasons for participating in the Service Learning pilot project. While many of them were interested in the concept of Service Learning and had previously either been involved in volunteer programmes or came from families who had been involved in volunteer programmes, others were attracted by the 'promised' academic benefit and found the idea of enhancing their studies while doing their 'good deed' motivating. Comments such as: *"I wanted to advance my learning"; "I wanted to learn about the South African communities"; "I'm going to change someone's life"*, echoed the enthusiasm felt by the students.

Even though students were informed during the information session that they were not there to be the "knight in shining armour"; that they should have no personal expectations and should not offer or agree to do anything outside of the set Service Learning curriculum outcomes, it was clear from comments such as *"...we are going to change someone's life"* that expectations were exaggerated and were not in line with Service Learning outcomes. From the interviews and reflections it became clear that the students did not entirely understand the context of Service Learning which potentially could set them up for a disappointing experience.

Partners in the Journey

Community Partner's (CP's) are a vital ingredient in the successful implementation of Service Learning. In our context, the whole concept of Service Learning was new and this resulted in an element of uncertainty in how to identify CP's.

---

3. Higher Education Quality Council

There were a total of four different CP's identified. A staff member involved with community engagement had a contact at a homework centre in a rural area not far from the campus. It was a centre that had been started by a church and was predominantly used as a youth centre where the youths were primarily involved in sports activities on weekends.

The horse riding school for the disabled (SARDA[4]) was also approached to be a CP. It was convenient as it was in close proximity to the campus. It was chosen for the Academic English course with the purpose of improving students' writing by founding their writing exercises on real life examples. They were to observe and report on any perceived changes and development of the physically challenged riders, as well as noting the experiences of the parents. The ultimate aim was to base their research on reality and describe their experiences and observations. I was also interested in finding out if this would result in some personal development in students and perhaps lead to a change in attitudes towards differences.

A school in one of the previously disadvantaged Townships was used by the students who were involved with maths tutoring.

One student (from Academic English) requested to do her Service Learning at SANCA[5] in Soweto as she had done volunteer work there before. They agreed to accommodate two to three students.

The marketing students were involved in the design of a marketing plan for a non-profit organisation as well as for the homework centre. The purpose was to design a marketing plan that the CP's would be able to utilise to improve their visibility in the community and infrastructure.

Reflections

The homework centre was chosen because it was convenient; it already had an infrastructure and learners from the surrounding schools went there for additional help with school work. Students from three courses did their Service Learning projects at this venue. The problem was that the centre was active mainly on Saturdays. This left the students with almost no contact with the learners during the week when they went there to carry out their engagement. (It seemed that there was little interest from the learners in school work, with major interest in the weekend sporting activities)

In addition to the fact that the centre was under-utilised during the week and the learners came mainly on Saturdays, the students only managed to get there about six times because of time and transport constraints.

There was also limited communication and probing toward identifying and understanding of the needs of the CP's. A short meeting with the CP did not properly identify the objectives or communicate our objectives. A follow up meeting was planned, but was never executed, with the exception of the Marketing unit.

4.South African Riding for the Disabled

5.South African National Council on Alcoholism And Drug Dependence

In addition there was another complex issue which had to be addressed in a sensitive manner and that was that the person in charge of the centre was concerned that the learners might feel even more 'disadvantaged' if there were these 'affluent' university students trying to meet their needs. There was a fear that the learners from the homework centre would not respond well to the students and as a result were not encouraged to meet the students.

This contributed to the student's feelings that in addition to the time being too short to accomplish what they were expected to achieve, they also had not learned much and that the whole programme was rather a waste of time as Service Learning goals were not met. The perception was that failure was due to a shortage of time as well as lack of effective planning on the part of the lecturers. Students felt that there was not enough time for them to implement and achieve Service Learning goals.

At SARDA, the students felt out of place. As one student put it: "*we feel like tourists*". In response to the question why, they stated that most of the volunteers were regulars and had formed a strong bond with each other and did not openly welcome the students.

Students involved with Service Learning at the riding school did not achieve the stated outcomes because they did not improve their writing. The students lacked confidence and so did not interview the physically challenged riders or their parents. As time was also an issue they were not involved long enough to see the therapeutic difference that the riding may have had on the physically challenged riders or the impact of any contribution they themselves may have had. They revealed that they had not learned much and that they were disappointed that they had not achieved their desired outcomes which on the one hand were Service Learning outcomes and on the other hand their expectations.

Although the students who went to the Township school enjoyed their project, they were also constrained by time limits and reported that they were frustrated because there was not enough time to achieve what they had set out to do.

SANCA was an ideal CP, as they had identified a real need which could be addressed by the Service Learning programme. They required that their manuals and policies be renewed and edited. The students were able to implement their writing and editing skills. Therefore both the students and the CP benefited from this relationship.

In retrospect, the selection of the CP's was done from an uninformed position. According to Mitchell and Rautenbach (2005:105) there are certain conditions that need acknowledgement and review to ensure successful partnerships. They talk about "agreed-upon missions, values, goals and measureable outcomes". Furthermore the relationship must be perceived to be one of shared trust whilst reliance on each others' value and commitment is potentially seen in the developing relationship. The roles should also be clearly defined and respected. My assertion is that none of these elements were present in the selection of CP's as they were chosen for the sake of convenience and existing contacts. There was also no development of relationships that would or could be sustained for future projects. As we were unequal partners yoked in this project, success was compromised.

To further support this view I refer to Uphoff's article (2005: 53-54). This paper discusses a Service Learning project where the CP was directly involved in all phases of the project. Both the researcher and community benefited in many ways, but the conclusion states that had the community not been involved, the success would have been minimal. This reinforces my argument that, if Service Learning is to truly succeed, the CP has to be "right" for the project, the student and the particular field of study.

Reflecting on the journey, it was clear that we followed a "nose in the air" approach and this resulted in being ill-prepared for the real Service Learning experience which resulted in students not being exposed to 'true' Service Learning. It has become clear that eagerness and enthusiasm are not the only ingredients for success, for a venture of such a nature. After careful consideration the following conclusions can be drawn:

- Lack of knowledge hampered the preparation of the students and course material.
- Lack of experience resulted in some unwise choices which made the experience less worthwhile.

Joseph and Anderson (1997: XI) state that "...well-designed, well-managed Service Learning can contribute to student's learning and growth while also helping to meet real community needs". Clearly our lack of experience and prior knowledge as well as ill-designed programmes resulted in a disappointing experience for the students.

The initial enthusiasm we felt about this project has somewhat subsided, but is still brewing in the background. The lessons learned are valuable and should be taken forward in planning for the next "trip" of Service Learning.

Perhaps it would have been prudent to spend at least six months planning the incorporation of Service Learning in existing curriculums. It is vital to plan exactly what outcomes you hope to achieve and how this can be done. If not, you could have the situation where students go out to the CP's and are not sure what they are expected to achieve, which results in wasted time.

More time should be spent in the search and selection for a community partner that:

- has definite identifiable and obtainable needs;
- is not only convenient, but suitable for the project and subject; and
- has needs that can be met within the course content.

It is evident that from comments made by many students about time being a constraint that:

- more time should be made available for achieving the goals; and
- CP's should be more accessible so that students can go during their free time and not have to wait for organised transport.

Furthermore, training for staff is very important in order to link outcomes to course content. If you are to embark upon a Service Learning project, register for training or find someone who will mentor you along your journey.

The most obvious, yet humbling admission, is that senior management were correct in being cautious with regards to our involvement in the Service Learning programme. Their experiences permitted them to be wary in allowing 'inexperienced staff' to embark upon such a major challenge.

Although the perception was formed among the volunteers that management showed their lack of commitment to the process of implementing Service Learning, by offering very limited support. This is also a clear indication that Service Learning was not and is not on the list of priorities to be discussed.

Instead of rushing ahead, as stated previously, we should have taken more time and utilised other internal and external experience, knowledge and expertise to guide our preparations.

It is clear though, that lack of institutionalisation[6] of Service Learning will hamper any future attempts to embark upon another Service Learning programme. This is an issue that will need to be addressed to ensure that there are policies and procedures in place which make it feasible to have more staff committed to Service Learning and funds made available to support and develop such projects.

Final Thoughts

We live in a world controlled by humans with personal agendas, ideas and aspirations. To think that we could embark upon a new paradigm / pedagogy that is so different from the theoretical base most academics stand by, is / was naïve.

If we are to embrace Service Learning, we will need to expect resistance. As Butin (2006:474) surmises, even though Service Learning has moved rapidly into the academic mainstream, the 'actual academic footprint' seems to be uncertain. The reason for this is that Service Learning is often considered to be a 'co-curricular' practice and viewed by 'serious' academics as an 'atheoretical' pedagogy which requires a lot of time and cannot be considered to have serious academic status.

6.Institutionalisation is the process of having service learning engraved into an institutions' mission, vision and policies. It requires staff to implement service learning in their units. Service learning outcomes are worked into the performance objectives of staff members and units and are consequently followed up and evaluated.

It is up to the champions of Service Learning to take this fight to the academic and promotion committees to promote Service Learning as a serious academic paradigm which can make valuable contributions to the performance of students. It is up to us to learn from others' experiences and to push for development and promotion opportunities for the lecturers involved in the practice, development and implementation of Service Learning programmes.

The Wingspread statement (Brukardt, 2004: ii in Butin, 2006) poses the question: *"Is higher education ready to commit to engagement?"* The answer is a glaringly obvious, no! It is evident from the struggles that Service Learning promoters have to endure to fight for a voice and a place in academic spheres, that the fight for Service Learning to be recognised as part of academia is far from over. If we are to find our place, we must fight for it and strive to institutionalise this pedagogy. The saying: *"Strike while the iron is hot"*, comes to mind. While Service Learning is in the minds and on the agendas of important meetings, it is important to promote and fight for advancement, before the imaginations of those in positions of power are captured by something else and all this hard work goes to waste.

Conclusion

In conclusion, the experience learnt was disappointing, yet challenging and one that has taught valuable lessons. To embark upon Service Learning, you need more than enthusiasm; you need a well designed curriculum and a careful selection of CP's to ensure a synergy between curriculum outcomes and community needs.

You will also need to identify the political nuances behind the scenes and address the issues pertaining to the initiation of the institutionalisation process for Service Learning. This will help to ensure not only the survival of such an approach as a pedagogy, but also ensure the promotion and development of Service Learning to further enhance its teaching capabilities and to allow all students to experience a holistic and sound education.

And finally to link my thoughts to the first quote I used: *"It is said that if you want to know reality, you must try to change it"* (Uphoff, 2005: 60). It has become quite clear from the struggles that are faced and challenges that are met that the our reality is not ready for reality of Service Learning, as many people do not want to change their "reality" to accept this pedagogy. But is the journey worth the effort? I would say a definite yes, but would also add that it is a very personal journey and a ride that may not be suitable for everyone. Even with my failed experiences, there is still a passion for Service Learning and for the benefits it holds and would state that unquestionably, it is well worth the fight and the journey.

References

Anderson, B.A., & Callahan, J. (2005), The Institutionalising of Service Learning in Pre-service Teacher Education. (P17 – 36). *Improving Service Learning Practice. Research on Models to enhance impacts.* Edited by Root.

Bender, C.J.G., Daniels, P., Naude, L., Lazarus, J. & Sattar, K. (2006). Service Learning in the curriculum. A resource for Higher education Institutions. *Higher Education Quality committee (HEQC) CHE Council of Higher Education.*

Bender, S. (2005). *Measuring the Impact of Service Learning at Monroe Community College: Designing and Implementing an Assessment Approach.* Available from www.cgr.org accessed January 2006.

Bringle, R.G. & Hatcher, J.A. (2000). Institutionalisation of Service Learning in Higher Education. *The Journal of Higher Education.* 71(3), 273-290.

Butin, D.W. (2006) The Limits of Service-Learning in Higher Education. *Review of Higher Education.* 29 (4).), (473-498). Available from ProQuest Education Journals database. Accessed October 2007

Erickson, J.A. & Anderson, J.B. (Editors). (1997). *Learning with the Community, Concepts and Models for Service-Learning in Teacher Education. American Association for Higher Education.* USA

Eyler, J. & Dwight E, G. (1999) *Where's the Learning in Service-Learning.* Jossey-Bass Publishers. San Francisco, California.

Fourie, M. (2003). Beyond the ivory tower: Service Learning for sustainable community development: Perspectives on higher education. *South African Journal of Higher Education.* 17(1):31-38. Available from SAEPublications. Accessed 12 December 2006.

Furco, A. & Billig, S.H. (Editors). (2002). *Service Learning, The essence of Pedagogy. A volume in advances in Service Learning Research.* . Information Page Publishing, USA

Kruger, E., Gravett, S., & Petersen, N. (2005). Learners' experiences of a Community Service Programme within the Therapeutic Massage Therapy Qualification. *Education as Change.* 9 (1)

Lategan, L. (2005). Research, monitoring and evaluation in Service Learning: the distinct characteristics of research into Service Learning. Acta Academica : Research and (Community) *Service Learning in South African Higher Education Institutions,* Supplementum 3: 99-115

Marais, L. & Botes, L. (2005). Putting the horse before the cart: policy research, partnerships and community service, Acta Academica: research and (Community) Service Learning in South African Higher Education Institutions, Supplementum 3: 178-202 Available from SAE Publications. Accessed 12 December 2006

Merriam, S.B. (1998). *Qualitative Research and Case Study Applications in Education. Revised and expanded from Case Study Research in Education.* Jossey-Bass Inc. A Wiley Company

Mitchell, C. & Rautenbach, S. (2005). Questioning Service Learning in South Africa: problematising partnerships in the South African context. A case study from the University of KwaZulu- Natal. *South African Journal of Higher Education.* 19 (1). : 101-112

Mitchell, C., Trotter, K. & Gelmon, S. (2005). A case study of a higher education institutional assessment on service learning. Acta Academica: Research and (Community) Service Learning in South African Higher Education Institutions, Supplementum 3: 51-177

Osman, R & Castle, J. (2006). Theorising service learning in higher education in South Africa. *Perspectives in Education.* Volume 24 (3) 2006.63-69

Pittman, K.J., Yohalem, N. & Tolman, J. (Editors). (2003). *When, where, what and how Youth Learn.* Blurring School and community Boundaries. *New Directions for Youth Development (97).* Wiley Periodicals, Inc.

Root, S, Callahan, J & Billig, SH, (Editors). (2005). *Improving Service Learning Practice. Research on Models to enhance impacts.* Information Age Publishing Inc, Printed in the USA.

Schensul, J.J., Berg, M. & Brase, M. (2002). Theories guiding outcomes for Action Research for Service Learning. Chapter 6 in *Service Learning, The essence of Pedagogy. A volume in advances Service-Learning research.* Information Page Publishing, USA Edited by Furco, A. & Billig, S.H.

Uphoff, N. (2005). The integration of rural development research and community service. Research and (Community) Service Learning In South African Higher Education Institutions, 3: 2005. Available from SAE Publications. Accessed 12 December 2006

Van Rensburg, W. (Ed.). (2004). Writing Partnerships: Academic Writing and Service Learning. *Education as Change.* 8(2)

Pryor, DE. (2005). Measuring the impact of Service Learning at MCC: Designing and implementing an assessment approach. *A report prepared for Monroe Community College.* New York,

Part II
Service-Learning Models

Overview

Chapters 4-6 make up Part 2 of the book, which focuses on models of service-learning. Chapter 4 looks at an effective service-learning model in higher education. Chapter 5 explores community-based learning as a core component to service-learning. Chapter 6 provides a look at a democratic civic education model.

Chapter 4
Service-Learning in Higher Education

A Model for Effective Service-Learning Design and Implementation in Private Higher Education

Regan Harwell Schaffer

Background and Problem Statement

The concept of pairing community service and academic learning has been around since John Dewey (1938) and his theory of democratic education, but the term "service-learning" was not coined until the 1960's in an attempt to give a name to a community service program students were involved in the US (Harkavy & Benson, 1998). Since then, service-learning has increased in population and proven to be an effective learning tool as demonstrated in numerous studies which has shown positive outcomes in students' GPA, writing skills, critical thinking skills and understanding of course content (Astin, Vogelgesang, Ikeda, & Yee, 2000; Rockquemore & Schaffer, 2000; Driscoll, Holland, Gelmon, & Kerrigan, 1996; Batchelder & Root, 1994). In 1990 over 147 variations of definitions of service-learning existed (Eyler & Giles, 1999). As a result, service-learning has grown into a widely recognized, but often misapplied, pedagogy. To further complicate matters, many educators have been using the term service-learning as an umbrella term for programs that are actually internships, field work, or volunteer efforts (Eyler & Giles, 1999; Howard, 1998). In such cases the accomplishments of the programs have been hindered in terms of learning outcomes and effectiveness since they did not encompass the attributes proven necessary for a service-learning course to meet its intended goals and impact student learning (Mintz & Hesser, 1996). The reason for this may be that many have not understood the difference between service-learning, volunteer work and internships and as a result are unaware of the guidelines for effective service-learning program quality. Another reason could be that given limited resources, institutions are not able to educate and train faculty and staff who could develop a service-learning program that maintains academic rigor while integrating quality community service (Morton, 1993; Singleton, Hirsch, & Burack, 1999). Regardless, clarity regarding this powerful pedagogy is needed.

Purpose

The purpose of this study incorporated two components. Since service-learning has many definitions and characteristics, the first component was to identify a working definition and set of attributes that have proven to be effective and useful according to the research and practitioners. Second, since effectual programs at private institutions exist, the final component was to explore several such "best practices" and discuss their programs. The culmination was a comprehensive definition of service-learning and a working model for designing service-learning in the private college or university context.

Research Questions

For the purpose of this study, the following research questions were addressed:

What might be a comprehensive definition of service-learning?

What are the best practices of effective service-learning programs at private liberal arts colleges and universities?

Based on the best practices discovered in Research Question Two, can a model be developed to design an effective service-learning program at private liberal arts colleges and universities?

Methodology and Results

To address the research questions, the researcher examined the findings of unpublished data from a survey on service-learning at private colleges (Schaffer, 2000) and conducted a thorough review of the literature on service-learning and higher education. Based upon these findings, program interviews were conducted with seven private colleges that exemplified best practices in service-learning. The subjects were those institutions that met the following criteria: (a) had an established service-learning program at their institution which had at least one full-time staff person (who was the contact for the interview); (b) the service-learning program must have utilized at least six of the seven characteristics identified in the literature as necessary for effective service-learning programs (which are outlined later in this article); and (c) the service-learning program must have been cited or recognized for its effectiveness outside of the college or university (through participation in a research study or cited in a service-learning or higher education publication). The interviews were transcribed and a content analysis was performed with the use of an inter-rater and the findings tabulated. Based upon the results, a summary was made of the data and conclusions were drawn to address the research questions.

A Comprehensive Definition of Service-Learning

The primary phase of the methodology enabled the researcher to address the first research question based upon the literature review and subsequent studies in program development for service-learning. The researcher examined 70 research articles or texts on program characteristics of *effective* service-learning in which seven characteristics were deemed "significant". The 70 articles represent a vast array of contexts, but were selected for their pedagogical implications in a service-learning course. In order for a characteristic to be considered significant it had to be identified in at least 30% of the 70 articles examined (Table 1). The researcher also considered the findings of the surveys and program interviews of best practices in service-learning when formulating a response to the research question. What resulted was the following comprehensive definition: Effective service-learning takes place when: (a) the service is tied to the learning objectives of a course; (b) the community is involved in the teaching and learning process; (c) the service performed by the students meets a need that is identified by the community;(d) guided reflection, both oral and written, is required of the students;(e) the service performed is meaningful and appropriate for the course;(f) there is assessment and evaluation of student learning and the service-learning program; and (g) the institution (college or university) provides support and incentive for service-learning.

Table 1: Characteristics of Effective Service-Learning Programs or Courses

Factor/characteristic of effective service-learning:	(n=70)	F	%
1. Reflection: Oral and Written	43		62
2. Service is tied to course learning objectives 3. Service performed is applicable and meaningful 4. Community defines need and is involved in the learning and teaching 5. Institutional support of service-learning (staff, resources, etc.) 6. Assessment/evaluation of student learning and program 7. Service meets a need within the community 8. Monitoring by university personnel 9. Relationship: Students build relationships with community members	39 28 24 23 23 22 11 10		56 40 34 33 33 31 16 14
10.Placement and service quality 11.Duration: Several interactions over time	10 10		14 14
12.Faculty: Students able to work closely with faculty 13.Diversity: Students work with people from diverse groups and backgrounds 14. Intensity: Length of each service experience 15. Orientation of students and community members	10 9 7 7		14 13 10 10

This comprehensive definition integrated previous explanations proposed by Howard (1998) and Kendall (1990), but incorporated an added dimension of institutional support. This seventh characteristic of institutional support was not only prevalent in the literature review, where it was stated by 33% of the sources, but also in the program interviews. As this article later explains, the responses in this area were significant and considered a necessary attribute in order for an institution to truly be able to have an effective service-learning program.

The program interviews with practitioners from private colleges and universities with best practices in service-learning corroborated many of the characteristics used in this definition. For instance, 86% of the respondents stated that the service should be tied to the learning objectives of a course (point 1 in the definition) and 71% stated that the service should meet a community need and that the community should be involved in the process (points 3 and 4 in the definition). Reflection was mentioned by 42% of the respondents (point 4 in the definition) and much discussion was given to the importance of designing purposeful service and the crucial role of institutional support (points 5 and 7 in the definition). Forty-three percent discussed the importance of meaningful work and ensuring that the service provided connections to the course content (point 5 in the definition). As a result, the comprehensive definition was supported by the literature review and the comments from the program interviews. Furthermore, it indicates that designing an effective service-learning component in a class is not enough, but the college or university administration must embrace and support service-learning so that resources are available to ensure success.

Best Practices of Service-Learning

The second phase of the methodology was designed to address the second research question and included data from numerous sources. The first was unpublished results of 90 private colleges from a population of 239 surveyed (Schaffer, 2000). The purpose was to determine the current knowledge and practices with regards to service-learning among private colleges and universities. The second source of data was the results of the best practices program interviews described previously. And finally, the literature review produced valuable data. Based upon this information, four key elements were evident in private colleges that were considered among the best. This included fifty percent or more of the colleges in the program interviews. The elements are presented in no particular order and include the following:

- Institutional Support
- Mission
- Definitions and Guidelines
- Academic Validity

Institutional support. One of the first attributes that enabled those colleges interviewed to be among "the best" was the institutional support for service-learning on their respective campuses. In these situations, institutional support included funding for an office, staff, and training as well as advocacy of service-learning by upper administration. In the program interviews, all (100%) of the respondents stated they had institutional support, which was defined as: operational funds, office space, salaries for at least one full-time staff person and resources for training and workshops.

This coincides with the literature review and program interviews. Thirty-three percent of the articles discussed the importance of institutional support in the health and success of a service-learning program (Table 1). Ed Zlotkowski (1998a) and others (Bringle & Hatcher, 2000; Caron, 1999; Astin, 1996; Mintz & Hesser, 1996; Ward, 1996) discussed specifically in their research the need for the leadership within a college or university to embrace the philosophical and pedagogical reasons for service-learning as a means to be a force for positive change in the campus culture and community. This form of headship provides the practical resources of facilitating the growth of service-learning on a college campus. Aside from operational and staffing funds, institutional support also included: formal encouragement from the administration to the faculty to integrate service-learning into their courses; resources to aid faculty in both coordinating their service-learning and teaching them how to properly design and evaluate a service-learning course; and recognition of service-learning as a criteria for rank, tenure, and promotion within the institution. This type of support was found in some form at all of the institutions interviewed. Not surprisingly, the research found that if the cornerstone of institutional support was lacking, service-learning remained dormant or nonexistent on campuses. As a result, this attribute was included in the comprehensive definition of effective service-learning practices stated previously.

Mission. Coinciding with institutional support was the importance of the mission statement of the organization being an impetus for action. The language of the mission statement and subsequent dedication to the statement were key components of the seven programs interviewed. When asked what they would do first if they were to start a service-learning program at their college, 71% said they would examine their mission statement because typically at a private institution emphasis has been placed on civic responsibility and service. This corresponds with the literature review, which indicated that most private college and university mission statements consisted of the same elements: language on heritage, teaching, research, and service (Holland, 1999; Hughes & Adrian, 1997). Since each word of the statement should have meaning, the mission is a powerful advocate for designing opportunities that engage students and the campus community in fulfillment of the mission. Furthermore, the literature showed that the greatest commitment to service-learning occurred when it was explicitly linked to the mission and thus made a priority within the institution (Wutzdorff & Giles, 1997).

Definitions and guidelines. While the definitions and guidelines for service-learning have varied greatly, the programs that were effective had some form of definition or set of guidelines to direct their service-learning efforts. When asked to state their definition of service-learning, the content analysis identified several themes that institutions used when defining service-learning at their college or university. These were used to inform the reasoning for the comprehensive definition stated previously.

The research did reveal that a definition or set of guidelines is needed to clarify the difference between service-learning and other forms of volunteer work. More important, however, was that the interviews and literature review both indicated that in order for service-learning to be effective as a pedagogical tool, a proper working definition and/or guidelines must be *followed* (Astin et al., 2000; Eyler & Giles, 1999; Zlotkowski, 1998b). For example, 71% of the respondents interviewed had a definition, written guidelines, and assessment tools designed to assess the effectiveness of the service-learning on their campus. As a result, the service-learning staff was able to ensure the quality of the service provided, that learning took place, and that the service-learning met the intended objectives because guidelines were clearly communicated. Definitions and guidelines are not used for only assuring quality, but also to educate. Eyler and Giles (1999), found that one of the barriers to faculty using service-learning was simply not knowing what it is or how to effectively use it.

Academic validity. Typically, what differentiates service-learning from other forms of experiential learning or volunteer work is its connection to course learning objectives. Further, what naturally attracts faculty to using service-learning is the academic and moral growth students experience while involved in service-learning. Enos and Troppe (1996) discussed this in their research, stating that service-learning gains its academic credibility based upon the precept that the service must be tied to the learning objectives of the course. As a result, the emphasis upon service-learning being an academic pursuit is part of the proposed definition stated earlier in this article and has been included in other definitions of service-learning (Kendall, 1990; Campus Compact, 1996; Howard, 1998). In fact, six of the seven colleges interviewed by the researcher have their service-learning program funded by the Academic Affairs portion of their institution and four of the seven report directly to the Chief Academic Officer. But unless the academic component to service-learning is communicated and integrated, it is difficult to comprehend why faculty and the institution should consider service-learning in curricular planning and pursuits.

A Model for Private Higher Education

Research question three required the researcher to design a model of service-learning specifically for private colleges and universities based upon the findings of the review of the literature, unpublished survey and program interviews. What resulted were eight guidelines that form a model intended to aid in the development of a service-learning program or for use in evaluating an existing program. Many of the guidelines in the model coincide with the four key elements of "best practices" outlined previously, but provide them in a context for overall service-learning program effectiveness. Each guideline in the model builds upon the previous; however, if colleges are already engaged in service-learning the model can be used to assess current practices or in accordance to the specific needs of a campus. Further, the guidelines are meant to address both the philosophical and practical implications in designing an effective service-learning course and program. As a result, the following eight guidelines are recommended as a model for designing an effective service-learning program at a private college or university:

- Examine the Mission
- Enlist Others
- Establish a Definition
- Educate and Train
- Develop Community Partnerships
- Pilot Test
- Reflect and Evaluate
- Gain Institutional Support

Examine the mission. The mission of private colleges and universities should shape not only the motivation behind wanting to serve, but provide learning opportunities that will challenge and develop students holistically. Therefore, the first guideline is to examine the mission statement of the institution and determine how the college or university is fulfilling the mission through the curriculum and co-curriculum. Questions to consider when reviewing the mission statement include:

- What is the purpose of our mission?
- How is service developed in the students?
- What intentional activities or experiences are available that will ensure that the students develop a worldview that includes service to others?
- Are only voluntary service activities provided?
- What does the mission statement call the college or university to expect of its student's, campus community and relationship to others?

These are not questions that can necessarily be answered by one person, but perhaps should be the impetus for dialogue with others who may be supportive of service-learning. Through examining the mission and asking these questions, the philosophical reasoning and efficacy of service-learning should be evident and a shared vision can be developed. Records should be kept on the outcomes of these discussions and used in shaping the program and assessing its effectiveness. Ultimately, it is the mission statement that in many cases provides the justification for service-learning and the commitment needed to see an effective program develop.

Enlist others. Most service-learning programs start with a few people who have a heart for service and want to combine it with a love for learning. Therefore, in starting a service-learning program proceed by soliciting the support of others through current programs already in existence. Many of the respondents interviewed said they developed their program by dialoguing with faculty, staff and students who were already a part of a service club, certain majors, or other volunteer organizations on campus. This is the group of people who should be part of the discussion on the mission and purpose of the institution. Moreover, these people may already have contacts in the community and a willing desire to assist in the design or implementation of a service-learning course. This group does not need to be large, but it is important to bring them together and have an open discussion and start to develop interest and support with people who already are committed to the same principle of service.

Once these partnerships begin to develop, recruit people from this group to serve as an advisory board to assist in fulfilling the subsequent guidelines. This board should also be representative of people who may not be currently involved in service, but may be an untapped resource. The advisory board should include faculty from each of the academic divisions, students, and key staff and community members who can provide visibility of the effectiveness of the service-learning program while offering valuable insight and feedback. The program will need longevity beyond the initial people involved and an advisory board can provide the sustenance needed to aid in the growth and commitment of service-learning on campus.

Establish a definition. Earlier in this article the researcher provided a comprehensive definition of an effective service-learning class and program. As argued previously, a definition serves to educate, clarify and communicate the components of an effective service-learning course. Further, a definition will provide the outline for strategic planning and program assessment. Therefore, it is crucial that a definition is established that represents sound principles for designing an effective service-learning program as opposed to just another service opportunity. It should also embody the mission and unique purpose of the institution and therefore may not be exactly the same as the definition at another institution.

Educate and train. Once interest has been developed and a definition established, those involved need to be educated and trained. Forty-three percent of the respondents in the interviews moved the faculty from *interest in* service-learning to *implementation of* service-learning by hosting a workshop on campus. Even if only a few faculty are interested, if these individuals can implement effective service-learning classes and have a positive experience they will recruit more faculty in the future. In many cases, the institutions interviewed hired an outside consultant for their first workshop introducing service-learning to their campus.

Develop community partnerships. The community organizations that receive the service by the students are a very important partner in the learning process. It is imperative that people from the community are involved in the process on two levels: identifying the need and designing appropriate service activities. In order to do this, partnerships need to be developed with people in the community. This can be achieved by enlisting the assistance of those on the advisory board who already have relationships in the community. For example, if the volunteer center already works with several social service organizations, ask for the names of the individuals at those service locations and make initial contacts. These people will already know the college or university, its mission, and hopefully will have had a positive relationship with the students. If they do not have appropriate service needs, they can provide other contacts.

The community partners should also be educated and trained as to what service-learning is and what their role is in ensuring that a program is effective. As stated previously, service-learning is different than volunteer work and may require different expectations of the community organization especially if they are used to working with students in simply a volunteer status. It is important that this differentiation is clearly communicated and the established definition and guidelines explained. Regardless, some venue for education, training and dialogue should be established, as the community partners must be able to discuss their needs and how service-learning classes might address those needs.

Pilot test. As the previous guidelines come to fruition, it is time to pilot test a service-learning class. Repeatedly, when asked about the best way to get a service-learning program started, the respondents interviewed stated to start with one class or one faculty member. While the temptation is to jump in and pilot a class immediately, it is better to work through the previous guidelines-especially in regards to mission and training-before doing so. The ultimate purpose for piloting a class is to establish a foundation from which to learn and grow. Therefore, a solid foundation built around a clear definition, a mission-driven purpose, an effective design, and community need establishes a solid benchmark from which to ensure some level of success.

The pilot is not only a test of the service-learning program, but of the sincerity of purpose and commitment of those engaged in the design and implementation of service-learning. Service-learning is not contained in a classroom environment where the only implications of a poorly designed pilot program are the disappointment of the faculty and lack of learning for the students. Service-learning has the potential to impact people's lives, both in the community and within the institution, by the quality and attitude of those providing the service. Therefore, the pilot course must be designed responsibly. It is not worth the risk to pilot an inadequately planned program that either demeans the act of service or lessens the academic validity of service-learning. Instead, the pilot should represent the best efforts of those involved in the planning with the intention of creating an outstanding first impression to the college and community about the legitimacy and power of service-learning.

Reflect and evaluate. Just as reflection and assessment are key components of an effective service-learning class, they also are essential components in designing a service-learning program. The reflection process actually should begin during the first guideline when discussions take place regarding the role service-learning plays in fulfillment of the faith-based mission. The process of reflection and evaluation should continue more formally with the pilot class or courses and be a regular part of a service-learning program. Further, it is through reflection that cognitive and moral development takes place, as those engaged must connect the service and the learning. Therefore, it is an important tool for those involved in the design and implementation process.

One means of reflection is self-reflection on the process. Self-reflection often deals more with the intangible and a change in perspective or attitude based upon what is being experienced. While the faculty member and students are more directly involved in the service-learning, it is still valuable to allow those who have supported the development of the course or program to reflect on the process. This reflection can take place through informal meetings, reflection activities by those involved, and continual dialogue on the process and if it is meeting its intended purpose. This is especially important when conducting a pilot test of a service-learning course.

The evaluation process tends to focus on the more tangible aspects of service-learning. It often includes determining if the learning objectives of a course have been met through the service, assess actual student learning, and measure the impact the service has on the community. Again, this is also an important aspect of the pilot program. To evaluate the process it is helpful to keep samples of students' work, especially any written work that would document a continuum of thoughts or growth. Exams, projects, and any evaluation tools should be kept for documentation. The community member(s) should evaluate the process, both in written and oral formats, as well. Based upon the reflection and evaluation process, those involved can make the appropriate changes and determine the direction for a strategic plan for the institutionalization of a service-learning program at a particular college.

Gain institutional support. While the design and implementation of a service-learning class can be accomplished with few resources, if service-learning is going to grow on a campus it must have greater fiscal and verbal support. Reality is that financial support rarely comes without proof that the investment will reap positive outcomes. Indeed, most institutions researched found they gained institutional support *after* they had proven that service-learning could be an effective tool on their campus. This underscores the need to implement the previously stated guidelines as a means to be prepared and provide a strong argument for institutional support. Each guideline is a step towards this ultimate goal by: beginning with the mission, enlisting support, establishing a definition, providing training, identifying community partners, pilot testing a course and through reflection and evaluation creating a strategic plan for service-learning. The demonstrated interest, effort, and dedication inherent in the fulfillment of these guidelines serves to communicate the depth of commitment by those involved. This commitment combined with the emphasis upon the connection between service-learning and the faith-based mission could potentially serve as a catalyst for gaining support. While institutional support may happen gradually, it should be a pursuit nonetheless to ensure quality and sustainability of service-learning.

Conclusion

This concludes this study outlining the best practices of effective service-learning at private colleges and universities. As outlined in the research questions, the researcher has identified a comprehensive definition of service-learning, key elements of best practices in private higher education, and provided a model using eight guidelines for use in designing a service-learning program. The model suggests that designing an effective service-learning class is not enough, but that the leadership within the administration needs to make service-learning a priority.

The research also indicates that service-learning has the potential to be an effective and meaningful learning tool which exemplifies the mission of private higher education when designed appropriately. This research is meant to assist educators in designing and implementing service-learning through the proposed definition and guidelines.

Bibliography

Astin, A.W. "The Role of Service in Higher Education." *About Campus,* (March-April 1996): 14-19.

Astin, A.W., L. J. Vogelgesand, E. K. Ikeda, and J. A. Yee. "How service learning affects students." *Executive Summary, Higher Education Research Institute, UCLA* (2000).

Batchelder, T.H., and S. Root. (1994). "Effects of an undergraduate program to integrate academic learning and service: Cognitive, prosocial cognitive, and identity outcomes." *Journal of Adolescence,*(1994): 341-355.

Bringle, R.G. and J.A. Hatcher. (2000). "Institutionalization of service learning in higher education [CD-ROM]." *The Journal of Higher Education,* (May/June 2000). Article from: ProQuest File: 00221546

Campus Compact. (1996). "Wingspread principles of good practice for combining service and learning." Retrieved November 20, 2002, from http://www.compact.org/csds/slbrochureprinciples.html

Caron, B. (Ed.). "Service Matters: The engaged campus." *Campus Compact* (1999)

Driscoll, A, B. Holland, S. Gelmon, and S. Kerrigan. (1996). "An assessment model of service-learning: Comprehensive case studies of impact on faculty, students, community and institutions." *Michigan Journal of Community Service-Learning,* (1996): 66-71.

Enos S.L. and M.L. Troppe. "Service-learning in the curriculum." In *Service Learning in Higher Education,* ed. B. Jacoby & Associates. San Francisco: Jossey-Bass.

Eyler, J. and D.E.Giles Jr. *Where's the learning in service-learning?* San Francisco, CA: Jossey-Bass Publishers, 1999.

Harkavy, I & Benson, L. "De-platonizing and democratizing education as the bases of service-learning." In *Academic service learning: A pedagogy of action and reflection,* ed. R.A. Rhoads and J.P.F. Howard. San Francisco: Jossey-Bass Publishers, 1998.

Holland, B.A. "From murky to meaningful: The role of mission in institutional change." In *Colleges and universities as citizens,* eds. R.G. Bringle, R.Games, and E.A. Malloy. Needham, MA: Allyn & Bacon, 1999.

Howard, J. "Academic service learning: A counternormative pedagogy." In *Academic service learning: A pedagogy of action and reflection.* eds. R.A.Rhoads and J.P.F. Howard. San Francisco: Jossey-Bass Publishers, 1998.

Hughes, R.T. and W.B. Adrian. *Models for Christian higher education: Strategies for survival and success in the twenty-first century.* Grand Rapids, Mich.: Eerdmans, 1997.

Ikeda, E.K. "How does service enhance learning? Toward an understanding of the process." Unpublished Dissertation, UCLA, 1999.

Kendall, J. *Combining service and learning*. North Carolina: Publications Unlimited, 1990.

Mintz S.D. and G.W. Hesser. Principles of good practice in service-learning." In *Service-Learning in higher education,* eds. B. Jacoby & Associates. San Francisco: Jossey-Bass, 1996.

Morton, K. "Potential and practice for combining civic education and community service." In *Rethinking tradition: Integrating service with academic study on college campuses,* ed. T. Kupiec. Providence, R.I.: Education Commission for the States, 1993. *A Model for Effective Service-Learning Design and Implementation in Private Higher Education.*

Rockquemore, K.A. and R.H. Schaffer. "Toward a theory of engagement: A cognitive mapping of service-learning experiences." *Michigan Journal of Community Service Learning,* (2000): 14-25.

Schaffer, R.H. *"Survey of Christian colleges and universities service-learning programs".* Unpublished study, Pepperdine University, 2000.

Singleton, S., D. Hirsch, and C. Burack. "Organizational structures for community engagement." In *Colleges and universities as citizens,* eds. R.G. Bringle, R.Games, and E.A. Malloy. Needham, MA: Allyn & Bacon, 1999.

Ward, K. (1996). "Service-learning and student volunteerism: Reflections on institutional commitment." *Michigan Journal of Community Service Learning,*(1996): 55-65. Wutzdorff, A.J. and D.E. Giles. "Service-learning in higher education." In *Service-learning: Ninety-sixth yearbook of the national society for the study of education,* ed. J. Schine. Chicago: University of Chicago Press, 1997.

Zlotkowski, E."A service learning approach to faculty development." In *Academic service learning: A pedagogy of action and reflection.* eds R.A. Rhoads and J.P.F. Howard. San Francisco: Jossey-Bass Publishers, 1998a.

_____. *Successful service-learning programs: New models of excellence in higher education.* Bolton, MA: Anker Publishing Company, Inc., 1998b.

Chapter 5

Service-Learning and Community-Based Education

Community Based Science

A Service Learning Model

C. Sheldon Woods

Abstract: "Science Seekers" is an after school science program that provides hands-on science activities for children. The program is a partnership between university professors, university students, community volunteers and children from community based organizations, such as congregations, schools, government housing buildings and ethnic associations. In this service learning models, pre-service teachers from universities, gain experience providing instruction to students. The university students are providing a needed service to the community and they are reinforcing the learning theories that they learn in class.

Service Learning

Service learning is not a new concept. It has a long history in education and is gaining increased attention as part of the curriculum (Giles & Eyler, 1994). This has been bolstered in part by the National and Community Service Act of 1990 and the National Service Trust of 1993 in an effort to rebuild communities and public education (Moore and Sandholtz, 1994). In addition, more recent national movements such as Americorps, have put service learning on the national agenda.

Service learning has numerous definitions and synonyms. The Alliance for Service Learning in Education Reform (1993) defines service learning as a method where young people learn and develop through active participation in thoughtfully organized service experiences that meet the actual community needs and that are coordinated in collaboration with the school and community. Ward (1996) defines academic service learning as the combining of academic learning with an identified community need. While Checkoway (1996), defines community service learning as learning activities that combine classroom work with social and service action to promote student development of subject matter, knowledge, practical skills, social responsibility and civic values. The 1990 Community Service Act defines service learning as a method of learning in which students render needed services in their communities for academic credit, using and enhancing existing skills with time to "reflect on the service activity in such a way as to gain further understanding of the course content, a broader appreciation of the discipline, and an enhanced sense of civic responsibility" (Bringle and Hatcher 1995:112). Even though some of the terms are different the definitions have the same principle at their core. There is a reciprocal relationship involving students and the community where students enter the community, provide a service and in the process strengthen their own learning.

History and Theoretical Framework

John Dewey (1938) developed the concept of experiential learning. Advocates cite experiential learning most often as the foundation of service learning (Boyer, 1983, 1987; Clark & Welmers, 1994; and Lipka, Beane, and O'Connell, 1985). According to Johnson and Notah (1999), experiential learning is based on two principles: the principle of continuity and the principle of interaction. The synergistic effect of these principles means that life/educational experiences and habits of a student influence the students' current and future educational experiences. As a result educational institutions must provide opportunities for students to apply learning to their community and the world.

According to Carver (1997), service learning addresses "the three major goals of 'experiential education': allowing students to become more effective change agents, developing students' sense of belonging in the communities of which they are members, and developing student competence" (p 143). Even though service learning or community service, as it is also called has its theoretical basis in experiential learning, its early proponents can be found as far back as the 1920's. According to Carver (1997), early advocates of service learning (Hatch 1923 and Rugg 1923) believed it to be a means to cultivate democracy through civics education. Service learning continues to be used to promote political and social goals (Lipka et al., 1985; Melchior 2000; Jay 2000; Mooney & Edwards 2001; and Baise & Sleeter 2000).

DePaul University and the School of Education

DePaul University is a private university located in Chicago, IL. It is the largest Catholic University in the United States with an enrollment of 20,000 students. The university offers over 130 academic majors in undergraduate, graduate, professional, and doctoral programs on seven campuses. DePaul University students and faculty are actively engaged with the culturally rich urban environments through curricular offerings, research, and more than 70 public service programs.

DePaul University has a set of core values based on the teachings of St. Vincent DePaul. These core values influence the educational process. The core values are: holistic, integrated, creative, flexible, excellent, person oriented, collaborative and focused (Sullivan, 1997).

The DePaul University School of Education affirms that contemporary educational settings require professional urban educators who exercise skills, understanding and, above all, sound judgment. The school embraces a holistic orientation toward education, and strives for the positive transformation of persons and society.

As an urban institution, the SOE is committed to improving education in the metropolitan area and, in particular, the city of Chicago, by training professional urban educators. Framed within a commitment to diversity the SOE prepares students to be "Urban Professional Multicultural Educators" who: 1) integrate theory and practice; 2) consider multiple perspectives; 3) exhibit Vincentian personalism; 4) promote positive transformation and 5) function as life long learners. These core values of the university, coupled with the SOE Urban Professional Multicultural Educator model, create a mission of working in the community in underserved and neglected areas.

History and Mission of ASAP

After School Action Programs (ASAP), a program of Alternatives, Inc., is a Network of 30 youth serving agencies on the north side of Chicago and exists to strengthen the capacity of its members to work effectively with youth. ASAP accomplishes this by providing support through program development, resource development, training, leadership development, advocacy, and networking, community building. Members include ethnic associations, congregations, tenant associations, and non-profits. The following are some of the not for profit organizations that are members of ASAP: Alternatives, Inc, Bosnian Herzegovinian American Community Center, Cambodian Association of Illinois, 850 W. Eastwood tenants Association, Centro Romero, Chicago Uptown Ministry, Chinese Mutual Aid

Association, Eastwood Tower Tenants Association, Ethiopian Community Association of Chicago, InterChurch Refugee and Immigration Ministries, Jesus People, USA, United Winthrop Tower Tenants Association and Uptown Community Youth Program.

ASAP was founded in 1993 out of a community initiative designed to link youth serving agencies, large institutions, businesses, and families together. Concerned community members wanted an organization with the power to leverage resources, the dedication to advocate for and on behalf of youth, and the knowledge to enhance youth programming, and the courage to affect change within the social service system. Since its inception, ASAP has worked toward collaboration and communication among youth serving agencies. Effects of this include less unintentional duplication in the community and more effective programming across the community.

The heart of ASAP's work is in its strategic presence and interventions in the community. Resource development is important in a community that, while rich in developmental assets, is poor in traditional resources. ASAP offers a resource pool to distribute small seed grants within the Network for new and emerging initiatives. The Network also takes advantage of a 15 passenger van to transport youth to and from after school programs. Further, ASAP provides volunteers to agencies to increase program staff and a library to increase members' knowledge in a wide range of topics. ASAP offers frequent trainings to support youth workers in their professional development. All training topics originate from the Network and cover such topics as Creating and Managing a Fiscal Budget and Speaking with Youth about Sexuality. Trainings are held at least four times a year and are facilitated by "experts" in the topic's field. While ASAP brings in outside individuals to share knowledge, ASAP also recognizes the unique gifts in the community. Often a traditional "expert" is paired with a community member to train youth workers.

Leadership Development and Advocacy is key to the Network's success. The ASAP Network is a self-determined body. A body of youth workers called the Leadership Team guides most staff functions. The Leadership Team identifies important potential programs, issues affecting youth, and strategies to strengthen the Network. Youth workers who serve on the Leadership Team find that they do have power in a society that does not always value their profession.

ASAP also provides opportunities for youth, youth workers, and families to come together. Youth workers come together to create a support system through social gatherings in the neighborhood. Families come together to complete youth's participation in programs. The community comes together to celebrate the hard work and dedication of all its members. These gatherings offer people the chance to create a sense of relatedness among each other. The rational is that if people are related, then they can unite to accomplish anything.

Finally, ASAP's strongest strategy area is Program Development. ASAP offers technical assistance to its member organizations to develop their own in-house programming. The program collaborates with businesses and institutions to create innovative programming that can be intentionally duplicated throughout the community. These programs offer variety to traditional educational and recreational programs. They also allow youth to stretch their minds and imagine possibilities that are not taught in a traditional classroom setting.

Science Seekers Purpose and Description

One of ASAP's most successful programs is Science Seekers. Science Seekers is collaboration with DePaul University's School of Education and is a 10-week science initiative geared toward teaching complex scientific concepts through hands on activities and experiments. Science Seekers is designed to introduce youth to science innovatively. Many schools have found that students struggle with math and science. Science Seekers is an alternative to traditional classroom activities. Science Seekers aims to not only teach youth about the world around them, but to also foster an appreciation for the sciences and scientific thought and analysis. The question that students ask most often is "why". Why is the sky blue? Why does it rain? Why can't you see the stars during the day? Why do some animals walk while others fly? This program is designed to empower youth to ask these questions and then find the answers through thought provoking activities. Answers and solutions are not given to youth via a lecture. Instead, youth explore their world and discover the answer under the guidance of adults.

The Partnership

The partnership between the SOE and ASAP has developed over a six-year period. It developed out of mutual needs and collaboration. Pre-service teachers (SOE students) are required to complete 100 hours of clinical hours of observation before they are allowed to student teach. SOE students traditionally complete these observations during the daytime by visiting classrooms around the city. It is a challenge to find clinical sites to meet the schedules of adult and graduate students who work during the day. It is also challenging to find alternative site where students can get meaningful experiences. This matter is complicated by the commuter population that makes up the majority of the student body in the SOE. Between work and commuting to and from school many of the student's schedules are taxed to their limits. As a result of this dilemma it became important to find alternative what would provide opportunities for students to do science clinical hours. Initial attempts were to have students volunteer at science museums, judging science fairs and providing tutoring to students in science. These were good activities but they did not provide the same experiences as a classroom setting.

As the SOE was looking for alternative sites for clinical observation, ASAP was seeking university students to volunteer in a newly formed after school science program. They were working with another university initially but there was a shortage of volunteers. After initial conversations, a symbiotic partnership was formed.

The initial goal from the SOE was an alternative clinical observation site that met in the evenings. For ASAP it was to staff the participating community sites with university students to run its program. Over time the relationship grew, with each partner taking a more active role and benefiting from the process. Initially the SOE students went to the site and taught their classes with a community liaison (an adult member from the community being served) and received clinical credit for it.

The program has now evolved to a point where there is collaboration on the Science Seeker's curriculum. The youth in the program provide feedback as to the topics they want to study each cycle. The cycles usually coincide with the university terms. A SOE faculty member and ASAP personnel get together to discuss the curriculum, share resources and discuss how the curriculum meets the state and district goals. An intern working for ASAP completes the curriculum. One of the benefits of this is that the curriculum now more closely matches what the pre-service teachers are learning in class and what the youth would see in school.

The SOE students visit their negotiated and/or assigned site each week and conduct science activities with youth from the community. The SOE students adapt the curriculum to meet the needs of the specific needs of the youth at each site. This is done in a fun, hands-on and informal manner. It is meant to be different and more relaxed than the traditional classroom setting. All of the activities are designed for active hands-on participation, primarily because it is an after school program and it is voluntary for the youth. This has in effect become a built-in formative evaluation for the university students. If the community youth do not like what is happening the Science Seekers or find it boring they will not attend future sessions. This puts pressure on the pre-service from the university to get to know the youth and present the curriculum in such as way that it is fun and exciting.

The students reflect on their experiences by journal writing and class discussions. This self-evaluation is the only type of evaluation for the university students. It is difficult to grade. A great deal of time is spent encouraging the students to do meaningful reflection about what they are experiencing. They are encouraged to do more then just write what happened, but to write about their feelings about what happened and how the children responded to certain activities and what could have been done differently. Some are better at this than others. There is also class time devoted to reflection. Other students who do not participate in the program benefit from the discussion and students compare the alternative site to the traditional clinical site and discuss the differences.

Benefits and Challenges

Service learning has some inherent benefits and challenges. Each service project will add unique circumstances to the milieu. The benefits to the university are greater visibility in the community, exposure to potential future students and aid in fulfilling Vincentian mission. DePaul University has a reputation of active community involvement and such activities attract students that seek opportunities for social justice.

This active community involvement does present challenges for the university, namely, it is time consuming for participating faculty members and it is difficult to for enough volunteers for the numerous service projects.

For the Pre-service teacher (SOE student) the benefits are numerous. Students gain personal growth, social, professional and practical development, as well as increased civic awareness coupled with cognitive real world linkages. While the students are in a program preparing for a professional career, they are still learning a great deal about themselves and the world around them. Many are facing the end of their dependence on their families while others are facing a change in careers. This service learning opportunity provides them with opportunities grow and develop.

The pre-service student is also faced with some challenges, many of which involve things beyond their control. Service learning is not a process that students traditionally encounter in education programs; as a result they are apprehensive and lack confidence initially. There are numerous surprises and perplexities involved in service learning. Emergencies can arise with the participating agencies or with the students, creating stressful and trying situations. Scheduling conflicts are initial hurdles for students. Students must juggle their schoolwork, job, family and their service project. Time management becomes a way of life. Another challenge for students is uncertainty in responsibilities. While the outcomes of the project are stressed and known to students when they volunteer, they are working with very diverse and different community agencies, each with different expectations. It takes some time for students to negotiate expectations with each agency.

ASAP and the community benefit from the partnership. ASAP gains direct aid in fulfilling its mission by having more opportunities for collaborations and enhanced programmatic offerings. ASAP saves money in that there is more effective use of resources, no need to hire additional staff, development of reusable curriculum and the ability to offer science activities at multiple sites. The community benefits from student investments of creativity and enthusiasm, which leads to community development and renewal.

ASAP faces a variety of challenges some of which have a direct impact on the community. There is inconsistency among sites and member organizations and this often leads to last minute changes and problems that ASAP must solve. ASAP is never sure how many SOE students will volunteer to participate with Science Seekers each program cycle and this affects program offerings. Science Seekers is an elective program for youth of the community and attendance and retention in the program can be sporadic. It is also challenging to develop a science curriculum for a multi-aged population with a diversity of needs.

Youth participating in Science Seekers benefit from the program in many ways. First and foremost, they have a safe place to be after school and develop critical thinking skills by reinforcing scientific concepts and principles. They have significant interaction with university students who serve as role models and they gain exposure to science careers through field trips. Lastly the students have fun while gaining a stronger sense of community and family interaction. Families are encouraged to attend a culminating activity where the youth have a quiz bowl and demonstrate science activities for their families.

The challenges that youth face are due mainly to the nature of the structure of Science Seekers. Students often have a short-lived relationship with the SOE student because of the relatively short duration of the program cycle. Youth have a longer school day because Science Seekers does occur after school. Science Seekers meets once a week and as a result the instruction is fragmented and time management becomes an issue.

The challenges are opportunities for growth and development if viewed in an affirming manner. They can become obstacles that dissolve partnerships if not addressed in a positive manner.

Personal Reflections

Involvement in this project is very rewarding professionally and personally for all participants. Students gain practical experience that cannot be duplicated in the classroom. The community becomes their classroom. Students are exposed to communities that they otherwise might not experience. Furthermore, the students actually teach the class and work with a very ethnically diverse group of youth. Where multicultural education is the focus of many teacher education programs, it is rare to find a program that offers practical experience for the students. Science Seekers provides students with an opportunity to put into practice much of the science methods and multicultural theories that they have learned. Instead of relying exclusively on readings, class discussions and passive visits to observe in a multicultural setting, students in Science Seekers deal first hand with issues, such as linguistic diversity, cross cultural classroom management, class issues and race relations. These are issues that students might not face until student teaching or later in their career.

As a professor, it is very rewarding to see students return to class excited about a lesson that they taught or something that they learned about the community. They very often learn a great deal of authentic information about different cultural groups. Misconceptions are shattered and students have a greater sense of the community and how they relate to it. Students are encouraged to reflect on their initial thoughts about the community and students. They are then encouraged to reflect on their new thoughts and critique what has changed and how they have grown. This self-reflection and critique is an ongoing process and should be encouraged by all parties involved in the process.

The experience is not always affirming. There have been instances where students have learned that they were not cut out to be teachers or that they do not want to teach in an urban setting or a multicultural setting. There have also been instances where it was apparent that a student still had a great deal of maturing both socially and professionally. It was good that these lessons are learned before they started their careers as educators.

Overall the SOE students that participate in Science Seekers enjoy the program a great deal. They also gain impressive experience to put on their resumes. They cannot only speak about things they learned in their academic program but they can speak about how they put these into practice in the community in their own class. This makes them very marketable in the job market.

Lessons Learned

Many of the difficulties encountered in this type of learning can be addressed through a few simple steps.

Orienting Students

One of the initial hurdles to cross each cycle of Science Seekers is recruiting students from the SOE and training them. Most of the students that volunteer are very eager to work with the program but still have some reservations because of the new style of learning. It is important to have community partners present the program and what it has to offer to the students. This provides students and opportunity to ask questions and gain knowledge of the program before they commit themselves to it. It is also important that the community partner provide written material about the program and the community. It is also critical to provide students with time to form questions and a vehicle to get in touch with community agency to get answers later. Some students might feel pressured to volunteer and providing a way for them to gain more information later reduces some of this pressure. It is also important to stress to students the seriousness of the project and the responsibilities that come with it. This should be in writing somewhere, either in the course syllabus or in a service contract.

Monitoring and Evaluating Students

This can be a time consuming and somewhat nebulous area. It is important to seek information from students on a consistent basis regarding their experiences and to provide feedback and guidance as appropriate. Refrain from being hasty to solve student problems, yet provide them with guidance and assistance in working through tensions they may have. It is important to do this is such a way that the student understands that you care about them and are not setting aside their problem but, rather you are encouraging them, with guidance, to work through it.

Because of the nature of service learning work, evaluation is not as clear as in traditional coursework. Expected outcomes need to be discussed ahead of time. Students should be assessed on the basis of these expected outcomes. In addition to this, some sort of formative assessment should be completed. This can take several forms such as reflected writing, class discussions, individual discussion and reports and/or a conference with the community partner to discuss progress. Whichever is used the students should be made aware of this from the beginning.

Sustaining the Partnership

Collaborations are not to be taken for granted. Any change with either partner can jeopardize the working relationship. Communication is paramount. It is important to communicate with all the parties involved know what is expected of them. This is especially important with the SOE students. They are still in student mode while acting in a professional role. Students make a commitment to be responsible for a group of youth and they must show up each week to meet those students. They are not able to skip this responsibility like they sometimes skip class. It is also critical that there be effective communication between the partners and the community sites. Small tensions between the partners can fester and become major tensions that strain the collaboration. It is important that any conflicts are quickly resolved.

Sustaining the partnership takes work. It is important to document progress and setbacks. Roles must be clarified and confirmed often. This is important because the network of sites is composed of very diverse ethnic and social groups from the community with different needs. Conflict resolution must be expedient to sustain the partnership and should be responsive to cultural differences. Furthermore, each party involved in the conflict sees it from a different perspective, which is colored by their own cultural norms. Each partner must be organized and able to provide the promised support. Failure to provide promised support can doom the partnership.

Strengthening the Partnership

Strengthening the partnership is relatively easy, but time consuming. The community voice must be heard and legitimized. Members of the community must be part of the learning experience and not just passive bystanders. This is why Science Seekers involves a community liaison at each site. This person is able to speak about the needs of the community and inform the community about what is happening with Science Seekers.

The university students must see the community beyond its needs. Students must be trained to see the strengths in the community and the assets that the community has to offer. If a student goes into the community with the notion that they are there to save it, they are going to have problems. This attitude will affect their behavior and the community will resent them.

Conclusion

In conclusion, the Science Seekers program is a successful model for public service learning. This program builds on the service learning history in education by pairing student experience, reflection and learning, with responsiveness to community needs. Overall the experience of the participants: students, SOE, ASAP, and not-for-profits, has been very positive, but there have been some developmental steps along the way to strengthen the program and avoid problems.

Communication is crucial. This cannot be stressed too much. Because of the number of parties involved, there are many opportunities for miscommunication. All parties involved should express their thoughts in regular discussions to avoid conflicts and solve problems.

This is only one model of service learning. There are numerous models and opportunities to provide students with experiential learning and give back to the community. Service learning provides practical experience for students, increases their civic awareness and helps to sustain and develop communities.

References

Alliance for Service Learning in Education Reform. (1993). Standards of quality for schoolbased service learning. Equity and Excellence in Education, 26 (2), 71-73.

Baise, M.B., & Sleeter, C. E. (2000). Community-based service learning for multicultural teacher education. Educational Foundations, 14 (2) 33.

Boyer, E. L. (1983). High School: A report on secondary education in America. New York: Harper & Row. Boyer, E.L. (1987). Service: Linking school to life. Community Education Journal, 15 (1), 7-9 Bringle, R. and Hathcer, J. (1996). Implementing service learning in higher education. Journal of Higher Education, 67 (2), 221-239. Carver, R.L. (1997). Theoretical underpinnings of service learning. Theory into Practice, 36 (3), 143-149. Checkoway, B. (1996). Combining service and learning on campus and in the community. Phi Delta Kappan, 77 (9), 600-606. Clark, S.N., & Welmers, M. J. (1994) Service learning: A natural link to interdisciplinary studies, Schools in the Middle, (7) 11-15.

DeJong, L., & Groomes, E. (1996). A constructivist teacher education program that incorporates community service to prepare students to work with children living in poverty. Action Teacher Education, 18 (2), 86-95.

DeVitis, J., Johns, R., and Simpson, D. (1998). To serve and learn: The spirit of community in liberal education. New York: Peter Lang.

Dewey, J. (1938). Experience and education. New York: Collier.

Giles, D.E. and Eyler, J. (1994). The theoretical roots of service-learning in John Dewey: Toward a theory of service-learning. Michigan Journal of Community learning, 1 (1), 77-85.

Hatch, R. W. (1923). A program for the social studies in the junior and senior high school. In G.M. Whipple (Ed.), National Society for the Study of Education yearbook 22. Bloomington, IL: Public School Publishing.

Jay, G. (2000). The community in the classroom. Academe, 86 (4), 33-37.

Johnson, A.M., & Notah, D. J. (1999). Service learning: History. Literature review, and a pilot study of eighth graders. The Elementary School Journal, 99 (5), 453-467.

Lipka, R. P., Beane, J.A., & O'Connell, B.R. (1985). Community service projects: Citizenship in action. Bloomington, IN: Phi Delta Kappa Educational Foundation.

Melchoir, A. (2000) Service learning at your service. The Education Digest, 66, (2), 26-32.

Mooney, L. A., & Edwards, B. (2001). Experimental learning in sociology: Service learning and other community-based learning initiatives. Teaching Sociology, 29 (2), 181- .

Moore, K.P., and Sandholtz, J.H. (1999). Designing successful service learning projects for urban schools. Urban Education, 34 (4), 480-498.

Rugg, H. (1923). Do social studies prepare pupils adequately for life activities? In G.M. Whipple (Ed.), National Society for the Study of Education Yearbook 22, Bloomington, IL: Public School Publishing.

Sullivan, L. (1997). The core values of Vincentian Education. New York: Niagara University.

Swick, K.J. (1999). Service learning helps future teachers strengthen caring perspectives. The Clearing House, 73 (1), 29-32.

Ward, K., (1996). Service learning: Reflections on institutional commitment. Michigan Journal of Community Service Learning, 3, 55-65.

Chapter 6

Service-Learning and Democratic Civic Education

Teachers as Involved Intellectuals in Society and the Community

A Democratic Civic Education Model

Esther Yogev, Kibbutzim College of Education, Israel
Nir Michaeli, Kibbutzim College of Education, Israel

Abstract: This article presents a uniqe model for teacher training which was deve-
loped at the Kibbutzim College of Education in Tel Aviv. The model is directed cre-
ates a comprehensive concept for training teachers to serve as involved intellectuals
in the community. Teachers acting in this fashion are those whose professional iden-
tity leans on robust intellectual self-esteem, a culture of active concern about other
people, awareness of social activism and a commitment to public activity. The mod-
el has taken shape over the last two years at the Kibbutzim College of Education. It
began as an overall conceptual system containing a guiding rationale and practical
experience of various types that are part of appropriate academic teaching and at-
tendant research observation. This article will describe the model from its theoretical
and applicatory aspects, and will comprise three main parts: The first part presents
the Israeli social, cultural and educational contexts in which teacher training takes
place and its effect on forming the professional identity of its graduates. The second
part presents a theoretical outline of the characteristics of the educator acting as an

*involved intellectual while employing the ideas of Antonio Gramsci as a basis to val-
idate teacher training which intensifies the sense of professional capability in novice
teachers. The third part presents the main points of the change introduced into the
training in two parallel application parameters: expanding the students' experiential frameworks in the community and changes in the academic syllabi and campus
life. The preliminary findings of the accompanying study present the influence of the
change on the perceptions of novice teachers.*

Introduction

A recent comprehensive empirical study has verified what has existed for
thousands of years, from Plato to the present day, at the core of educational
philosophy and is perceived intuitively by the public: the fact that the teacher is the key to educational endeavor.[1]

This recognition has caused researchers, practitioners and public figures
to consider the question of the contemporary teacher's function and status.
Numerous countries have introduced varied reforms that participate in the
effort to find the practical golden mean whereby top-quality people will be
attracted to the teaching profession.

The study states that investment in teacher training was observed as
being more effective in leveraging students' achievements than similar investment in school reform.[2] As education researcher Michael Fullan put it:
'Teacher education has the honor of being the worst problem and the best
solution in education'[3].

Recognizing the importance of teacher training on the one hand, and
the challenges currently facing it on the other, this article presents a different training model – an attempt to train teachers as 'involved intellectuals'
in society and the community. Teachers acting as involved intellectuals are
those whose professional identity leans on robust intellectual self-esteem, a
culture of active concern about other people, awareness of social activism
and a commitment to public activity. This attempt has taken shape over the
last two years at the Kibbutzim College of Education. It began as an overall
conceptual system containing a guiding rationale and practical experience
of various types that are part of appropriate academic teaching, and attendant research observation.

1. *How the World's Best-performing School Systems Come Out on Top*. McKinsey & Company, September 2007. http://www.mckinsey.com/clientservice/socialsector/resour-
ces/pdf/Worlds_School_Systems_Final.pdf

2. Darling-Hammond, L., & Ball, D., *Teaching for High Standards: What Policymakers
Need to Know and Be Able to Do*, Philadelphia, PA: National Commission on Teaching and America's Future Consortium for Policy Research in Education, 1998.

3. Fullan, M., "Why Teachers Must Become Change Agents", *Educational Leadership*,
50 (6) March 1993, 16, 12-17.

The article will describe the training model from its theoretical and applicatory aspects, and will comprise three main parts. In the first part we will briefly present the Israeli social, cultural and educational contexts in which teacher training takes place and its effect on forming the professional identity of its graduates. It will present the artificial division that has been created between educational endeavor and social critique of the reality of life in Israel, and will raise the need for teacher training that nurtures a position of pedagogic activism in novice teachers. In the second part we shall present a theoretical outline of the characteristics of the educator acting as an involved intellectual while employing the ideas of Antonio Gramsci[4] as a basis to validate teacher training which intensifies the sense of professional capability in novice teachers. In the third part we will present the training model for involved-educators that was developed at the Kibbutzim College of Education. This part will present the main points of the change introduced into training in two parallel application parameters: expanding the students' experiential frameworks in the community and changes in the academic syllabi and in campus life. The preliminary findings of the accompanying study will present the influence of the change on the perceptions of novice teachers.

Teacher Training in Israel in Social, Cultural and Educational Contexts

Teacher training and the educational system work within broad social, cultural and economic contexts and therefore any discussion of teacher training mandates a basic knowledge of these contexts. This knowledge serves as a basis for an understanding of the problem inherent in the prevailing training model and of the proposed solution in training teachers acting as involved intellectuals.

The Israeli educational system works within a complex social context: Israeli society lives in the reality of a prolonged regional conflict and is also characterized by wide socio-economic gaps and intercultural and religious tensions.

In its early decades Israel developed a social-democratic structure and its society enjoyed high standards of cohesion and mutual commitment and responsibility. In the last three decades, it has undergone comprehensive

---

4.Antonio Gramsci (1891-1937) was an Italian philospher, writer, politician and political theorist. A founding member and and onetime leader of the Communist Party of Italy, he was imprisoned by Mussolini's fascist regime. Gramsci wrote more than 30 notebooks and 3000 pages of history and analysis during his imprisonment. These writings, known as the *Prison Notebooks*, contain Gramsci's tracing of Italian history and nationaliusm, as well as some ideas in Marxist theory, critical theory and educational theory. He is renowned for his concept of cultural hegemony as a means of maintaining the state in a capitalist society and for his ideas about the role of the intellectuals in society.

change. From a society of solidarity, it has become individualistic and alienated. Since the end of the 1970s, Israeli society adopted the principles of neo-liberal economics and embarked on privatization and decentralization processes in government and public institutions. These processes created a socio-economic reality of widening gaps, erosion of the welfare state and massive growth in private spending required for health services, education and basic subsistence[5]. In general terms, suspicion of public institutions in general and state-owned ones in particular become prevalent in Israeli society. As a substitute and solution for increasing social difficulties and needs, we are seeing the flourishing of the 'third sector'.[6] In tandem with these processes, the Israeli public harbors feelings of frustration, despair, and even revulsion towards anything identified with politics.

These social processes are deeply influenced by the global post-industrial trends prevailing in the Western world. These include the consolidation of an exhibitionistic consumer society that justifies hedonism and living for the moment and displays sentiments of rejection and contempt for any aspiration towards social reform[7].

Together with a culture of social nihilism fostered by a flamboyant consumer culture, global trends also led to a breach of traditional national boundaries and redrawing them in a particular, tribal and local direction. Zygmunt Bauman termed this phenomenon 'glocalization'[8].

5.Shafir, G., Peled, Y., *The New Israel: Peacemaking and Liberalization*. Colorado, West View Press, 2000.

6.Gidron, B., "The Evolution of Israel's Third Sector: The Role of Predominant Ideology", *Voluntas: International Journal of Voluntary and Nonprofit Organizations*, 8 (1).1997, 11-38; Gidron, B., Bar, M., Katz, H., *The Israeli Third Sector: Between Welfare State and Civil Society*. New York, Kluwer Academic Publishers, 2004.

7.The philosopher-sociologist Christopher Lasch called it the 'culture of narcissism', which in his view spawned a 'me' generation devoid of social direction and compass, which spouted empty 'freedom' slogans and is characterized by detachment, boredom, violent tendencies and civil and political apathy. See, Lasch, C., *The Culture of Narcissism, American Life in An Age of Diminishing Expectations*. New York, W.W. Norton and Company, 1979/1991, 13-27, 66-71.

8.Glocalization according to Bauman theory is a social division between the globally mobile and the locally stationary: the economic, technological, educated, political and successful elites move from one end of the world to the other while physically and mentally detaching themselves from the specific identity space of their country. On the other hand, there is a growing stratum in local population, which due to the weakening of the welfare state, feels abandoned and nurtures universal tribalism on the basis of ethnicity, religion, gender, etc Bauman, Z., *Liquid Modernity*. Cambridge, Polity Press, 2000.

The weakening of the public education system intensifies the process of uprooting the political aspects from the educational endeavor and discourse, focuses teaching and learning on instrumental objectives, and subjugates them to narrow and measurable standards[9].

Analysis of the changes in the educational system in this spirit is commensurate with the findings of McPhail and Kaur who hold that an educational system adapts itself to the political climate in which it exists. For example, public education at the beginning of the twentieth century existed under the aegis of political trends characterized by an optimistic, even utopian, view of democracy. Accordingly, public education adopted the progressive educational aims of John Dewey, which perceived schools as democratic cooperative communities. In contrast, at the beginning of the twenty-first century, the educational system is influenced by a neo-liberal political spirit which demands a free market logic and narrow achievement-oriented standards. The authors seek a way of restoring the progressive spirit and the nurturing of democratic citizenship to the educational system by instilling changes in teacher training[10].

The existing training methods employed by the majority of colleges preserves the conventional positions and educational methods extant in the Israeli education system and thwart any attempt to change them. The majority of teachers perceive their mission in the system as training their students for an efficient and beneficial integration into society as it is today. The educational system avoids social and political issues and cloaks itself in a mantle of false neutrality acquired at the cost of separating social critique and educational endeavor.

Any attempt to change the Israeli education system mandates a change in educators' professional self-definition and the training that shapes them. We would like to see an educator who perceives himself as an educational leader and involved intellectual who does not seek solely to reproduce the extant but also seeks to mark the worthy and the possible.

The Teacher as an Involved Intellectual

Antonio Gramsci spoke of the need for 'organic intellectuals'. He thought that civil society is the main sphere of activity of politics. He stressed that no economic factor can act without passing through human consciousness. 'Organic intellectuals,' according to Gramsci, are people who are not de-

9.Nichols, S. L. & Berliner, D. C., *Collateral Damage: How High Stakes Testing Corrupts America's Schools*. Cambridge, Harvard Education Press, 2007. It is worthy of note that these forces lean on the findings of various international comparative studies that position the Israeli education system at the bottom of the scale of developing nations in everything pertaining to gaps and achievements. See, for example, the 2008 OECD Report.

10.McPhail, J. C., Kaur, B. "In Search of a Participatory Democratic Vision in Teacher Education", in Freeman-Moir, J., Scott, A., (eds.), *Shaping the Future - Critical Essays on Teacher Education*. Rotterdam, Sense Publishers, 2007, 235-256.

tached from the very thin fabric of public life but strengthen the dimension of knowledge within it. They are the appropriate link between intellectual critique of the extant and those sections of the public that have not detached themselves from the consciousness boundaries of the hegemony.[11] Gramsci's concept of an 'organic intellectual' marks a different possible option for describing the desirable characteristics of the educator as an educational leader. It is not our intention to propose the direct application of Gramsci's ideas here. We will use the term as a basis to justify teacher training reinforces the novice teacher's intellectual self-image and nurtures in them a philosophy of pedagogic activism and public responsibility.

According to Gramsci, hegemony is a complex arrangement of values and meanings which accord legitimacy to social and political reality. A project becomes hegemonic when certain ways of life become the natural way of observing and accepting reality. At the same time, other ways of conceptualizing are removed from the compass of public legitimacy and presented as inconceivable. To achieve its objective the hegemonic group positions itself at the center of social life as a kind of 'core' of society and fills the entire space of public consciousness.

There are groups within the fabric of civil society for which the tension between the picture of reality offered by the hegemony and their real experiences is increasing. Against the backdrop of this gap, foci of opposition to hegemonic order are constantly being formed[12]. The hegemony of the forces of change is the condition and objective for the success of change, and here Gramsci accords great weight to the active role of the 'organic intellectual':

> "The mode of being of the new intellectual can no longer consist in eloquence, which is an exterior and momentary mover of feelings and passions, but in active participation in practical life, as an constructor, organizer, "permanent persuader" and not just simple orator... from technique-as-work one proceeds to technique-as-science and to the humanistic conception of history, without which one remains "specialized" and does not become "directive" (specialized and political)"[13].

Since Gramsci assumed that in every human being lies a potential intellectual[14] and that this potential can also be fostered in the weak strata that are not within the bounds of the hegemony, there is no field more appropriate for achieving this aim than education.

11.Gramsci. A., *Selections from the Prison Notebooks*, (edited and translated by Hoare, Q. and Smith, G. N), London, Lawrence and Wishart, 1971, 5-23.

12.Gramsci. A., *op.cit.*, 12-13, 55-60, 261, 404.

13.Gramsci, A., *op. cit.*, 10.

14.Gramsci, A., *op. cit.*, 323.

But to lay the foundations for change, educators must abandon their role as lackeys of the ruling hegemony and take upon themselves the responsibility to act as 'organic intellectuals' within the community and the nation.[15]

Gramsci's idea of the 'organic intellectual educator' is reinforced by the epistemological-existential elements lying at the basis of critical pedagogic perception. Like Gramsci, leading critical pedagogy thinkers such as Paolo Freire, Henry Giroux, Peter McLaren, Ira Shor and others[16] view the formal educational system as a political forum which plays a leading role in shaping a public consciousness in which the hegemony can reproduce itself. In his book, *Teachers as Intellectuals: Towards a Critical Pedagogy of Learning*, Giroux proposes a critical concept of education in the sense of the educational praxis incumbent upon the intellectual as set out by Gramsci. He views educators as responsible for raising an involved, critical citizen with a developed sense of justice and of concern about others. Critical education should empower and reinforce the learner so that he can decipher the language of the hegemony, identify through a critical reading of reality the factors and forces influencing his life, and develop for himself an informed direction and appropriate skills which will enable him to lead his life for his own benefit and that of his community[17]. The problematic limitation in this context is that teachers in the education system usually act in their "comfort zone" or as Bourdieu puts it, in the framework of their professional 'habitus of the field'. Bourdieu's 'habitus' is the categories of consciousness that are internalized through socialization and which activate people in everyday social situations. This activity is characterized by a low level of awareness and does not exist in a conscious adherence to rules, calculation, consideration and clarification. In other words, the professional field of education, despite its being a locale of hegemonic conflict, is characterized by a political language not identified as political. This language is characterized by rhetoric of neutrality and is validated by its avoidance of trenchant debate and a denial of the existence of the political struggle per- se[18].

15. Gramsci, A., *op. cit.*, 26-43; Smith, M.K., *Local Education: Community, Conversation, Praxis*. Buckingham, Open University Press, 1994, 127.

16. Freire, P., *Pedagogy of the Oppressed*, trans. Ramos, M.B., New York, Herder & Herder, 1970; Giroux, H. "Postmodernism and the Discourse of Educational Criticism", *Journal of Education*, 1988; McLaren, P., *Life in Schools*. New York & London, Longman, 1989; Shor, I., *Empowering Education, Critical Teaching for Social Change*. Chicago, Chicago University Press, 1992.

17. Giroux, H., *Teachers as Intellectuals: Towards a Critical Pedagogy of Learning*. New York, Bergain & Garvey, 1988.

18. Bourdieu, P., *In Other Words: Essays toward a Reflective Sociology*. Stanford, CA, Stanford University Press, 1990; *Practical Reason: On the Theory of Action*. Stanford, CA, Stanford University Press, 1998.

In order to empower the critical literacy of teacher training and reinforce the basis for cultivating a democratic culture, experiential locales and learning patterns must be created that will equip novice teachers with the tools required for advancing socio-political education[19] in the education system such as ways of dealing with current affairs for discussion in the public arena; group study; developing curricula linked to the students' real life questions; making the students partners in shaping the school community, familiarization with and activity in non-formal education systems, and so on.

The training model presented below was designed to nurture professional consciousness and identity in teachers that will enable them to act as involved intellectuals in their schools.

Model for Training Teachers Involved in Society and the Community

Nurturing teachers to be involved intellectuals and the intellectual, consciousness and pedagogic empowerment from which it draws its justification as described above, finds expression in the 'service-learning' model. The aim of this teacher-training model is twofold: to create meaning for practical personal knowledge within a context that does not leave learning solely on the theoretical level and to enable students to experience the community and move in addition to the school experience. The basic premise of an experiential setup such as this is that the students' three spheres of study – the academic sphere at college that provides them with theoretical knowledge, the school sphere that introduces them to formal education, and the non-formal education sphere that introduces them to the community and society, will nourish their learning in various aspects and endow it with broader meaning. This combination of the three learning spheres also provides pedagogic enrichment and variety since it enables the students to be exposed to non-formal teaching and learning approaches based on active participation and involvement.

The students' experience with a training model that connects formal and non-formal education comprises three components: a link between theoretical knowledge and reality; cultivating commitment to and empathy with pupils; and increasing professional capabilities.

1. **Teaching that links academic-theoretical knowledge with reality**. Lave and Wenger speak of learning with authentic participation attended by a theoretical-professional discourse as the creation of new knowledge

---

19. Galston William A, "Civic Knowledge, Civic Education, and Civic Engagement: A Summary of Recent Research". *International Journal of Public Administration*. Vol. 30 (6 & 7), 2007. pp. 623 – 642; Macedo Stephen, *Diversity and distrust: civic education in a multicultural democracy*. Harvard University Press, 2003; Syvertsen, Amy K.; Flanagan, Constance A.; Stout, Michael D. *Best Practices in Civic Education: Changes in Students' Civic Outcomes*. Center for Information and Research on Civic Learning and Engagement, (CIRCLE).2007. In: http://eric.ed.gov/ERICDocs/data/ericdocs2sql/content_storage_01/0000019b/80/36/29/6d.pdf.

in the professional training of 'communities of practice'. Their premise is based on a contextual approach that views such learning processes as a renewed and subjective interpretation of reality in the immediate context of professional training.[20] The teaching trainee becomes aware of the community structure, learns to read its cultural codes and norms, knows the central figures active in it, is exposed to its unique forces and dark corners, identifies its place in Israeli society and maps its needs. Confronting the students' previously held assumptions while examining them in the field of a different culture can challenge their familiar cultural conventions and raise essential questions regarding the educational endeavor and their professional identity[21]. Students' practical work in the community and academic study of the social context enables them to create personal-practical knowledge and expose it to and connect it with theoretical knowledge.

2. Teaching that fosters commitment to and empathy with pupils. Training students through service to the community seeks to implant in their developing professional identity a sense of commitment to and concern for the educational endeavor. Non-formal educational encounters are usually characterized by a personal relationship between teacher and student. In this kind of relationship, competitiveness, alienation or achievement orientation is absent. Practice and learning in an informal framework allows the teacher trainee to shape a supportive attitude that meets the needs of pupils[22].

3. Teaching that enhances professional capabilities. A professional training program while serving the community and accompanied by reflective and informed observation of the process undergone by the students will reinforce their sense of professional capability and enhance their real ability to decipher, analyze and propose solutions for difficult situations and conflict.[23] Teacher training that requires students to leave the classroom and which familiarizes with experience in the community strengthens their personal and intellectual confidence, expands their critical thinking and heightens their sense of responsibility. A training model such as this will position the future teacher at the center of his/her professional community and heighten the sense that s/he can lead change in it.

At the Kibbutzim College of Education, the vision of training teachers as involved intellectuals was translated into two parallel tracks: expanding the novice teacher's practical experience in the community in the formal and

20. Lave, J. & Wenger, E. *Situated-Learning: Legitimate Peripheral Participation*. Cambridge, Cambridge University Press, 1991.

21. Anderson, J. B., "Service Learning and Preservice Teacher Education". *Denver: Education Commission of the States, Learning in Deed Issue Paper*, 2002.

22. Buber, M., *I and Thou* (trans. R. Gregory Smith), Edinburgh, T. & T. Clark, 1958; Noddings, N., *The Challenge to Care in Schools: An Alternative Approach to Education*. New York, Teachers College Press, 1992.

23. Pearson, S., *Finding Common Ground: Service Learning and Education Reform*. American Youth Policy Forum, U.S.A, 2000.

non-formal educational frameworks and deepening social knowledge, critical thinking and cultural infrastructure while combining non-formal pedagogic aspects with the curriculum and maintaining academic campus life:

Learning in the Community and in Society: Extending Community Experience and the Social Involvement Program

Developing Community-involved Pedagogic Training

One of the unique and central components of teacher training is pedagogic instruction that comprises the novice teacher's practical experience in the classroom and the attendant didactic-academic workshop. While recognizing the centrality and importance of pedagogic instruction in the training process[24] premised upon educational methods emphasizing reflectivity, knowledge construction and community exposure[25], we sought to extend the borders of pedagogic instruction to the social and community arenas.

To enable experiences such as these, a two-stage organizational measure was instituted that included concentrating all of them into specific communities and integrating partial ones that deviate from disciplinary and classroom experiences.

The first stage, as noted above, concentrated the experiences into specific communities: up to that point, classroom-disciplinary logic mandated broad experiences. Each student underwent his practical experience in a school close to home, while the pedagogical instructor moved from school to school. The desire to leave the classroom space and experience school and community activities required students to concentrate in defined communities. Thus, alliances were forged between the College and specific cities and neighborhoods. These alliances were formed at the administrative level (between the College administration and mayors), the intermediate level (between the heads of training tracks and heads of municipal departments), and the executive level (between the pedagogical instructors, school principals and community center directors). The premise was that concentrating the practical work would almost certainly give rise to new possibilities for activities based on familiarity and deeper relations between the instructors and community educators and institutions.

---

24. Koster, B. F., Korthagen, A. J. & Wubbels, T., "Is There Anything Left for Us? Functions of Cooperating Teachers and Teacher Educators". *European Journal of Teacher Education*, 21 (1), 1998, 75 – 89.

25. Shulman, S. L., "Knowledge and Teaching: Foundations of the New Reform", in Leach, J. and Moon, B. (eds.), *Learners and Pedagogy*, Open University, Sage, 1999, 61-77; Hargraves, A. & Fullan, M., "Mentoring in the New Millennium", *Theory into Practice*, 39 (1), 2000.

In the second stage of the three-year training process, each of the College training tracks was requested to include either practical work in non-formal organizations, educational and social activities for the school community and the surrounding community or individual tutoring of students that does not stop at learning support but deals with holistic monitoring and support. These changes mandated a change in the perception of the pedagogic instructors' role and function. They were required to extend their sphere of involvement and activity and to redefine the aims of their instruction objectives.[26]

The intermediate findings of the evaluation study accompanying the innovations in the training program in general, and the specific projects born in it in particular (hereinafter 'the accompanying study'), established that the model increased the presence and involvement of the pedagogic instructors and cemented cooperation between groups of students and the staff of the educational institutions. These changes heightened the students' sense of individual confidence and capability. The students discussed the various problems they encountered and made productive suggestions for problem solving. Cooperative instruction in the group showed an increase in the students' sense of individual capability in the group process and constituted a cornerstone for empowerment of their consciousness as people able to generate change in the school.[27]

Founding the Program for Social Involvement at the College

The supplementary component for the changes undertaken in pedagogic instruction is the inclusion of experiencing extracurricular social activity as an integral and binding part of the College's training program. This component seeks to develop a consciousness of and commitment to democratic civics in student teachers.

---

26. To this end, and in parallel with the abovementioned two stages, seminars were held for all the instructors, as were separate intensive encounters for all the track instructors. According to the preliminary findings of evaluation studies that examined changes in the positions of the track heads and the pedagogic instructors regarding the new training approach, it was clearly evident that in the first stages there was a sense of suspicion, but at the same time they were willing to cooperate. The changes in the training program are accompanied by an evaluation study conducted by the Kibbutzim College of Education Research Unit, led by Dr. Smadar Donitsa-Schmidt. The study was commenced in 2007 and its partial preliminary findings were published in the course of 2008. Completion of the study together with deepening the program's application will, in the future, mandate its study and discussion afresh. See, *Study Abstracts*, Tel Aviv, Kibbutzim College of Education Research Unit, 2008, 33-40, 53-60 (Hebrew).

27. Donitsa, S., *op.cit.*, 53-60 (Hebrew).

Educational research is a partner to the understanding that meaningful education towards democratic civics cannot settle for theoretical teaching or practical experience, but must combine them[28].

This concept led to the development of a social involvement program which combines theoretical and experiential components. Every student at the College is obliged to work in a social organization for 60 hours and, at the same time, take part in an academic course accompanying that activity.

The innovation of the social involvement program is its introduction into the core training as the College's social message and as an everyday endeavor binding all the teacher-training students. The project's working assumption is that close acquaintance with varied populations, particularly marginal populations such as labor emigrants, refugees, the deprived strata of society, the elderly, new immigrants, etc., will help students to develop a social and political understanding and an empathetic and respectful attitude. This understanding and attitude will constitute a basis for nurturing a professional identity that views the educational endeavor as an act of social reform and influence.

A Social Involvement Unit was established and made responsible for the program's application while each of the existing training tracks was granted a great degree of autonomy in developing the program in accordance with its concepts and preferences.

The program comprises three components:

Accreditation: The social activity gains academic points. This recognition is essential and conveys the message to the students that, to all intents and purposes, social activities are part of the academic program. Accreditation obliged the various tracks to restructure their schedule and thus the program became part of the track core rather than an addendum to it.

Academic supervision: The assumption is that practical work alone, as experiential and meaningful as it might be, cannot create significant and lasting roots in the students. The attendant courses should inculcate the theoretical contexts of the practical work and draw upon the fields of sociology, philosophy, culture, economics, education and so forth. The courses' role is to arouse thinking, encourage critique and nurture hope.

---

28. Mathews, D., "Reviewing and Previewing Civics", in Parker W. C., *Educating the Democratic Mind*. Albany, New York, State University of New York Press, 1996, 265-286. An IEA international study on civic education found that in the twenty-four countries studied there is broad agreement on the ways its should be undertaken. The study also found an aspiration to teach civics by multidisciplinary, activating, interactive and life-relevant ways, that takes place in a non-authoritarian environment, deals with various social challenges, and is conducted together with the community, the parents and third sector bodies. The study proposes an octagonal model presenting the close circles of influence (micro) and the distant ones (macro) that should be addressed when shaping civic education. See, Torney-Purta, J., Schwille J., Amadeo, J., (eds.), *Civic Education Across Countries: Twenty-four National Case Studies from the IEA Civic Education Project*. Amsterdam, IEA, 1999.

Psychological support: Experiential practical work in social activity in marginal populations creates stress and dilemmas that must be discussed and processed. These activities frequently require skills that must be acquired and therefore a social involvement program must meet these needs. The attendant courses should provide the students with an opportunity to share their experiences, difficulties and the tensions that arise in the course of their practical work. For their part, the social organizations that absorb the students must provide professional backing and maximal support. The joint support of the College and the organizations is vital in creating conditions for a beneficial experience and fruitful learning.

The preliminary findings of the evaluation study that accompanied the early application of social involvement showed that participation in the program significantly increased awareness of social issues, the students reported on a high degree of satisfaction with the activity and its attendant course, and that it made a considerable contribution to both the personal and teaching aspects[29].

Democratization in Learning and Campus Life: Learning Communities and Extending Partnership Circles

Developing Lessons using the 'Learning Community' Model

In light of the pedagogic platform outlined above and on the basis of constructive models[30] the College developed a wide range of courses employing the 'learning communities' concept.[31] These courses emphasize workshop-style teaching and learning methods – discussions on multidisciplinary research, performing reflective cognition, varied didactic methodology, etc.

These courses achieve two goals: (1) practical application of the pedagogic concepts while providing room for thinking, expression, formulating a position, and developing students' values and professional identity, and (2) employing an alternative teaching and learning model that the students can adopt and apply as teachers.

The accompanying study indicates a high degree of student satisfaction with this learning method, and their opinion that the study's weight in the curriculum should be increased. In the framework of this study, the

---

29. Donitsa, S., *op. cit.*, 33-40.

30. Perkins, D., "The Many Faces of Constructivism". *Educational Leadership*, 57 (3), 1999, 6-11: Stone, W. M. (ed.), *Teaching for Understanding: Linking Research with Practice*. San Francisco, Jossey-Bass.

31. Bereiter, Carl. *Education and Mind in the Knowledge Age*, London: Lawrence Erlbaum. 2002 ; Harpaz, Yoram & Adam , Lefstein, "Communities of thinking", *Educational Leadership*, 58 (3).2000. pp. 54-57; Perkins David. "Teaching for understanding" in, Arthur L. Costa (Ed). Developing Minds: A resource book for teaching thinking, 3ed edition, Alexandria' Verginia : ASCD, 2000. pp. 446-450.

students noted that the lessons encouraged them to be more involved in planning and action and did not allow the development of indifference or passivity towards the studied content.[32]

Opening Student and Faculty Partnership Circles

On the basis of Michael Apple's distinction between an open and hidden curriculum[33], the new training model posited that the desire to establish and heighten involvement, participation and responsibility in the public sphere also create the possibility of such activity on the College campus. A training program cannot demarcate itself solely within the bounds of the 'open' curriculum with its traditional academic frameworks but must look at the entire gamut of student life and strive to reduce the gap between the training model's verbal messages and statements and everyday experiences.

Accordingly, as an integral part of the training concept the need arose to create arenas for cooperation with the students, encourage and support their independent initiatives, all of which will go beyond the student association's routine activities.

The following are three examples of such involvement:

Greening the Campus. As a continuation of one of the social courses, organization students sought to place environmental issues on the College agenda. The group created an awareness of this subject in the College community and led real changes in College management in this direction. The College supported the group's activity and a year later established a 'Green Council' comprised of students, lecturers, and administrative staff. They studied the issues together and created plans for their implementation.

Students sitting on the Teaching Committee. The College Teaching Committee is a formal body responsible for the advancement and development of the College's core experience and deals with fundamental issues of teacher training and with questions regarding teaching and learning. Although this body is comprised exclusively of lecturers, it was decided to include student representatives from all fields of study to participate in the fundamental discussions.

The students' struggle for the College's cleaning and security staff. The social awakening that runs through the College by dint of specific training tracks and the training model gave birth to a joint organization of students and lecturers that sought to address the terms of employment of the College's cleaning and security staff. The students undertook three initiatives: an open campaign for a pay raise, collecting money to buy holiday presents for the staff on 'Operation White Night' where the students gathered before the Passover festival; and cleaned the College, to allow the

---

32. Shemer-Elkayam, T., "Evaluation of a Research Learning Community at the Kibbutzim College of Education", in Donitsa-Schmidt, S., (ed.), *Study Abstracts*, Tel Aviv, Kibbutzim College of Education Research Unit, 2008, 54-55 (Hebrew).

33. Apple, M. W., *Ideology and Curriculum*, New York, Routledge, 1979.

cleaning staff to enjoy a free morning. The College cooperated in this undertaking and congratulated the students on this important activity. This activity also influenced the employment terms of College staff.

These three examples illustrate a significant change in the College's culture and its willingness to nurture its students' genuine experience and involvement in educational and social activism. These opportunities for involvement complement the experience and insights gathered in lectures and practical teaching and are a greenhouse for empowering the students as involved intellectual leaders.

Summary

A training model seeking to nurture teachers as intellectuals involved in society and the community focuses the process on an attempt to empower the novice teachers with intellectual self-confidence, reinforced their sense of self-esteem in their ability to lead change and nurture pedagogic-didactic dialogical skills.

The training model presented above blurs the borderline between formal and non-formal education and takes the students out of the classroom to bring them into contact with the community and society and to introduce democratic conduct into the academic life of the College.

This model constitutes an alternative to the accepted learning tracks at teacher training institutions:

1. Unlike conventional teacher training, the model presented above seeks to equip teachers with a critical approach to reality and to prepare them to act in it as pedagogic activists.

2. Unlike conventional teacher training, the new training model views the students as partners in the structuring of teaching and learning, in designing the curriculum and in shaping campus academic life.

3. Unlike conventional teacher training, the new training model seeks to expand the pool of experiences and viewpoints to additional circles of community and society. This broader and varied experience strengthens the novice teacher's ability to observe the educational endeavor in the social and political fields and it influences and heightens his/her human and social sensitivity.

The training model presented in this article is in its third year of application at the Kibbutzim College of Education. The accompanying study is still in its early stages. It it remains to be seen whether the study's findings support our hypothesis that the model can generate change in the perception of the vocation and instruct novice teachers to be involved intellectuals. The research examines the following questions:

A. Was there any change in the students' concept of the teacher's duty between the beginning and the end of the student's training?

B. Were there any changes in the teachers involved in the program' concept and attitudes?

In spite of our support for this training policy, we are aware of the difficulties in its applications and we are not certain it can achieve all its aims and purposes. Ongoing research on these graduate teachers and their work would be highly beneficial.

An educational system with teachers acting as involved intellectuals with human and social sensitivity will nurture the complex human fabric of a multicultural society and an awareness of active democratic civics and will ensure a relevant and meaningful teaching and learning experience.

Part III

Service-Learning and Diversity Education Outcomes

Overview

Chapters 7-10 make up Part 3 of the book, which focuses on service-learning and diversity education outcomes. Chapter 7 explores the need for diversity education in an increasingly diverse society, from a sociological perspective. Chapter 8 looks at the role of service-learning in transnational learning. Chapter 9 explores usung service learning as a means to broad one's world-view and understand diverse cultural perspectives. Finally, Chapter 10 explores using service-learning to promote a sense of belonging.

Chapter 7

A Sociological Approach to Diversity Education

Education in Today's Diverse Society

A Sociological Approach

Barbara Sposet, Baldwin-Wallace College, Ohio, USA

Abstract: In the past ten years, the K-12 classroom has changed dramatically in the United States. Institutions of higher education engaged in the preparation of teacher candidates have responded by enhancing their current curriculum with new/revised courses focusing on this diversity. The paper will focus on the uniqueness of an undergraduate, three-semester-hour education course at a small, liberal arts college in northeast Ohio. While students explore eight distinct areas of diversity, the course also requires the completion of a community scan as well as a non-school service learning field experience. Both activities provide students the opportunity to recognize the human variety of experiences, the challenges of living in a diverse world, and the impact of this diversity in the classroom setting. The paper will include data from a sample of 22 students (instructor's section) as well as recommendations from the presenter/instructor for institutions seeking to implement a similar experience for its teacher candidates.

Introduction

In the past 10 years, the K-12 classroom has changed dramatically in the United States as a result of the country's newest wave of immigrants. Demographic data from the U.S. Department of Education indicate that more than four of 10 students in K-12 schools today are students of color (2006). And, by 2020, the number of Asian American, Latino and African American children are projected to be nearly half of the elementary and secondary population. One of the major institutions impacted by this change from a predominantly white European population to one that is substantially non-white is the K-12 classroom. With close to 85% of the teachers in today's P-12 classrooms being European American (Gollnick & Chinn, 2009 p. 2), institutions of higher education engaged in the preparation of teacher candidates have responded to the mismatch between teacher and student by adding one or more courses addressing this diversity primarily from a content-knowledge approach.

Significance of the Paper

This paper focuses on the uniqueness of an undergraduate, three-semester-hour required multicultural education course offered at a small liberal arts college in northeast Ohio. Data represents one section taught by the author in spring, 2009 following a 'master' syllabus created by four members of the education faculty. (Three of the four instructors volunteered to teach the course; two of the three had previously taught a similar course at other institutions.) While students explore eight distinct areas of diversity through assigned readings, chapter reflections, a chapter presentation (all from the main course textbook) and a philosophy on diversity, each class member must also complete a community scan assignment as well as a non-school service-learning experience. The results of this data will be used to determine the effectiveness of the two out-of-school experiences as it relates to one or more of the seven course outcomes. It is the belief of this writer that the two activities provide students the opportunity to recognize the human variety of experience, the challenges of living in a diverse world, and the impact of this diversity on the classroom setting. In so doing, the activities sets this course apart from other multicultural education courses in teacher education programs by providing a sociological perspective as defined by I. Robertson (1981) in that students are given the opportunity to look at his/ her familiar surroundings in a fresh way by examining areas of society that one might otherwise have ignored or been misunderstood.

Both qualitative and quantitative data from a sample of 23 students gathered upon the completion of the two out-of-classroom activities were collected and analyzed by the researcher. The paper concludes with recommendations for both the presenter's institution as well as other institutions seeking to implement a similar experience for its pre-service teacher education candidates.

Class Demographics

The demographics of this particular section of EDU 211D closely mirror Gollnick's (2009) statistics about today's classroom teachers. Of the 23 students, 20 or 96% were Caucasian; 19 (87%) were female; all 23 students were born and raised in Ohio. While eighteen (80%) of the students had traveled to countries outside the United States including Canada (8), Europe (4) Mexico (3), Jamaica (2) and China (1), only eight students (45%) of the class had any previous experience or interaction with a culture/cultural identity different than their own through travel to countries whose official language is not English (Canada and Jamaica).

Course Outcomes/Activities/Assignments

The seven outcomes for the course entitled *Exploring Education in a Diverse Society* include:

1. Students will define and apply multicultural vocabulary to discuss concepts in multicultural education;
2. Students will critically examine their beliefs, values and assumptions about cultural differences and cultural identity;
3. Students will discuss the dynamics of privilege, economic oppression and school practices that contribute to social inequity;
4. Students will understand the relationship among language, culture and learning;
5. Students will research and investigate the histories and contributions of diverse groups represented in today's society;
6. Students will define the meaning and discuss culturally-relevant pedagogy; and
7. Through instructor modeling, students will be able to explain instructional strategies sensitive to cultural and linguistic variations.

As previously mentioned, students explore eight distinct areas of diversity including race/ethnicity; class and socioeconomic status; gender and sexual orientation; exceptionalities; language; religion; geography; and age. Three activities that enhance the learning experience of content knowledge used by this instructor included a group poster presentation of one of the eight chapters; a Pause to Reflect activity; and the reading of the novel "When I Was Puerto Rican" by Esmeralda Santiago. The novel was chosen as there is a very large Puerto Rican population in a urban city school district located only 15 minutes away from the college. The K-8 buildings in this school district serve as one of many sites for the completion of methods and student teaching. The novel served as an application, analysis and evaluative activity for the terms presented in the class textbook.

The two activities that take students outside the college classroom and that align to the outcome of "research and investigate the histories and contributions of the diverse groups represented in today's society" are 1) the community scan and 2) the service-learning requirement.

The Community Scan

A community scan assessment focuses on local assets, resources and activities as well as gaps, barriers or emerging needs. It is a broad look across agencies, systems and community members with the purpose of identifying and appraising information to help a) understand the context in which families live and possible issues that need to be addressed; b) locate hidden strengths or underutilized resources that could be developed; and c) design effective strategies that engage children and families (North Central Regional Educational Laboratory, 2004).

After students completed a survey of familiarity (either personal or through a family member) with a number of communities within a 30-mile radius from the college, the instructor randomly assigned the community students were to investigate using 30 questions including:

1. What are the age demographics of your community?
2. How many single-parent households are there?
3. What languages are spoken in the homes of the people in your community?
4. What ethnic groups are represented in your community?
5. What are your community's three largest employers? What do they do? How many people do they employ? How is it likely to be different in five years?
6. What is the median income?
7. What are the homes, streets and sidewalks like in your community?
8. What percentage of families falls below the poverty level?
9. What institutions (i.e. library, hospital, youth center) does your community have?
10. List the number and type of schools in your community. Are they public or private?
11. What percent of people (25 & older) have at least a high school diploma or equivalent? Some college? Four years of college?
12. What types of religious institutions are there in your community?
13. Where do residents go for their basic commercial/business needs?
14. What are the challenges (price, accessibility, culture etc.) residents have in using neighborhood-based businesses?
15. What are the various crime rates for your community?

Students were encouraged to drive to the city and spend at least 4-5 hours gathering information from primary sources including the library, restaurants, city hall, recreation center, board of education office, and individuals. Students then orally shared their information using a visual aid (a collage or poster) to highlight within 5-10 minutes what they felt were significant points of interest. For example, one student cut out her visual in the shape of the community as it appears on the street map for that area. Another student presented his photographs on a circle that was wrapped in Duct tape demonstrating that city's primary employer. Yet a third student chose the shape of a quarry stone as his community was built on the work of quarrymen.

In addition, students presented to the instructor responses to the 30 questions. Each student was also asked to write a minimum one-page reflection discussing his/her views a) before and b) after visiting his/her assigned community. A third question focused on the strength and challenges of the community in general. A rubric for both the presentation and essay were distributed at the time the assignment was presented to the class.

Community Scan Reflection

As previously mentioned, each student enrolled in *Exploring Education in a Diverse Society* is required to complete a community scan of a city or township within a 30-mile radius of the college. At the end of that activity, each student is asked to write a reflective essay focusing on three questions explaining his/her views before and after the visit as well as what each one perceived as the strengths and weaknesses of the community. A class discussion was held following all the presentations to discuss in general the impact of those resources and their future as a teacher in that particular community. The specific category/field in the rubric entitled "Reflection/Future Impact" was used to assess the three questions utilizing the rating scale of 1/Needs Improvement; 2/Meets Expectations; and 3/Exceeds Expectations. The 'expectations' being measured would be those appropriate for students who have had no previous teaching experience or interaction with a culture/cultural identify different than their own. The verbiage describing the ratings of 1, 2 and 3 appears below. Table 1 shows the aggregated scores for each of the three ratings.

Category	1/Needs Improvement	2/Meets Expectations	3/Exceeds Expectations
Reflection/Future Impact	NO reflection provided or information is missing as asked for in the prompt. The information provided lacks depth and/or has the appearance of being hastily prepared.	Reflection is included with answers given as asked for in the prompt.	A thoughtful and well-detailed reflection is included with answers given as asked for in the prompt.

Table 1: Data from Community Scan Reflection Essay

Total 'N'	1/Needs Improvement	2/Meets Expectations	3/Exceeds Expectations
23	5	10	8

While the quantitative data indicates that the responses of 78% of the class either met or exceeded expectations by the definition given above, the author believes more can be gathered from some of the written responses themselves. They include:

- "The community places a premium on education...They also organize every opportunity for enrichment for all ages...As a future teacher, I believe I would have no end of parental support..."
- "The strengths of the city are obvious. There are many upper-middle class residents that invest in the community, particularly theater and art...the city's plight to maintain their town center, ensuring no litter or vandalism, and keeping the center filled with small, family-owned businesses, is noble. The community values small town ideals.
- "...Taking the time to learn about the community and residents that a teacher or administrator will be serving will play a vital role in their success within the classroom, school and community."
- "One major attraction that I was impressed with was the city's nature center. This would be an amazing place for a teacher to bring a young class for a field trip."
- "I witnessed the most diversity in the different religious temples and churches. The city seemed to have a large Ukrainian population with two Orthodox churches. I also saw many Christian churches as well as a Hindu temple. I think this diversity is a strength for the city because of the variety of tradition and values...The city would appeal to a variety of people who may be moving into the area and looking for a location that is accepting of their previous culture."
- "I found this project to be very beneficial to me as a future teacher. I learned a lot about a local community that I had little familiarity with. When I am a teacher I need to become familiar with all aspects of the community I work in order to understand what local opportunities are available to my students and their families as well as what challenges the community may face."

Service Learning Field Experience

According to the Corporation for National and Community Service, "Service learning is a teaching and learning strategy that integrates meaningful community service with instruction and reflection to enrich the learning experience, teach civic responsibility and strengthen communities" (p. 1). Two of the characteristics of this strategy is that service learning 1) promotes deeper learning because the results are immediate and uncontrived; and 2) challenges values as well as ideas thus supporting social, emotional and cognitive learning and development (p. 2).

A critical issue in teacher education today, according to Ukpokodu (2005) is the mismatch between racially homogeneous teachers and students from increasingly diverse cultural backgrounds. In the United States, 40% of the students represent minorities while close to 85% of the teaching population represent the white, middle class (Gollnick, 2009, p.2). Numerous studies, Ukpokodu states, indicate that negative dispositions by white teachers toward diverse students combined with lower expectations are major factors contributing to the widespread academic failure among diverse students. Providing prospective teachers the opportunity for authentic experiential encounters with diversity in context can lead these candidates to challenge their preconceived notions and ultimately transform their attitudes (Ukpokodu, p. 20).

With this in mind, the diversity course was specifically designed to include a 15-hour service learning experience in a non-school setting that would engage the teacher candidate with persons and/or groups that do not represent the candidate's culture or cultural group. In this particular class, students were assigned to hunger centers, Alzheimer centers, a teen pregnancy clinic, senior centers and homeless shelters. Before starting the field experience, all students were required to attend a one-hour orientation conducted by the college's Office of Community Outreach (OCO) relative to format of the visits, potential reactions to the experience, and reporting procedures during and following each visit.

Service Learning Reflection

Following the completion of the 15-hour service learning experience, students were asked to complete a reflective essay consisting of 10 questions. Of those 10, questions #6 through 10 provide a sociological perspective to the activity. Those questions included:

1. Overall, what was the most challenging aspect of the experience?
2. What did you learn from the experience?
3. What did you learn about yourself from the experience?
4. How and why did your assumptions change from the beginning? If they did not, why do you think that is so?
5. How will this experience make a difference in your classroom? How will this experience make a difference on you as a teacher? If you don't think it will, why not?

Two of the four fields in the rubric provided to students to guide them in completing the essay were scored again using the scale of 1/Needs Improvement; 2/Meets Expectations; and 3/Exceeds Expectations. The 'expectations' being measured would be those appropriate for students who have had no previous teaching experience or interaction with a culture/cultural identify different than their own. The verbiage describing the ratings of 1, 2 and 3 appear below. Aggregated data for the two fields is included in Table 2.

Category	1/Needs Improvement	2/Meets Expectations	3/Exceeds Expectations
Overall Reaction to Experience	Not included/weak explanation provided by students. Response does not address all of the questions asked.	Adequate response provided by student explaining his/her feelings about the overall experience. All of the questions asked are addressed.	Extensive response provided by student explaining his/her feelings about the overall experience as outlined in questions #6-9
Application to Future Career	Not included/weak explanation provided by student to the three parts of the questions.	Emerging level of application of experience to future career. While all three parts of the question are addressed, response not overly-developed and/or lacks specific details connecting experience to future career choice.	There is evidence of a 'proficient' level of application of experience to future career choice. The response is well developed and includes specific details connecting the experience to future career goals. All three parts of question #10 are addressed.

Table 2: Data from Service Learning Reflective Essay (N = 23)

Category	1/Needs Improvement	2/Meets Expectations	3/Exceeds Expectations
Overall Reaction to Experience	0	11	12
Application to Future Career	1	14	8

Analysis of the Data

The data indicates that 100% of the class either met instructor expectations (48%) when reflecting on their overall experience to the service learning experience or exceeded the instructor's expectations (52%) in this part of the reflective essay.

The scores from the second field in the rubric indicate that 60% of the subjects were able to appropriately apply the knowledge gained from the experience to their future career as a teacher and another 35% exceeded expectations in their responses. Five percent (5%) earned scores of '1' indicating they could not apply OR did not find any future application of the service learning experience to their future profession.

When coding the responses used to determine the scores of '1', '2' or 3, the predominant themes gathered from the application to one's future career included: 1) new knowledge of a culture different than one's own (including race/ethnicity, age, socio-economic status, gender and/or geography); 2) perceptions by people of others who were different than themselves; and 3) perspective-taking. Not only do these themes meet the second learning outcome for the course (i.e. "Students will critically examine their beliefs, values and assumptions about cultural differences and cultural identity"), they also fall into the hierarchy of culture learning developed by Kleinjans in 1971.

Culture learning, as defined by Damen (1987), is a particular type of human learning related to the patterns of human interaction and identification . One of the three ways in which the process can be viewed is in varying stages of awareness, understanding and acceptance. In 1971 Kleinjans developed a hierarchy of culture learning utilizing the domains similar to the work of Bloom (1956) and others in educational psychology (Sposet, 1997, p. 32). The most superficial level involves information, perception and awareness (the first and second coding themes mentioned above). The second level involves observation and the management of data from the experience. At the third level (synthesis), patterns and themes emerge whereas the fourth level calls for understanding and valuing of change and action. The final level involves the feeling of being inside the head of others especially those who do not share one's own cultural patterns (Damen, 1987, p. 219). This final level represents the third coding theme of perspective-taking as demonstrated in 14 of the 19 reflection essays

Specific comments that speak to Kleinjans' hierarchy include:

- "I have learned that hard times can fall upon anyone at any given time..."
- "Physically pushing the wheelchair was not hard or particularly interesting, but this experience did make me think about what it would be like for a person who doesn't have control over their body, is no longer able to walk, or is confined to a bed..."
- "I experienced not only their hunger but got to see how they rely on the facility for shelter and emotional support from the workers and their friends that join them."
- "The most challenging aspect of the experience...was worrying that those boys would have no dinner that evening since the Hunger Center is only open for breakfast and lunch."
- "I learned...that everyone is prejudiced to some degree and that people possess extremely different values and morals from each other."
- "Through this experience I learned that it's not always the individual's fault for their position in life-sometimes they get thrown into that life."

99

- "I realized that poor teen mothers had a different approach to life...that they live in an alternate world where stability and love may be missing.
- "It made me feel thankful that I have never had to wonder where or when I would get my next meal."
- "I now have the ability to understand a student's position if their family is poor or struggling..."
- "I was exposed to a different experience with many different types of people (senior centers). It was a means for me to try to understand the specific problems they were going through and facing. It allowed me to put myself in their shoes and sympathize with their own situations and problems. I can adapt this experience to my classroom as it will enable me to understand and better communicate with all different sorts of students."

Conclusions

Did the community scan and the service learning experience provide the students in this section of *Exploring Education in a Diverse Society* with a sociological perspective to diversity? According to the work of Robertson, Mills and Kleinjans (1972), I believe they did.

At the onset, the goals of both the community scan and the service-learning experience were to have the students "take a new look at the world we have always taken for granted" (Robertson, 1981, p. 2). The use of primary and secondary resources (i.e. a half-day visit to the community and the use of Internet resources) provided the students with the opportunity to "assess both the opportunities and constraints that characterize our lives" (Mills, 1959, p.18). In this case, the follow-up essay revealed that 78% of the class scored **at or above** the expectations of the instructor when asked to reflect on the impact of their community's opportunities and constraints as it pertains to their chosen career of teaching (i.e. "As a future teacher, I believe I would have no end of parental support...").

The service-learning experience, in particular, exposed the students to areas of society "that might otherwise have been ignored or misunderstood" (Robertson, 181, p. 3). For this class, those areas of society included the homeless, under-resourced schools, the elderly, teens in crisis, and the hungry. The coding of responses from the reflection essay revealed a change in attitudes ranging from a heightened level of awareness or knowledge about a culture different than the candidate's own to perspective taking or 'getting into the head of another' (Kleinjans, 1972, p. 12).

An unexpected outcome of this paper is that the data from the reflection essays for the service learning experience indicates that the rubric used to assess the question of the impact of the experience on one's future career directly relates with the description provided by the instructor for the score of '2' or Meets Expectation. Further use of the rubric by a larger sample would be needed, however, to determine statistical significance, reliability, and validity.

Limitations of the Study

While not intended or written as research using control and experimental groups, there are limitations to this quantitative report. They are: a) the instructor's interest in diversity and the preparation of pre-service candidates for teaching in a more diverse classroom than those of her tenure; and b) the subjectivity of the evaluation of the findings as the data came from the students in the writer's section of this required course.

Implications for the Future

When asked to rank the nine major activities of the class as they related to helping the student meet the course objectives, the mean score for the community scan was 3.8 while the mean score for the service learning experience was 3.6. (A Liekert scale of 1-5 was used with 1 representing the term 'strongly disagree'; 2 'disagree'; 3 'neither agree or disagree': 4 'agree'; and 5 'strongly agree.') Using the explanation provided for the ratings, the community scan was closer to approaching 'agree' by the class than the service learning experience. One reason explaining the difference, I believe, could be that this was the first time any of the 23 students had conducted a community scan. However, upon further discussion with the class, two issues came to the forefront regarding the service-learning project. The first was the site placement. In several cases, students were matched up with a site according to their non-class hours only to find the residents were not available. In other cases, the supervisors were not prepared for the students' visits. As a result, the students had nothing to do for a period of one to two hours. Thus, one goal for the next academic year is to work with the Office of Community Outreach and be more intentional about matching the student with the site and the site's times of availability.

Secondly, as a means of assessing the experience itself, a set time for discussion needs to be allotted during the seven weeks of field experience to help students analyze what is occurring at the site in lieu of the outcomes for the course.

In regards to the community scan, one major recommendation would be to assign the same community to two to three students. There would be one group presentation with three individual papers and individual reflections. While students were originally limited to 10 minutes and the presentations were spread out over five class periods, 230 minutes (approximately four hours) is a large amount of time to devote to this aspect of the activity. Instead, time could be better spent discussing the opportunitie and constraints of a particular community as it relates to benefits for the school as well as opportunities for engagement with the community on behalf of the school and individual teachers.

Lastly, a longitudinal study to determine the degree to which these two particular activities assisted in developing the dispositions needed to teach in culturally diverse settings is recommended.

References

Corporation for National and Community Service (2002). *Students in Service to America,* Washington, D.C.

Damen, Louise. (1987). Culture learning: The fifth dimension in the language classroom. Reading, MA: Addison-Wesley Publishing Company.

Eyler, Janet & Giles, Dwight E. Jr. (1999). Where's the learning in service-learning? Edison, NJ: Jossey-Bass Publishing.

Gollnick, Donna M. and Chinn, Philip C. (2009). Multicultural education in a pluralistic society. Upper Saddle River, NJ: Merrill-Pearson Publishing.

Kleinjans, Everett. (1972). On culture learning. Honolulu: East-West Culture Learning Institute.

Mills, C. Wright. (1959). The sociological imagination. NY: Oxford University Press.

North Central Regional Educational Laboratory. (2004). Conducting a community assessment." Retrieved from http://www.ncrel.org. on 4/26/09.

Robertson, I. (1981). Sociology. NY: Worth Publishing.

Santiago, Esmeralda. (1959). When I ws Puerto Rican. NY: Knopf Doubleday.

Sposet, Barbara. (2003). The affective and cognitive development of culture learning during the early and middle childhood curriculum. NY: The Edwin Mellen Press.

Ukpokodu, Omiunota Neilly. (2005). The impact of shadowing culturally different students on pre-service teachers' dispositions toward diversity. *Multicultural Education,* Winter, 19-28.

U.S. Department of Education, National Center for Education Statistics. (2006). *The condition of education 2006* (NCES 2006-071). Washington, DC: U.S. Government Printing Office.

Chapter 8
Service-Learning and Transnational Learning

Crossing Borders

Academic Service Learning as a Pedagogy for Transnational Learning

Loshini Naidoo, University of Western Sydney, NSW, AUSTRALIA

Abstract: The paper examines the implications of an academic service learning program "Crossing Borders" on transnationalism and the internationalization of higher education. For individuals coming into Australia from other cultural and linguistic backgrounds, education arguably plays an especially significant part in the negotiation and construction of their understandings of Australian culture and identity. Transnational students are encouraged to disregard standards and norms developed in their home country and adopt those of the host country. This process is clearly complex since cultural norms and beliefs are embedded into the student and thus putting these aside is difficult. As a result, cultural differences exist in the student-lecturer relationship. Transnational students tend to be more reluctant to question the opinions of a lecturer as this is a position of authority. Students coming from cultures where study is very much teacher-led may find the transition to an academic environment with a strong emphasis on independent learning difficult. Using Bourdieu's theory of social capital and cultural reproduction as a conceptual framework, this study explores the role of the "Crossing Borders" program in enabling transnational learning communities generate and sustain empowering knowledge networks. Such insight might inform educators and policy makers at some point in the future so that other transnationals will benefit from an increased understanding of the challenges and opportunities involved in crossing cultures. Further benefits of transnational education are that it helps in the development of university involvement with other nations and also provides the opportunity for cross-cultural experiences for domestic students.

Introduction

Today, universities around the world, are increasingly affected by the process of globalization. Globalization, for the purpose of this paper will be defined as "the intensification of world-wide social relations which link distant localities in such a way that local happenings are shaped by events occurring many miles away and visa versa" (Giddens, cited in Naidoo. 2007, p. 54). In conceptualizing globalization, two important characteristics emerge: the first is that the world is viewed as a single space, a whole and the second revolves around the concept of time-space reordering. Featherstone, (cited in Naidoo. 2007, p. 54), believes that globalization "entails the sense that the world is one place, that the globe has been compressed into a locality, that others are neighbours with whom we must necessarily interact, relate and listen". Some of the important socio-economic dimensions of globalization are transnational transportation and migration of people or increased transportation of labour across the globe (Castles & Miller, 1998, cited in Robinson & Jones- Diaz 2005).

Transnational students are using the 'internationalisation of higher education' to acquire skills geared towards a knowledge economy. Taking Appadurai's (1996, p. 33) notion of 'global cultural flows' as a point of departure, it might be argued that the global/national/local movements of transnational students (and academics), and their imaginings about moving, constitute a key feature of the current transitions in the practices of globalisation.

Australia has become a popular destination for international students particularly from Asian countries. This is attributed to its geographical proximity to Asian countries, its English language, reputation and flexibility of study, work arrangements and prospects for immigration. It is argued therefore that research on educational and cultural awareness of transnational students as fieldworkers is an important step in the discourse of internationalisation in Australian institutions. As Portes (1998, p. 2) points out, the concept [Transnationalism] 'may actually perform double duty as part of the theoretical arsenal with which we approach the world system structures, but also as an element in a less developed enterprise, namely the analysis of the everyday networks and patterns of social relationships that emerge in and around those structures.'

The purpose of this paper is to provide the research community with knowledge derived from a professional experience (academic service learning) strand undertaken in the Masters of Teaching (Secondary) at the University of Western Sydney (UWS). The Crossing Borders Program is a project of engagement through academic service learning which aims to provide (online and off-line) peer-mentoring to overseas trained pre-service Master of Teaching students in order to facilitate academic transition. The Master of Teaching (secondary) is an 18 month post-graduate qualification, within which there are three professional experiences or practicum. Two of these could be described as traditional student teaching placements, where pre-service teachers, under the supervision of a qualified teacher, are assigned a series of classes to teach. The focus of these placements is to essentially provide a means to instruct pre-service teachers in the art and the mechanics of teaching, and to gain some understanding of the daily functions of schools. The third professional experience (PE3) which comprises sixty hours of service learning is essentially a community engaged practicum and requires pre-service teachers to extend their knowledge and experience beyond the classroom, using their pedagogical and inter-personal skills to support young people in different ways.

The service learning practicum is intended to instil in students an appreciation for the community's strengths, resources, perceived needs and expectations through service-oriented experiences. The students have the opportunity to collaborate with local agencies to define needs and to participate in service delivery. Students also develop an awareness of the importance and value of combining academic learning with identified issues related to education in the community and they develop an appreciation for the relationship between personal and professional growth in developing leadership skills. The alternative practicum emphasizes reciprocal learning where traditional definitions of "school," "teacher" and "learner" are intentionally blurred. It also emphasizes reflective practice - reflection facilitates the connection between practice and theory and fosters critical self-reflection.

Review of the Literature

Models of heterogenous and conditional adaptation (Gans, 1997; Portes and Zhou, 1993; Rumbaut, 1997), suggest that effective adaptation can occur without fully relinquishing native cultural practices and that the success of adaptation depends on how an immigrant's characteristics interact with the circumstances he or she finds in the host country (Zhou and Bankston, 1998). According to Cameron and Meade (2002), there is a tendency to view international students, as a homogenous group. Thus, while it is important to be aware of the heterogeneity of the international student population, recent research suggests that there are a number of common difficulties which many international students face in terms of their adjustment and well being. These include homesickness, financial difficulties, language difficulties, problems dealing with university staff and other authorities, loneliness, isolation from other classmates and anxiousness about speaking in the classroom in front of classmates and lecturers (Leder and Forgasz 2004; Novera 2004; Robertson et al. 2000; Scheyvens et al., 2003).

A number of studies suggest that many international students prior to coming to Australia have spent many years learning to speak English and thus enter the country unaware of the extent to which local accents, fast speech and Australian colloquialisms are going to reduce their ability to speak and understand English in Australia (Scheyvens et al., 2003). It is not only English language that prevents students from speaking and mixing with local students but also knowing what to speak about (Novera 2004, p. 480). Essentially in Novera's (2004) study, students rated the non academic support which they got much more highly than the academic support which they received. The cross-cultural 'mismatching' between international students and their new academic environment does result in some discontent from both sides (Handa, 2004) and lack of engagement on the part of international students becomes an issue for their institutes (Scott, Bond & Webb, 2005). Students' active involvement and their sense of belonging at university has been claimed as the most effective factor in their learning; as their engagement with the academic environment seems to translate in "a range of outcomes including persistence, satisfaction, achievement and academic success" (Krause, 2005, p.1)

Handa (2004), in her study of international non-English speaking students at UWS, indicated that there "was a clear lack of interaction between the local and the international students. Most of the questionnaires that were returned show a clear absence of any solid interaction between the two cohorts inside or outside the classroom. The reasons seem to be the obvious ones, lack of language, lack of time and local students' disinterest in them". Transnational students, according to Handa (2004) showed a lack of confidence in their own ability to form intelligent questions or to engage in classroom discussions. A few of them also showed their frustration with tutors who presented local examples to start discussions in the class, disadvantaging students who were not familiar with certain topics. Difficulties in adjusting to university can be exacerbated by the extra demands of adjusting to life and study in a new language and a different cultural setting (Armitage, 1999; Smart, Volet & Ang, 2000). Universities may need to provide direct teaching of skills, support, and opportunities for local and overseas students to interact productively (Smart et al., 2000). Peer support programs in higher education, can be effective in "achievement gains, reduced student stress, graduation outcomes and dropout rates" (in Kowalsky & Fresko, 2002, p. 262).

Theoretical Framework

Using Bourdieu's theory of social capital and cultural reproduction as a conceptual framework this paper will explore the role of the peer-mentoring program at UWS in the acculturation of overseas trained and overseas born students. Central to Bourdieu's theory are the concepts of "habitus" and "field." Bourdieu (1977, p.487) defines habitus as "that system of dispositions which acts as a mediator between structures and practice". An individual's habitus is influenced by external "conditions of existence, which in turn become the basis of perception and appreciation of all subsequent experience" (Bourdieu & Passeron, 1977, p. 78). As such, one's habitus shapes one's expectations and orientations toward the future. The positions on a field are influenced by the symbolic capital held by different individuals. Bourdieu described symbolic capital as "capital—in whatever form—insofar as it is represented, i. e., apprehended symbolically, in a relationship of knowledge . . . [that] presupposes the intervention of the *habitus*, as a socially constituted cognitive capacity" (1986, p. 255). Since habitus is generative of practice, Bourdieu allows that habitus can be modified in the face of other fields, or due to "an awakening of consciousness and social analysis" although it is not easy (Bourdieu & Wacquant, 1992, p. 167).The challenge is to help people learn to recognize how the existing order co-creates their experiences via habitus and to help them internalise new dispositions.

Further, Bourdieu identifies cultural capital and social capital as forms of symbolic capital. According to Bourdieu, cultural capital can exist in three forms, in the embodied state (in the form of dispositions of the mind and body), the objectified state (in the form of material goods with cultural value), and in the institutionalized state (in the form of societal institutions). The concept of habitus involves the perspective of power as cultural capital for the dominant (ethnic majority) and as symbolic violence towards subordinate groups.

Adler and Kwon (2000) refer to social capital as the '*collective good*', which they associate with benefits, such as access to information which brings with it benefits. Schuller et al (2000, p. 35) believes that the concept is powerful, as a tool for exploration and can handle complex and multidimensional investigations. Therefore, they recognise its key merit as '*the way it shifts the focus of analysis from behaviour of individual agents to the pattern of relations between agents, social units and institutions*'.

This type of symbolic capital is linked to membership in a group which "provides each of its members with the backing of the collectively-owned capital," a "credential" which entitles them to credit, in the various senses of the word (Bourdieu, 1986, p. 249). One's social capital depends on "the size of the network of connections" an individual can mobilize for his or her social benefit. One of the effects of cultural reproduction is "symbolic violence," a concept Bourdieu describes as social power imposing existing social limitations on those who do not have the cultural capital required to combat challenge the privileged social classes (Bourdieu & Passeron, 1977). One of Bourdieu and Passeron's (1977, p.5) central tenets is that "pedagogic action is, objectively, symbolic violence insofar as it is the imposition of a cultural arbitrary by an arbitrary power".

Bourdieu's (1991) concept of symbolic violence can be linked to his theory of linguistic power where minority languages are invalidated as part of the social discrimination and where the dominant – or rather 'legitimate' – language is an instrument of power. The 'legitimate language' has symbolic value and functions as 'cultural capital', convertible into material resources and positions of structural power. As such students in Australian universities are expected to conform to the demands of language teaching that values such a view.

For Bourdieu, the extent to which agents can attain knowledge of, and negotiate, various cultural fields is dependent on, and can be explained in terms of, what he terms a "practical sense" or a "logic of practice" (Bourdieu 1990, 1998; Bourdieu & Wacquant 1992). This, he explains further, can be characterized as an ability to comprehend and negotiate cultural fields, that is, a knowledge of the various rules (written and unwritten), genres, discourses, forms of capital, values, contexts and imperatives which inform and determine their practice, and are, simultaneously, continuously being transformed by them.

This knowledge provides agents with specific literacy that allows them to make sense of what is happening around them, and to make decisions as to how that field should be negotiated (in other words, what practices, genres or discourses are appropriate in certain circumstances). Moreover, Bourdieu insists (Bourdieu & Wacquant 1992) that, in certain circumstances this practical sense can be extended to include what he refers to as a "reflexive" dimension or disposition. In other words, reflexive knowledge allows agents to respond to their knowledge of the particular set of circumstances (the conditions that produce and delimit what meanings and ideas are available to an agent) and factor it in to their ability to read and make sense of a situation.

Background to the Program

The Crossing Borders strand of Academic Service Learning is offered to any UWS Master of Teaching student who was trained overseas, whose previous degrees were obtained overseas and who is expecting to work in education in NSW. About ten local students volunteered to mentor ten overseas trained students. Most of the students who were mentees were from the Asian and Indian sub-continent. The peer-mentor is an equal with just a little more experience than the mentee. Although some commentators point to the importance of matching mentors for commonalities other research says that as relationships develop unanticipated coincidences often strengthen rapport (Cox, 2005). The success of such scenarios appears to depend on putting time and effort into developing the relationship, the reliability of mentor and mentee to adhere to agreed appointments, the flexibility of the program and whether or not participation is actually meeting the needs of the mentee. (Boyle, 2005; Conway, 2005).

The pilot program which begun in 2007 initially consisted of structured social activities; English conversation; helping newcomers find their way around Sydney; learning about aspects of Australian history and culture; clarifying expectations in the Australian higher education system and giving guidance where appropriate. This year (2008) Crossing Borders has been extended to include academic support to overseas trained students who then also have an opportunity to practice their literacy skills in a collaborative environment with guidance and feedback from mentors selected from the same cohort of students. The central component of the academic support is a weekly seminar group session which is available to all students in need of academic support. Students who have been identified as in need of support are assigned to a mentor. An adapted version of the Measuring the Academic Skills (MASUS) instrument is used to identify students who require additional linguistic and cross-cultural support. The seminar groups meet weekly for approximately sixty minutes, depending on the nature of the needs of participants. The mentors work with the Learning Skills Unit to prepare academic learning skills lessons and the participants are given the opportunity to evaluate their mentees over the course of the semester via an online site. Participation in the program is voluntary and there is no fee to participate.

The program is intended to support the development of critical thinking skills; raise self awareness and understanding of others; provide opportunities for refining a wide range of interpersonal skills; help define the elements of effective group interactions; encourage transnational students to reflect on aspects of their own culture and those of others. Novera (2004, p. 475) claims that further benefits of international education are that it helps in the development of university involvement with Asian nations and also provides the opportunity for cross-cultural experiences for domestic students. He goes on to say that while academic success may heighten a student's confidence, social and cultural adjustment can be important factors which lead to this academic success (Novera, 2004, p. 475).

Seminar sessions focus specifically on basic instruction about reading, interpretation, note-taking, preparing for class, participating in class, structuring assignments and time management. Seminar sessions also assist students to develop the basic analytical and critical reasoning skills needed to succeed in teaching. Given that the group participants are all enrolled in the M. Teach course, the groups can be tailored somewhat to draw on the specific substantive doctrines taught in that course. UWS is a community of staff and students whose purpose is to foster academic growth and equal access to education for all students through creating a welcoming, inclusive, comfortable environment and nurturing students' identity development and personal and academic growth. The Crossing Borders program with its focus on providing academic and social and cultural support for overseas trained students through peer tutoring programs therefore works with the university's mission statement by demonstrating a strong commitment not only to diversity but also to advancing student learning and success.

Analysis of Data

In 2007, 24 students were involved in the Crossing Borders program. Twelve were mentors and twelve were mentees. The data obtained was in the form of an online evaluation and weekly learning log where participants recorded their evaluations and reflections of the weekly peer mentoring program. This provided the data for analysis in this section. There are some potential methodological limitations of this study in that the study has a small sample size and an external validity problem because I conducted the research at one university. The small sample size is not surprising given the fact that this program requires voluntary participation. As a result of this, I am aware that generalizations cannot be made about diverse students in other institutions.

'Non-traditional' students and in this case, transnational students from the Indian sub-continent, are said to have lower reserves of cultural capital than more traditional students; they are perceived and perceive themselves to be both economically disadvantaged and as social and academic outsiders. With regard to education, Bourdieu also emphasizes how the resources of the dominant class can provide advantages that goes beyond the ability to purchase access to better educational settings or additional supports such as tutoring. By accepting the validity of the concepts of cultural capital and habitus the Crossing Borders Peer-Mentoring Program attempts to prepare students for the rigours of university life through the creation of informal support networks, revising expectations of university life and providing studies skills support. One effective way in which students can be empowered is to see themselves as part of a learning community and then act accordingly.

Social capital, including programs like peer-mentoring, play a particularly important role in helping transnational students navigate the complexities of university life. Social capital is created when mentors and mentees establish norms in their weekly meetings. During online discussions and monthly meetings, mentors form relationships with other mentors and the coordinator of the program to ensure that their mentees maximize their access to the cumulative knowledge, skill sets, and resources (i.e., information channels) available through the entire mentor network.

Furthermore, students who successfully negotiate the educational system come out on the other side with increased cultural capital, which they can then employ in their efforts to obtain valued societal positions. At this most basic level, cultural capital exercises an influence on educational attainment that goes beyond such factors as ability and effort. Success at university is not simply a matter of students demonstrating their academic abilities. In order to be successful, students need to know how to successfully navigate the university – not just the physical layout of the campus, but the culture of the higher education that ultimately shapes the interactions that can promote or hinder student success. In Bourdieu's terms, the mentoring acts as a kind of "imported" cultural capital, increasing the likelihood of these students success at university. By "channelling" the students' into a select "path of action", the peer mentoring empowers the student and leads to a greater likelihood of academic success at the university while at the same time encouraging social integration. One mentee commented:

Navin: When I first arrived at the university, I felt alone and almost regretted my decision to study overseas........however through the Crossing Borders program, my attitude changed and I became very positive about living and studying in Sydney.

Developing greater levels of social capital may also help transnational students to counteract the influence of a hostile campus climate and provide access to academic information and opportunities within institutions of higher education. Another peer tutor said that she shared with her mentee personal experiences of starting high-school in mid Year 7 in Australia;

Emet: I could speak and write English well, I experienced disorientation adjusting to the 'Australian colloquialism' used by teachers and 'slang' used by students. I had to train myself to distinguish the language of the text from the language of instruction. This interaction was very enriching as we discovered that we had a lot of things in common and that we could also learn a lot from each other.

Suzan: My mentee has transformed from a quiet person to a person "with voice". This has and will be a positive growth for her as a teacher. Having a familiar face on campus and someone to discuss both personal and academic issues meant a growth in understanding the different ways of approaching things in a different country.

The strength and utility of these relationships may depend upon students' own orientations, as students with higher levels of academic performance and more life experiences generally derive greater rewards from their social networks. In the context of our study, the connections that transnational students might cultivate with institutional agents may increase the chances that they would learn about unique opportunities and similar experiences.

Mary: I have developed a friendship with my mentee and I believe that this has been a two-way mutually beneficial experience. I have been able to prepare her for the practical and expanded her concept of the practical by sharing with her my own experiences, challenges and breakthroughs. She has found this insight to be helpful to her in the prac. I have found my mentee to be a very intellectual and self-resourceful person therefore; I was able to acquire a different perspective as we discussed several topics. It was nice to provide feedback, advice, suggestions and also be listened to and realise that someone else is going through similar challenges and hardships.

Ravi: Overall, this opportunity has helped me to appreciate and understand what mentoring should be about- building respectful relationships and friendships..... the rapport that my mentee and I have is one that I consider to be at an equal level of status, we are ultimately two intellectuals who are sharing similarities and differences in regards to our knowledge acquisition, cultural experiences and concepts in the context of the course and beyond.

Sarah: Working closely one on one enabled me to develop a close relationship with my mentee. This allowed me to arrive at a deep understanding of the challenges new Australians experience not only with their studies but also in other areas of their lives. I have also developed a lovely friendship with a beautiful family.

Similarly, mentees may draw upon their peers for access to information and opportunities especially if they are unable to rely on family for support. Furthermore, the strength of the relationship can affect the scope of the resources gained through the relationship. This continues to highlight the need for students to be *both* academically and socially integrated in the university environment. This in turn construes habitus – of both mentor and mentee – as a raw material, and mentoring as a labour process to reform habitus as a saleable commodity. As Stella (mentee) commented:

The mentoring program is essential for us (international students)...if we get lost, we can find our way back.

Recommendations

The main problem with the mentoring program is that it is voluntary and there is therefore no way of ensuring that students of international and overseas trained backgrounds build and sustain the social and cultural capital they need to succeed at university. I suggest therefore that there needs to be some strengthening of the norms of the program, a strengthening of structures to ensure that students who require assistance do actually volunteer for the program and some form of sanction to ensure that students participate actively and with good intentions in the mentoring process. A commitment by all staff in the school of education to the mentoring process will allow the mentors to network and meet with other key people in the faculty and at the university to help build social networks.

Conclusion

In the current era of globalization, it is more important than ever for students to succeed academically in order to access increased opportunities (Suárez-Orozco, 2001). Like all immigrants, transnational students, face the challenge of learning English as well as acquiring an understanding of how Australian institutions work as social and academic institutions: i.e., how to behave in formal and informal settings, what the rules are, and how to relate to peers and lecturers. Therefore increased acculturation to the university as a social setting is essential for students who are attempting to understand how to negotiate their transitions from university to work, especially for those who are seeking to explore the options available in terms of teaching in Australia.

Bourdieu's habitus, social capital, and cultural reproduction are concepts that are useful in studying the experiences of transnationals rebuilding their lives in Australia, but they do not reflect the nuances of the complex personal and cultural identities of individuals who may feel marginalized between two cultures, who may be struggling with an oppositional bicultural identity, or may be simultaneously negotiating two cultures with different peer groups. Nevertheless Bourdieu's theory of social and cultural capital is important in understanding the academic and adjustment experiences of transnational students who have not been academically successful. Thus, Bourdieu's ideas on cultural and social capital can also offer further understanding as to how mentoring can exert power and influence to shift margin and centre. Since education is recognised as playing a key role for the future of transnationals, programs such as "Crossing Borders" is obviously important for educators and policymakers to know. Education offers the key to roles in the future and the culture learning that accompanies educational experience is essential to the acculturation and adjustment of transnational students.

References

Appadurai, A. 1996 Modernity *at Large, Cultural Dimensions of Globalization,* University of Minnesota Press, Minneapolis.

Armitage, L. 1999 *Factors Affecting the Adjustment of Koreans Studying in Australia,* Australia Korea Foundation, Australia.

Bourdieu, P. 1977 Cultural reproduction and social reproduction. In J. Karabel & A. H.Halsey (Eds.), *Power and ideology in education* (pp. 487-511), Greenwood Press, New York.

-----------.1986 The forms of capital. In J. G. Richardson (Ed.), *Handbook of theory and research for the sociology of education* (pp. 241-258), Greenwood Press, New York.

-----------.1990 *In other words* (M. Adamson, Trans.), Stanford University Press, Stanford, CA.

-----------.1991 *Language and symbolic power,* Harvard University Press, Cambridge.

----------- 1998 *Practical Reason: on the Theory of Action,* Polity Press, Cambridge, UK.

Bourdieu, P., & Passeron, J.C. 1977 *Reproduction in education, society, and culture.* Sage, Beverly Hills, CA.

Bourdieu, P and L Wacquant. 1992 *An Invitation to Reflexive Sociology,* University of Chicago Press, Chicago, USA.

Boyle, M. 2005 Most mentoring programs stink – but yours doesn't have to, *Training,* 42 (8):12-15.

Cameron, B.and P. Meade. 2002 Supporting the transition to university of international student: issues and challenges, in D Nulty (ed), *Changing Agendas 'Te Ao Hurihuri', proceedings of the Sixth Pacific Rim conference on First year higher education,* University of Canterbury, Christchurch, New Zealand.

Conway, K. (2005). Mentoring; Back to the basics. *Training,* 42 (8): 42-42

Cox, E. 2005 for better, for worse: the matching process in formal mentoring schemes. *Mentoring and Tutoring: Partnerships in Learning,* 13 (3): 403 – 414

Gans, H. 1997 toward a Reconciliation of 'Assimilation' and 'Pluralism': The Interplay of Acculturation and Ethnic Retention. *International Migration Review,* 31: 875-92.

Handa, N. 2004. What else did I need to bring with me? International students and their dilemma, Paper presented at the 15th*ISANA Conference of the International Students Advisors' Network of Australia (ISANA)*, Melbourne.

Kowalsky, R. and Fresko, B. 2002 Peer Tutoring for College Students with Disabilities. *Higher Education Research and Development*, 21 (3).

Krause, K. L. 2005 Understanding and promoting student engagement in university learning Communities. Paper presented as a keynote address *'Engaged, inert or otherwise occupied? Deconstructing the 21st century undergraduate student'* at the James Cook University Symposium 2005, Retrieved May 2006 from http://www.cshe.unimelb.edu.au/pdfs/Stud_eng.pdf

Leder G.C., and H. J. Forgasz. 2004. Australian and international and mature age students: the daily challenges. *Higher Education Research and Development*, 23(2):184-198.

Naidoo, L. 2007 Re-negotiating Identity and Reconciling Cultural Ambiguity in the Indian Immigrant Community in Sydney, Australia. In A. Singh (2007) (Ed) *Indian Diaspora- The 21st Century- Migration, Change and Adaptation,* Kamla-Raj Enterprises, New Delhi.

Novera, I. S. 2004 Indonesian Post graduate students studying in Australia: An examination of their Academic, social and cultural experiences. *International Education Journal,* 5(4): 475.

Portes, A.1998 Globalisation from below: the rise of transnational communities, *ESRC Transnational Communities Programme Working Paper* No. 1.

Portes, A. and Zhou, M. 1993 the new second generation: Segmented assimilation and its variants among post-1965 immigrant youth. *Annals of the American Academy of Political and Social Science,* 530: 74-96.

Robertson, M., Line, M., Jones, S. and Thomas, S., 2000 International Students, Learning Environments and Perceptions: a case study using the Delphi technique. *Higher Education Research and Development,* 19(1): 89-102.

Robinson, K. and Jones-Diaz, C. 2005 *Diversity and Difference in Early Childhood Settings.* UK: Open University Press

Rumbaut, R. 1997 Assimilation and its discontents: Between rhetoric and reality. *International Migration Review,* 28: 748-94.

Schuller T., Baron, S., Field, J. 2000 Social capital: A review of critique. In: *Social Capital: Critical Perspectives,* edited by S. Baron, J. Field and T. Schuller, pp.1-38, Oxford University Press, Oxford.

Scott, G., Bond, N., & Webb, C. 2005 'What retains students and promotes productive learning in higher education?' *UWS Quality forum: 8* September, UWS

Smart, D. Volet, S. and Ang, G. 2000 *Fostering Social Cohesion in Universities: Bridging the Cultural Divide,* Commonwealth of Australia, Canberra.

Scheyvens, R., Wild, K. and Overton, J., 2003 International Students Pursuing Postgraduate Study in Geography: impediments to their learning experiences, *Journal of Geography in Higher Education*, 27 (3): 309-322.

Suárez-Orozco, M. 2001 Globalization, immigration, and education: The research agenda, *Harvard Educational Review,* 71: 345-365.

Zhou, M. and Bankston, C. L., III.1998 *Growing up American: How Vietnamese children adapt to life in the United States,* Russell Sage Foundation, New York.

Chapter 9

Service-Learning and Diverse Perspectives

Teaching Diversity Perspectives in Spanish Language Classes through Service-Learning

Jodie Parys, University of Wisconsin-Whitewater, Wisconsin, USA

Abstract: In an increasingly globalized world, borders, both literal and figurative, are being crossed as cultures intersect, collide, and collaborate. The resultant multiculturalism requires that all parties become versant in and cognizant of the cultural, linguistic and sociological differences between individuals with the aim of forging respect for the increasingly diverse world in which we all live. One way to foment such diversity perspectives is through education. Many colleges and universities across the United States recognize this vital aspect of education in their academic missions and have made it their responsibility to prepare students for our multicultural society by incorporating diversity perspectives into both general education courses and specific area studies as students progress toward a degree. What varies, however, is how diversity perspectives are presented and incorporated into the curriculum. This paper looks specifically at teaching diversity perspectives in university-level Spanish language courses geared toward students whose primary language is not Spanish. I illustrate the vitally important role that diversity perspectives play in Spanish lan-

guage instruction to produce not only bilingual, but also bicultural, graduates who are adept at working with the rapidly growing Spanish-English bilingual population in the U.S. I argue that the most effective way to do this is vis-à-vis the incorporation of service-learning into Spanish language programs. Through the use of service-learning as a way to cross the boundary between the campus and surrounding community, students are given an invaluable opportunity to cement the knowledge gained in the classroom while serving the community and interacting with people of diverse backgrounds. This article will trace the use of service-learning as a pedagogical tool, showing how it is an ideal way to teach diversity perspectives in the college Spanish language classroom while producing students who will have a greater ability to be effective professionals with increased respect for our multicultural society.

Introduction

In an increasingly globalized world, borders, both literal and figurative, are being crossed as cultures intersect, collide, and collaborate. The resultant multiculturalism requires that all parties become versant in and cognizant of the cultural, linguistic and sociological differences between individuals with the aim of forging respect for the increasingly diverse world in which we all live. One way to foment such diversity perspectives is through education. Many colleges and universities across the United States recognize this vital aspect of education in their academic missions and have made it their responsibility to prepare students for our multicultural society by incorporating diversity perspectives into both general education courses and specific area studies as students progress toward a degree. What varies, however, is how diversity perspectives are presented and incorporated into the curriculum.

This paper looks specifically at teaching diversity perspectives in university-level Spanish language courses geared toward students whose primary language is not Spanish. I illustrate the vitally important role that diversity perspectives play in Spanish language instruction to produce not only bilingual, but also bicultural, graduates who are adept at working with the rapidly growing Spanish-English bilingual population in the U.S. I argue that the most effective way to do this is vis-à-vis the incorporation of service-learning into Spanish language programs. Through the use of service-learning as a way to cross the boundary between the campus and surrounding community, students are given an invaluable opportunity to cement the knowledge gained in the classroom while serving the community and interacting with people of diverse backgrounds. This article will trace the use of service-learning as a pedagogical tool, showing how it is an ideal way to teach diversity perspectives in the college Spanish language classroom while producing students who will have a greater ability to be effective professionals with increased respect for our multicultural society.

The Importance of Teaching Diversity Perspectives

Regardless of course of study, every student can gain intellectually and so-cially from a well-rounded curriculum that includes diversity perspectives. It not only helps students prepare for work in a globalized economy where interactions with individuals from a multitude of nations are increasingly becoming the norm, but often, it allows students to gain a broader appreci-ation for their peers as they gain an understanding of some of the cultural and societal issues that affect people from different racial, social and eco-nomic groups. This, in turn, can help students become more self-aware as they begin to examine their own histories in light of those of the people and communities around them. When successful, incorporating multicul-tural and other diverse perspectives into the curriculum has the potential to forge cultural understanding and bring about positive social change rooted in cooperation rather than conflict.

The potential to positively impact social justice issues through the incor-poration of multicultural and diverse perspectives is examined by O'Grady, who asserts that "when students can learn to analyze, to critically reflect on, and ultimately--if they choose to--to transform oppressive situations through action, they are engaged in a form of political activism inherent in social reconstructionist multicultural education" (2000, 5). O'Grady pro-posed a two-pronged approach, arguing that, on the one hand, students must have the opportunity to critically engage with the material that is presented in a multicultural curriculum. The responsibility for this first as-pect falls on the instructor to appropriately frame the material in a way that allows for analytical reflection. Secondly, it is imperative that students have the opportunity to act upon the information they learn, not only in the classroom setting, but in a way that connects with the community being studied, thus shifting the responsibility to enact change onto the student. O'Grady argues that the vehicle for this activism is service-learning, noting that, when combined with multicultural education, it can potentially result in profound systemic change (2000, 6).

Increasingly, both diversity perspectives and service-learning are being incorporated into college curricula, reflecting the growing understanding of the critical value of both approaches to creating a well-rounded edu-cational experience and producing graduates prepared to engage with the rapidly-evolving society we inhabit. Even a cursory examination of the mis-sion statements of various colleges and universities reflects this reality. How that mission is carried out, however, varies vastly across schools, colleges, departments, and programs. As I argue, it is my position that one of the most effective ways is through the incorporation of service-learning pro-jects that engage students with the communities around them and provide the opportunity to meaningfully interact with diverse populations.

Since the scope of my project occupies itself with the incorporation of diversity perspectives in Spanish language courses, it is important to exam-ine diversity in the realm of foreign language teaching, looking specifically at Spanish. Spanish holds a particularly important place in language programs on campuses across the nation because of its relevance and in some markets, absolute necessity, to many fields of study. The dramatic growth of the Hispanic population in the U.S. has been well-documented, with the Pew Hispanic Center estimating that as of 2007 (the most recent year for which statistics were compiled), there were approximately 45.3 million Hispanics living in the U.S, reflecting a 28.9% increase in population from 2000-2007. (http://pewhispanic.org/files/factsheets/hispanics2007/2007%20Hispanic-%20Profile_Final.pdf). Add to that number the estimated 12 million illegal immigrants in this country from Spanish-speaking countries (http://pewhispanic.org/reports/report.php?ReportID=61) and it becomes clear that for students graduating in an array of fields today, it is not a luxury, but often a necessity, to be bilingual in Spanish and English. Spanish education programs across the country are increasingly recognizing this need and as a result, one notes an increased emphasis on the use of functional, communicative language pedagogies that highlight diversity perspectives as they strive to produce bilingual and bicultural graduates.

To accomplish this, many Spanish programs across the country incorporate some, if not all, of the American Council on the Teaching of Foreign Language (ACTFL) standards into their educational missions. ACTFL identifies 5 key areas that should be incorporated in all foreign language programs. The "5 Cs", as they've come to be known among language instructors, are broadly envisioned to allow each program to develop specific guidelines that take into consideration the needs of their students and communities. They include communication, cultures, connections, comparisons, and communities and are articulated in the ACTFL standards statement.

Examined more closely, it becomes clear that the concept of diversity is interwoven throughout these 5 Cs and is an inherent part of language learning and must be incorporated into Spanish language classrooms to offer a comprehensive language-learning experience that takes into consideration not only the structure and use of the language, but also the meaning of language in a variety of contexts. For communication to occur, students must develop an ample lexicon that enables them to interact linguistically with Spanish speakers from diverse backgrounds. Part of that process involves arriving at the understanding that language does not exist in a void. It is essential to integrate the cultural elements of language to be an effective communicator. Spanish is spoken as the official language in 21 countries and as a secondary language in a handful of others[1]. Clearly, each of these nations has unique cultural elements that influence the way the language is spoken and dictate variations in meaning that are essential to truly mastering a language and having the ability to use it with such a population as diverse as the world's Spanish speakers.

Bilingualism provides an avenue to make connections with people in the community and around the world to which students wouldn't have access without the linguistic ability. It is not uncommon for students to enter col-

---

1.http://www.spanishprograms.com/spanish-speaking-countries.htm

lege after living their entire lives in small, rural communities in which there is little to no linguistic or cultural diversity. For many, Spanish becomes a tool to make connections with people from diverse cultural, linguistic, and racial backgrounds and allows students to experience true diversity that is often absent in their upbringings, thus better preparing them for a globalized economy. This fosters comparison and contrast between viewpoints, lifestyles, cultures, and societies, providing a variety of perspectives and challenging students to re-examine previously held beliefs as they compare the points of view that they brought with them to college with those of others from vastly different backgrounds. This ability to view the world and take into account a range of viewpoints, particularly in relation to complex issues, reflects an academic maturity that is often lacking when students begin their studies. It is also an important characteristic of well-rounded graduates who will enter an increasingly diverse workforce and ideally, with have the ability to forge connections throughout their communities.

The mark of a true bilingual professional is one that is not only linguistically and culturally competent in both languages, but has also established connections with both language communities and can serve as a liaison between groups. Language programs that encourage participation in multilingual and multicultural communities, both on and off campus, effectively guide students in the subtle art of integrating oneself into diverse groups and finding connections that foster a level of comfort and cooperation so that no one feels like an "outsider". Each campus incorporates this in different ways, whether through language clubs, language houses or dorms, multicultural groups, study abroad programs or other initiatives. Another method that is particularly useful in helping students become a part of multilingual communities, as I will elaborate below, is service-learning. I offer a brief overview and history of service-learning, before focusing on best practices that enhance both the teaching of diversity perspectives and Spanish language in college classrooms vis-à-vis service-learning.

Service-Learning: An Overview

According to Stanton, Giles & Cruz, the term *service-learning* was first invented by Southern Regional Board members in 1969, who described it as "the accomplishment of tasks that meet genuine human needs in combination with conscious educational growth" (Stanton, Giles & Cruz, 1999 in O'Grady, 2000). The tradition of marrying civic engagement with learning, however, is much more deeply rooted in our society. In fact, Benjamin Franklin's writings from 1749 asserted that the fundamental purpose of higher education was an "inclination joined with an ability to serve" (cited in *New Times Demand New Scholarship*, 2005, 5). Since Franklin's time, the connection between scholarship and service has taken on many forms and been called by many names, but many scholars agree that the field as it is known today draws largely from the early work of John Dewey, who believed that when people are actively engaged in solving the problems facing their society, they also tend to make large advances in the knowledge base related to the issue being studied (*New Times...*, 2005, 8; Stanton, Giles & Cruz, 1999). According to Hale, Dewey's "theoretical and philosophical study of experience-based learning provides a broad rationale for the application of service-learning in college curricula today" (1999, 14). Since these early articulations, the concept has come to be known by various names. Some refer to "engaged scholarship" (New Times...., 2005, 9), while others prefer "civic engagement" (Raill, S., & Hollander, E, 2006, 3; Kiesa, A., et al., 2008, 1). A majority of practitioners, however, have incorporated the term "service-learning" into their work and use it to describe a pedagogical approach that integrates a course-appropriate service component and reflection activities into the academic curriculum to allow students to apply course content to real-world situations.

Despite the common term, there are nuanced differences to how various practitioners define service-learning. From the selections presented below, it is possible to piece together a comprehensive definition that encompasses all of the vital components of service-learning. One of the most complete characterizations of the practice is offered by Barbara Jacoby, who posits that

> Service-learning is a form of experiential education in which students engage in activities that address human and community needs together with structured opportunities intentionally designed to promote student learning and development. Reflection and reciprocity are key concepts of service-learning (in Rosenberger, 2000, 25).

Jacoby's definition highlights three key components of successful service-learning: projects that address a true need and are not simply fabricated to serve the needs of the class; connection of the project to student learning; and reflection activities that require students to actively draw parallels between what they are experiencing in the community and what they are learning in the course. In the absence of any one of these elements, the project will suffer and will fail to achieve the unique symbiotic relationship exemplified by service-learning in which educational outcomes and student learning are balanced with meaningful service that meets a demonstrated social need.

Other practitioners expand upon Jacoby's definition, noting that "within the service-learning paradigm, the four walls of the traditional classroom open themselves to a new classroom without borders, one that integrates students as participants in real-world contexts" (Caldwell, 1997, 466). This "classroom without borders" is a key concept to service-learning in that the community agency is seen as a fundamental partner in the educational process, often collaborating with instructors and reinforcing in the field lessons that are taught in the traditional classroom. In fact, there is an entire body of research devoted to gleaning the perspective of community partners to improve the relationship between higher education institutions and community agencies in a way that is beneficial to all involved, producing both desirable educational outcomes for students participating on-site in service-learning while meeting the needs of the agency and the individuals it serves (Leiderman, et. al, 2002; Sandy & Holland, 2006; *University + Community Research Partnerships*, 2003).

Sandy & Holland elaborate on the discourse mentioned above regarding the borderless classroom when they note that "a common metaphor used by service-learning practitioners to frame their thinking about the service-learning experience is "boundary crossing" or "boundary work," entering another world where different rules apply" (Hayes & Cuban, 1997; Keith, 1998; McMillan, 2002; Skilton-Sylvester & Erwin, 2000; Taylor, 2002, all cited in Sandy & Holland, 2006, 31). Because of the intense nature of "boundary crossing" and the potential for misunderstanding, "the role of the teacher is crucial in fostering critical assessments and reflection of the student experiences in the community. Both the curriculum and the way it is taught affect the meaning students make of their interactions with community members who have different life experiences" (Westheimer & Kahne, 2007, 99). This caution reminds practitioners of the vitally important role of the instructor, and I would add, the community partner, in framing the experiences in an educationally meaningful way and even more importantly, of helping students process the work they perform, the interactions they have and the often unfamiliar things they witness. A service-learning program that is devoid of this crucial guidance could potentially reinforce stereotypes (Westheimer & Kahne, 2007, 99). This is because without well-guided reflection activities, which Eyler (2001) contends are the "hyphen in service-learning" (cited in Caldwell, 2007, 468), and the opportunity to discuss what they witness, students are unable to adequately process their experiences, many of which put them in the position of outsider or minority for the first time in their lives.

However, with the proper guidance and well-structured projects, service-learning has the potential to positively impact the student in myriad ways. There is a wealth of research related to the benefits of service-learning programs on students personally, socially, academically and professionally. Below I've highlighted a few of the findings from research in the last decade, particularly noting areas that are not only related to overall student learning and growth, but also illustrate why service learning is particularly useful when teaching about multiculturalism and diversity perspectives. Numerous studies have shown a positive impact of service-learning on academic achievement (Billig, 2002; Meyer, 2003; Billig & Meyer, 2002, in *The Impact of Service-Learning...*, 2007, 1; Vogelgesang & Astin, 2000; Strage, 2000) while others notes that "engagement in the first year yields especially powerful benefits for historically underserved students" (Kuh, et al., 2007 in *How Can Engaged Colleges...*, 2008, 2). In addition to academic benefits, service-learning also positively impacts student personal development in terms of moral growth, development of personal identity, and sense of personal efficacy (Wang, 2000; Astin, Sax & Avalos, 1999). It leads to an enhanced ability to work well with others and improves leadership and communication skills (Vogelgesang & Astin, 2000; Astin & Sax, 1998). Furthermore, it appears that service-learning begets more service, evidenced not only during college study but after graduation, as well (Astin & Sax, 1998, Vogelgesang & Astin, 2000; Astin, Sax, & Avalos, 1999).

Research has clearly shown that the personal, educational, and social impact of service-learning is overwhelmingly positive. The question at hand, however, is how service-learning relates to teaching diversity perspectives. What impact does it have on facilitating cultural and racial understanding and/or reducing or challenging stereotypes and prejudicial thought and actions? In those regards, much of the research concludes that service-learning demonstrates a positive impact in this area, with students often demonstrating a much greater sensitivity towards different cultures and races or questioning some of their previously-held beliefs, particularly those related to stereotypes (Astin & Sax, 1998; Astin, Sax & Avalos, 1999; Boyle-Baise, 1998; Boyle-Baise & Kilbane, 2000; Eyler & Giles, 1999; Vogelgesang & Astin, 2000).

Despite the positive results observed post-service-learning, some research cautions that poorly designed service-learning projects, particularly those lacking adequate reflection opportunities, can have a contradictory effect, and actually reinforce stereotypes (Anderson & Guest, 1994; Berry, 1990; Kretzmann & McKnight, 1993; Levinson, 1990; Reardon, 1994; Tellez, Hlebowitsh, Cohen, & Norwood, 1995; Waldock, 1995, all cited in O'Grady, 2000, 12). To help mitigate this issue and maximize the potential benefits that service-learning can offer in curricula that strive to incorporate multicultural and diversity perspectives, McPherson and Kinsley (1995) recommend that service-learning programs:

1. Must not reinforce old stereotypes and perpetuate a duality between the server and the recipient, perpetuating paternalism;
2. Must address significant issues that are real social justice issues;
3. Must not be trivialized through rote or repetition;
4. Must involve real collaboration with the community; and
5. That service learning practitioners must be clear about their deeper motivations for utilizing service learning (cited in O'Grady, 12).

Taken as a whole, the literature reveals that when practitioners work closely with their students and community partners to carefully design, communicate, and execute their projects, taking into consideration the advice and experience of the pioneers in the field, they have a powerful pedagogical tool that is a valuable means to teach students in a multicultural, pluralistic society. Furthermore, service-learning "serves as a vehicle through which to examine in depth personal bias and racism and to better understand the meaning of diversity" (Baldwin, Buchanan, & Rudisill, 2007, 315). Interestingly enough, however, despite the seemingly natural fit between service-learning and multicultural education, there is a lack of articulation from scholars and practitioners of service-learning on how to forge a strong relationship between the two fields (IDEAS Report, 2009, 2). This article aims to take a small step towards addressing that gap in the field of Spanish language.

Service Learning in Spanish Language Courses: Multiple Border Crossings

Service-learning is a beneficial tool for teaching diversity perspectives in Spanish language courses precisely because of the pluralistic nature of language learning. I concur with Hale that:

> Service-learning, when applied to the teaching of language and culture, has the potential to reach far beyond the acquisition of academic subjects. It has the power to reshape attitudes not only toward these subjects, but, even more important, toward the people those subjects reference, thus alleviating some of the significant cultural and linguistic barriers that prevail in our society today" (1999, 22).

As mentioned above, a majority of Spanish programs adhere to the ACTFL standards and incorporate to some degree the "5 Cs" into their language instruction. However, according to Hellebrandt & Varona, "despite a slew of approaches, methods, and strategies for teaching and learning a second language that have emerged in the last 20 years, student learning has basically remained confined to the classroom (1999, 1). Hale goes on to explain that "a missing link yet to be extensively explored is the application of service-learning to the foreign- or second-language curriculum. For example, few universities have integrated the concept of having students work in Spanish-speaking communities as a means of learning Spanish" (1999, 9). In my opinion, the failure on the part of second language and/or foreign language programs to integrate service-learning into their curricula in a more consistent and widespread manner prevents language instructors from maximizing the potential for language acquisition and cultural awareness that service-learning offers. In the course of a typical semester, students undertake a veritable journey in their language learning, crossing multiple borders as they learn about linguistic, cultural and racial diversity. Service-learning is an ideal vehicle to allow students to approach that diversity from a perspective of cooperation rather than one of conflict. Below, I discuss each of the aforementioned diversity perspectives that are typically encountered by Spanish students when they engage in service-learning and how these learning projects effectively address each realm.

Linguistic Diversity

At the crux of all second language- or foreign-language acquisition programs is the goal of helping students develop proficiency in the language of study. Linguistic development focuses on four skills: speaking, reading, writing, and listening, applied in an array of situations. Language-acquisition theory provides numerous perspectives on methods that are most beneficial for acquiring various skills. While the purview of this article does not include a historical analysis of language-acquisition,[2] there are certain precepts that do lend themselves well to our discussion of service-learning and its ap-

---

2. See Mullaney for a succinct historical review of salient language-acquisition theory and her analysis of its relation to service-learning pedagogy.

plicability to teaching linguistic diversity in language classes. Specifically, Peregoy & Boyle (1993) contend that "language comprehension develops as a result of opportunities for social interaction with speakers of the new language" (56) and that "all language skills....are best developed when students are using those skills to achieve communication goals that are interesting and meaningful for them" (1993, 153, cited in Mullaney, 1999, 52). Although there are many ways to try to *recreate* authentic environments in the language classroom (through videos, tape-recordings, language labs, interactive CDs, language partnerships, internet, etc), none is truly authentic in the way that interacting and speaking with Latinos in a service project in the community is. Short of studying abroad, students simply do not have the opportunity in the course of a regular semester to communicate meaningfully and for a significant period of time with heritage speakers of Spanish if they are not directly involved with the community.

Service-learning provides the means to tie that direct involvement into the classroom goals, allowing for students to develop their linguistic abilities as they negotiate meaning with native speakers in an authentic environment. This enables them to hear different accents and experience first-hand the difference in dialect between speakers from various countries of origin. It allows them to hear different registers of Spanish, and makes real the concept of formal vs. informal speech that previously was confined to verb conjugation charts and simulated conversations. They see that even native speakers speak with incorrect grammar at times or employ code switching in their speech patterns, thus revealing authentic language patterns that cannot be replicated in the classroom. What results is a much deeper first-hand understanding of some of the linguistic diversity of the Spanish speaking population of this country. Clearly, this varies depending on the project, but my experience has shown that often a single project has a more profound impact in this regard than multiple classroom lessons that try to replicate the same concepts.

Cultural Diversity

When thinking about cultural diversity, the experience recounted by Jonathan F. Arries echoes my own and reveals one of the many challenges facing language instructors:

> When asked what they want from their...college Spanish course, they typically describe their travel in Latin America or Spain and say they want to learn more about Hispanic culture. However, the students' use of that noun in the singular form suggests that they have not had an opportunity to think critically about culture as a concept; they seem unaware that there is no such thing as a single Hispanic culture. Also troubling in these students' comments is the connotation of "foreignness" that their travel experience leads them to associate with the concept of Hispanic cultures; they may easily overlook the more than 20 million [sic] Hispanic Americans in the United States" (1999, 33).

This myopic vision of "Hispanic culture" is often shared by my own students, many of whom are not even able to differentiate between "Spanish" culture and "Mexican" culture, much less the many vast and subtle differences between countries of the same region or continent. Furthermore, it comes as a shock to a majority of students that the United States is consistently ranked in the top 5 in terms of countries in the world with the largest number of Spanish-speakers.[3]

Although there are many wonderful texts, movies and "realia" that can be brought to the language classroom to *show* students about culture, service-learning allows students to *experience* culture. The often visceral reaction of being able to see, feel, touch or taste cultural elements while interacting with Hispanic members of the community tends to produce a level of comprehension not seen while simply introducing "realia" into the classroom. This is particularly true in communities with individuals from a variety of Spanish-speaking countries, thus providing students with the opportunity to experience traditions from multiple countries of origin. As a result, many students express not only a greater understanding of cultural diversity, but also a greater respect for distinct cultural traditions.

In the case of one of my former students, the effect was even more profound. As a bicultural and biracial woman of African American and Puerto Rican descent, Lola[4] always identified herself as "black" and felt more at ease with the African American community than with the Puerto Rican community. However, through her service learning project, she became involved in a project that put her in direct contact with both the Puerto Rican and Mexican communities in her hometown. By the end of the semester, the effects were profound: her level of confidence in speaking Spanish had skyrocketed, she had reconnected with the Puerto Rican side of her family, she had learned how to cook various Puerto Rican dishes (which she shared with the class), was invited to family and community celebrations of Puerto Rican heritage, and had even fallen in love with a Puerto Rican man, to whom she is now engaged. Lola recounted to me that service-learning allowed her to reclaim an entire part of her cultural, linguistic and racial heritage that was previously unknown to her. She says she is eternally grateful for the experience.

Such personal outcomes in cultural diversity are one potential product of service-learning programs. They also facilitate the development of cultural competency. The respect for diverse cultures that often results from service-learning experiences is an integral step to developing cultural competency, which is operationally defined as "the integration and transformation of knowledge about individuals and groups of people into specific standards, policies practices, and attitudes used in appropriate cultural set-

---

3.http://www.nationmaster.com/graph/lan_spa_spe-language-spanish-speakers, http://wiki.answers.com/Q/What_countries_have_the_largest_Spanish_speaking_population

4.I have changed the name of my former student to protect her identity.

tings to increase the quality of services, thereby producing better outcomes" (Davis, 1997; Herbert, 2006, both cited in Wehling, 2008, 298). The development of cultural competency is vital not only to achieving one of the primary aforementioned ACTFL standards of language instruction, but is essential for working effectively and empathically in our multicultural society.

Racial Diversity

Lola's experience highlights not only the importance of cultural and linguistic diversity, but pinpoints the often complex racial issues facing many Hispanics today. Much the same way that students spoke about "Hispanic culture" in the singular in Arries' quote above, they also tend to envision all Hispanics as sharing a singular racial identity. Many students fail to realize that people from different Spanish speaking nations represent a vast racial diversity that runs the gamut from African ancestry to many different Indigenous roots to European descent. Furthermore, in appearance, Spanish speakers, particularly those hailing from Caribbean nations, encompass every variation in skin tone, eye color, hair color and physique possible.

Again, texts and other classroom materials can certainly be used effectively to educate students on the racial variety found in Spanish-speaking nations (and I include the U.S. in that category), but true enlightenment is often borne from the opportunity to collaborate with people who may look either very similar or very different racially and to come to the realization that the previously conceptualized "Hispanic race" is really a diverse group of people whose appearance is tremendously varied. Furthermore, for many college students, particularly those who are light-skinned or of European ancestry, service-learning projects that afford them the opportunity to work side-by-side with Latinos in predominantly Latino neighborhoods are often the first time they have ever found themselves in the position of racial minority. McBrien affirms the importance of this for developing empathy, stating that "cognitive knowledge about the experiences of refugee and immigrant children and families is helpful in creating...empathy, but it's not a substitute for experiencing firsthand the confusion, fear, and emotions of being an outsider" (2009, 337). The experience of being the "other" and the work done processing it, both on site and in the classroom, often has a profound impact on students' perspectives regarding race in this country and tends to lead to more open-mindedness and understanding. While "crossing the 'us-them' border", students pass through a "personalizing phase, in which a diverse social group that students have only read about in a textbook actually becomes real for them (Howard & Rhodes, 1998, cited in Wehling, 2008, 303).

This developmental process is only possible through experiential learning, illustrating precisely why service-learning is such a tremendously effective pedagogical method for teaching diversity perspectives in Spanish language classes. It is the experiential nature of these projects that drive home lessons presented in class and make them "real" and tangible in a way that other methods simply do not. Students exhibit personal and intellectual growth that advances them on their language learning journey. To be certain, as some of the aforementioned studies indicate, there is a vast array of approaches to service-learning in Spanish language classrooms, with each type of project having the potential to affect one or more of the diversity perspectives mentioned above to greater or lesser degrees. As would be expected with such a pluralistic pedagogical method, the specific outcomes of service-learning on individual students will vary, depending on the practitioner implementing it, the community in which it is performed and the students performing it. In the end, however, as we have seen, the outcomes are largely positive, affecting both students and community in overwhelmingly positive ways.

In fact, it is this plurality of approaches that opens up one possibility for future research. Now that so much work has been done exploring *what* service learning is, *how* it came about and *why* it is effective, it would be particularly informative to see more studies focusing on precisely *how* it is implemented in specific disciplines, especially Spanish.[5] Another area of inquiry that would be fruitful to pursue involves the long-term impact of service-learning. We have seen the potential for impact within the timeframe of a semester-long class, but it would be enlightening to examine if those effects continue to be exhibited months or even, years after completing a service-learning experience. I intend to continue to explore these questions as I continue to incorporate service-learning in my Spanish language classroom and I will work to encourage my colleagues to do the same in their classes because I have found that the results are profound and have an enriching effect on the classroom environment, student learning and the community at large.

References

Arries, J. F. (1999). Critical Pedagogy and Service-Learning in Spanish: Crossing Borders in the Freshman Seminar. In J. Hellebrandt & L. T. Varona (Eds.), Construyendo Puentes (Building Bridges): Concepts and Models for Service-Learning in Spanish. Washington, DC: American Association for Higher Education.

Astin, A. W., & Sax, L. J. (1998). How Undergraduates are Affected by Service Participation. Journal of College Student Development, 39(3), 251-263.

---

5. In fact, I have produced an expanded version of this study that focuses on service learning in my own intermediate-level Spanish language classes and draws conclusions from student feedback about the impact that service-learning has in the three areas of diversity mentioned here. That article is forthcoming.

Astin, A. W., Sax, L. J., & Avalos, J. (1999). Long Term Effects of Volunteerism During the Undergraduate Years. Review of Higher Education, 22(2), 187-202.

Baldwin, S. C., Buchanan, A. M., & Rudisill, M. E. (September/October 2007). What Teacher Candidates Learned About Diversity, Social Justice, and Themselves from Service-Learning Experiences. Journal of Teacher Education, 58(4), 315-327.

Boyle-Baise, M. (1998). Community Service Learning for Multicultural Education: An Exploratory Study with Pre-service Teachers. Equity & Excellence in Education, 31(2), 52-60.

Boyle-Baise, M., & Kilbane, J. (2000). What Really Happens? A Look Inside Service-Learning for Multicultural Teacher Education. Michigan Journal of Community Service Learning, 7, 54-64.

Caldwell, W. (2007). Taking Spanish Outside the Box: A Model for Integrating Service Learning Into Foreign Language Study. Foreign Language Annals, 40(3), 463-471.

Eyler, J. S., & Giles, D. E., Jr. (1999). Where's the Learning in Service-Learning? San Francisco, CA: Jossey-Bass, Inc.

Eyler, J. S., Giles, J., Dwight E., Stenson, C. M., & Gray, C. J. (2001). At a Glance: What We Know about The Effects of Service-Learning on College Students, Faculty, Institutions and Communities, 1993-2000: Third Edition: Vanderbilt University.

Hale, A. (1999). Service-Learning and Spanish: A Missing Link. In J. Hellebrandt & L. T. Varona (Eds.), Construyendo Puentes (Building Bridges): Concepts and Models for Service-Learning in Spanish. Washington, DC: American Association for Higher Education.

Hellebrandt, J., & Varona, L. T. (1999). Introduction. In J. Hellebrandt & L. T. Varona (Eds.), Construyendo Puentes (Building Bridges): Concepts and Models for Service-Learning in Spanish. Washington, DC: American Association for Higher Education.

How Can Engaged Campuses Improve Student Success in College? Research Brief #1. (Research Brief #1 No. in the Building Engaged Campuses series) (2008). Boston, MA: Campus Compact.

Issue Brief. The Impact of Service-Learning: A Review of Current Research. (January 2007). www.nationalservice.gov.

Kiesa, A., Orlowski, A. P., Levin, P., Both, D., Kirby, E. H., Lopez, M. H., et al. (2008). Millennials Talk Politics: A Study of College Student Political Engagement, Executive Summary: CIRCLE: The Center for Information & Research on Civic Learning & Engagement.

Leiderman, S., Furco, A., Zapf, J., & Goss, M. (2002). Building Partnerships with College Campuses: Community Perspectives: Consortium for the Advancement of Private Higher Education's Engaging Communities and Campuses Grant Program.

McBrien, J. L. (2009). Soy la Otra: A white middle-class American woman experiences being "the other" and learns lessons that apply to U.S. schools. Phi Delta Kappan, January, 333-337.

Mullaney, J. (1999). Service-Learning and Language-Acquisition Theory and Practice. In J. Hellebrandt & L. T. Varona (Eds.), Construyendo Puentes (Building Bridges): Concepts and Models for Service-Learning in Spanish. Washington, DC: American Association for Higher Education.

New Times Demand New Scholarship: Research Universities and Civic Engagement. A Leadership Agenda. (2005). Paper presented at the Conference on Research Universities and Civic Engagement, Tufts University.

O'Grady, C. (2000). Integrating Service Learning and Multicultural Education: An Overview. In C. O'Grady (Ed.), Integrating Service Learning and Multicultural Education in Colleges and Universities (pp. 1-19). Mahwah, New Jersey: Lawrence Erlbaum Associates.

Raill, S., & Hollander, E. (2006). How Campuses Can Create Engaged Citizens: The Student View. Journal of College & Character, VII (No. 1), 1-7.

Raschio, R. (2004). Adams Spanish Immersion and The Ascension Parish Project: Two Service-Learning Projects, Two Levels of Success. Hispania, 87(1), 122-127.

Rosenberger, C. (2000). Beyond Empathy: Developing Critical Consciousness Through Service Learning. In C. R. O'Grady (Ed.), Integrating Service Learning and Multicultural Education in Colleges and Universities. Mahwah, New Jersey: Lawrence Erlbaum Associates, Publishers.

Stanton, T.K., Giles, D.E., Jr., & Cruz, N.I. (1999). Service-learning: A movement's pioneers reflect on its origins, practice and future. San Francisco, CA: Jossey-Bass.

Strage, A. (2000). Service-Learning: Enhancing Student Learning Outcomes in a College Level Lecture Course. Michigan Journal of Community Service Learning, 7, 5-13.

Tilley-Lubbs, G. (2004). Crossing the Border through Service-Learning: From Practice to Theory. Hispania, 87(1), 135-136.

University + Community Research Partnerships: A New Approach. (2003). Richmond, VA: Pew Partnership for Civic Change.

Vogelgesang, L. J., & Astin, A. W. (2000). Comparing the Effects of Service-Learning and Community Service. Michigan Journal of Community Service Learning, 7, 25-34.

Wang, W. (2000). Service Learning: Is it Good for You? Paper presented at the Annual Meeting of the American Educational Research Association Conference Roundtable, New Orleans, LA.

Wehling, S. (2008). Cross-Cultural Competency Through Service-Learning. Journal of Community Practice, 16(3), 293-315.

Westheimer, J., & Kahne, J. (2007). Introduction. Equity & Excellence in Education, 40(2), 97-100.

Chapter 10

Service-Learning and Sense of Belonging

An Alternative Approach to Preventing Student Alienation and School Violence through Teacher Education Curricula

Using Service-Learning to Promote a Sense of Belonging that Embraces Human Diversity

Dr. Carroll R. Tyminski

Abstract: What can teacher educators do to prepare future teachers to address complex issues inherent in our schools today? Young people characterized as outsiders inflict deadly violence in our schools. They are often alienated, socially isolated, and devoid of social responsibility.

Fixing this problem requires community partnership. Teacher education programs and schools must incorporate service-learning and sensitivity training into their curricula.

The most recent case of deadly school shootings in the U.S. occurred in a junior high school in Red Lion, Pennsylvania this April. A principal was murdered and a student committed suicide in front of hundreds of witnesses. An interview with the Assistant Principal of the school provides a focal point for discussion of school violence and the vital role of teacher educators.

Introduction

What can teacher educators do to prepare future teachers to address complex issues inherent in our schools today? Young people characterized as outsiders inflict violence upon our communities. They are often alienated, socially isolated, and devoid of social responsibility.

Fixing this problem requires community partnership. Teacher education programs and schools must incorporate service-learning and sensitivity training into their curricula. Future teachers graduating from our teacher education programs must be part of the solution, not part of the problem. As teacher educators, we have a social responsibility to ensure that this is indeed the case.

This paper will discuss the problem of violent crime in U.S. schools and will chronicle a recent school homicide-suicide in Red Lion, Pennsylvania that has implications for teacher educators worldwide.

Enormity of the Problem in the United States

The U.S. Department of Justice (2002) reports that incidences of crime in schools have declined from a reported high of 5.9 % of students reporting "violent victimization" in 1993 to a low of 2.6 % of students reporting "violent victimization" in 2000. Granted, this is an improvement. However, when we consider that there are approximately 52 million students in American schools, we are still talking about over 1.3 million students who are victims of violence within the walls of their own schools!

Reporting agencies downplay the severity of the school crime problem by implying that an American has a greater chance of being struck by lightning than child has of being victimized by violence in his school. Nevertheless, the level of violence in U.S. schools is grossly "out of proportion to the levels of violence in (schools of) other developed nations", at least according to interviews of diplomats assigned to embassies in Washington, D.C. (Haynes & Chalker, 1999, p.23). Reports indicate, for example, that American teenagers are ten times more likely to commit acts of lethal violence than Canadian teenagers (Hinds, 2000).

School-Related Violent Crime

A small but significant amount of lethal violence occurs within American schools, on school property, or at school-sponsored events. Therefore, we must understand what is meant by school-based violence. Definitions of violence vary greatly. Violence may include actual or perceived threats, bullying, name-calling, harassment, "disruptive" behavior, drug use, fighting, carrying weapons with the intent to inflict aggression against school property or persons, suicide, and murder.

In the United States, gun-related death by suicide or homicide in the schools has received dramatic publicity. The most recent case to attract national publicity took place in April, 2003 in a small, peaceful, rural community of Red Lion, Pennsylvania. Unfortunately, this case did not make it into the official statistical records because there were no police arrests. Mr. Kurt Fassnacht, Assistant Principal of Red Lion Junior High School granted the author an extensive interview to discuss the case and its implications for future practice. He discussed his perspectives concerning causes of deadly school violence, effectiveness of preventative measures, and implications for the future.

Mr. Fassnacht knew the shooter, and he was standing nearby when the murder/suicide took place. The basic facts are as follows:

Where? Red Lion Middle School in Red Lion, Pennsylvania.

When? April 24, 2003 about 7:30 a.m.

Who? James Robert Sheets, age 14, and Principal Gene Segro, age 51.

What? In the presence of almost 400 students, James "Jimmy" Sheets walked into the school cafeteria and pulled one of three guns from his backpack. He fired a .44 caliber revolver point blank at the chest of his principal, Gene Segro. Then he pulled a .22 caliber handgun from his backpack and shot himself in the temple. Students ran screaming from the cafeteria. Teachers led them to the nearby senior high school. James Sheets died at the scene. Gene Segro died on the way to the hospital.

Why? Reason unknown.

Public Reaction to Tragedy

Following the tragic school shooting in Red Lion, Pennsylvania, local school teachers as well as the general public cried out for something to be done.

Following more well-known cases of lethal school violence such as in Littleton, Colorado (1999), Conyers, Georgia (1999), Springfield, Oregon (1998), and Jonesboro, Arkansas (1998), the public also demanded that something be done. When questioned by reporters, Red Lion Junior High School Assistant Principal Kurt Fassnacht, said there was no warning of a threat; he does not know how the school could have prevented these shootings. Prevention of future tragedies is a topic of ongoing discussion in Red Lion and elsewhere in the United States.

Letters to the local newspaper following Red Lion's tragedy indicate that the public has a few ideas about what caused the shootings as well as what should be done. The following comments are representative:

"I am the parent of a young woman who was a student at Columbine High School on April 20, 1999. The fourth anniversary of the worst school shootings in the U.S. just passed a few days ago. I want to send my heartfelt sympathies to the community of Red Lion, especially to the families of the deceased. The shootings at their school this morning bring to light the tragedy of school violence and the need for better understanding of the needs of our children. Certainly the young boy needed something that he felt he wasn't getting. Why choose the school to vent his anger and frustration? We may never know. And that is a tragedy too. In Colorado there are still questions about this. The debates go on about what could and should have been done to prevent this tragedy. I pray that we find answers and that those in Red Lion find answers too." Lorre Gibson, Littleton, Colorado.

"I think they need to put metal detectors at each door and more security to check these kids out before they get into the school. A lot of parents are getting to the point where they're afraid to send their kids to school." Valerie Marrs, Brogue, Pennsylvania.

"I think the problem with all the school and with everything today is that they took God out of the school and let the Devil in. I think we need to do more on that kind of thing instead of letting the devils in there get these kids and getting all this stuff accomplished. They took God out of schools and let everything else in and the Devil's in there making this stuff." Donna Grove, Loganville, Pennsylvania.

Why Did Lethal School Violence Occur in Red Lion, Pennsylvania?

Local, state, and federal investigators have been unable to determine a motive in this case. James Sheets did not fit the profile of the "typical shooter" who is often characterized as a bullied loner, fascinated with violence and destruction. Unfortunately, we are learning that "there is no simple explanation as to why these attacks have occurred. Nor is there a simple solution to stop this problem" (Vossekuil, Fein, Reddy, Borum, & Modzeleski, 2002, p.4).

Nevertheless, we continue to compile data that profiles the "troubled" student who commits acts of violence. For example, statistics indicate that males are more likely to carry a weapon to school than females. At the same time, with the exception of Hispanic or Latino students, minorities are more likely to carry weapons to school than Caucasians. Furthermore, students in grade 9 are more likely to carry a weapon than those in grade 12 (U.S. Department of Justice, 2002).

The following table shows some of the most recent data available from nationally representative surveys of the same 1,234 public and private high schools throughout all fifty states and the District of Columbia collected every two years from 1993 through 2001 (U.S. Department of Justice, 2002):

Students in Grades 9-12 who Reported Carrying a Weapon on School Property
at Least Once in the Past 30 Days

	1993	1995	1997	1999	2001
Total Respondents	11, 410	6, 540	11, 247	10, 098	8, 568
Male	17.9%	14.3%	12.5%	11.0%	10.2%
Female	5.9%	4.9%	3.7%	2.8%	2.9%
Caucasian	-	-	-	6.4%	6.1%
African American	-	-	-	5.0%	6.3%
Hispanic/ Latino	-	-	-	7.0%	5.7%
Native American/ Alaska Native	-	-	-	11.6%	16.4%
Pacific Islander	-	-	-	9.3%	10.0%
Asian	-	-	-	6.5%	7.2%
Multiple	-	-	-	11.4%	13.2%
Grade 9	12.6%	10.7%	10.2%	7.2%	6.7%
Grade 10	11.5%	10.4%	7.7%	6.6%	6.7%
Grade 11	11.9%	10.2%	9.4%	7.0%	6.1%
Grade 12	10.8%	7.6%	7.0%	6.2%	6.0%

More research is necessary in order to draw conclusions from the data. This is just a sample of survey results focusing on behaviors that put youth at significant risk for "mortality, morbidity, disability, and social problems during both youth and adulthood" (U.S. Department of Justice, 2002, p.150).

In addition, carrying a weapon or even threatening to use it does not mean that the weapon will be used. For example, more weapons are carried in the schools by minority students. And yet, according to the U.S. Secret Service and the U.S. Department of Education, three-quarters of school attackers using weapons have been described as "white" (Vossekuil, Fein, Reddy, Borum, & Modzeleski, 2002).

To answer the question concerning why the shooting occurred in Red Lion, Pennsylvania, we need more information. Like the students profiled by the U.S. Secret Service, James Sheets was a young, "white" male. However, these facts do not provide the answers we need.

Access to guns? Media? Drugs? History of disciplinary problems? Victim of bullying?

Easy access to guns is often blamed for school shootings (Haynes & Chalker, 1999). In the Red Lion Junior High case, however, this was not the situation. James Sheets searched his house, found a hidden key, and unlocked his step father's gun case. Then he took three guns and placed them in his backpack without telling anyone. Red Lion is a rural community in which hunting is a way of life. Therefore, ownership of guns is commonplace.

Violence in the media, in musical lyrics, on the internet, and in video games is often targeted as another cause of violent behavior (Boal, 1999; Capozzoli & McVey, 2000; Steyn, 1998). In this case, law enforcement officials took James Sheets' computer as well as personal belongings from his bedroom and from his home. No evidence of graphic and violent influences or fixations emerged from the investigation.

In addition, students who commit acts of lethal violence are often portrayed as drug-crazed zombies. Post-mortem analyses of James Sheets' body, however, revealed no evidence of alcohol or drug use. He had no history of psychiatric disorders. He had not been labelled clinically depressed, bi-polar, learning disabled, Attention Deficit Hyperactivity Disorder, or anything else. As far as anyone knew, he was a "normal" adolescent. Therefore, we cannot even blame use of legally prescribed drugs such as Prozac or Ritalin for his behavior.

Also, the public perception is that the student who commits an act of deadly violence has a history of disciplinary problems at school. However, James Sheets had never been a behavior problem in school. In recent months, he had been marked late to his first period class a few times because he was walking his girlfriend to her class each morning. Nevertheless, there were no disciplinary issues that caused teachers or administrators to become alarmed. Indeed, research indicates that two-thirds of violent attackers have never or rarely been in trouble in school (Vossekuil, Fein, Reddy, Borum, & Modzeleski, 2002).

Recently, much attention has been given to research on bullying and the development of anti-bullying programs in schools (Sullivan, 2000; Vail, 1999). The general assumption is that students who commit acts of violence have suffered, in some cases, years of abuse in the form of bullying. According to Kurt Fassnacht, however, no evidence has been uncovered that would indicate that James Sheets, was either the victim of bullying or the perpetrator of bullying behavior.

The bottom line is that no known reason exists for the heinous murder/suicide that took the life of Principal Gene Segro and James "Jimmy" Sheets on April 24, 2003

What can the Red Lion School District do now?

During the interview with the author, Kurt Fassnacht indicated first of all what Red Lion Schools were *not* going to do. They are *not* going to install metal detectors in every building. They are also *not* going to ban book bags and backpacks from the schools. Mr. Fassnacht believes that if students are intent on sneaking weapons into school, they will find a way to do so – even if it means wrapping them in cloth and putting them in their underwear. Besides, he believes that using punitive measures will only make school seem like a prison and perpetuate a sense of fear.

His views are supported by others who believe that "the intensifying and automatic use of punishment, as opposed to prevention of behavior and violence in schools, makes the schoolhouse toxic for too many children" (Hyman & Snook, 2000, p.491). Dependence upon fear of punishment as a deterrent to crime requires power and control which can lead to maltreatment of students. As a result of being subjected to disciplinary measures that resemble the criminal justice system, "a growing number of young people see themselves as outcasts, as 'bad'" (Wachtel, 1997, p.123). This domination certainly does not lead to the type of caring, child-centered, learning community that encourages students to trust teachers and others in authority when they need help.

Red Lion School District has already taken several positive steps following the recent tragedy. For example, the district created a "hotline" for anyone in the community to use if threats or perceived threats of school violence are discovered. Systems for reporting threats are generally supported as a means to prevent violence (Capozzoli & McVey, 2000). The danger is that students can misuse them as a means to "get back at" others. This, in fact, occurred at Red Lion School District on two occasions in the weeks following the shootings. In both instances, thorough police investigation indicated that the reports of threats were merely pranks.

Another positive step that the district has taken is to allow students the opportunity to create a "wall of hands" in the junior high cafeteria where the murder/suicide occurred. The cafeteria is wrapped in a painted yellow band upon which almost one thousand students have chosen to place their painted purple handprints as memorial to their beloved principal who touched their hearts. Assistant Principal Kurt Fassnacht says that each student in the school can readily point out his particular handprint. This wall of hands continues to be therapeutic for the students and adults who return to the scene of the tragedy each day. The community has responded by selling T-shirts and bumper stickers that read "I Support Red Lion" to raise money for a memorial to the slain principal.

Plans for the Future

A study of thirty-seven separate school shootings and school attacks that occurred between 1974 and 2000 has resulted in ten key findings that can be used to develop violence prevention plans for the future.

Key Findings of *Safe School Initiative*

Incidents of targeted violence at school *rarely* are sudden, impulsive acts.

Prior to most incidents, other people knew about the attacker's idea and/or plan to attack. In most cases, those who knew were other kids...this information rarely made its way to an adult.

Most attackers did not threaten their targets directly prior to advancing the attack.

There is no accurate or useful profile of students who engaged in targeted school violence.

Most attackers engaged in some behaviour, prior to the incident, that caused others concern or indicated a need for help.

Most attackers had difficulty coping with significant losses or personal failures. Many had considered or attempted suicide.

Most attackers had access to and had used weapons prior to the attack.

In many cases, other students were involved in the attack in some capacity.

Despite prompt law enforcement responses, most attacks were stopped by means other than law enforcement intervention and most were brief in duration. (Vossekuil, Fein, Reddy, Borum, & Modzeleski, 2002, pp.34-40)

These key findings do not make the job of preventing school violence any easier. Nevertheless, if we are truly as child-centered as we like to think we are, we can focus on the clues contained within these findings to locate and help "at-risk" students. We cannot afford to be surprised once again by the "kid ... who just comes out of the woodwork" (Rasicot, 1999, p.18).

One concern expressed by Mr. Fassnacht is that schools today have become so large that they can become somewhat depersonalized. He believes the ideal size for a middle school or junior high school is no more than five hundred students. Red Lion Junior High is a consolidation of two smaller schools, and today its enrolment is nearly one thousand. Research reinforces Mr. Fassnacht's concern. Students tend to perform better academically in small schools. Furthermore, small schools foster the human connections that allow students to form strong bonds with their teachers and with each other (Capps & Maxwell, 1999; Holms & Horn, 2003; Lewis, 1999). When it comes to schools, many now believe that bigger is not better.

The question then becomes one of how to make a large school feel like a small community in which no one "falls through the cracks".

One alternative being discussed is the establishment of collaborative teams or "academies" of teachers who all teach the same group of students on a daily basis.

Another alternative is a "school within a school" model; the large junior high would essentially become a seventh grade school and an eighth grade school, each with its own cadre of teachers.

Still another approach is an "advisory system" in which all professional personnel are assigned a small number of students for whom they are "responsible" during their two years in the junior high. Each "advisor" and his assigned group of students develop community service-learning projects together and engage in various school-related activities together over an extended period of time.

Each of these alternatives has been tested and shown to be successful as secondary school reform strategies (Boss, 2000). In fact, any strategy that allows the same group of teachers to have contact with a cohort of students for more than one year is believed to increase "student visibility" and "combat violence" (Klonsky, 2002). As Red Lion School District makes future plans, these and other alternatives are likely to be considered.

Alienation: Social Isolation, Powerlessness, and Normlessness

For many years, researchers have studied adolescent alienation as a major problem of contemporary society (Calabrese, 1987; Calabrese, 1989; Calabrese & Raymond, 1988; Calabrese & Poe, 1990; Calabrese & Schumer, 1986; Tyminski, 1995). The words "alienation" and "alienated" are now being used to describe youth who are at risk for committing school violence (Capps & Maxwell, 1999; Hardy, 1999; Kohn, 1999; Rosenberg, 1999; Vail, 1999). Therefore, it is important to make sure we have shared understanding of the concept.

Alienation is a concept rooted in sociological tradition, and it is often described using three components: social isolation, powerlessness, and normlessness. Social isolation is viewed as a lack of social participation or a feeling of isolation from the group; powerlessness is viewed as a sense of helplessness or a lack of power to control the events upon which happiness depends; and normlessness is viewed as a sense of separation from group standards or a conflict of norms in relation to the majority cultural community (Tyminski, 1995). All three components have been used to describe students who commit acts of school violence. Therefore, it is imperative that we find ways to reduce or eliminate adolescents' sense of alienation. This is a task that the school cannot accomplish alone. Mr. Fassnacht is correct in recognizing the necessity of creating a caring community that is responsive to the needs of the students, the teachers, the parents, and the community at large. This is an immense task that the school cannot achieve singlehandedly. The school and the university that prepares future teachers must work in partnership since traditional approaches to eliminating school violence have failed.

What can teacher educators do?

Teacher educators have historically prepared preservice teachers in early childhood and in elementary education to create "caring" learning environments in which children feel a sense of belonging. We teach students to meet the individual needs of all learners as they employ pedagogical techniques utilizing multiple intelligences or adaptations for children who receive special education services. But, how well are we preparing our secondary education preservice teachers to meet the emotional needs as well as the academic needs of their students?

With that said, we are aware that U.S. secondary education majors, by necessity, must focus on their content areas so that they will pass their PRAXIS exams and so that they will develop appropriate levels of expertise. Of course, they also take their required education courses including teaching methodology. But, there is limited time, if any, for curricular topics that may contribute to the prevention of school violence.

During an interview shortly after the deadly shootings in Red Lion, Pennsylvania, Kurt Fassnacht expressed surprise that "anti-bullying curricula", for example, is not routinely taught to preservice teachers. As much as teacher educators would like to have courses in anti-bullying and other "peace promotion" information, this is not a realistic accomplishment within the four years of most secondary education programs. Still, there are options to help secondary education preservice teachers become more attuned to their students' emotional development.

An option that works well at Elizabethtown College in Lancaster County, Pennsylvania is service-learning incorporated into already existing required curricula. Elizabethtown College has as its motto, "Educate for Service", so faculty have been encouraged to incorporate service-learning into their courses for years. College students discover a real need in their community that pertains to the course they are taking; they develop a meaningful way of meeting that community need; they therefore extend their learning beyond the classroom walls and enhance what is taught by their professors; they plan structured time to think, write, and/or talk about their experiences. Reflection is the added component that makes service a learning experience (Silcox, 1993). Through this practice, service-learning is therefore taught experientially as a teaching methodology. Benefits reported by preservice teachers include an increased sense of caring, recognition that their actions make a difference in the lives of people in their community, and increased sensitivity to the feelings of others. These reports are consistent with studies showing that service activities reduce adolescent alienation (Calabrese & Schumer, 1986).

The curricular component of service-learning at the university level also has implications that pertain to the prevention of school violence. The benefits that preservice teachers experience can also be experienced by their students in the schools. In addition, the interpersonal relationships developed between teachers, students, and members of the community reduce the social isolation that many at-risk students feel. A sense of powerlessness is reduced as students recognize that they are important in the lives of others in their community. As relationships build, students feel a sense of belonging that encourages acceptance of community norms; accordingly, normlessness is reduced. A statistically significant reduction in alienation as a result of service-learning curricula has been documented in studies with students at the university level and at the secondary school level (Calabrese & Schumer, 1986; Tyminski, 1995). Feelings of alienation have been linked with school violence (Klonsky, 2002). Programs that provide opportunities for students to communicate and connect with adults whom they perceive to be "caring" also reduce violence (Vossekuil, Fein, Reddy, Borum, & Modzeleski, 2002). Therefore, any practice such as service-learning that reduces alienation will have an effect on students' tendency to resort to violent behavior.

Another aspect of service-learning curricular programming is a unique form of sensitivity training. A significant number of elementary education and secondary education preservice teachers at Elizabethtown College elect to perform service-learning activities with at-risk students who receive special education services. Many of them have never worked with students who have readily apparent physical or mental differences. As part of their preparation, these preservice teachers experience various simulation activities in which their mobility, hearing, vision, or speech capacity is reduced or eliminated for an extended period of time. They may be required to complete a series of tasks as they venture into the downtown community, a shopping mall, or go about their regular campus schedule while in a wheelchair, for example. Their verbal and written reflections indicate that these activities are often transformative experiences. Comments such as the following are typical:

> "With the uneven pavements and not being able to locate an easily accessible bathroom, I am shocked that someone isn't improving these conditions! This experience was an awakening and has given me greater awareness and compassion."

> "I found it very frustrating to see such disregard for people with disabilities. I felt isolated. Seeing people looking at me, in a different way, also made each little thing I did more difficult."

> "I definitely will be more sensitive to people with disabilities because of this experience!"

Afterwards, preservice teachers often express heightened awareness of the needs of students with special needs who will be included in their regular classes. They report increased empathy for others. The same is true for students in secondary schools who undergo disability simulations as part of their preparation for community service with the elderly or with people who have disabilities. Simulations or "sensitivity training" sessions are also part of *Magic Me*, for example, an international service-learning program for "troubled" middle school children that originated in Baltimore, Maryland.

Again, when university students and school students participate in service-learning, they develop a sense of connectedness with their school and with their communities. McPherson (1997) reports that this teaching methodology is "associated with greater student engagement with schools, better attitudes towards schools, better attendance, fewer disciplinary actions, and fewer behavior problems" (p.11).

Finally, in the opinion of the author, teacher educators should embrace service-learning as a key element of the professional development of future teachers. This methodology provides opportunities to incorporate key elements of communication, active listening, conflict resolution, and problem solving and – who knows – perhaps even the anti-bullying information about which Mr. Fassnacht inquired. No one knows if service-learning would have prevented the deadly school violence in Red lion. However it has been proven to reduce the social isolation, the sense of powerlessness, and the sense of normlessness that disconnected, violent youth often feel. It is at least a step in the right direction.

References

Boal, M. (2000). The shooters and the shrinks. In D. M. Bonilla (Ed.), School violence (pp.103-106). New York: The H. W. Wilson Company. (Original work published 1999).

Boss, S. (2000). Big lessons on a small scale. Northeast Education Magazine, 6(2). Retrieved July 6, 2003 from http://www.nwrel.org

Calabrese, R. L. (1987). Adolescence: A growth period conducive to alienation. Adolescence, 22 (88), 929-938.

Calabrese, R. L. (1989). The effects of mobility on adolescent alienation. The High School Journal, Oct./Nov., 41-45.

Calabrese, R. L., & Raymond, E. J. (1988). Alienation: Its impact on adolescents from stable environments. The Journal of Psychology, 123(4), 397-404.

Calabrese, R. L., & Poe, J. (1990). Alienation: An explanation of high dropout rates among African American and Latino students. Educational Research Quarterly, 14(4), 22-26.

Calabrese, R. L., & Schumer, H. (1986). The effects of service activities on adolescent alienation. Adolescence, 21(83), 675-687.

Capozzoli, T. K., & McVey, R. S. (2000). Kids killing kids. New York: St. Lucie Press.

Capps, W. R., & Maxwell, M. E. (1999). Where everybody knows your name. The American School Board Journal, 186(9), 35-36.

Haynes, R. M., & Chalker, D. M. (1999). A nation of violence. The American School Board Journal, 186(3), 22-25.

Hyman, I. A., & Snook, P. A. (2000). Dangerous schools and what you can do about them. Phi Delta Kappan, 81(7), 489-501.

Klonsky, M. (2002). How smaller schools prevent school violence. Educational Leadership, 59(5), 65-69.

Lewis, A. C. (2000). Listen to the children. On D. M. Bonilla (Ed.), School Violence (pp.82-85). New York: The H. W. Wilson Company. (Original Work published 1999).

McPherson, K. (1997). Service learning: Making a difference in the community. Schools in the Middle, 6(3), 9-15.

Rasicot, J. (1999). The threat of harm. The American School Board Journal, 186(3), 15-18.

Silcox, H. (1993). A how to guide to reflection: Adding cognitive learning to community service programs. Philadelphia: Brighton Press.

Steyn, M. (2000). Virtual violence. In D. M. Bonilla (Ed.), School violence (pp.86-90). New York: The H. W. Wilson Company. (Original work published in 1998).

Sullivan, K. (2000). The anti-bullying handbook. Oxford: Oxford University Press.

Tyminski, C. R. (1995). Effects of an intergenerational service-learning curriculum on refugee/immigrant students. UMI No. 9535815.

U. S. Department of Justice (2002). Indicators of school crime and safety (NCJ 196753).

Washington, DC: Author. Vail, K. (1999). Words that wound. American School Board Journal, 186(9), 37-40. Vassekuil, B. Fein, R. A., Reddy, M., Borum, R., & Modzeleski,

W. (2002). The final report and findings of the Safe School Initiative: Implications for the prevention of school attacks in the United States. Washington, DC: U. S. Secret Service and U. S. Department of Education.

Wachtel, T. (1997). Real justice. How we can revolutionalize our response to wrongdoing. Pipersville, PA: The Piper's Press.

Part IV

Service-Learning and Teacher Education Outcomes

Overview

Chapters 11-13 make of Part 4 of the book, which focuses on service-learning and teacher education outcomes. Chapter 11 explores service-learnings role in "authentic academics." Chapter 12 looks at how service-learning increases a teacher's capacity to meet the needs of diverse learners. Chapter 13 looks at the role of service-learning in teacher preparation and professional development.

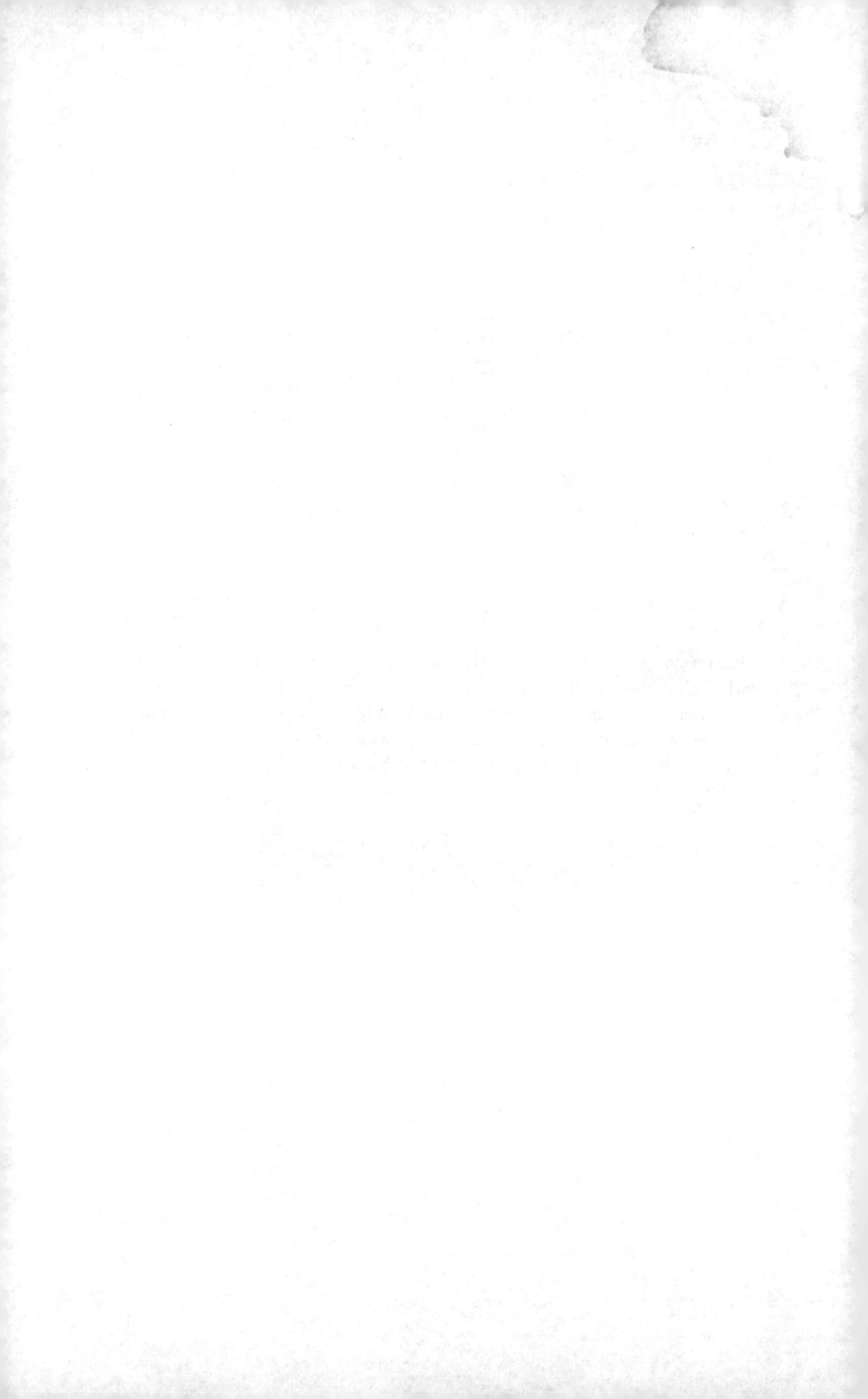

Chapter 11
Service-Learning and Authentic Academics

Authentic Academics

Service Learning in Teacher Education

Sharon Kossack, Eric Dwyer and Hilary Landorf

"Yea, we nuked "em!" replies an eighth grade student in a Lafayette, Indiana class during a unit on Japan. Others stand up and high-five each other. Leila Meyerratken (2003), the teacher of this course, feels personally insulted as she remembers her own experience in Japan, when an elderly man walked from his hometown many miles away to meet the visiting American teacher and give her a bag filled with candy, origami, and rice seeds, to take to her students as a simple gift of hospitality. Burning with a desire to reach her students in a meaningful way, Ms. Meyerratken embarks on a multi-faceted journey with them, the centerpiece of which is service-learning. After preparing the project by reading Yoshiko Uchida's The Bracelet, a book about the imprisonment of U.S. citizens of Japanese descent during World War II, and constructing a twelve-foot-high poster, "An Injustice to Remember," honoring U.S. World War II veterans of Japanese ancestry, Ms. Meyerratken and her students design and build a Zen garden in the school courtyard. They enlist the participation of many family members, who help shovel, measure, and level the ground. They look into building codes in order to include a six-foot deep miniature pond. They raise funds, give presentations, and keep track of incoming donations. At the end, their hard work yields a magical Japanese garden, and the rooting of a commitment to civic engagement.

On the Explorer, an ecotour cruise ship hosting tourists roaming the Galapagos Islands, a volunteer for the U.S. Peace Corps in a small Ecuadorian village accompanies 15 children on board. There her students perform a play they composed in both Spanish and English about the history of the Galapagos-a retrospective including a look at evolution, the arrival of Darwin, his examination of the animals of the island, and the subsequent human presence on the islands. At the end of the story is a description of pollutants and impact of human presence on the islands, both historical and current, as well as attitudes the children wish the on looking tourists to leave with. The final bows, music, and applause are accompanied by children asking for donations that go to various preservation societies that support the Galapagos Island-money the tourists seem pleased and honored to hand out.

Service Learning Philosophy

These two examples may be described as *service learning*, an instructional method with an underlying philosophy of education. The service learning philosophy is essentially grounded in Dewey's (1938) notion that experiential education forms the foundation of moral, intellectual, and civic life. Based on the process of making meaning out of experience, experiential education for Dewey replaces the dualisms of experience and knowledge, mind and body, with an emphasis on the unifying process of communication. Accordingly, the primary purposes of education for service learning students include the development of social responsibility, and preparation for active involvement in a democratic civic life. According to Heffernan (2001), the synergy of the intellectual, moral, and civic dimensions is what distinguishes service learning from vocational education, whose primary purpose is to prepare students for a viable professional occupation.

Service Learning Instructional Method (Pedagogy)

As an instructional method, service learning is the serious, deliberate and integral infusion of community service within the context of an academic course in ways that ensure that the service so relates to the educational goals and process that the academic goals/objectives are learned through the service itself. The uniqueness of service learning is that it links academic course objectives with real community needs. In service learning, course materials inform student service, and service informs academic dialogue in an ongoing reflective practice.

AUTHENTIC ACADEMICS

The Alliance for Service Learning in Education Reform (ASLER) provides the most commonly used definition:

Service Learning is an educational experience: [Through which] students learn and develop through active participation in thoughtfully organized service experiences that meet actual community needs and that are coordinated in collaboration with school and community That is integrated into the students' academic curriculum or provides structured time for a student to think, talk, or write about what the student did and saw during the actual service activity. That provides students with opportunities to use newly acquired skills and knowledge in real-life situation in their own community and That enhances what is taught in school by extending service learning beyond the classroom and into the community to foster the development of a sense of caring for others (ASLER, 1993, p. 1)

Through the authentic community benefit, learning is enriched as students master serious academic information while concomitantly providing public service. This deepens academic learning by rendering it more authentic, and builds a sense of commitment to citizenship. When service is a deliberate part of academic learning, schools and universities become an integral part of the whole, contribute to the solution, while at the same time meet (and exceed) academic goals.

History

Service learning in the United States emerged from the Progressive Education movement in the 1920's and the sense that experience should form the foundation of learning. Dewey (1938, 1963) urged that learning be grounded in purposeful activity-based curricular experiences that provided opportunities for social interactions authentically linked to community needs. Such philosophy substantiated Kilpatrick's (1918) Project Method suggestion that learning should occur in settings outside school and address needs within the community.

Long dormant, service learning again emerged in the 1970's when significant professional organizations took issue with the academic curriculum taught in isolation from authentic life links (National Association of Secondary School Principals, 1972, National Panel on High School and Adolescent Education; Martin, 1976). Courses offered in alternative contexts, using community involvement, were thought to increase curricular relevance for young adults.

Momentum increased in the 1980's when "A Nation at Risk" challenged teacher effectiveness prompting service-based experiences to be a required part of student academic experiences. Boyer, for example, urged that students "reach beyond themselves and become more responsibly engaged," (1983, p. 209) suggesting that a Carnegie unit focused on service be added to the academic curriculum of high schools.

153

But in the 1990's we see serious interest and research associated with service learning. There was legal precedent set as the National and Community Service Act (1990) became law, followed by the National and Community Service Trust Act (1993), which provided funding for service learning partnerships statewide to students in grades K-12, through the Corps for National Service. Campus Compact, started in 1985 by the presidents of Brown, Georgetown and Stanford Universities, along with the president of the Education Commission of the States, is a coalition of colleges and universities whose primary purpose is to help students develop citizenship values and skills through active involvement with their communities. Campus Compact now has a membership of over 900 public and private two and four year colleges and universities. The Compact has developed a vast array of resources, including toolkits and institutes, a consulting corps, a service learning syllabi project, a list of funding resources, and a program model database, all which can be accessed from its website, at http://www.compact.org.

Purpose of Service Learning

Berger Kaye (2000) describes service learning as a "dynamic and practice teaching method... that connects classroom content and skills to meeting actual community needs" (p. 4). To accomplish such, she details six outcomes of such a framework:

> Students apply academic, social, and personal skills to improve the community.
>
> Students make decisions that have real, not hypothetical, results.
>
> Students grow as individuals, gain respect for peers, and become better citizens.
>
> Students of all abilities succeed.
>
> Students retain and reflect on their learning and service experience to have greater understanding of themselves, their community, and society.
>
> Students develop as leaders who take initiative, solve problems, work as a team, and demonstrate their abilities while helping others. (Berger Kaye, 2000, p. 4)

Corrigan (2000) notes that the result of such concentration is a change in attitudes in schools. He proposes that the purposes of service learning programs include 1) the bringing of social action, 2) the establishing of value-free communities in classes and on campuses, and 3) the generation of students' active citizenship.

Of Corrigan's purposes, the second and third are particularly noteworthy when we consider the demographics of new English learners in the US. The Education Commission of the States (ECS) issued a paper (Anderson, 2000) stating that potentially 1.1 million students in K-12 programs throughout the

US could be participating in service learning projects should all 1325 teachers education programs nationwide incorporate service learning into their curricula.

Heffernan (2001) broke service learning into two categories: delivery of service, and curricular connections. Delivery of service refers to the structure of the service to the community. The result of service learning is always measurable in an observable change in the community, but to determine the delivery system being considered, questions must be asked such as: Will the service solve a problem, or will it be service for service's sake? The category of curricular connections asks educators to consider the placement of the service in a course. Is it a part, a way of learning, or the entire course itself?

Heffernan proposed a model (see Figure 1) that allows educators to analyze the place service learning would hold in academic contexts, ranging from minor, tangential links, to fully and significantly imbedded projects. Heffernan's models include 1) service learning for service's sake, 2) subject-based materials, 3) problem solving, 4) culminating experiences, and 5) action research. The following figure describes these five models in terms of their conceptualization and gives examples.

Models of Service Learning

Model 1. Servce iLearning for Service's Sake
Model Conceptualization: Field experience, volunteers, citizenship.

Example: Students in Florida International University's undergraduate elementary education program have a minimum of two hours per week application (with K-5 students) of what they have been learning within their methods courses.

Model 2. Subject Based.
Model Conceptualization: Students are out in the community on a regular basis; focus is the course content; reflection the mode of deepening course.

Example: Secondary students taking the undergraduate content area reading course are required to apply weekly, two-hour lessons involving text-based strategy learning activities with at-risk, academically struggling students in local middle and high schools. After delivering clusters of instruction, students process the experience with reflections on cluster content, student reactions and performance. Pre- and post-test comparisons indicate the middle and high school students' performance within their classes improved significantly.

Pretest Posttest Pretest Posttest
(# Correct) (# Correct) (% Correct) (% Correct)
3.4 of 7 5.85 of 7 51.4% 87.5%

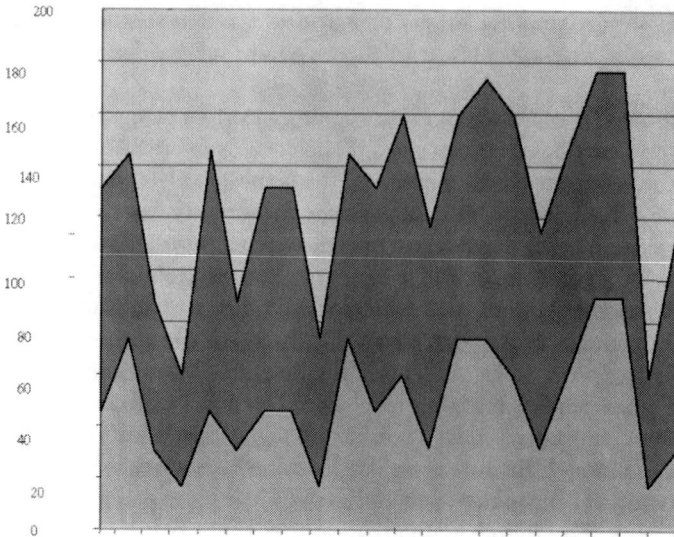

Figure 1: Mean At-Risk Student Gains after 16 hours of Mentoring (Fall 2002)
At-Risk Student Performance Changes after 18 hours of Mentoring (Fall 2002)

Student Posttest Performances (Percentages) on Mock FCAT
Student Pretest Performances (Percentages)
Participating Students

Figure 2.Fall 2002 Individual At-risk Student Performance Gains on simulated Florida state mandated test after 16 hours of Mentoring

At-risk public school students consistently show such gains, semester after semester. Spring, 2003, at risk high school students nearly doubled their average performance on a simulation of the required state test (pretest X =43% correct, posttest mean of 80% correct) after only 16 hours of mentoring (see figure 3).

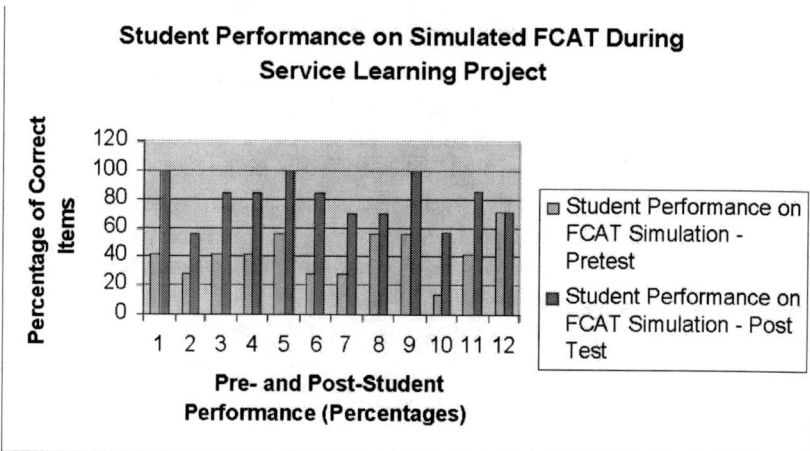

Figure 3: Effects of 16 hours of strategy-based subject area teaching on student performance on simulated state test (Spring, 2003)

The undergraduates gained many forms of awareness through this experience Having concrete evidence of student improvement, they realized 1) that at-risk students, in spite of their negative bravado demeanor, wish to achieve and succeed, 2) that the undergraduates pre-teachers have deliberate strategies which initiate this improvement for the most challenging learner in their future classes, and 3) that the learners learn the subject area when the reading strategies are the focus of instruction (Kossack, 2001). Additionally, they felt as if they had positively contributed to the pressing issues of high stakes testing.

However, student learning of subject area information stands as the content area teacher's primary objective. Strategy-based teaching, in which students learn how to learn, and performance on the state mandated te3st should not overshadow student knowledge of subject. Post-semester assessment of students' of subject area knowledge was also administered, via a self-assessment. Students were asked to rate themselves on a scale of 1 (indicating little knowledge) to 5 (suggesting great knowledge). At pretest, the students felt their subject area knowledge was at a "F" level (48%) while after the study-skills intervention they felt their knowledge rose to almost a "B" level (78%) which showed an average subject-knowledge gain of 30% after approximately 20 hours of intervention (see figure 4).

At-Risk Student Self Perception of Subject Area **Knowledge**

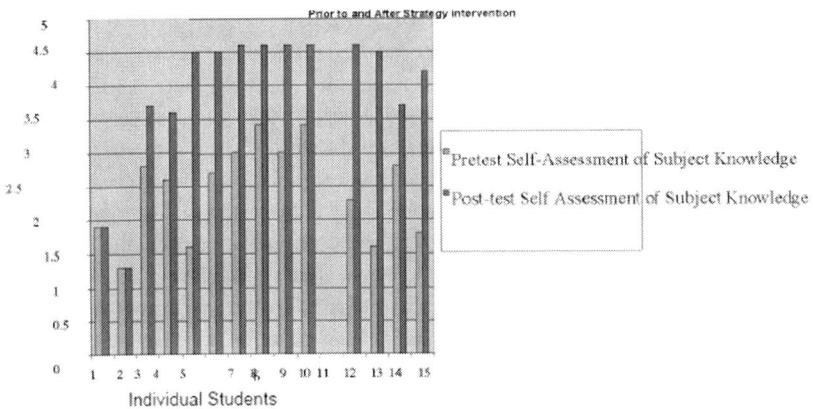

Figure 4: Effects of strategic teaching on perceived subject area information

Model 3: Problem solving

Model Conceptualization: Community is the client. Significant identified problem becomes the target for solution.

Example: Problem. Students in an inner city elementary school (Gardendale Elementary) were vandalizing the bathroom in their wing of the school. School staff and training consult met with the students who used the bathroom, collaboratively clarifying the problem using a de Bono thinking skill process called PMI (Plus, Minus, Interesting) to dispassionately explore the effects of the destruction. What emerged is that students were irritated that the bathroom on another wing was nicer and felt that if they damaged their bathroom, the school would provide them with similar renovations.

Using another technique (P/S: Problem/Solution), students brainstormed ways they could solve the problem. The group then examined each of the suggested alternatives, choosing to involve a local business, Home Depot, to enlist their (donation of materials and demonstration of techniques for repairing the damage). Students worked on the weekend alongside the Home Depot employees, planning, measuring, plumbing, painting, tiling, and learning numerous home repair skills.

Students reflected on the whole process, exploring more positive ways for solving problems and getting what they want; how mutual, positive problem solving can result in greater good. From this experience they learned problem identification and positive problem-solving, numerous academically related skills (measurement, estimation, life skills) and with the ownership of renovation, they would proudly maintain the improved condition of the facility

Model 4: Culminating Experiences

Model Conceptualization: A capstone experience at the end of the program synthesizing all that was learned in the program, thus bridging theory and practice

Example: Paired Diagnosis and Remediation courses provide a culminating, guided clinical application for graduate students enrolled in a Reading M.S. The 22 educators focused on academically struggling students who have repeatedly failed the state competency examination, earning the school a lower ranking. Educators nearing the end of their 2.5 year program, worked intensively with at-risk students designated by the school, beginning their problem-identification with a performance profile provided by the school as performing at or below the twenty-fifth percentile. They assessed and targeting their teaching in ways that significantly improve student performance ranging from five months to 4 years of improvement in reading after 30 hours of intervention (Kossack 2002, see figure 5). These improvements held for two clusters of predominantly second-language students.

Authentic Academics
Sharon Kossack, Eric Dwyer, and Hilary Landorf

The Effects on Student Performance of Student-Embedded Teacher Development

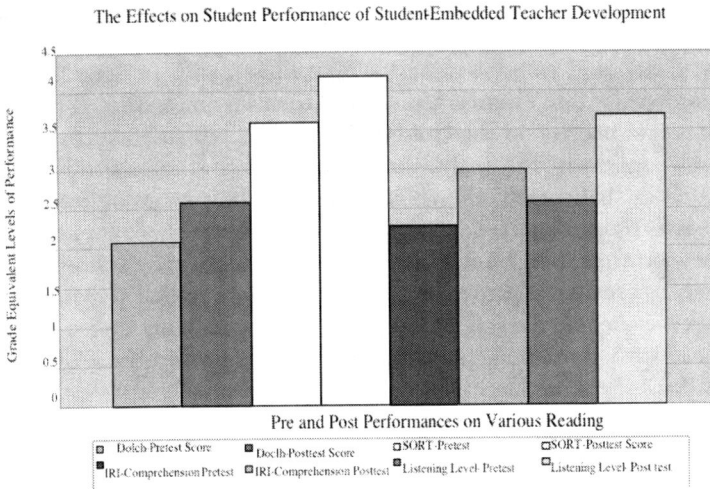

Pre and Post Performances on Various Reading

- Dolch Pretest Score
- Dolch Posttest Score
- SORT-Pretest
- SORT-Posttest Score
- IRI-Comprehension Pretest
- IRI-Comprehension Posttest
- Listening Level-Pretest
- Listening Level-Post test

Figure: 5 Progress of Clinical Child with Targeted Teaching *

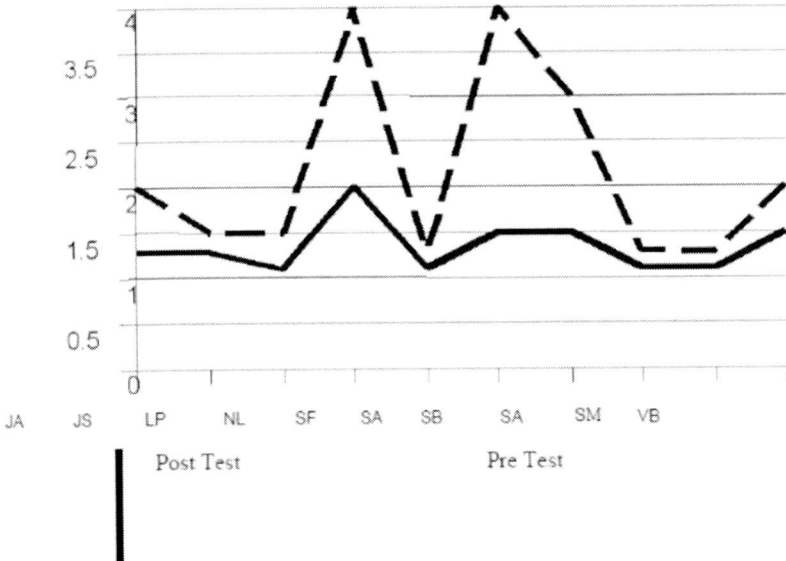

Post Test   Pre Test

Figure 6: Student pre-post reading improvement after 8 hours of intervention

Model 5: Service internship;

Model Conceptualization: Students do community work for 10-20 hours per week, the culmination of which is a product that is of real value to the community. Self-reflection is an ongoing part of service internships, allowing students to analyze their experiences using discipline-based theories. Reflective activity may take the form of peer group get-togethers, one-on-one meetings with the instructor, or electronic communication with all class members present in a chat room.

Golden Glades Elementary is a severely impoverished inner city elementary school whose children are at-risk underachievers. Its school plant is dirty, dusty, and run-down. The school linked with undergraduates at a local university (St. Thomas University) to study butterflies. The undergraduates met and found the children were attracted to butterfly gardens. As a result, following the analysis of what attracted students to butterflies and a look at their needs, the children wrote a how-to guide for creating home butterfly gardens. They raised money to buy the plants and equipment needed to sustain a butterfly garden and beautify the school, coming weekends to create the garden, arranging the plants so that they beautified the school, enriching the soil, painting areas of the building that were soiled or defaced with graffiti. Participants reported the project brought pride of ownership to the school.

Then the students sought small containers, bought soil, and planted (with clippings from their plants) potted versions of the plants in their garden. When the plants had bushed out and looked healthy, students colorfully covered the pots tied it on with jaunty bows. These were taken to a local nursing home to give to the patients there. The students shared their reports on butterflies, their nature and needs and the creation of the school's butterfly garden. Then they gave the residents their own colorful potted plant, which of course meant more when they understood the genesis of it.

The hours spent on this project dwindle in importance with the multilayered gifts to the children, the school, the nursing home residents, and the community.

Model 6: Action Research;

Model Conceptualization: Guided practice or independent study with an experienced practitioner, as when students work with faculty member to link subject knowledge/expertise with research techniques for community change agency. Issues are of importance to the community.

Example: Action research is an integral part of the Reading Master's program at Florida International University, a public university which serves a multilingual urban community. Students take a course named Research in Reading, giving them research background supporting the development of the problem to focus their Action Research project. The project focus must then be on change agency in a context over which they have some control, i.e., assuring that implementation will be effective and sustained, at the child, class, grade, school, or district level. Results are shared with the group as a whole so others may benefit from their findings.

Reported Results of Service Learning

The following list and review of researchers' conclusion reveals results of service learning and three key outcomes:

Students treat each other well. They help others do their best (Berkas, 1997)

Students report greater empathy and cognitive complexity (Courney, 1994)

Students report greater acceptance of cultural and racial diversity (Melchior, 1999; Berkas, 1997)

Students increased their own awareness of cultural differences and attitudes toward helping others (Shaffer, 1993; Stephens, 1995)

Ss felt more comfortable within ethnically diverse groups (Loesch-Griffin et al, 1995)

Teachers and students report cohesiveness and more positive relationships (Weiler et al, 1998).

Students more likely to increase self esteem (Shaffer, 1993).

Reduced levels of alienation and behavioral problems (Stephens, 1995; Yates and Youniss, 1996)

Students less likely to be sent to the principal's office (Follman, 1997; 1998)

Students less likely to participate in dangerous sexual or violent activities (O'Donnell et al, 1999)

Students less likely to drop out of school (Supik, 1996; Rolzinski, 1990).

Students more likely to initiate questions (Loesch-Griffin et al, 1995)

Student academic learning improvements Service learning associated with higher scores on high stakes tests (Anderson et al, 1991) and higher grades (Shumer, 1994; Shaffer, 1993; Dean and Murdock, 1992; O'Bannon, 1999; Follman, 1999)

Students show improved problem-solving skills in real-world situations (Stephens, 1995; Bacon, 1997; Balazadeh, 1996; Cohen and Kinsey, 1994; Eyler and Giles, 1999; Fenzel and Leary, 1997).

Standards

Faculty and students who have never participated in service learning often think of it as a co-curricular model of altruism, an add-on supporting positive "town-gown" relationships and enhancing students' sense of fulfilling social and moral responsibilities. As we have seen, service learning does foster the development of social and personal responsibility (Root, 1997) and promotes a sense of caring (Middleton, 1993), but service learning encompasses much more than service. Myers and Pickeral (1997) argue that service learning supports many school reform efforts. Anderson (2000) notes a number of Interstate New Teacher Assessment and Support Curriculum (INTASC) standards for undergraduate teacher preparation that are directly addressed through use of service learning projects in teacher education. The links of these specific standards with the above-cited projects are direct and evident, thus suggesting that service learning need not diminish standards-based focus or delivery, but, in fact, enhances it.

INTASC (Interstate New Teacher Assessment and Support Consortium)Anderson (2000), page 3
The teacher understands and uses a variety of instructional strategies to encourage students' development of critical-thinking, problem-solving and performance skills.
The teacher plans instruction based upon knowledge of subject matter, students, the community and curriculum goals.
The teacher fosters relationships with school colleagues, parents and agencies in the larger community and curriculum goals.
The teacher understands how students differ in their approaches to learning and creates instructional opportunities adapted to diverse learners.

Challenges

Anderson (2000) and Heffernan (2001) cite the following challenges toward making service learning a regular feature:

Service learning is not perceived as aligned with institutional mission, goals, roles and rewards or resist curricular changes and rewards are narrowly biased toward scholarship.

Some faculty and administrators are not interested in service learning, academic professionalism becoming increasingly insular.

Faculty members are unprepared to use service-learning as a teaching method.

Teacher education faculty lack time and flexibility within teaching load.

The preservice teacher education curriculum is already overcrowded.

Recommendations

To meet these challenges on the school level, Anderson (2000) recommends the following: Include knowledge and commitment to service learning as required factors in hiring teachers and administrators. Develop school board policy Hire or designate a district- or school wide service-learning coordinator Provide release time for teachers working with pre-service teachers Provide on-going professional development opportunities

Anderson, 2000, p. 11

On the university level, Heffernan (2001) argues that, before embarking on a commitment to service learning, faculty must consider the following three variables: **Institutional Memory:** The institution's place in the maintenance and growth of the community must be evaluated. Questions such as, "What experiences have led to trust or mistrust between the institution and the community?" and "What events have served to consolidate partnerships, and what events have strained campus-community relationships?" must be asked and honestly answered. **Organizational Literacy within Institutional Culture:** The key conflict addressed here is the often unseen or denied disconnect of campus and community. In simple terms, what happens on campus is not necessarily what happens in the community. To address this conflict, Heffernan suggests finding out who the leaders of the community are, what the level of buy-in for service learning is, and how faculty members on campus may influence the leaders' commitment to service learning. **Engendering Institutional Support:** In addition to learning about the resources the university already offers for faculty interested in service learning (a service learning office, departments that have institutionalized service learning, services offered by the community service center), the general methods the university most often uses to responds to community concerns must be considered. Is the university centralized or decentralized in terms of responding to community concerns? If decentralized, who does the community most often look to for negotiation? For which problems? Knowing the leaders of university-community partnerships and problems is essential.

As a result, Quality Service Learning should include the following checklist of elements:

Integrated Learning. The project should have a clearly defined knowledge base, skill, or goals that derive from broader class or school goals. What is learned through the project should be processed back in the class so it is a meaningful and authentic link to the curricular objectives of the course in a way that there is added mutual depth to the service project and the course content.

High Quality Service. The project should fit the age and abilities of the recipients, reflect a high degree of planning and organization. It should be a real and significant need and the project should offer evident benefit to the recipients.

Collaboration. There should be mutual benefit to both participants and recipients. The development of the project (or at least the means of delivery) should reflect, as much as possible, input from all involved.

Student Involvement. Students should be able to choose and plan the service project, assuming roles and activities that are age-appropriate. Planning, processing, and evaluation sessions should be integral parts of the project.

Civic Responsibility. There should be evidence that the project builds a sense of responsibility to community on the part of the students. They should leave the project committed to a sense that they are responsible for solutions of problems in their neighborhood and are capable and able to find those solutions.

Reflection. Before, during, and after processing helps to link the learning experience and the academic goals.

Evaluation. Everyone --participants and recipients --should have evaluative input as, together, they gauge how well the learning-service goals were met.

Resources

The following annotated list of web sites offers links to service learning agencies.

American Association for Higher Education Service Learning
http://www.aahe.org/service/srv-lrn.htm Includes a Series on service-learning in the disciplines, links to service-learning resources , models of good practice for service-learning programs, and the full report of an AAHE initiative for service learning.

The Big Dummy's Guide to Service-Learning www.fiu.edu/-time4chg/ Library/bigdummy.html
This site is organized around frequently asked questions and divided into faculty and programmatic issues. Includes "101 Ideas for Combining Service & Learning" in various disciplines.

Campus Compact http://www.compact.org
A comprehensive site that includes resources for service-learning practitioners, including faculty, presidents, and administrators.
Includes a calendar of events, extensive links to web resources, job listings, news, model programs and sample syllabi, a section dedicated to "Building the Service-Learning Pyramid," and much more.

The National Service-Learning Clearinghouse http://www.servicelearning.org/
This site contains a library of service learning research, guides, and projects, a database of K-16 literature and links, and information about events, jobs, funding resources, listservs, and Learn and Serve America Online Project forms.

National Society for Experiential Learning http://www.nsee.org
Promotes experienced-based approaches to teaching and learning, including service-learning. Contains publications, resources center, conference information, and membership materials.

References

Alliance for Service-Learning in Education Reform: ASLER. (1993). *Standards of quality for school-based service-learning.* Chester, VT: ASLER.

Anderson, V., Kinsley, C. Negroni, P., and Price, C. (1991). Community Service-Learning and School Improvement in Springfield, Massachusetts. *Phi Delta Kappan*, 72, June, 761-764.

Anderson, J. B. (2000). Service-Learning and Preservice Teacher Education. "Learning In Deed" Issue Paper. Denver: ECS Distribution Center.

Bacon, N.A. (1997). The Transition from Classroom to Community Contexts for Writing. Unpublished dissertation, University of California, Berkeley.

Balazadeh, N. (1996). Service Learning and the Sociological Imagination: Approach and Assessment. Paper presented at the National Historically Black Colleges Faculty Development Symposium, Memphis, TN, October 10-13.

Berger Kaye, C. *The Service Learning Bookshelf.* 2nd Edition. Los Angeles: ABCD Books.

Berkas, T. (1997). *Strategic Review of the W. K. Kellogg Foundation's Service-Learning Projects, 1990-1996.* Battle Creak, MI: W. K. Kellogg Foundation.

Cohen, J. and Kinsey, D. (1994). Doing Good and Scholarship: A Service-Learning Study. *Journalism Educator,* Winter, 4-14.

Corrigan, R. (2000). The Service Learning Imperative Teacher Education. Keynote address at Service-Learning Institute for Faculty of the California State University, Oct. 12-13, 2000. Los Angeles, CA.

Courney, J. (1994). An Evaluation of the Native American School's Water Quality Testing Program. In M. Neal, R. Shumer, and K. Gorak (Eds.), *Evaluation: The Key to Improving Service-Learning Programs.* Minneapolis: Minnesota Department of Education and the University of Minnesota.

Dean, L. and Murdock, S. (1992). The Effect of Voluntary Service on Adolescent Attitudes Toward Learning. *Journal of Volunteer Administration,* Summer, 5-10.

Dewey, J. (1938/1963). *Experience and education.* New York: Macmillan Publishing Co.

Eyler, J. and Giles, D.E. (1999). *Learning with the community: Concepts and models for service-learning in teacher education.* Washington: AAHE.

Fenzel, L, Mickey, L., and Leary, T. (1997). Evaluating Outcomes of Service-Learning Courses at a Parochial College. Paper presented at the Annual Meeting of the American Educational Research Association, Chicago.

Follman, J. and Muldoon, K. (1997). Florida Learn and Serve: What Were the Outcomes? *NAASP Bulletin,* 29-36.

Follman, J. (1998). *Florida Learn and Serve: 1995-96: Outcomes and Correlations with 1994-95 and 1995-96.* Tallahassee, FL: Florida State University, Center for Civic Education and Service.

Heffernan, K. (2001). Service-learning in higher education. *Water Resources Update.* Issue 119, February.

Kilpatrick, W. (1918). The project method. *Teachers College Record,* 19, 320.

Kossack, S. (2001) *Training Cycles: In-service Training for Mastery of Craft,* Proceedings, European Reading Conference, Dublin, Ireland
Kossack, S. (in press). Student Embedded Teacher Training. *Journal of Reading Education.*

Loesch-Griffin, D., Petrides, L.A., and Pratt, C. (1995). *A Comprehensive Study of Project YES-Rethinking Classrooms and Community: Service-Learning as Educational Reform*. San Francisco: East Bay Conservation Corps.

Melchior, A. (1999*). Summary report: National evaluation of Learn and Serve America*. Waltham, MA: Center for Human Resources, Brandeis University.

Meyerratken, L. (2003). A Zen-Garden at Tecumseh: From Mocking to Honoring. *Middle Level Learning.* 17: May/June, 8-10.

Middleton, E. (1993). *The psychological and social effects of community service tasks on adolescents*. Unpublished doctoral dissertation, Purdue University.

Myers, C., & Pickeral, T. (1997). Service-learning: An essential process for preparing leaders in the reform of public education. In J. Erikson & J. Anderson (Eds.), *Learning with the community: Concepts and models for service-learning in teacher education*, 13-41. Washington, DC: American Association for Higher Education.

National Association of Secondary School Principals (1972). *American youth in the mid-seventies* (Conference Report). Reston, VA: N.A.S.S.P.

National Commission on Excellence in Education (1983). *Nation at risk: the imperative for educational reform*. Washington DC : U.S. Government Printing Office.

O'Bannon, F. (1999). Service-Learning Benefits Our Schools. *State Education Leader 17*, 3.

O'Donnell, L., Stueve, A., San Doval, A., Duran, R., Haber, D., Atnafou, R., Johnson, N., Grant, U., Murray, H., John, G., Tang, J., and Piessens, P. (1999). The Effectiveness of the Reach for Health Community Youth Service Learning Program in Reducing Early and Unprotected Sex Among Urban Middle School Students. *American Journal of Public Health, 89*(2), 176-181.

Rolzinski, C. (1990). The Adventure of Adolescence: Middle School Students and Community Service. Washington: Youth Service America.

Root, S. (1997). School-based service: A review of research for teacher educators. In J. Erikson & J. Anderson (Eds.), *Learning with the community: Concepts and models for service-learning in teacher education*, 42-72. Washington, DC: American Association for Higher Education.

Shaffer, B. (1993). *Service-Learning: An Academic Methodology*. Stanford, CA: Stanford University Department of Education. Cited in R. Bhaeman, K. Cordell, and B. Gomez (1998). *The Role of Service-Learning in Educational Reform*. Raleigh, NC: National Society for Experiential Education and Needham, MA: Simon and Schuster, Inc.

Shumer, R. (1994). Community-based learning: Humanizing education. *Journal of Adolescence.* 17, 357-67.

Silcox, H. (1993). Experiential environmental education in Russian: A study in community service. *Phi Delta Kappan,* 74(9), 706-9.

Stephens, L. (1995). *The Complete Guide to Learning Through Community Service, Grades K-9.* Boston: Allyn and Bacon.

Supik, J. (1996). *Valued Youth Partnerships: Programs in Caring.* San Antonio: Intercultural Research and Development Association.

Uchida, Y. (1996). *The Bracelet.* New York: Paper Star/Penguin Putnam.

Waterman, A. (1993). Conducting research on reflective activities in service-learning. In H. Silcox (Ed.), *A hot to guide to reflection: Adding cognitive learning to community service programs.* Philadelphia, PA: Brighton Press, 90-99.

Weiler, D., Crane, E. LaGoy, A., Rovener, A. (1998). *An evaluation of K-12 service-learning in California: Phase II final report.* Emeryville, CA: RPP International and the Search Institute.

Yates, M. and Youniss, J. (1996). Perspective on Community Service in Adolescence. *Social Development,* 5, 85-111.

Chapter 12

Service-Learning and Diverse Learners

Service-Learning Prepares Teachers to Meet the Needs of Diverse Learners

Virginia Jagla, National-Louis University, IL, UNITED STATES

Abstract: This action research project at The Dodge Renaissance Academy (TDA) in the inner city of Chicago was conducted with two middle level mentor teachers and their residents, who are National-Louis University graduate students. The two main undertakings of the 2006-07 academic year were a composting and global warming awareness project in a sixth grade classroom and a photography/beautification project with a group of seventh graders. Few service-learning studies involve inner city young adolescents as the producers of the project. The additional layer of involvement by our university students in this project enhances the benefit as they have contracted to teach in underperforming schools in Chicago for at least five years after they receive their degrees. Gaining firsthand knowledge of the powerful pedagogy of service-learning as preservice teachers enables them to utilize the pedagogy in classrooms throughout the city.

Inner city schools face problems of poor attendance, disengaged students, high drop out rates, bullying and gang involvement. Teachers in the inner city often "burn out" or lack the energy and vitality necessary to continue to deal with the day to day necessities of coping with the myriad of problems within their schools and communities. Preservice teachers aspiring to fill the need for well prepared urban teachers are often lacking in experience with proven best practice strategies. The middle grades are the last best hope to reach students in elementary school. Middle level is a pivotal age for student development.

I was involved in an action research project at The Dodge Renaissance Academy in the inner city of Chicago. As the National-Louis University (NLU) Liaison to the Academy for Urban School Leadership (AUSL), I interact regularly with the principals, mentor teachers, and residents at the elementary professional development schools which comprise AUSL. This project was conducted with two middle level mentor teachers at Dodge.

Initially I engaged the mentor teachers to enhance understanding of the pedagogy of service-learning and the civic mission of schools. Through dialogue and conference attendance we immersed ourselves in the culture of service-learning as we gained knowledge of the wide array of projects presented by teachers and students from around the state.

I set up a site visits for the resident teachers to a service-learning leader school in similar situations as theirs. As the mentor teachers and residents became more familiar with the various aspects of service-learning pedagogy they involved their 2006-07 classes of students in designing, planning, and implementing their service projects. Young adolescents learn by doing. Through their involvement with the service projects the middle level students developed and enhance practical skills, self esteem, and a sense of civic responsibility.

The students were involved in designing the service-learning projects which took them into the wider community. Research suggests that effective service-learning programs improve grades, increase attendance in school, and develop personal and social responsibility. Curriculum integration naturally occurs as social issues are addressed in middle schools.

Research abounds regarding the use of service-learning in K-12 schools. Much of the research addresses academic learning. Various studies have been done to gain more insight into the pedagogy. One such study found that students in quality service-learning schools showed moderate to strong positive gains on student achievement tests in language arts and/or reading, engagement in school, sense of educational accomplishment and homework completion (Weiler, et. al., 1998). Other studies have found that students who participated in service-learning have achieved higher scores on the state test of basic skills (Anderson, et. al., 1991). Further research indicates that elementary and middle school students who participated in service-learning had improved problem-solving skills and increased interest in academics (Stephens, 1995). In their comprehensive book, Serve and Learn: Implementing and Evaluating Service-Learning in Middle and High Schools, Pritchard and Whitehead (2004) show how service-learning can improve intellectual development because of its constructivist nature. They further illustrate how service-learning increases academic achievement and can be instrumental in accelerating school reform. As an aspect experiential learning, service-learning enhances the relevance of the knowledge. Students are actively involved in the process of constructing their own knowledge and see how it relates to the real world as opposed to just learning the theoretical concepts in isolation. These natural connections enhance understanding and retention of the facts and data required through the standards and benchmarks of the school district and state board of education. The interdisciplinary nature of service-learning enhances understanding throughout the curricular areas.

This is one of a growing number of service-learning studies involving inner city young adolescents as the producers of the project (Gomex, 1996; Lakin & Mahoney, 2006; Moore & Sandholtz, 1999; Scales et al, 2006). The additional layer of involvement by our university students in this project enhanced the benefit since they have a contract to teach in underperforming schools in Chicago for at least five years after graduation. Gaining firsthand knowledge of the powerful pedagogy of service-learning as preservice teachers enables them to better utilize the pedagogy in classrooms throughout the city. The AUSL program provides field coaches who interact with the university graduates for years to come. Thus we will be able to track their progress to proliferate the pedagogy in the public school system.

The intention of service-learning is to experience democracy in action. Adolescents learn through the experiences themselves as well as reflection on the process. The powerful pedagogy of service-learning empowers those who participate. Some think of inner city youths as the recipients of service. Students in any neighborhood strengthen their sense of altruism and self esteem through helping others. Preservice teachers need to learn more about this powerful pedagogy to assist in teaching students in similar situations. By providing preservice teachers with service-learning experiences in which they work with teachers in a school setting to design and implement service-learning projects with the young adolescents, we impart the knowledge, skills, and dispositions to empower these future teachers to be able to develop such projects in their future schools in other blighted neighborhoods in Chicago for years to come.

Service-learning offers a unique opportunity for middle level students to get involved with their communities in a tangible way by integrating service projects with classroom learning. Service-learning engages students in the educational process, using what they learn in the classroom to solve real-life problems. Students not only learn about democracy and citizenship, they become actively contributing citizens and community members through the service they perform.

Service-learning is a proven strategy to address many of the problems typically found in inner city schools. (Learn and Serve, 2007)

A national study of Learn and Serve America programs suggests that effective service-learning programs improve grades, increase attendance in school, and develop students' personal and social responsibility. A growing body of research recognizes service-learning as an effective strategy to help students by:

- Promoting learning through active participation in service experiences;
- Providing structured time for students to reflect by thinking, discussing and writing about their service experience;
- Providing an opportunity for students to use skills and knowledge in real-life situations;
- Extending learning beyond the classroom and into the community; and
- Fostering a sense of caring for others.

Service-learning also strengthens both education and local communities by:

- Building effective collaborative partnerships between schools or colleges and other institutions and organizations.
- Engaging parents and other adults in supporting student learning
- Meeting community needs through he service projects conducted
- Providing engaging and productive opportunities for young people to work with others in their community

The National Service-Learning Partnership (2005) defines service learning as "a teaching method that engages young people in solving problems within their schools and communities as part of their academic studies or other type of intentional learning activity. Service-learning helps students master important curriculum content by supporting their making meaningful connections between what they are studying and its many applications."

Middle Level Educators agree on the relevance of service learning programs for young adolescents. The original Turning Points: Preparing American Youth for the 21st Century (1989) and Turning Points 2000 (2000) promote good citizenship, service to others, experiential learning, ethics, and diversity. National Middle School Association has publications (Fertman, White, & White, 1996) supporting service learning in middle schools. NMSA and others argue that middle level curriculum should be interdisciplinary and exploratory. James Bean (1997) delineates how curriculum integration naturally occurs as social issues are addressed in middle schools. In their significant book, *Social Issues and Service at the Middle Level*, Samuel Totten and Jon Pedersen (1997) proclaim that "a study of social issues and involvement in service are ideal ways to begin to interweave a meaningful exploratory component throughout the curriculum." (p. 9). Totten & Pedersen's book highlights a wide array of middle level service learning projects which are both interdisciplinary and exploratory.

Infusing service-learning into the curriculum at the professional development school entails working with the mentors (Dodge teachers), the residents (university students) together with the middle level students. The middle level students were involved in much of the decision making. The two main undertakings of the 2006-08 academic year were a composting and global warming awareness project and a photography/beautification project.

By actively involving students in the process of constructing their own knowledge they more readily see how it relates to the real world as opposed to just learning the theoretical concepts in isolation. These natural connections enhance understanding and retention of the facts and data required through the standards and benchmarks of the school district and state board of education. The interdisciplinary nature of service-learning enhances understanding throughout the curricular areas.

I worked with two Chicago Public School master teachers to instruct them in the pedagogy of service-learning. We began with basic introduction to service-learning pedagogy. I gave each teacher a copy of Cathryn Berger Kaye's influential book, *The Complete Guide to Service-learning: Proven, Practical Ways to Engage Students in Civic Responsibility, Academic Curriculum, and Social Action* (Kaye, 2004) along with other literature and videos. Together we worked with their middle level students to formulate relevant service projects to fit needs in the community and enhance their own learning. The middle level students benefited academically, socially and emotionally. Through the service-learning endeavors the middle level students developed skills, explored career options, came to value civic responsibility, actively participated in their local community, and became more globally aware.

Each of the master teachers was responsible for mentoring National-Louis University graduate students working toward their Master of Arts in Teaching degree and certification through the state of Illinois. The collaboration of these colleagues with the Dodge students developed exciting curriculum and fostered a culture of altruism. The graduate students were a part of my middle level courses during the winter and spring terms of 2007. They helped me share the ongoing service projects with the rest of the graduate students. These students are placed in underperforming Chicago Public Schools for at least the next five years. As new teachers, they, in turn, are now versed in the powerful pedagogy of service-learning and are able to continue the cycle within their new schools and communities.

The projects at Dodge offered a pedagogy which encouraged students to engage in and advocate for their own communities. These projects have far reaching ramification throughout the City of Chicago as our graduate students become teachers well versed in the powerful pedagogy of service-learning and utilize this method in numerous underperforming schools with future students. Students, teachers and community members are affected and influenced in positive ways.

The service-learning project which involved the sixth graders at Dodge was entitled *Our Environmental Impact: Our Responsibility to the World.* This project was linked to the curricular standards for science, with emphasis on environmental science. Students viewed the Al Gore video, *An Inconvenient Truth*, to set up the discussion regarding the human impact on the environment. Students studied biodiversity, Pangaea, continental drift, the carbon cycle, decomposition, and composting. Students experimented with factors that affect decomposition of matter through a long term, hands-on investigation involving vermicomposting in their classroom. Decomposing worms lived in their classroom in receptacles so the students could observe the decay of plant matter.

This highly engaging project spawned from the mentor teacher's interest in gardening. Earlier in the academic year the sixth grade teacher expressed the desire to engage his students in planning and implementing a community garden on a tract of land adjacent to the school. This neighborhood beautification project was embraced by all involved within the school. Plans and ideas were discussed, with the thought of becoming fully engaged in the early spring. These plans came to an abrupt halt after a search for the owner of the property uncovered the fact that this plot of land was now up for sale. The sixth grade students still learned through the process of research. The disappointment motivated the sixth grade teacher to apply for a grant to build a greenhouse within the school. This has now materialized, and provides for further service-learning projects. One such venture is to grow herbs, harvest them, and donate them to local soup kitchens. The links to units on homelessness and hunger are readily apparent.

Initially, the vermicomposting was thought of as a way to enrich the soil in the vacant lot for the intended garden. For the 2006-07 year the decomposition project was the catalyst for students to study renewable and non-renewable resources. The students gained knowledge through research and class work about the human impact on the environment. They enacted an environmental agenda, deciding on a local and national course of action. The sixth grade students enacted a school-wide campaign persuading other students to sign a petition on global warming to send to Illinois Senator Barack Obama. Students wrote persuasive letters encouraging Senator Obama to make environmental issues a cornerstone of his national presidential campaign.

Some of the questions investigated throughout this project were: Why are we studying all this? What is a global threat? How is the climate changing? What are some of the consequences of global warming for Chicago? Illinois? The USA? Whose problem is it anyway? What is the human impact on our environment? How can we make a difference? In Dodge? In Chicago? In our country? What can WE do? Who should we tell? Are we ready to tell others? Where do we go from this?

After researching and gathering data, the students made graphs on climate change and increasing CO_2 emissions. They reviewed the Kyoto Protocol. They were highly engaged in the workshop on persuasive writing taught in conjunction with this unit because they understood some of the implications of good persuasive essays and letters in this regard. The sixth grade students prepared a presentation which they delivered to all fifth, seventh and eighth graders in their homeroom classrooms at Dodge. Their new found powers of persuasion paid off as they gathered student signatures from each classroom. The sixth grade students then prepared a package with the signatures, essays and graphs. This package was delivered to Senator Obama's press coordinator. The students recently acquired skills boosted their self esteem and confidence. The project engaged the students in understandings far beyond the science and math skills learned through the unit. The natural integration of language arts and social studies aspects of the endeavor allowed the students to experience the utility of the subject matter in addition to simply "knowing it for the test."

The second service-learning project, known as the *Neighborhood Beautification Project*, was carried out by the seventh graders at Dodge. Earlier in the year the seventh and eighth grade language arts and social studies teacher thought she would like to incorporate photography into language arts lessons planned to discover interesting and "beautiful" aspects of the community surrounding Dodge.

The mentor teacher and residents came up with their own answers to the question: What is service-learning? They viewed service-learning as an integration of academic curriculum and physical "work" with a purpose, a way to involve students in their learning, student centered teaching, a means to provoking a life long interest in community work, instilling responsibility and ownership in one's community, and development of a cohesive unit as a classroom. This particular service-learning project at Dodge was to understand what "beauty" is, be able to use places and things to represent something personal, and learn how to communicate feelings and ideas through pictures.

It was particularly exciting to see the residents in this classroom become so fully involved with seeing this project through. There was a mad dash at the end of the school year to produce final results for this project. Due to a variety of set backs, crucial equipment was not delivered in a timely fashion. We had a small grant in conjunction with this project. We did not receive the cameras originally ordered; although we kept getting messages that they were "on their way." I finally went store to store to procure a quantity of inexpensive digital cameras so each student would be able to take a camera home to capture images of personal interest. Printers and mounting supplies were also procured. The residents worked hard to organize the equipment so cameras could be signed out to all the students.

Some initial classroom discussion revolved around the question: What is beauty? Students talked in small groups about what it means to be beautiful. This provided the context that beauty is not just something that is aesthetically pleasing. Once they had a better understanding of what kind of beauty they were looking for, it was time to have a discussion about how photography could communicate their ideas. Students learned how to "read" photographs, how to compose images and how to "speak" to their audience through images.

Some of the goals of this project were to: have students understand what true beauty is, have students take digital cameras home to document through pictures what is beautiful to them, mount and display photos in a community building or school, beautify the community surrounding Dodge. Most of these goals were realized. The students waited a long time for the cameras. Although this aspect was unintentional, it served to create a sense of excitement and anticipation. Students studied photography and thought about the photos they would eventually take. The results were phenomenal. The photos were displayed in a local community library a few blocks from Dodge, then at the school.

The seventh graders wrote brief reflections of some of their favorite photos. Some relate to these simply what they see in the picture:

- "I love the way they cursive wrote their names on the top of the windows."
- "I took this picture because I just liked how the colors looked and I never really saw that many bird feeders before."

Many wrote why they took the particular image:

- "This building always creeps me out at night. It looks like a haunted house I use to tease my cousin Kyle and tell him it really was haunted."
- "My dad doesn't live with us anymore and I miss him a lot. I remember him taking us, me and my brother, to this barbershop to get a haircut before Easter. It has been here a long time. Even all of the other buildings closed down, but not the shop."
- "My cousins in the burbs come all the way to the city to see the Sears Tower and downtown. On my block we can see the downtown from the front porch. That's what's up!"
- "One of my favorite people is my best friend Aisha. I can always go to her for advice. She acts so shy but she knows that she ain't shy for real."
- "This makes me think about something old because it's black and white. The picture looks like two kids kissing; I think that's kinda cute!"
- "People always think thugs and gangbangers make graffiti but these show Martin Luther King in graffiti so it can't be negative because he is a positive man."

Some students wrote longer reflective pieces regarding the whole project. Here is an example of one such reflection which tells the whole story:

> I always used to say when I saw postcards and magazine pictures that 'I could do that!' I didn't know that taking pictures was so hard. Maybe I should say that taking GOOD pictures is so hard. When Ms. Hay and Mr. Morris first told us about the project, everybody was geeked because we thought that we were going to get our own cameras. We also thought that this was going to be like having free time in school because we got to take pictures in place of writing for a few days. WRONG!
>
> Ms. Hay and Mr. Morris had shown us pictures from something they did called a community walk. I was kind of shocked because I saw some places that I didn't even know existed. I was the first one to talk about things that could be inspiration for photos. They showed one picture of a man in the doorway of a restaurant and everybody laughed because they knew exactly where it was. What we didn't know was some of the history behind the restaurant and why they chose to take this picture. We had a few mini-lessons that talked about how 'beauty is in the eye of the beholder' and how really good photographers capture moods, emotions and feelings that you can relate to even if you don't know the place in the picture.

I said before that it was hard taking some good pictures. We had a hard time trying to figure out the focus buttons because some pictures were blurry, too small, too far away and all kinds of stuff. Then we had to learn about what degradation of picture quality was and how just because we can see everything in the window when we take the picture doesn't mean that the picture is going to turn out good. We learned about all types of stuff that I may not remember next year but it may come to me next time I take some pictures. I really enjoyed the project and I think that we should do things like this more often. Students always say that teachers are boring and even the fun ones only have us doing school stuff. I know that Ms. Hay and Mr. Morris said that this was still school stuff but it didn't feel like it and that felt good.

Another seventh grader wrote:

My mom used to always say that 'beauty is in the eye of the beholder' when I would call someone ugly. I didn't really understand what this meant at the time but this was the quote that they showed us before we started our project. They gave us a chance to talk about and write down what this phrase meant to us and many people said that it was all about how people have differences in how they see beauty. When we first learned that we would be given cameras to take thoughtful shots of things that we saw to be beautiful about our neighborhood, everyone thought that they were going to have these extra nice photos. Not many of us knew how much you actually have to think about why you take certain pictures. It is as much an art as it is a skill.

I write poetry and this is what I compared it to when we talked about it in class after our first day with the cameras. When I write, I am inspired by events, people and feelings. This was the same thing that we learned about photography. I took some pictures that I really liked but my favorite was one that my friend took of our friend Aisha. She has a good personality; she is really funny and kind of silly at times. In the picture she has her back turned like she is trying to be shy. We all know that she isn't but this picture shows exactly what we know about her personality. It was really simple but I like it most. I enjoyed working with them on this project and I think that I understand why they talk so much about students using higher order thinking. They want us to understand the deeper meaning of things that we see and do. This project was pretty cool in doing that because we were not criticized for our ideas but they showed us how to think more critical about our decisions and photos. We should do this again next year because we didn't have a lot of time to really get into it.

The residents involved in this project reflected on the service-learning venture as well. One of the residents wrote:

The students were extremely eager to get the cameras and even mentioned a number of things that they had in mind to take pictures of. Some of those subjects included sibling's unkempt rooms, old classic cars in parent's garages and so on. This was a clear indicator of how much instructional time and modeling would be necessary to give the students a clear understanding of what the nature of the project was. Time is the key word here because we were operating on a fixed amount...We ultimately had to take a leap of faith in arming the children with limited knowledge and trust their creativity and inferential abilities. There is one lesson that I will take away from this experience that supersedes all others: service-learning requires the same attention, preparation and content knowledge that go into effective lesson planning. The attention to detail, level of differentiation and general focus needs to be considered heavily while executing such a project.

In the end, there were a number of extremely successful students... The rationales provided by students showed some growth in the student's awareness of the activity purpose and artistic critical thought. One particular shot comes to mind where a student photographed a graffiti mural painted on the outside of a local boys and girls club. While photographs focused on the aesthetic appeal, conversation with this student revealed that he was attentive to the theme of the piece and had even memorized quotes that were sprinkled throughout. In summing the experience, like all teaching experiences, metacognition will enable a more successful project in the future.

Another resident wrote:

When I reflect on my experience with this beautification service-learning project there are many events and people I think of. First, the idea of service-learning is absolutely essential to the development of thoughtful, hardworking, and empathetic human beings. Students feel a sense of ownership with activities that place them in the center of a project. Second, middle school students are constantly feeling that they are not given the ability to make their own decisions and take control of their learning; therefore a learning opportunity where they are able to choose and develop their own goals, organize their own thoughts and ideas, and be responsible for an activity that will be enjoyed and observed by some of the most important people in their lives, their neighbors, is an absolutely appropriate activity! As middle school education students we are constantly told that young adults need to express themselves, it is part of their personal and social development; necessary to creating a positive self esteem. Service-learning is the best way I have found to allow young people to take control and take risks with their learning.

On the subject of the actual service-learning that I took a leadership role in, a community beautification project, I learned that you CAN integrate service-learning into curriculum. What I also realized was that service-learning projects must be organized because the student centered classroom, project, or activity is already in itself an element chaos, of course it is that chaos that makes these theories so effective and refreshing. Being organized by having materials well in advance, having a clear vision what it is you want students to learn; having clear cut objectives and providing effective scaffolding requires backwards planning and fair amount of time to introduce and progress as a class.

The students were very excited about this project and were really looking forward to starting to take pictures, they all had a variety of ideas on what they were going to capture and express on camera. I know that I could have done so much more with this service-learning project; I could have combined it with a writing lesson and a publishing party, it could have been a great community building project that allowed all students, including the timid or shy, to show their classmates a side of their personality, or it could have part of an entire unit on photography and the media focusing on the power of a photo, propaganda, tone, and audience, and even been a hook to begin practice with extended response! Even though I feel that I could have done so much more, I am glad that I had this preliminary experience because now I can add this service-learning skeleton to my current units and fill it up in years to come with teaching!

Although each of these projects had some challenges, ultimately many of the goals of service-learning were met with having the students civically engaged while learning important areas of the curriculum. The residents involved with these projects acquired a wealth of experience and now have a good conception of what these types of projects entail. They experienced firsthand the integrative properties of the pedagogy of service-learning and are ready to fine tune such ideas in future classrooms. Each of these residents presented to classes of other residents to inform them of these particular projects and further explain the pedagogy of service-learning. The mentor teachers involved continue to utilize service-learning pedagogy with new residents and middle level students. As the students progress from year to year: Will there be a community garden? A greenhouse growing herbs for the local soup kitchen? There are budding photo journalists writing and illustrating books for younger students at Dodge.

There are knowledgeable, nascent teachers learning their way and attempting new service-learning projects in the underperforming schools in Chicago. As one of the residents put it, "I have decided to make service-learning a staple in my future curricula and will be an advocate for the acceptance and growth of the service-learning movement... an educator is responsible for one thing: finding the most relevant, efficient, and meaningful ways to teach children, to enlighten young people, and inspire our future leaders."

References

Anderson, V., Kinsley, C., Negroni, P. & Price, C. (1991). Community service-learning and school improvement in Springfield, Massachusetts. *Phi Delta Kappan*, 72, June, 761-764.

Bean, J. A. (1997). "Social issues in the middle school curriculum: Retrospective and prospective," in *Social Issues and service at the middle level.* Totten, S & Pedersen, J. E. (eds). Needham Heights, MA: Allyn & Bacon.

Fertman, C. I.; White, G. P.; & White, L. J. (1996) *Service learning in the middle school: Building a culture of service.* Westerville, OH: NMSA.

Gomez, B. (1996) "Service-Learning and School-to-Work Strategies for Revitalizing Urban Education and Communities" in *Education and Urban Society* v28 n2 p160-166

Jackson, Anthony W. & Davis, Gayle A. (2000). *Turning Points 2000: Educating Adolescents in the 21st Century.* New York: Teachers College Press.

Kaye, C. B. (2004). *The complete guide to service-learning: Proven, practical ways to engage students in civic responsibility, academic curriculum, and social action.* Minneapolis, MN: Free Spirit Publishing, Inc.

Lakin, R. & Mahoney, A. (2006). "Empowering Youth to Change Their World: Identifying Key Components of a Community Service Program to Promote Positive Development" in *Journal of School Psychology*, v44 n6 p513-531

Learn and Serve America (2007). http://www.learnandserve.org/about/service_learning/index.asp

Moore, K.P. & Sandholtz (1999). "Designing successful service-learning projects for urban schools" in *Urban Education*, v34, n4 p480-498

National Service-Learning Partnership (2005). http://www.service-learning-partnership.org/site/PageServer.

Pritchard, F. F. & Whitehead, G. I. III (2004). *Serve and learn: Implementing and evaluating service-learning in middle and high schools. Mahwah, NJ: Lawrence Erlbaum Associates, Publishers.*

Scales, P.C.; Roehlkepartain, E.C.; Neal, M.; Kielsmeir; Benson, P.L. (2006). "Reducing academic achievement gaps: The role of community service and service-learning" in *Journal of Experiential Education, v29 n1 p38-60*

Stephens, L. (1995). *The complete guide to learning through community service, grades K-9. Boston, MA: Allyn and Bacon.*

Totten, S. & Pedersen, J. E. (1997). *Social issues and service at the middle level. Needham Heights, MA: Allyn & Bacon.*

Weiler, D., LaGoy, A., Crane, E. & Rovner, A. (1998). *An evaluation of K-12 service-learning in California: Phase II final report. Emeryville, CA: RPP International with the Search Institute.*

Chapter 13
Service-Learning and Teacher Preparation

A Sample Implementation on Teacher Candidates' Pre-Service Learning

Pinar Girmen, Eskisehir Osmangazi University, Turkey

Abstract: Lifelong learning involves conscious and purposeful continuation of learning throughout life. Lifelong education is a very broad concept aiming for individuals' personal, social and professional development and for continuing that all through life.Public education centers are widespread educational institutions in support of lifelong education within Turkish educational system. Therefore, public education centers play a key role in meeting educational needs of the people of our developing country. Especially the adult literacy courses offered in these centers has had a pioneering role in literacy campaigns in society. Students of primary school education departments of faculties of education were provided with hands-on experience tasks in literacy courses offered in public education centers so that their training could be enhanced and their social awareness could be increased. In this study, each student attending literacy program was paired with a teacher candidate ensuring that they would collaborate. The duration of the project was planned as 60 days and teacher candidates and students worked together twice a week for a period of studying hours determined by the pairs themselves. 26 primary school teacher candidates participating in the project were interviewed to determine the efficiency of the project in terms of teaching profession. The descriptive analysis method was used to analyze the data obtained. Two field experts and the researcher conducted independent studies in forming the interview coding key. The final draft of the coding key was formed in light of the agreement reached between the experts and the researcher. The findings and interpretations were shaped in accordance with the themes and sub-themes formed and quotes from the statements made by the interviewee teacher candidates were included. The conclusion and suggestions were developed based on the findings.

Introduction

Training teachers is a multidimensional matter. Issues such as choosing teacher candidates, their pre-service training, school practices and in-service training are entirely involved in the concept of teacher training. Considering the fact that an efficient and quality teaching can only be achieved by the teacher, it is undeniable that the teacher is the most significant component in an educational system. Whether or not an educational system will be successful or not depends highly on teachers, who will actually run and implement it. In order to raise the quality of the teaching profession, the general and specific professional competencies supposed to be possessed by teachers should be determined first of all and then these competencies should be acquired by teacher candidates and teachers through pre- and in-service training programs. It is essential that teaching competencies be given and improved up to the desired levels in teacher training programs by means of theoretical and practical studies offered to students (YOK/The Higher Education Council of the Turkish Republic, 1998).

In Turkey, pre-service training of teachers is under the responsibility of educational faculties of universities. As the teaching profession is an occupation that requires unique knowledge and skills, teacher candidates are supposed to receive a 4-year professional training after high school. Teacher training programs are continuously revised and updated according to the contemporary requirements and expectations of the society from teachers. These programs are categorized under four groups: general culture, subject matter knowledge, subject matter teaching and professional knowledge. General culture aims to develop knowledge and abilities based on general culture. Subject matter knowledge is intended for having candidates acquire the knowledge, skills, attitudes and values required in the field in which teaching will take place. Subject matter teaching involves the knowledge, skills, attitudes and values concerning how subject matter teaching will be performed while professional knowledge includes the acquisitions unique to teaching (Küçükahmet, 1993). These programs are supplemented with elective courses, social responsibility projects and social activities designed to raise teacher candidates' sensitivity towards society and their knowledge about the society they live in.

In this study, a project was developed so that teacher candidates' social awareness could be increased, they could learn better about the society they lived in and they could have the opportunity to become involved in teaching literacy practices. Adding variety to the learning environment and moving the learning environment outside the classroom are considered to be significant in terms of raising teacher candidates' quality. Therefore, this project was designed in a way that would keep students in rich learning environments.

Lifelong learning means conscious and purposeful continuation of learning throughout life. Lifelong education is a very broad concept intended for individuals' personal, social and professional development and for continuing that all through life. In Turkish educational system, public education centers are widespread educational institutions supplementing lifelong education. Public education centers therefore play a key role in meeting educational needs of the people of our developing country. Particularly the adult literacy courses offered in these centers has taken on a pioneering role in literacy campaigns in society. The aim of literacy courses is to let all citizens older than primary school age who are completely illiterate or who can hardly read and write learn to read and write under the supervision and responsibility of the state and in accordance with the objectives and fundamental principles of Turkish National Education or to let them receive a primary school level education. Literacy courses consist of two stages:

Stage I Literacy Course: This type of literacy courses can be organized anywhere appropriate under the supervision of public education centers. They are free of charge and last for 90 class hours. They are intended for those illiterate citizens who are older than primary education age (older than 14). Number of participants is not a prerequisite to start this type of literacy courses. Applying to a public education center or any other educational institution in neighborhood is enough to enroll in classes. Stage I Literacy courses is aimed at having illiterate people acquire the skills necessary for literacy, Turkish language, basic mathematics and civics and gain the knowledge and abilities needed in everyday life. Those adults proving successful Stage I literacy courses are granted a "Certificate of Literacy" and qualified to attend Stage II courses.

Stage II Literacy Course: This type of literacy courses is intended for those adults who have Stage I literacy certificate or who can prove in documentation that they left school without finishing the fifth grade of any primary school. They are also free of charge and last for 180 class hours. In order for a literacy course to be started, the number people applying for a literacy course in a center should be a minimum of ten people. Application is made to a public education center. Those people proving successful Stage I literacy courses are granted a "Stage II Certificate in Adult Education" and this document is recognized as equivalent to the first five years of primary school. As a matter of fact, people completing this program are considered to have acquired the knowledge and skills normally given during the first five years of primary education. People having this certificate are qualified to attend the sixth grade of primary education.

In this study a literacy teaching project was designed. This project was intended for supporting students attending literacy courses offered in Public Education Centers and to provide students of primary school education departments with hands-on experience tasks in literacy courses so that their learning environment could be enhanced and their social awareness could be increased.

Literacy Project

A literacy project was developed so that the pre-service training of the students of primary school education departments of faculties of education could be enhanced and their social awareness could be increased. The project was designed in a way ensuring that students attending literacy program and teacher candidates would work in collaboration with each other. A total of 84 students taking literacy teaching course on a voluntary basis were assigned tasks in the project. Each student attending the literacy program was paired with a teacher candidate ensuring that they would collaborate. The duration of the project was planned as 60 days and teacher candidates and students worked together twice a week for a period of studying hours determined by the pairs themselves. In this project, the teacher candidates helped literacy course students do their assignments do exercises and with the necessary issues about reading and writing.

Research Objective

This study aims to find out teacher candidates' opinions about the efficiency of an adult literacy teaching project in which they participated actively. To achieve this general objective, this study tried to provide answers to the following questions:

1. What are the professional gains of the teacher candidates who participated in the project?
2. What are the gains of the teacher candidates who participated in the project in terms of social awareness?
3. What are the suggestions of the teacher candidates about the project?

Method

Aimed at determining the efficiency of an adult literacy teaching project based on the opinions of the teacher candidates who participated in the project actively, this study was carried out by adopting descriptive method. Also, this study made use of qualitative research approach in collection, analysis and interpretation of data.

184

Participants of the Research

A type of purposeful sampling methods was used in qualitative research: convenience sampling. This sampling method normally gives a research speed and practicality because in this method the researcher chooses a close and convenient case (Yıldırım and Şimşek, 2006). The reason why convenience sampling was chosen for this study was that it was conducted with those students with convenient class hours. The research sampling comprised a total of 26 third-year students of Department of Primary School Education, Faculty of Education, Eskişehir Osmangazi University who participated in literacy project. Students chosen for the research sampling was assigned numbers instead of their names.

Data Collection

The research data was collected by means of a type of qualitative research data collection methods: semi-structured interview method. The interview, in general definition, involves the process in which the researcher's oral questions are orally answered by those participating in the interview. Traditionally interviews take place face to face, one to one and at a time. According to Stewart and Cash (Stewart and Cash, 1985; quoted in Yıldırım and Şimşek, 2005), interview is "a process of dyadic, relational communication with a predetermined and serious purpose designed to interchange behavior and involving the asking and answering of questions." The questions in the interview form were examined by a field expert and the interview form took its final form after the necessary adjustments. The interviews were performed one by one with each participant. In addition to the written consents, the researcher obtained verbal consents of the participants and recorded them by a voice recorder. Then, the participants were asked the questions in the interview form in numerical order. The teacher candidates were allowed to address the questions in the space they wish and the researcher paid particular attention so as not to manipulate the participants. In the semi-structured interviews, a separate cassette tape was used for each participant. The interview dates and names of the teacher candidates interviewed were written on the cassettes. The interviews were conducted in the researcher's office.

Data Analysis

Recording the data in the interview form: The data from each interview record was written on the interview form without any changes. The interview form includes parts such as participating person/case, contextual data like place and time, descriptive index, descriptive data, the researcher's comment and page comment. Transferred into the relevant forms, the data was presented to another expert for evaluation in its original version. The expert checked whether there was a difference between the recordings and written documentations.

Forming the interview coding key: The main aim of this phase, in principle, is to decide under which themes the research data will be grouped and presented. The researcher and two experts independently filled in the interview coding keys. Then, the researcher and the experts worked together and examined the response for each question one by one. The coding key took its final form in accordance with the agreement reached between the researcher and the experts.

Thematizing interview data: The researcher and two experts independently formed the themes and sub-themes. Then, these themes and sub-themes were compared with each other. The themes were finally shaped through the mutual agreement between the researcher and the experts. The interview data was arranged and interpreted according to the themes and sub-themes formed.

Research Reliability: There was an agreement for each theme designed based on interviews conducted to determine the efficiency of the literacy teaching project for teacher candidates. However, comparing sub-themes yielded two differences between the researcher and two field experts. The reliability of the findings of the interviews conducted in this way was found to be .98

$$\text{Reliability} = \frac{\text{Agreement}}{\text{Agreement} + \text{Disagreement}}$$

Findings

The findings obtained through the interviews were grouped under three main themes: "the professional gains of the teacher candidates," "the gains of the teacher candidates in terms of social awareness" and "the suggestions of the teacher candidates about the improvement of literacy projects." The findings then were represented in tables in the form of frequency distributions and summarized by direct quotations from participants' statements about their opinions.

Professional Gains of Teacher Candidates

The opinions of the teacher candidates who participated in the project about their professional gains are shown in Table 1.

Table 1: Professional Gains of Teacher Candidates

Professional gains of teacher candidates	f
Developing professional self-confidence	26
Gaining experience about teaching literacy skills	26
Implementing a variety of methods in teaching literacy skills	23
Realizing the importance of communication in education	22
Realizing the importance of primary education	20
Gaining experience about the differences of adult education	14
Developing a perspective on illiterate parents	9
N= 26	

Table 1 shows that all of the teacher candidates involved in the project stated that the developed professional self-confidence and that they gained experience about teaching reading and writing. Almost all of the teacher candidates (23) claimed that they had the opportunity to implement a variety of methods in teaching reading and writing. The number of those teacher candidates stating that during the project they realized the importance of communication in education and that they realized the importance of primary education is 22 and 20 respectively. 14 teacher candidates emphasized that they gained experience about the differences of adult education while 9 candidates said they developed a perspective on illiterate parents.

The following are some of the candidates' statements about this theme, their professional gains: teacher candidate 10, "*It was through this project that I realized how important the skills acquired in primary education are. Obviously, primary education means a base for everything and it plays a significant role in people's having a better life as well as their learning literacy skills*" (L. 10.5-10.7); teacher candidate 23, "*This project proved very useful for us; we had the chance to implement the theoretical knowledge we learnt in teaching literacy course*" (L. 23.3-23.4); teacher candidate 7, "*It was the first time I felt like a teacher. I enjoyed being a teacher. I literally contributed to someone's learning something. This hands-on experience gave me concrete evidence that teaching profession is exactly for me. Everything was fun and also the cakes the ladies in the course made for us were really delicious*" (L. 7.2- 7.6); teacher candidate 3, "*The lady who I helped learn to read and write found me too young to become a teacher at first. She was not convinced that I could help her and it took some time till I could persuade her about me as a teacher. For example, I came up with songs and sang them so that she could feel the sounds but she just thought they were so funny and she did not take me seriously. Meanwhile, I lost my motivation but things got better after a while. It was only then that I realized why adult education is different from others and that communication does really matter in this kind of education*" (L. 3.2-3.12).

Gains of Teacher Candidates in terms of Social Awareness

The opinions of the teacher candidates who participated in the project about their gains in terms of social awareness are shown in Table 2.

Table 2: Gains of Teacher Candidates in terms of Social Awareness

Gains of teacher candidates in terms of social awareness	f
Happiness from doing something in return for nothing	26
Happiness from making someone's life easier	23
Sharing someone's sense of achievement	20
Collaborating with somebody one has just met	20
Realizing the differences among people's life qualities	17
Realizing the life difficulties of social groups with disadvantages	15
Satisfaction from being a person who is being appreciated	14
Sense of leaving a positive trace in someone's life	5
N= 26	

Considering the opinions of teacher candidates about what they thought they gained in literacy project, it is clear that all of the participants expressed their happiness from doing something in return for nothing. Also, 23 teacher candidates mentioned their happiness from making someone's life easier. Both the number of the candidates talking about the feeling caused by sharing someone's sense of achievement and the number those mentioning the feeling of collaborating with somebody one has just met is 20. 17 candidates commented they realized the differences among people's life qualities while 15 candidates claimed that they realized the life difficulties of social groups with disadvantages. Finally, 14 teacher candidates stated that they enjoyed the satisfaction from being a person who is being appreciated and 5 candidates highlighted how beautiful the sense of leaving a positive trace in someone's life was.

Some of statements of the teacher candidates about this theme, their gains in terms of social awareness are the following: teacher candidate 1, *"It was a nice feeling to become involved in this project; I want to join in and do something if it is held again. I think feeling that you are really useful and doing something without wanting anything in return is good, especially when the person you help is somebody you don't know"* (L.1.8-1.10); teacher candidate 18, *"You know what, people we taught to read and write could not believe that we did that job in return for nothing. My partner-student always tried to buy me presents or a cup of tea for example. She offered to compensate my travel cost. She says she has never seen anyone in her life that helps for free. After a while she quit that kind of offers but she brought me home-made cakes and cookies"* (L. 18.10-18.21); teacher candidate 2, *"Being appreciated by someone was a cool feeling. After every class hour, the lady I worked with was forever blessing me"* (L. 2.5-2.6) and teacher candidate 15, *"It was not until my involvement in this project that I literally learnt about what difficulties being illiterate could bring about and how unfair life conditions when we are born could be. Of course what we hear counts for something but first-hand experience of being surrounded by harsh conditions of life is something different. Life is really hard for those people who cannot read or write and whose life skills are limited. Just think about it... doing shopping, getting on the bus, going to the hospital and so on. My involvement in the project made it possible for me to feel empathy with them"* (L. 15.7-15.14).

Suggestions of Teacher Candidates about the Improvement of Literacy Projects

The suggestions of the participant teacher candidates about the improvement of the project are shown in Table 3.

Table 3: Suggestions of Teacher Candidates about the Improvement of Literacy Projects

Suggestions of teacher candidates about the improvement of literacy projects	f
Making the working environment more functional	26
Preparing reading materials	23
Designing activities for learning in real life	20
Preparing programs for learners that develop basic life skills	20
Keeping the duration of literacy projects longer	17
N= 26	

As can be seen in Table 3, 26 teacher candidates who participated in the project expressed the need for making the environment they worked in more functional. 23 teacher candidates claimed that more diverse materials should be produced while 20 candidates emphasized the need for designing activities for learning outside the classroom in real life. The number of teacher candidates pointing out the need for considering programs for learners that develop basic life skills within the project is 20. On the other hand, 17 teacher candidates suggest that the duration of literacy projects should be longer.

The following are some of the candidates' statements about this theme, their suggestions regarding the project: teacher candidate 9, "*This project was good for teaching literacy skills but those people need much more than just learning to read and write. Maybe if the learning environment was outside the classroom, we could have taught them how to withdraw money from a cash dispenser. Just think about it for a moment; those people have to get on the same tram with us, go to the supermarket, adapt to the people they live with in a society and protect themselves*" (L.9.20-9.26); teacher candidate 25, "*It is true that they learnt to read and write but there should certainly be an additional course which provides further improvement because their skills need to be strengthened especially in writing*" (L.25.18-25.20); teacher candidate 8, "*I believe that the duration of the course is not long enough. Most of the students are female and mothers, so they cannot attend classes regularly as their kids get sick or they have guests. I think the duration of the course should be longer*" (L.8.18-8.21) and teacher candidate 4, "*It was necessary to bring to the classroom the materials that could attract their attention; daily newspapers, for example, could have been more functional if they had come regularly*" (L.4.16-4.17).

Conclusion

The teacher candidates think that the literacy project they participated in on voluntary basis contributed to their professional development. They emphasized that this experience helped them develop professional self-esteem, feel like a teacher and gain experience in teaching literacy skills.

The teacher candidates also stated that the literacy skills teaching project increased their social awareness. Particularly helping a group handicapped by disadvantages is an aspect highlighted by those teacher candidates willing to make an individual's life easier.

The teacher candidates made the following suggestions concerning the literacy project in which they participated: adding variety to the learning environment, creating extra learning environment apart from the classroom, considering programs for learners that develop basic life skills within the project and making the duration of the project longer.

Suggestions

Education faculties of universities and civil society organizations could collaborate and develop new projects for the groups faced with disadvantages. The win-win outcomes of this project will increase the efficiency of this project.

Some projects could be developed to make life easier for groups handicapped by harsh conditions and to increase their life qualities.

Guiding teacher candidates through the projects in which they could have opportunities to practice teaching will add to their professional development.

Teaching the practice courses in educational faculties outside the faculties will increase teacher candidates' professional competency.

References

Gürkan, T. and Gökçe, E. *Primary Education in Turkey and Several Countries: Program-Student-Teacher* Ankara: Siyasal Publications, 1999.

Küçükahmet, L. (1993) Teacher Training Programs and Practices. Ankara.

Miles, M. B. and Huberman, A. M. *An Expanded Sourcebook Qualitative Data Analysis.* (Second Edition). California: Sage Publications, Inc., 1994.

Yıldırım, A. and Şimşek H. *Qualitative Research Methods in Social Sciences,* Ankara: Seçkin Publications. 2005.

YÖK. (1998). "Faculty-School Cooperation" YÖK (Higher Education Council) / World Bank Pre-Service Teacher Training Project", Ankara.

Part V
Service-Learning and Other Student Outcomes

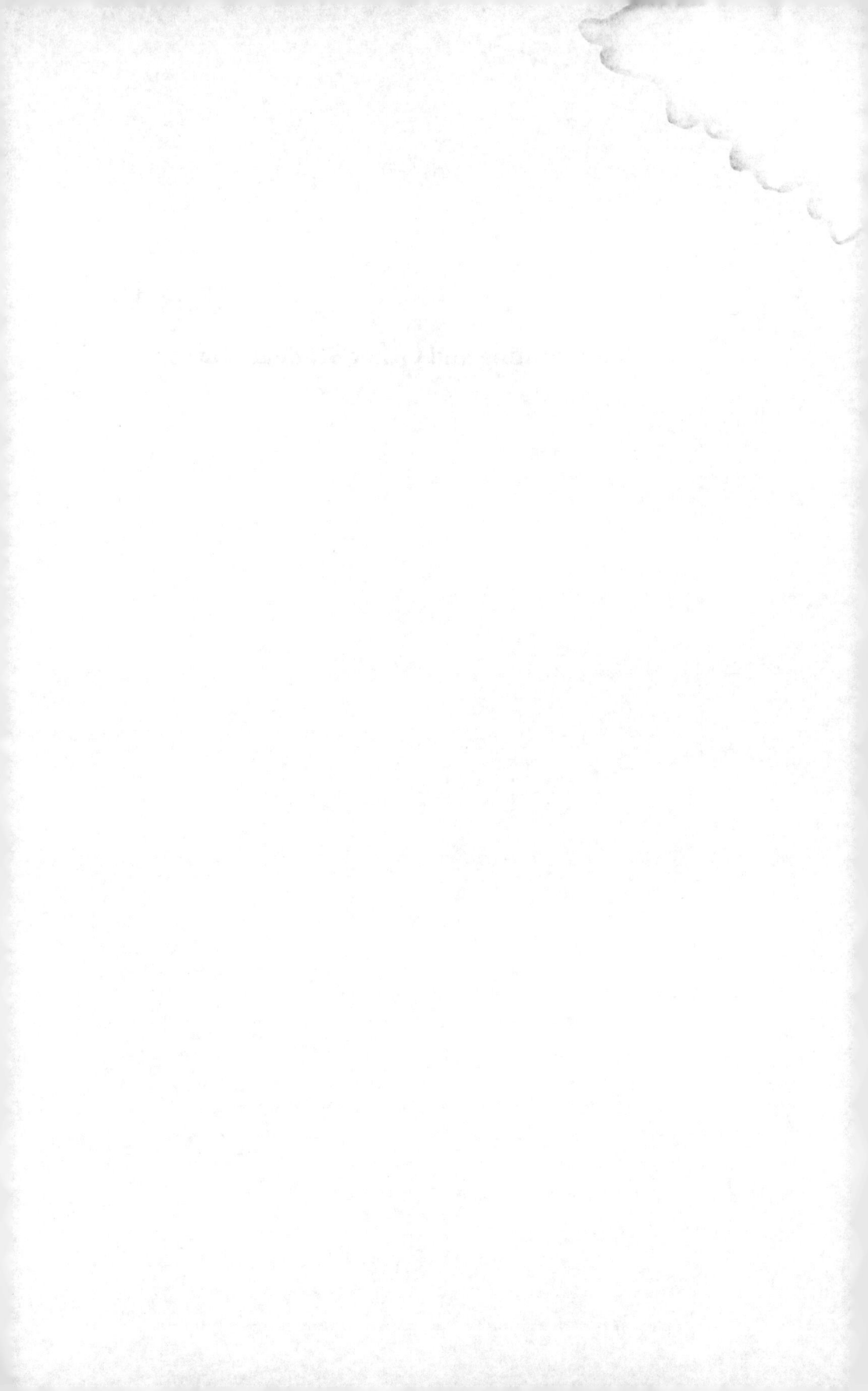

Overview

Chapters 14 and 15 make up Part 5 of the book, which focuses on service-learning and other student outcomes not previously discussed. Chapter 14 looks at using service-learning as a learning mechanism to promote citizenship education and promote social justice. Chapter 15 explores service-learning's role in preparing students for the global workplace.

Chapter 14

Service-Learning and Social Justice

Using Citizenship Education, Adolescent Literature, and
Service Learning to Promote Social Justice

Leisa Martin, The University of Akron, Ohio, USA
Lynn Smolen, The University of Akron, Ohio, USA

Abstract: Promoting social justice is an important part of social studies education and is essential in preparing students for citizenship in the 21st century. In the Partnership for 21st Century Skills' framework for learning (2004a), two interdisciplinary themes are mentioned as key elements of the report. They are: (a) using global awareness to "understand and address global issues" and (b) civic literacy (Partnership for 21st Century Skills, 2004b, para. 1). Leaders in government and education emphasize the importance of preparing students to be more globally aware and better prepared to join the domestic and international workforce. This preparation begins in the schools and one way schools can help students learn content and prepare for active citizenship is to incorporate service learning and global adolescent literature into the school curriculum in the study of social justice issues such as hunger and poverty. Students can study historical events using adolescent literature, and respond to the issues and injustices they learn about by taking action to address a social justice issue.

Promoting social justice is an important part of social studies education and is essential in preparing students for citizenship in the 21st century. Social justice examines the use of power in terms of gender, racial or ethnic background, and socioeconomic status (Botelho & Rudman, 2009, p. 1). Citizenship education, adolescent literature, and service learning can be used in the classroom to advance social justice. This article describes how these three curricular components increase students' understanding of social justice using the example of the Irish Potato Famine.

Social injustice has been pervasive throughout the world's history. An excellent example of social injustice is the Irish Potato Famine, a tumultuous event that occurred from approximately 1845 to 1852. This event played a significant role in the history of Ireland and the United States.

After the Catholic Irish lost in battle to the English Protestant King William of Orange in 1690, the king and the English parliament enacted the Penal Laws to prevent future Irish uprisings.

> Under the Penal Laws, [Irish] Catholics were forbidden to vote, hold political office, carry or own firearms, engage in certain trades or professions, or provide their children with a Catholic education. They could not purchase land or bequeath their land as they wished. They were also forbidden to possess a horse worth more than five pounds (Bartoletti, 2001, p. 13).

The Penal Laws resulted in much suffering and oppression of the Irish. Approximately 155 years after the enactment of these laws, the Irish Potato Famine took place. This epic famine was a result of the English oppression of the Irish, as well as numerous other factors, including agricultural disease. During this catastrophic famine, approximately one million Irish perished from hunger and disease and approximately two million Irish immigrated to the United States, Canada, and Australia to escape the consequences of this event (Bartoletti, 2001; O'Neil, 2009).

The act of addressing social justice issues can improve peoples' quality of life on the domestic and international level. In the course of studying the Irish Potato Famine in a world geography or world history course, students could learn about social justice issues such as hunger and poverty. To introduce the topic, teachers could provide background knowledge by using a combination of lectures, videos, and nonfiction literature. The nonfiction books could provide factual information about events that led up to the Famine as well as consequences of the Famine. The students could then read historical fiction to gain deeper insight into the human suffering and the challenges people faced during this horrific historical period. In response to what they read, they could take action to address social issues such as hunger on the domestic and international levels today and thereby display active citizenship. This article discusses adolescent literature books on the Irish Potato Famine and provides suggestions for ways students can respond to these books by taking action against hunger in today's world, thereby working to achieve social justice and taking steps towards developing the skills of domestic and international citizenship.

Citizenship Education

Citizenship education prepares students with the knowledge, attitudes, and skills to play an active role in the decisions that affect the political and social life of their community, nation, and world. Instead of being passive recipients of the privileges of citizenship, active citizens take an active role in the social and political life of their local community, nation, and world. Citizenship preparation has played a fundamental role in the American educational system. United States schools were originally designed to prepare students for citizenship (Carnegie Corporation of New York & The Center for Information and Research on Civic Engagement and Learning, 2003). Recent United States legislation in the No Child Left Behind Act of 2002, section 2342, requires schools to "to foster civic competence and responsibility" (United States Dept. of Education, 2001, para. 2). In addition, Wade (2007b) states that "schools are the sole institution available to society as a whole to train our youth in the theory and practice of democratic citizenship" (p. 13).

The skills and knowledge involved in active citizenship are not innate; they need to be developed (Altoff, 2008; Cogan, 1999; Farman & Hollins, 1981; Hartoonian, 1982). Due to globalization, leaders in government and education emphasize the importance of preparing students to be more aware of and to be better prepared to join the domestic and international workforce. This preparation begins in the schools. Domestic and international citizenship education seeks to prepare students to study issues, solve problems, and take action; likewise, "the mission of social studies education is informed and active citizenship" (Wade, 2007a, p. 3). Similarly, in their citizenship framework, Westheimer and Kahne (2004) suggest that there are three levels of citizenship. Personally-responsible citizenship, the first level, is where individuals serve as volunteers in the local community and follow society's laws. Participatory citizenship, the second level, is where an individual assumes a leadership role in a community organization or a community project. In justice-oriented citizenship, the highest level, individuals take action to address the root causes of injustice.

Understanding active citizenship can be enhanced in the social studies classroom when students engage in reading adolescent literature. The National Council for the Social Studies defines social studies as "the integrated study of the social sciences and humanities to promote civic competence" (National Council for the Social Studies, 1994, p. vii), and they believe that a fundamental aspect of understanding and taking action to address issues is the integration of multiple disciplines (National Council for the Social Studies, n.d., para. 3). Botelho and Rudman (2009) argue that:

> ...texts are sites for negotiation. The more we know, the more we are able to interrogate texts. The more we are exposed to multiple experiences, the more we are able to juxtapose what we have lived and read against those experiences. One text and one author cannot do it all; it is the reading of multiple texts and the juxtaposition of these texts against the lived experience and secondary sources that is central. Children's literature can redress injustice as much

as reflect it. It can inspire readers to reflect on their lived experience, re-imagine socially just worlds, provide new ways of exercising power, and offer tools for building cultural and historical understanding. (p. 266).

Social Studies and Literature

There are benefits to supplementing social studies content with adolescent literature. By reading different literature books on the same topic, students gain a more complex understanding of an issue or cultural group and develop insight into social justice issues (Botelho & Rudman, 2009, p. 265). Additionally, "children's literature puts a human face on sociopolitical circumstances" (Botelho & Rudman, 2009, p. 262). For example, literature such as *Time Travelers: How I Survived the Irish Famine: The Journal of Mary O'Flynn* (Wilson, 2001), *Journey to America: Fiona McGilray's Story: A Voyage From Ireland in 1849* (Pastore, 2002), and *Famine Secret at Drumshee* (Harrison, 2003) discuss the harsh consequences of social justice issues like hunger through the lens of different young adolescents.

In *Time Travelers: How I Survived the Irish Famine: The Journal of Mary O'Flynn,* Wilson (2001) creates a fictitious journal to describe the life of twelve-year old Mary O'Flynn and her family who live on a four-acre farm. The O'Flynn family includes Mary's dad, mother, grandmother, and five siblings. After the late blight fungus destroys the family's potato crop, the family suffers from hunger and the deaths of Mary's grandmother and baby sister, Annie. One day, Mary walks to a neighbor's home to discover that the mother, father, and five children have all died. When the landlord gives Mary's family the chance to sail to America in exchange for leaving their home, they accept. During the seven-week ocean passage, the passengers suffer from fever which breaks out throughout the ship, lack of water, death, and unrelenting stench. Mary is affected personally when her sister, Margaret, dies aboard the ship. When the ship arrives in New York, the customs doctor examines the passengers, sending the sick ones back to Ireland. Fortunately, Mary's family passes the health inspection, giving them the opportunity to establish a new life in the United States. The story is complemented by many photos of a young girl reenacting life during this time period.

Another historical novel on the Irish Potato Famine is *Journey to America: Fiona McGilray's Story: A Voyage From Ireland in 1849* by Pastore (2002). In this novel, readers meet young Fiona, her mom, dad, and four siblings. At the beginning of the novel, Fiona's family is better off than other Irish families because her father works as a field hand for a flax farm. While poorer families are starving, Fiona has a flower garden and her family eats apple tarts. When the flax farm does not make a profit, Lord Conray decides to stop planting flax, and Fiona's father loses his job. Because jobs are scarce, Fiona's father is only able to find work as a ditch digger. Hunger becomes a daily part of life, and Fiona's "stomach screamed for food" as their food supplies dwindle (Pastore, 2002, p. 19). In desperation, Fiona's family hires a bleeder to bleed a cup of blood from their cow so her mother can add blood to the cooking pot of water and cabbage. Fiona's sister, Maeve, dies of typhus which she contracts doing charity work at a Catholic church. In the midst of their hunger, Fiona's family learns that the English Prime Minister has had cornmeal shipped in from the United States; however, the food has been locked up in a warehouse. Acting out of desperation, Fiona and her brother break into the warehouse and steal some of the cornmeal. Again and again, Fiona's family and neighbors continue to steal grain, but one night, two police officers discover Fiona and her family stealing grain and chase them away. Fearful of the police, the family sends Fiona and her brother, Patrick, on a ship to America. In America, they have enough food, but they face harsh discrimination. Bullies call Fiona "an Irish pig" (Pastore, 2002, p. 105), and store shops post signs with NINA, or "no Irish need apply" (Pastore, 2002, p. 97).

Famine Secret at Drumshee (Harrison, 2003) is another historical novel that reveals the suffering of the Irish during this devastating period. This story, set in 1845, describes the life of eleven year-old Fiona and her family who tend a twenty-acre farm raising oats and potatoes. Their life becomes desperate when the blight destroys the potatoes. "The outside of the potato was good, round, and fat and healthy; but that was only the outside. The inside was a putrid, slimy mess" (Harrison, 2003, p. 5). Fiona loves school and wants to be a school teacher; however, her father does not know how long they can continue to pay the school fees for Fiona and her siblings. By November, 75% of the local school is empty because the parents cannot afford the school fees; by December, the school is closed. The situation in Ireland worsens. "Everywhere she [Fiona] went, she saw thin pale faces and skeletal bodies" (Harrison, 2003, p. 13). People become sickened from black and yellow fever. Fiona's mother dies at home from black fever. Their sickened father abandons the family so that the children will not catch the fever. After the potato crop fails again, Fiona and her siblings go to the dreaded workhouse where Fiona's sister, Dierde, spins wool into thread, makes lace, and escapes from a woman who tries to stab her in the hand with scissors. Fiona's brothers come down with yellow fever, and in the workhouse infirmary, "men and boys lay huddled on the floor, some with only straw to lie on. Many of them are writhing and groaning in pain. There was filth everywhere, and the smell of sickness filled the air." (Harrison, 2003, p. 61). During the winter at the workhouse, "the inmates shivered with cold and slowly starved from the lack of good nourishing food" (Harrison, 2003, p. 72). Fiona and her siblings escape the workhouse and return home, but they worry about paying a year's rent. Dierde makes lace and sells it, Fiona writes stories and sells them, and their brothers grow crops on the farm. They are temporarily spared when Fiona finds a gold necklace hidden in the clay wall of their storeroom and the family is able to pay rent for the following year.

Bartoletti (2001) observed that,

...one of the saddest things about the Famine years is that for each horrible story, there is always another more tragic and dreadful. Yet for each tragic story, you will also meet people who held on to hope, who committed heroic acts of self-sacrifice, and who fought to survive and to preserve their dignity (p. 3).

These adolescent literature books paint a grim picture of the suffering and misery that occurred during the Irish Potato Famine in the 1800's and help students gain insight into what it is like to suffer from starvation. Each of these novels examines the Irish Potato Famine from a youth's perspective and provides context for the event, helping students imagine what life was like during the Famine. By reading these books, students can make personal and emotional connections to the characters and events while imagining what it was like to suffer during this devastating period. According to Rosenblatt (1982), thought and feelings are legitimate elements of literary interpretation. There are both efferent (learning) and aesthetic (feelings) responses to text. An aesthetic response is "driven by personal feelings and attitudes that are stirred by the reader's transactions with the text" (Vacca & Vacca, 2008, p. 23). When students assume an aesthetic stance, they construct their own knowledge of the world they are reading about and vicariously experience what the characters are experiencing.

Teaching Social Studies and Literature

To explore the literature on the Irish Potato Famine, the teacher can ask students to form literature circles (Applegate, Quinn, & Applegate, 2006; Sandmann & Gruhler, 2007; Schlick Noe, & Johnson, 1999) and assign a different novel on the topic to each group to read. Literature circles are small, student-led discussion groups in which students gather together to discuss a book in-depth. The students share their responses to what they have read and discuss what they have learned about such elements as the characters, events, theme, author's craft, or personal connections to the literature (Applegate, Quinn, & Applegate, 2006; Sandmann & Gruhler, 2007; Schlick Noe & Johnson, 1999). Each literature circle group can then share what they learned from the novel on the Irish Potato Famine with the rest of the class and thus the entire class can gain different perspectives on the topic.

Teachers can then have students discuss the social issues related to hunger during this historical period and make text-to-world (Harvey & Goudvis, 2007) comparisons to countries around the world today where people are suffering from the devastating effects of hunger. For example, hunger is prevalent today in the Republic of the Congo, Haiti, Bangladesh, Ethiopia, Somalia, Pakistan, and Indonesia as well as a number of other countries. In response to their discussions of the literature and comparisons to conditions today, students can engage in active citizenship and promote social justice by engaging in service learning projects. Service learning combines classroom instruction with the needs of a service agency (Alliance for

Service-Learning in Education Reform, 1995). While service learning gives students the opportunity to practice thoughtful, active, civic participation, it also encourages students to construct knowledge by studying a socially relevant issue in a personal way and to develop their problem solving skills (*RMC Research Corporation, 2005*). According to the Alliance for Service Learning in Education Reform (1995), service learning should provide "concrete opportunities for youth to learn new skills, to think critically, and to test new roles in an environment that encourages risk-taking and rewards competence" (p. 5). Service learning should also involve meaningful service to the community and encourage the service learner to reflect on the experience.

Student engagement in planning is an important part of service learning (RMC Research Corporation, 2005). After reading and discussing the literature on the Irish Potato Famine and making connections to world hunger today, teachers can lead students in planning a service learning project on the issue of hunger on the local level or the international level. For example, on the domestic level, the class could raise money and provide vegetable plants and gardening supplies for local families in need. From the plants, families could obtain needed food and sell leftover vegetables at a farmer's market. On the international level, the class could create a fundraiser to support Heifer International (n.d.). This organization provides impoverished individuals around the world with a hen or a goat. The eggs or milk produced by these animals can provide food as well as an income source for the family, and the family then repays the organization by providing one of the hen's or goat's offspring to another family.

Reflection is also an important part of service learning as it encourages students to analyze and evaluate their service learning experiences and consider ways to design even more effective activities in the future (Learn and Serve America's National Service-Learning Clearinghouse, 2010; RMC Research Corporation, 2005). Teachers can have students write their reflections in journals to think more deeply about what they are experiencing and to focus on important social justice issues. At the end of the project, students can write a short essay summarizing what they learned from doing the project and describing ways they might improve it. The teacher could then use data from the summative essays to improve the project in future years.

To celebrate the accomplishments of the class, the students could submit an article or a series of articles to the school newspaper describing what they learned from their readings, discussions, and service learning experiences. Alternatively, they could invite a reporter from their town's local newspaper to write an article that discusses the class' efforts and achievements in addressing social justice.

Conclusion

Well-written adolescent literature on a social topic, such as starvation during the Irish Potato Famine, touches the heart and develops empathy for those who suffer injustices. This literature inspires students to take action to right wrongs and engage in civic activities that improve the lives of individuals less fortunate than themselves.

When engaging students in social action activities, teachers may face challenges such as reluctant students, resistant parents, or unsupportive administrators. To overcome these challenges, teachers must provide students, parents, and administrators with a detailed explanation of the benefits of the service learning project for student learning as well as the ultimate positive social outcomes for the community. Teachers must also work with their students to carefully plan and organize the service learning project so that it is a meaningful experience for them.

To guide the process effectively, it is important that teachers engage students in meaningful discussion of the literature they read to develop a deeper understanding of social issues. Furthermore, it is important that teachers guide students to design meaningful response activities that lead towards social action. Engaging in service learning activities related to a social issue students have read about and discussed, helps them to develop an understanding of what it means to be a good citizen. Furthermore, reflecting on service learning activities develops students' analytical and critical thinking and helps them develop deeper understanding of the importance of working to achieve social justice. Ultimately, social studies teachers should strive to develop more responsible citizens and to keep in mind that the "...primary purpose of social studies is to help young people develop the ability to make informed and reasoned decisions for the public good as citizens of a culturally diverse, democratic society in an interdependent world" (National Council for the Social Studies, 1994, p. vii).

References

Alliance for Service-Learning in Education Reform. (1995). *Standards of quality for school-based and community-based service-learning.* Alexandria, VA: Alliance for Service Learning in Education Reform/ Close Up Foundation.

Altoff, P. (2008). Citizenship must not be the last of the three "C's." *Social Education, 72*(7), 379.

Applegate, M., Quinn, K., & Applegate, A. J. (2006). Profiles in comprehension. *The Reading Teacher, 60*(1), 48–57.

Bartoletti, S. C. (2001). *Black potatoes: The story of the Great Irish Famine, 1845-1850.* Boston, MA: Houghton Mifflin Company.

Botelho, M. J., & Rudman, M. K. (2009). *Critical multicultural analysis of children's literature:Mirrors, windows, and doors.* New York, NY: Routledge/Taylor and Francis Group.

Carnegie Corporation of New York & The Center for Information and Research on Civic Learning and Engagement. (2003). *The civic mission of schools*. New York, NY: The Center for Information & Research on Civic Learning and Engagement and Carnegie Corporation of New York.

Cogan, J. J. (1999). Civic education in the United States: A brief history. *International Journal of Social Education, 14*(1), 52-64.

Farman, G., & Hollins, E. (1981). Citizenship and the infusion game. *Phi Delta Kappan, 62*(7), 510-512.

Harrison, C. (2003). *Famine secret at Drumshee*. Dublin, Ireland: Wolfhound Press.

Hartoonian, H. M. (1982). The courage to be literate and free. *The Social Studies, 73*(1), 37-40.

Harvey, S., & Goudvis, A. (2007). *Strategies that work: Teaching comprehension for understanding and engagement*. Portland, ME: Stenhouse.

Heifer International. (n.d.) Our work. Retrieved from http://www.heifer.org/site/c.edJRKQNiFiG/b.201470/

Learn and Serve America's National Service-Learning Clearinghouse. (2010). Retrieved from http:/www.servicelearning.org.

National Council for the Social Studies (n.d.) About National Council for the Social Studies. Retrieved from http://www.socialstudies.org/about

National Council for the Social Studies. (1994). *Expectations of excellence: Curriculum standards for social studies. (National Council for the Social Studies Bulletin 89)*. Washington, DC: National Council for the Social Studies.

O'Neil, J. R. (2009). *The Irish Potato Famine*. Edina, MN: ABDO Publishing Company. Partnership for the 21st Century Skills (2004a). *Overview core subjects and 21st century themes*. Retrieved from http://www.21stcenturyskills.org

Partnership for the 21st Century Skills (2004b). *Overview global awareness*. http://www.p21.org/index.php?option=com_content&task=view&id=256&Itemid=120

Pastore, C. (2002). *Journey to America: Fiona McGilray's story: A voyage from Ireland in 1849*. New York, NY: Berkley Jam Books.

RMC Research Corporation. (2005). *Curriculum development for K-12 service-learning*. Santa Cruz, CA: National Service-Learning Clearinghouse. Retrieved from http://www.servicelearning.org/instant_info/fact_sheets/k-12_facts/curriculum/

Rosenblatt, L. M. (1982). The literary transaction: Evocation and response. *Theory into Practice, 21*, 268-277.

Sandmann, A., & Gruhler, D. (2007). Reading is thinking: Connecting readers to text through literature circles. *International Journal of Learning, 13*(10), 105-113.

Schlick Noe, K. L., & Johnson, N. L. (1999). *Getting started with literature circles.* Norwood, MA: Christopher-Gordon.

United States Department of Education (2001). *Public law print of PL 107-110, the No Child Left Behind Act of 2001.* Retrieved from http://www.ed.gov/policy/elsec/leg/esea02/index.html

Vacca, R. T., & Vacca, J. A. L. (2008). *Content area reading* (9th ed.). Boston, MA: Allyn & Bacon.

Wade, R. C. (2007a). Introduction. In Rahmina C. Wade (Ed.), *Community action rooted in history: The CiviConnections model of service-learning.* (pp. 3-4). Silver Spring, MD: National Council for the Social Studies.

Wade, R. C. (2007b) Community service learning for democratic citizenship. In Rahmina C. Wade (Ed.), *Community action rooted in history: The CiviConnections model of service-learning.* (pp. 12-19). Silver Spring, MD: National Council for the Social Studies.

Westheimer, J., & Kahne, J. (2004). What kind of citizen? The politics of educating for democracy. *American Educational Research Journal, 41*(2), 237-269.

Wilson, L. (2001). *Time travelers: How I survived the Irish Famine: The journal of Mary O'Flynn.* New York, NY: Harper Collins Publishers.

Chapter 15

Service-Learning and Preparation for the Global Workplace

Preparing College Students for the Global Workplace

A Curriculum of Service Learning Projects, Intercultural Experiences, and Communication-Intensive Courses

Dr. Doreen Geddes

Introduction

The 21st Century workplace offers new challenges to college graduates and to those of us who educate them. The landscape of the business world is rapidly changing. New technologies become obsolete ever so quickly; the dynamics of the marketplace grow increasingly more complex and global; while the consumer, producer, worker, and manager become progressively more culturally diverse. Consequently, the college graduate entering this new world of work must possess considerable job savvy and experience. The subject of this paper is creating educational experiences for college students so they can more easily penetrate and successfully navigate the workplace of the 21st Century. Learning through experience or "experiential education" is at the core of students' preparation. Three forms of experiential education will be discussed: Service Learning projects, Intercultural Experiences, and Communication-Intensive courses.

The National Society for Experiential Education Foundation's Document Committee includes cooperative education, internships, and service learning as some of the learning activities that are considered experiential education. They note that, based on the educational philosophy of John Dewey, experiential education connects experience and knowledge through the process of dialogue or reflection. The cycle of experience and reflection forms the foundation of experiential education (NSEE, 1997). The Document Committee also notes that educational psychologists acknowledge the importance of experiential education for long term memory or as stated in their document "the more active our learning, the more we retain" (p. 7). The Committee points out:

> "In a highly competitive global market, our society can no longer afford to cultivate minds untested by and indifferent to concrete practical problems. [In] Experiential Education, we find a proven approach moving both our educational system and our society into a prosperous 21st century" (p. 7).

The importance of experiential education is echoed in an article by Gardner & Tyson (1994), in the *Journal of Cooperative Education*. They note that it is a challenge for both educators and employers to help students make the transition from school to workplace. They argue that experiential learning programs can facilitate this process. Gardner and Tyson maintain that "Without these types of experiences, socialization in the workplace is difficult. It takes longer to learn work tasks, to integrate into social groups and work teams, and longer to understand the informal decision networks throughout the organization" (p. 12). By gaining work experience, learning about the work environment, and developing a successful work ethic, students are better prepared to enter their professions.

Yet another article entitled "Experiential Education in the Undergraduate Curriculum," (Katula & Threnhauser, 1999), discusses the importance of "experiential education" programs for college students. The authors note that the "expanded classroom" is a significant trend in higher education taking the form of co-ops, internships, study abroad, and service learning.

> What is described above as experiential learning, could also fit Boyer's description of the "New American College." What I'm describing might be called the "New American College," an institution that celebrates teaching and selectively supports research, while also taking special pride in its capacity to connect thought to action, theory to practice. . .Undergraduates at the college would participate in field projects, relating ideas to real life. Classrooms and laboratories would be extended to include clinics, youth centers, schools and government offices. . .[A] new model of excellence in higher education would emerge, one that would enrich the campus, renew communities, and give new dignity and status to the scholarship of service. (Boyer, 1994, p. A48)

Service Learning

One form of experiential education is service learning which Bringle & Hatcher (1996, p. 2) define as a "...credit-bearing educational experience in which students participate in an organized service activity that meets identified community needs and reflect on the service activity in such a way as to gain further understanding of course context, a broader appreciation of the discipline, and an enhanced sense of civic responsibility."

Numerous college educators and researchers have discussed the benefits of service learning. Hunter & Brisbin (2000) note proponents of service learning claim that it helps students connect theory and practice, involves students in their communities, teaches students interpersonal and social skills, helps students develop critical thinking ability, and provides a lesson in citizenship. Communication scholars have written about the benefits of incorporating service learning in the communication curriculum (Artz, 2001; Braun, 2001; Gibson, Kostecki, & Lucas, 2001; Keyton, 2001; O'Hara, 2001). The Spring 2001 issue of The Southern Communication Journal is devoted to service learning.

Effectiveness of Service Learning

Beckman (1997) cites quantitative research that supports the effectiveness of service learning. For instance, (Markus, Howard, & King, 1993) measured the effect of a service component in political science classes at the University of Michigan. They report that those students who engaged in the service component, compared to students who just attended the class lecture, were significantly more likely to report that they learned to apply course material and that their grades were significantly higher statistically.

Hunter & Brisbin (2000, p. 623) evaluated the effects of service learning by conducting a pre test/post test study of students at three West Virginia institutions of higher learning. They found students generally felt positive about their service experience, often subsequently participated in other service, and said the service made the class more relevant. When service learning was discussed in class, "92% of students ranked the service experience as the most important part of the course, and 90% ranked the service experience as the most important part of their overall university education" (p. 624).

Carpenter & Jacobs (1994, p.97) describe the success of the Southern University System in Louisiana where service learning has been a requirement for students to graduate since 1990. Students have worked with over eighty service agencies playing a significant role in the lives of numerous adults and at-risk youth. Some students have subsequently taken jobs with the service agencies, while many others have continued to volunteer. Additionally, the students' journal writing and oral reflection on their service learning reinforced their requirement of participation in the university's writing-across-the-curriculum program.

Similarly, Tucker, McCarthy, Hoxmeier, & Lenk (1998) found students' communication skills were improved through a communication across the curriculum program which included community service learning projects.

Collins (1996) describes a program of service learning for MBA students enrolled in business ethics classes at the University of Wisconsin-Madison where students have been volunteering in homeless shelters and low-income communities developing projects (eg. starting a grocery co-op, credit union, day-care program, job resource center, and transportation service.) In addition, students developed service networks linking the low-income communities with student organizations, other university professors, and United Way volunteers. Collins reports students became more sensitive to issues of poverty, realized they can create change, applied course concepts, and brought positive visibility to the business school.

Morton & Troppe (1996, p.22) report findings from their three-year, national project on service learning supported by the Ford Foundation. They suggest that based on their research, ". . . service learning is an effective pedagogy for teaching both course content (academic concepts) and values." Similarly, Easterling & Rudell (1997) incorporated service learning into marketing courses in the form of internship assignments, consultancies, or participant/observer volunteer. They found students developed leadership and problem-solving skills, connected theory to practice, and built citizenship awareness.

While some faculty may say that service learning does not apply to their discipline, Zlotkowski (1996), founder/director of the Service Learning Project at Bentley College and senior associate at the American Association of Higher Education (AAHE), would disagree with them. His response to faculty who say that service learning is not relevant to their discipline is ". . . such alleged lack of relevance almost always lies not so much in the disciplinary area itself as in the way a given individual frames that area" (p. 25). Therefore, it is not surprising that Steven Madden (2000), editor of *Service Learning Across the Curriculum: Case Applications in Higher Education,* includes chapters from faculty practitioners of service learning at Clemson University in a variety of disciplines. In his book faculty in psychology; sociology; horticulture; landscape architecture; public health; parks, recreation & tourism management; marketing; organizational communication; business writing; science; education; and technical writing describe their use of service learning in their courses.

Service Learning Reflection

As mentioned earlier, reflection or dialogue grounds experiential education. Consequently, reflection is a key part of service learning. Anderson (1995) describes a program where students take 30 minutes per day to discuss and reflect on their service.

Likewise, Ogden & Claus (1997) contend reflection helps students understand material, it promotes responsibility, and it empowers them. Easterling & Rudell (1997) discuss the importance of student reflection to connect service to coursework and to the future of their communities. Consequently, service learning along with reflection can be a powerful method to help prepare students for their future professions.

International Exposure

Another form of experiential learning that can contribute to students' transition into the workplace is exposure to international cultures and experiences. Katula & Threnhauser (1999) mention study abroad as an example of the "expanded classroom" in their discussion of the growing trend of experiential education in higher education. Certainly, as the workplace becomes more global, college graduates need to develop an awareness and sensitivity to various cultures, politics, and economics around the world. In many instances, U.S college students are too insulated to be fully aware of the affairs in other parts of the world. A report by the American Council on Education (1995, p.1), argues that higher education is not preparing students to "function effectively in a global environment" and "calls for major changes in how colleges and universities educate their students about the rest of the world."

Similarly, Patterson (2000) laments the fact that American students lack knowledge and concern for international issues. She cites research that indicates college-aged Americans consistently rate last in their knowledge of global events among young adults in industrialized countries. She notes that while a number of college students "...are uninterested and uninvolved in domestic and international politics, the corporate world is increasingly demanding that college graduates have international experiences, cross-cultural training, and exposure to global economic and political issues" (p. 817).

Praetzel (1999) is another advocate of international exposure for college students. He notes the lack of internationalization in the undergraduate business curriculum. Most initiatives, he says, have focused on study of a foreign language. He calls for a major rethinking of how to incorporate an international perspective for students in curricular and extracurricular activities. His list of recommendations, in addition to intercultural activities on campus, includes study abroad, student exchanges, and international service learning as ways to "build the foundation for a comprehensive internationalized learning experience" (p.137).

Apparently, the public also believes in the importance of global competence for college students. A national telephone survey of 1,006 people conducted by the American Council on Education (A.C.E.) "found that more than 70 percent of those polled think that students should have an international experience as part of their college education and that students should be required to study a foreign language" (The Chronicle of Higher Education, November 17, 2000, p.A74). An additional study conducted by

A.C.E. and supported by the Ford Foundation showed that foreign language study has dropped from a high of 16 percent in the 1960's to an average of about 8 percent currently. Additionally, they report that only a small minority of students are "globally competent" (*The Chronicle of Higher Education*, November 17, 2000, p. A74).

Some schools are making sure that their students are globally literate. "When freshmen arrive at Tufts University, a world atlas is included in the orientation packets... a not-so-subtle nudge to think about studying beyond the Medford, Mass., campus" (*The Chronicle of Higher Education*, November 22, 2002, p. 63). Its emphasis on global education has brought national recognition to the university. The Chronicle article goes on to quote Todd M. Davis, Director of the Higher Education Resource Group at the Institute of International Education. "Tufts has a strong commitment to educating global citizens. Globalization is infused though all the activities of the institution – not just the responsibility of the study-abroad office or the international student office" (p. 63).

Goucher, an independent college of arts and sciences in Baltimore, is another example of a college committed to international experiences for its students. In the 1970's Goucher "faculty voted to require all students to complete at least three credits in an off-campus experience in order to graduate. Students can fulfil this requirement in several ways, such as by student teaching, study abroad, and internships" (Duggan & Cohen, 1992, p. 84). By working with international companies with offices in Baltimore, Goshen has created a program where students can intern abroad. Duggan and Cohen report that employers consider an international internship as a sign that an applicant has some knowledge of working in another culture (p. 86). As a result of Goucher's efforts, students have interned all over the world and alumni work in 24 countries across the globe.

Yet another college intent on exposing their students to an international experience is Goshen College. Wilbur Birky, Director of the International Education Program at Goshen, describes their program (*The Chronicle of Education*, June 7, 2002).

> Goshen College sends students to countries likely to challenge North American perceptions about issues of power, wealth, and development—countries like China, Cuba, and Ethiopia... Students spend half their semester abroad living with host families in an urban setting where they not only study language, but hear national lectures on the problems and special opportunities of the host culture in a global setting. In the second half of the semester, students move to smaller towns or rural areas, where they live with a second host family and work in service-related positions supervised by host nationals... alumni often tell us that while the immersion experience was profound in some way at the time, it was not until years later that they understood their experiences in global and economic terms (p. 4).

An article in *The Chronicle of Higher Education* notes that while business schools have led the trend of globalizing their graduate programs, engineering schools are not far behind. Old Dominion University in Virginia has teamed with eight engineering school in Europe to set up a master's degree in global engineering (*The Chronicle of Higher Education*, October 12, 2001, p. 50).

International Service Learning

One way of maximizing students' exposure to the outside world is to fuse service learning with an international experience. Chisholm (1997) suggests there is a growing demand for employees who are effective communicators in intercultural and international situations. She describes ways students can participate in international service learning, including ways to finance it. She cites testimony from faculty and students who describe how the experience changed them and helped them become global citizens. Similarly, Crabtree (1998) describes the effectiveness of two programs in El Salvador and Nicaragua. She says the experience of adapting to another culture along with the service learning component were successful in enhancing the communication skills of participating students.

One U. S. program that unites service learning with international travel is the International Partnership for Service Learning (IPS-L). "IPS-L is a not-for-profit organization which serves educational and service organizations around the world by fostering programs that link community service and academic study. IPS-L runs community-based experiential programs... hosted by higher educational institutions in these countries" (Monard-Weissman, 2003 p. 165). IPS-L has undergraduate programs in 14 countries such as Ecuador, India, Russia, Thailand, and more (http://www.ipsl.org/).

Monard-Weissman (2003) assessed the effects of the international service learning experience from reflections of IPS-L students working in an IPS-L summer study program in Ecuador. She concludes from her findings that, "The IPS-L experience helped students acquire a deeper understanding of their world and reassure their commitment to service. The experience became an awakening to the needs that exist in various parts of the world, and through reflection, they examined their roles as citizens in a diverse and global world" (p. 170). Clearly, exposure to other cultures and international experiences can add to a student's repertoire of abilities for the global marketplace.

Importance of Communication Competence

It is widely accepted that the ability to communicate effectively is critical for professional success. Tucker & McCarthy (2001) cite numerous sources that reinforce the importance of communication proficiency for effective job performance, career advancement, and organizational success. They also note a number of studies that indicate communication skills are pivotal for managerial success and that oral communication competence is especially important in job interviews.

Despite the importance of communication competency, many employees and college graduates entering the workforce lack effective communication skills. Additionally, some types of organizations and positions require greater proficiency in oral skills, while others rely on written ability (Roebuck, Sightler, & Brush, 1995). Also, Scudder & Guinan (1989) report that superiors' perceptions of subordinates' performance is linked to their perceptions of subordinates' communication competence. Clearly, communication competence affects employees' success in a variety of ways. It is not surprising, then, that a study of the 32 top-ranked MBA programs in the U.S. showed that communication education is an important aspect of their programs (Knight, 1999). Consequently, career success for MBA's is often directly related to the ability to communicate effectively.

Communication Across the Curriculum

One way to assist students with their communication proficiency is through a program called Communication Across the Curriculum (CAC). Tucker, McCarthy, Hoxmeier, & Lenk (1998) argue that students' communication skills can be enhanced through (CAC) programs where opportunities to communicate are repeatedly provided for students in various classes and projects. These communication-intensive courses provide opportunities for students to communicate as they might in their professional lives. According to the Clemson University CAC website (http://www.clemson.edu/programs/CAC/index.htm), Communication Across the Curriculum "is a teaching method that encourages students to become not only better writers and better speakers but also better thinkers and problem-solvers. CAC integrates oral, written, visual and electronic communication in all disciplines." CAC is included in courses across a variety of disciplines at Clemson University ranging from architecture, biology, engineering, horticulture, psychology, sociology, math and more.

While CAC programs typically include both written and oral communication, some may not incorporate visual and electronic communication as well. Also, various institutions of higher learning have different names for their programs. For instance, some may have a Writing Across the Curriculum (WAC) as well as a Speaking Across the Curriculum (SAC) or Oral Communication Across the Curriculum (OCXC). Still others may refer to their programs as Writing and Speaking Across the Curriculum. For continuity in this article, I will use CAC to refer to programs that strive to improve students' ability to write and speak.

Although the Writing Across the Curriculum (WAC) initiative and writing labs have a long history at many institutions of higher learning, CAC is a relative newcomer and less prevalent at colleges and universities. While effective writing skills are important for success in the workplace, effective oral communication skills are equally important for college graduates to possess. For instance, in their survey of 354 managers, Maes, Weldy, &

Icenogle (1997) report managers rated oral communication, problem solving, and self-motivation as the top three competencies needed by potential employees.

Among existing CAC programs in the U.S., there are vast differences in services, staff, resources, and facilities available. Some institutions have staff to offer workshops and assistance for faculty, peer tutors to assist students, and a facility with electronic or audio visual equipment and written resources for students. Other CAC programs may be limited to a resource person and website with resources listed. Also, some CAC programs may focus on helping students develop proficiency in public speaking alone, while others additionally offer resources for students to develop other communication skills such as interpersonal, listening, group discussion, and task groups.

Appendix A lists U.S. colleges and universities with CAC program websites. While the list is not exhaustive, it presents an overview of the services, facilities, and resources available at CAC programs. Additionally, numerous articles and scholarly papers have been written on CAC. Appendix B presents a sampling of papers related to Communication Across the Curriculum.

Numerous scholars report the effectiveness of CAC or communication-intensive courses for improving students' communication skills. While CAC, service learning, and international exposure taken separately are helpful to prepare students for the workforce, a program that includes all three would multiply those benefits. One university program that did is described in the final section of this paper.

Clemson University in South Africa (CUSA)

In July, 2001, Clemson University (CU), a land grant school in Upstate South Carolina, USA, and The University of Wittwatersrand (Wits) in Johannesburg, collaborated on projects in the South African bush. The primary project was to develop and install a clean water system for a South African village and its health clinic. At that time, the village got water, when it was available, from a bore hole. The dirty water was making many villagers sick. Engineering students and faculty at CU and Wits collaborated on developing and installing the clean water systems. Additionally, the community's health clinic had few medical supplies and needed everything from band aids to aspirin. Another concern was the lack of adequate educational resources. The local schools needed basic instructional material, had no recreational or sports equipment and no playground. Consequently, another project revolved around the needs of the schools and health clinic. Communication students, faculty, and staff from CU along with Architecture students and faculty from Wits planned and built two playgrounds at different school locations. All of the students from Wits and CU solicited building materials, educational supplies, sports equipment, and medical provisions or would seek financial contributions to purchase these items. Ultimately, the project included international service learning, communication-intensive coursework and experiences. It also involved collaboration among students and faculty from three disciplines with another university in a different country.

The CU portion of the project was divided into three phases: pre-trip, trip, and post-trip. A Clemson University professor in engineering, a professor in communication, and the director of the international office worked with CU students to plan and carry out the projects and the trip. In the pre-trip phase, the communication and engineering student participants enrolled in a special topics class team taught by the two faculty members and the international director.

The purpose of the class, which met one night a week, was to prepare students for the trip, develop students' group and intercultural communication skills, and plan the respective projects. To prepare for the trip students heard from practitioners about health precautions. Faculty who had participated in projects in the African bush spoke to them about the culture and environment. To learn about South African culture, history, politics, language, geography, and more, students researched and made power point presentations to the rest of the class. They read and discussed books by classic apartheid authors and also viewed a documentary about one apartheid hero.

Communication instruction and activities pervaded the course. Students learned about being an effective group member and conducting efficient meetings. Additionally, in order to help group members bond and work together effectively, the entire group participated in a groups' initiative course sponsored by the Clemson University Outdoor Laboratory. Also, everyone went on an overnight camping trip in a wilderness area to simulate working together in a Spartan environment.

Throughout the semester students worked in various groups. Each student worked either with the water project or the playground project group. Students formed additional groups to plan trip details, develop public relations materials, create a fundraising strategy, construct a trip web site, promote the trip, solicit donations of supplies and funds, and communicate with their counterparts at Wits. Consequently students practiced communications skills ranging from public speaking, small group communication, intercultural communication, public relations, and persuasion. A few days before our departure students gathered to finalize trip details and to pack the boxes upon boxes of medical and educational materials they collected.

During the trip CU students were enrolled in a small group communication course. In addition to successfully working with the respective groups, they were required to keep a journal for reflecting on their cultural, group, and project experiences. Additionally, the entire group was scheduled to meet daily to discuss their experiences and sort out any problems that occurred. Once the group arrived in Johannesburg, South Africa, they met their counterparts from Wits. Groups from both universities finalized project details and travelled north to the bush, an unfamiliar world for Wits and CU students alike. Here students experienced villages with no running water, no electricity, no sewage treatment systems, and dirt roads. While the bush area came under the new South African legal system, many villages maintained their tribal chiefs and councils. Consequently, one of the first items of business in the village was meeting with the tribal leaders for their input and blessing of the projects. During the time in the bush, either working on the water system or playgrounds, students experienced and learned about tribal rituals and culture. Using local translators students communicated with the villagers and worked along side them on the playground and water projects. At the end of the week when the children now had playgrounds, the schools had educational and recreational resources, the health clinic had medical supplies, and the village had clean water, the local women prepared a traditional feast for villagers and guests to celebrate the accomplishments we had made together. The celebrations included local tribal dancing, games, music, presentations, and much fanfare.

Despite the lack of physical comforts, the students were sorry to leave the village. Student journals and discussions indicated they were overwhelming moved that the villagers were so poor yet seemed so friendly and happy. They watched out for one another and each other's children. The villagers had a powerful sense of community like nothing the students had ever seen. Children and adults alike in the village seemed to have a strong sense of self and connection. The CU students commented that the Western culture's focus on material items brings us little happiness. Some of the students seemed to envy the lives of the people they had previously pitied.

Upon return to the U.S. and the beginning of a new semester, some of the students took the post-trip course. Here they created a report including pictures to send to the various donors and sponsors of the trip. They also created a power point presentation which one student presented to the major funding organization. The power point included numerous pictures of the students working with the villagers on the projects and would be used for raising funds for future similar trips. Students agreed the trip changed the way they viewed the world. They gained appreciation for a simpler and slower life without the conveniences of Western society. They learned about working with diverse people in a setting that was not textbook perfect. They understood the importance of the ability to improvise and to be flexible. And they practiced communicating in a variety of contexts. Without exception, students said they would welcome the opportunity to do a similar venture in the future. While time intensive, the benefits of a project that combines service learning, international exposure, and communication-intensive courses and experiences offers college students a way to help prepare them for the global workplace.

References

American Council on Education report. (1995). *Educating Americans for a World in Flux: Ten Ground Rules for Internationalizing Higher Education. Washington*, D.C.: American Council on Education.

Anderson, J. D. (1995). Students' reflections on community service learning. *Equity & Excellence in Education*, v28, 38.

Artz, L. (2001). Critical ethnography for communication studies: Dialogue and social justice in service learning. *The Southern Communication Journal*, 66, 239.

Beckman, M. (1997). Learning in action: Courses that complement community service. *College Teaching*, 45, 72-76.

Birky, W. (2002, June 7). Study-Abroad programs may have a lasting impact on students' lives. *The Chronicle of Higher Education*, p. 4.

Boyer, E. (1994, March 9). Creating the new American college. *The Chronicle of Higher Education*, v40, n27, p. A48.

Braun, M. J. (2001). Using self-directed teams to integrate service learning into an organizational communication course. *The Southern Communication Journal*, 66, 226.

Bringle, R. G. & Hatcher, J. A. (1996). Implementing service learning in higher education. *Journal of Higher Education*, v67, n2, 221-240.

Bringle, R. G. & Hatcher, J. A. (2000). Institutionalization of service learning in higher education. *Journal of Higher Education*, v71, i3, 273.

Carpenter, B. W. & Jacobs, J. S. (1994). Service learning: A new approach in higher education. *Education*, v115, n1, 97.

Chisholm, L. A. (1997). International service learning for a world of difference. *The Black Collegian*, v27, n2, 149-152.

Collins, D. (1996). Serving the homeless and low-income communities through business & society/ business ethics class projects: The University of Wisconsin-Madison plan. *Journal of Business Ethics*, 15, 67-85.

Crabtree, R. D. (1998). Mutual empowerment in cross-cultural participatory development and service learning: Lessons in communication and social justice from projects in El Salvador and Nicaragua. *Journal of Applied Communication Research*, 26, 182.

Duggan, E. P. & Schlossberg, H. M. (1992). Routes to working overseas. *Journal of Career Planning & Employment*, v LIII, n1, 72-81.

Easterling, D. & Rudell, F. (1997). Rationale, benefits, and methods of service learning in marketing education. *Journal of Education for Business*, v73, n1, 58-61.

Gardner, P. D. & Tyson, V. K. (1994). Diversity, work and education: A case for experiential learning during times of change. *Journal of Cooperative Education*, v29, n2, 11-26.

Gibson, M. K., Kostecki, E. M. & Lucas, M. K. (2001). Instituting principles of best practice for service learning in the communication curriculum. *The Southern Communication Journal*, 66, 187.

Hunter, S. & Brisbin, R. A. (2000). The impact of service learning on democratic and civic values. *PS: Political Science & Politics*, v33, i3, 623.

Katula, R. A. & Threnhauser, E. (1999). Experiential education in the undergraduate curriculum. Communication Education, v48, i3, 238.

Keyton, J. (2001). Integrating service learning in the research methods course. *The Southern Communication Journal*, 66, 201.

Knight, M. (1999). Management communication in US MBA Programs: The state of the art. *Business Communication Quarterly*, v62, i4, 9.

Madden, S. J. (2000). *Service learning across the curriculum: Case applications in higher education.* New York: University Press of America.

Maes, J. D., Weldy, T. G. & Icenogle, M. L. (1997). A managerial perspective: Oral communication competency is most important for business students in the workplace. *Journal of Business Communication*, 34, 67-80.

Marcus, G. B., Howard, J. P. & King, D. C. (1993). Integrating community service & classroom instruction enhances learning: Results from an experiment. *Education Evaluation & Policy Analysis*, v15, n4, 410-419.

Monard-Weissman, K. (2003). Fostering a sense of justice through international service learning. *Academic Exchange Quarterly*, v7, i2, 164-170.

Morton, K. & Troppe, M. (1996). From the margin to the mainstream: Campus Compact's project on integrating service with academic study. *Journal of Business Ethics*, v15, n1, 21-33.

NSEE Foundations Document Committee. (1997). Foundations of experiential education [Electronic version]. *National Society for Experiential Education.*

Ogden, C. & Claus, J. (1997). Reflection as a natural element of service: Service learning for youth empowerment. *Equity & Excellence in Education*, 30, 72-81.

O'Hara, L. S. (2001). Service learning: Students' transformative journey from communication student to civic-minded professional. *The Southern Communication Journal*, 66, 251.

Patterson, A. (2000). It's a small world: Incorporating service learning into international relations courses. *PS: Political Science & Politics*, v33, p817.

Praetzel, G. D. (1999). Pedagogical recommendations for internationalizing the undergraduate business curriculum. *International Advances in Economic Research*, v5, i1, 137.

Roebuck, D. B., Sightler, K. W. & Brush, C. C. (1995). Organizational size, company type, and position effects on the perceived importance of oral and written communication skills. *Journal of Managerial Issues*, v7, 99-116.

Scudder, J. N. & Guinan, P. J. (1989). Communication competencies as discriminators of superiors' ratings of employee performance. *The Journal of Business Communication*, v26, n3, 217-230.

The Chronicle of Higher Education. (2000, November 17). More students study abroad, but their stays are shorter. American Council on Education. p. A74.

The Chronicle of Higher Education. (2000, November 17). Snapshot of report on study-abroad programs. p. A74.

The Chronicle of Higher Education. (2001, October 12). p. 50.

The Chronicle of Higher Education. (2002, November 22). Keeping the study in study abroad. American Council on Education, p63.

Tucker, M. L., McCarthy A. M., Hoxmeier J. A. & Lenk M. M. (1998). Community service learning increases communication skills across the business curriculum. *Business Communication Quarterly*, v61, 88-100.

Tucker, M. L. & McCarthy, A. M. (2001). Presentation self efficacy: Increasing communication skills through service learning. *Journal of Managerial Issues*, v13, i2, 227.

Zlotkowski, E. (1996). Linking service-learning and the academy. *Change*, 28, 20-28.

Appendix A

Sample of U.S. Colleges and Universities with Communication Across the Curriculum Web Sites
A.   Clemson University, Clemson, South Carolina, 29634 (http://www.clemson.edu/programs/CAC/index.htm)
B.   Hamline University, St. Paul, Minnesota (http://www.hamline.edu/depts/commdept/oralcm.html.)
C.   Mary Washington College, Fredericksburg, VA 22401 (http://www.mwc.edu/spkc/resources/faculty/assignments.htm)
D.   Mount Holyoke College, South Hadley, MA 01075 (http://www.mtholyoke.edu/acad/programs/wcl/saw/)
E.   North Carolina State University, Raleigh, NC 27695 (http://www2.chass.ncsu.edu/CWSP)
F.   Ohio Wesleyan University (http://www.csus.edu/indiv/s/stonerm/SpeakingAcrossCurriculumHomePag e.htm)
G.   Radford University, Radford, Virginia (http://www.radford.edu/)

H. Randolph-Macon College, Ashland, Virginia, 23005
    (http://www.rmc.edu/directory/offices/hac/SAC/SAC.asp)
I. S.E. Missouri State Univ, Cape Girardeau, MO, 63701
    (http://ustudies.semo.edu/oralcom/)
J. Southern Illinois University, Carbondale, Illinois
    (http://www.siu.edu/departments/cac/guideone.htm)

Appendix B

A Sampling of Articles and Papers on Communication Across the Curriculum

Cronin, M. & Glenn, P. (1991). Oral communication across the curriculum
    in higher education: The state of the art. *Communication Education*
    40, 356-367.
Dannels, D. P. (2001). *An assessment protocol for Communication Across the
    Curriculum*. Paper presented at the National Communication As-
    sociation Convention, Atlanta, Georgia.
Dannels, D. P. (2002). *Building a solid communication across the curriculum pro-
    gram*. Paper presented at the National Communication Associ-
    ation Convention, New Orleans, Louisiana.
Morello, J. (1999). Comparing speaking across the curriculum and writing
    across the curriculum programs. *Communication Education*, 48, 1-15.
Morreale, S., Shockley-Zalabak, P. & Whitney, P. (1993). The center for ex-
    cellence in oral communication: Integrating communication
    across the curriculum. *Communication Education*, 42(1), 10-21.
National Communication Association. (1996). *Policy platform statement on
    communication across the curriculum*. Annandale, VA.
Palmerton, P.R. (1990). *Speaking across the curriculum: The Hamline experience*.
    Presented at the Conference on College Composition and Com-
    munication, Chicago, IL.
Palmerton, P.R. (1991). Speaking across the curriculum: Threat, opportun-
    ity, or both? *ACA Bulletin, 76*, 1-10.
Strohmaier, M., Novak, D. & Stratto, M. (1992). Implementing speaking
    across the curriculum: A case study. *ACA Bulletin*, 81, 32-52.
Euan Hague, "Nationality and Children's Drawings – Pictures 'About Scot-
    land' by Primary School Children in Edinburgh, Scotland and
    Syracuse, New York State", *Scottish Geographical Journal*, 117 (2),
    (2001): 77-99.

Part VI

Assessment of Service-Learning

Overview

Chapters 16-18 make up Part 6 of the book, which focuses on service-learning assessment. Chapter 16 first addresses the need for effective service-learning assessment strategies. Chapter 17 explores different service-learning assessment methods. Chapter 18 looks at the importance of student reflection in service-learning.

Chapter 16
The Need for Effective Service-Learning Assessment Strategies

Linking University and High School Students

Exploring the Academic Value of Service Learning

Duncan MacLellan, Ryerson University, Ontario, Canada

Abstract: While universities and colleges aim to become more inclusive and welcoming to students from a variety of backgrounds, major gaps remain in relation to particular high school students being admitted to postsecondary institutions. Located in Toronto, Canada's most culturally diverse city, Ryerson University is committed to both academic and applied learning. Building on that commitment, this paper focuses on one service learning project involving both university students enrolled in a senior level Ryerson course and high school students enrolled in a Grade 12 course located in downtown Toronto. This particular Toronto high school has not scored well in province-wide standardized tests and so few of its students apply to college or university. Bringing together these high school and university students in different activities over one semester will enable both groups to gain insights from each other. In addition, by using reflective assignments, Ryerson students can use course concepts to help ground their interactions with these high school students. Service learning has the potential to build linkages that help both university and high school students.

Introduction

Service learning has been identified as an effective mechanism to engage university students in a variety of learning opportunities (Day, 2008; Webster, 2007). For this study, Ryerson University students, in a senior-level course, were linked with students enrolled in a Grade 12 course at Maple Heights High School.[1] This particular urban high school has not fared well in provincial standardized tests, and few of its students continue to pursue academic studies after high school. A number of scholars have pointed to the troubling fact that many urban high school students may be prone to disconnect from their academic studies, which could limit their future career options (Elson, Johns, and Petrie, 2007; Kenny, Simon, Kiley-Brabeck, and Lerner, 2002; Webster, 2007).[2]

Webster (2007) notes that a significant body of literature related to service learning focuses on white middle-class suburban schools. Only of late, has the focus begun to move toward demystifying university and college programs for youth from under-represented urban communities. Well-designed service learning projects in urban schools have the potential to provide university students with opportunities to link with high school students; therefore, enabling both groups to exchange ideas and views on a range of formal and informal topics (Brown, Heaton, and Wall, 2007; Webster, 2007).

The goal of this paper is to present a practice-based case study, which describes an innovative service learning project involving high school and university students. The research question is: Can service learning be a positive means for linking university and high school students?

Review of Literature Related to Service Learning

Bringle and Hatcher's definition of service learning, referenced in Zlotkowski (2003), offers a useful lens to situate this study:

> We view service learning as a credit-bearing educational experience in which students participate in an organized service activity that meets identified community needs and reflects on the service activity to gain further understanding of the course content, a broader appreciation of the discipline, and an enhanced sense of civic responsibility.... (p. 64)

O'Quin (2003) refers to the *National and Community Trust Act*, which defines service learning '[a]s a method whereby students learn and develop through active participation in thoughtfully organized service that is conducted to meet the needs of communities' (2003, p. 3697). Some researchers relate service learning's pedagogy to John Dewey's scholarship, which views educa-

---

1. Please note that Maple Heights is a pseudonym.

2. The author would like to extend appreciation to Ryerson University's Service Learning Office, Ryerson's service learning students, and students and teaching staff at Maple Heights for their cooperation in this project.

tion as means for promoting democracy and engaging students in their communities (Ramsdell, 2004). More specifically, having a "good fit" between the course and the service learning experience, enables students, faculty, and community partners to see a project's value (Gupta, 2006; Hollander, Saltmarsh, and Zlotkowski, 2002).

Service learning can help students increase community awareness by applying their academic learning, knowledge, and skills to pre-identified local needs (Campus Contact, 2003; Frazer, Raasch, Pertzborn, and Bradley, 2007; Pearce, 2008). For service learning to be considered a viable pedagogic approach, it has to link with specific academic course content. The following quote from Eyler and Dwight, cited by Pearce (2008), responds to the question: Why service learning?

> I can honestly say that I've learned more in the last year (service learning) than I probably have learned in all four years of college. I have learned so much, maybe because I found something that I'm really passionate about, and it makes you care more to learn about it-and get involved and do more. You're not just studying to take a test and forget about it. You're learning and the experiences we have are staying with us. (p. 116)

In addition, as Pearce notes, "well designed, well-managed service learning can contribute to a student's learning and growth, while also helping to meet real community needs" (2008, p.119). The goal is to integrate service with the academic enterprise, so service reinforces and strengthens learning and learning reinforces and strengthens service. One primary goals of service learning is the use of reflection to help connect the broader context of service experience with course content (O'Quin, 2003).

Connecting an Urban University to Service Learning

This project aimed to link university and high school students in a series of informal and formal activities that would help familiarize high school students to university. Given Ryerson's evolution, this current service learning project builds on a strong foundation of applied learning. Ryerson University began as a polytechnic school shortly after World War Two, and its mission remains to link academic studies with practical applications. In the mid-1990s, Ryerson was granted standing as a university but maintained its emphasis on career-focused education. The 2008-2009 Ryerson University Calendar notes the following description:

> The special mission of Ryerson University is the advancement of applied knowledge and research to address societal need, and the provision of programs of study that provide a balance between theory and application and that prepare students for careers in professional and quasi-professional fields. As a leading centre of applied education, Ryerson is recognized as Canada's leader in career-focused education.... (Ryerson University, 2008, p. 14)

To help guide the organization of this service learning project, the instructor relied on the following definition provided by the Ryerson University Faculty of Arts Service Learning Office:

Service Learning is a form of experiential learning that links classroom teaching and course readings with meaningful voluntary experiences and critical reflective practices. Students engage in projects and activities in the community in addition to their course work. Learning is facilitated through individual and collective critical reflection in course lectures and assignments that help students integrate 'real world' experiences with course concepts. Service Learning differs from volunteer work and internships/practica in that it focuses on both community priorities and student learning, rather than just on community need (volunteer work) or just on student learning....(Ryerson University, 2008a)

To provide context for this service learning project, a brief overview of significant demographic and socio-economic figures that relate to Toronto and Ryerson University will be helpful.

- During the past decade, close to 50% of Toronto's population of 2.5 million residents were born outside of Canada (City of Toronto, 2009).
- Approximately 25% of the 1 million immigrants that came to Canada from 2001-2006 settled in Toronto (City of Toronto, 2009).
- The 2006 national survey results indicate that 47% of Toronto's 2.5 million residents report themselves as being part of a visible minority (City of Toronto, 2009).
- The 2006 national survey also notes that Toronto's population is made up of residents who claim identity with one or more of the 200 distinct ethnic groups that reside in Toronto (City of Toronto, 2009).
- On Toronto's socio-economic front, during the past few decades, the proportion of middle-income neighborhoods has fallen from 50% to 32%. Yet the proportion of low and very-low income neighborhoods increased from 19% to 50% (MacLellan, 2008).

Ryerson's student population reflects Toronto's ethno cultural mosaic. In 2007, 42.6% of Ryerson's first-year student population came from the City of Toronto. The four suburban areas surrounding Toronto are referred to as the Greater Toronto Area (GTA), and with a combined population of 2.3 million residents, Ryerson drew another 40% of it first-year student population from the GTA. In 2007, close to 12% of Ryerson's first-year student population came from outside Toronto and the GTA but still within Ontario. Approximately 3.8% of Ryerson's first-year students came from a non-Ontario province or territory within Canada (Ryerson University, 2008b).

Maple Heights High School was selected as the site for this service learning project. To a certain degree, Maple Heights's student population is similar in composition to the City of Toronto and Ryerson University. In spring 2008, Maple Heights reported that close to 32% of its students have resided in Canada for less than five years (Toronto District School Board, 2009). Maple Heights's 2007-2008 school profile is presented in Table One.

Table 1: A selected Profile of Maple Heights High School 2007-2008

	Maple Heights High School	Province of Ontario
Parentage of students who live in lower-income households	31%	16.5%
Percentage of students whose parents have some university education	21%	36.9%
Percentage of students who receive special education services	24%	12.5%
Percentage of students identified as gifted	0.1%	21.8%
Parentage of students whose first language is not English	56%	21.8%
Percentage of students who are new to Canada from non-English speaking country	21.3%	3.2%
Percentage of students who achieved provincial standard in academic math	19%	75%
Percentage of students who achieved provincial standard in applied math (2007-08)	15%	34%
Percentage of students in grade 10 who passed literacy test on their first attempt (2007-08)	42%	84%
These percentages are based on Ontario province-wide averages (Ontario Ministry of Education, 2008).		

Methodology: Education Politics, Urban Schooling, and Social Capital

This qualitative study was prompted by a desire to utilize service learning as the vehicle to connect high school and senior university students. The instructor was contacted by a Ryerson University Faculty of Arts Service Learning staff member to inquire if there was interest in "twinning" his "Education Politics and Policy" course with a Grade 12 course at Maple Heights High School. The "Education Politics and Policy" course relies on cultural and social capital theories to help students understand the social context within which educational decisions are made. In particular, Pierre Bourdieu's work on cultural capital is utilized to explore the idea that schools draw unevenly on social and cultural resources of members of society. Often cultural experiences at home facilitate children's adjustment to both school and academic achievement. This in turn, converts cultural resources into what Bordieu refers to as cultural capital (Lareau, 1987).

Within this course, we discuss how social capital is utilized to enable certain people to gain access to powerful positions through direct and indirect employment of social connections (Oakes, 2005). Howard (2006) contends that social capital promotes linkages that are both formal (volunteering at your local school for a committee) and informal (inviting your neighbors to a barbeque). The benefits from these opportunities can result in personal as well as academic gains for parents and their children. Howard (2006) then asks the following research question: If schools included service learning programs, would these help to close the achievement gaps among different racial and ethnic groups? In his case study of a Seattle middle school, Howard's results, while limited, found that by engaging students in service learning activities, these students spent less time watching television. While Howard's sample size was small, it did offer the potential for service learning to assist academic learning (2006). In summary, both cultural and social capital theories were used to help structure a significant portion of the "Education Politics and Policy" course.

Service Learning at Maple Heights: Research Design and Reflective Assignments

In the lead up to organizing the research design for this service learning project, the instructor benefited from valuable insights offered by Ryerson's Service Learning Office and educators at Maple Heights. The core of this project relied on Ryerson students submitting three reflective assignments that enabled them to offer their thoughts and knowledge with regard to both informal and formal aspects of their placement at Maple Heights over five weeks. To present the observations that emerged from both the reflective assignments and informal conversations that the instructor had with Ryerson students regarding their placement at Maple Heights, it became important to organize these findings in an organized manner. After reviewing a number of scholarly works, the instructor chose to adopt Sterling's (2007) subheadings of Knowledge, Activities, and Reflections because of the appropriate fit provided for this service learning project.

Knowledge

For this paper, we can consider knowledge as concepts, facts, information, and prior experience in the context of experiential learning (Sterling, 2007; Terry, 2005). More specifically, two aspects of knowledge can be considered. First, upon agreeing to participate in this service learning project, the instructor wanted to become informed about the principles of service learning. Second, the instructor was eager to gain "on the ground knowledge" related to Maple Heights High School. The course instructor and one of Ryerson's service learning liaison staff members met with Ms. Banks (pseudonym), the teacher responsible for Maple Heights's Grade 12 university-preparatory course, "Challenge and Change in Society" that was to be "twinned" with the "Education Politics and Policy" course. This meeting also offered Ms. Banks an opportunity to become familiar with the "Education Politics and Policy" course, and Ms. Banks provided the instructor with the following description of the "Challenge and Change in Society" course:

This course examines theories and methodologies used in anthropology, psychology, and sociology to investigate and explain shifts in knowledge, attitudes, beliefs, and behavior, and their impact on society. Students will analyze cultural, social, and biological patterns in human societies, looking at the ways in which these patterns change over time. Students will also explore the ideas of classical and contemporary social theories, and will apply those ideas to the analysis of contemporary trends. (Ontario Ministry of Education, 2002, p. 1)

The instructor also attended a professional development workshop on evaluating reflective assignments. This workshop offered the instructor an opportunity to engage with other faculty in relation to constructive approaches to assessing reflective assignments. To create the three reflective assignments for the "Education Politics and Policy" course, attention was given to O'Quin's (2003) comment that one must consider course goals and objectives when designing reflective assignments that connect service learning with a course's academic content. Furthermore, there does not appear to be one "right" way for students to process and assimilate the learning that takes place through their service learning experiences. For this reason, faculty are best suited to select methods of assessment and reflection that meet course goals and learning objectives (Day, 2008; O'Quin, 2003).

As Young, Shinnar, Ackerman, Carruthers, and Young (2007) note, service learning must be more than community service, service-learning assignments must include two components: continuity and interaction. Continuity refers to connections between course materials and assignments-the application of skills and concepts learned in a course to real life situations. Interactions refer to the link between the objective nature of the assignment and the subjective experience-the impressions and thoughts of the student. The link is achieved through reflection. Reflection can come in the form of class discussions, journal writing, term papers, or other assignments that require students to critically reflect upon their experiences. Ramsdell (2004) contends that for service learning courses to be successful, the academic component must be equally as important as the service. The implications of this are that the volunteer work must be directly tied to the course curriculum.

The service learning component of the "Education Politics and Policy" course was voluntary. Nine of 29 students submitted applications for service learning at Maple Heights High School. Due to the fact that students would be working with young adults, the Toronto District School Board (TDSB) required each student who applied to complete a Police Reference Check (PRC). All nine students were accepted for the service learning project at Maple Heights. Shortly thereafter, Ryerson's Service Learning Office organized a half-day orientation session for Ryerson students involved in service learning at Maple Heights. A few days before the visit, an altercation occurred near Maple Heights School property that led the Principal to initiate a school lockdown. This item generated media attention, and a few Ryerson students emailed the instructor regarding the safety of Maple

Heights. Ryerson's Service Learning Office sent an email to its Maple Heights service learning students, assuring them that all precautions would be taken to ensure their safety.

The visit remained as scheduled, and Ryerson university students gained a first-hand look at Maple Heights High School. Ryerson students were able to meet with Maple Heights's Principal and teaching staff involved with service learning. At this meeting, Ryerson students asked questions related to the school, and the Principal responded that many of the students attending Maple Heights are first-generation Canadians and a significant number are from low-income families. In addition, according to the Principal, some Maple Heights students are living on their own due to difficult family situations. The Principal also stated that the size of Maple Heights's English as a Second Language (ESL) Program reflects that many of its students are not fluent in English, in part, because of their recent entry into Canada. Geographically, the Principal noted that Maple Heights is located between two high-achieving secondary schools; therefore, it has the stigma of being the school where students who cannot gain entry into the other two schools end up. Next Ryerson students met informally with the students they would be working with, this was followed by lunch in the school cafeteria, and then a student-led school tour.

Two weeks later, Maple Heights's service learning students were given a half-day orientation to Ryerson University. The aim of the visit was for these students to see the campus and to help demystify some aspects of higher education. The visit to Ryerson University involved meeting with Student Services personnel. Then Maple Height students met with a group of first-generation Ryerson students to chat informally about university life. A campus tour was organized and this was followed by a brief lecture from the instructor to enable Maple Height students to "experience" a university class.

Activities

Ryerson university students enrolled in service learning at Maple Heights were required to spend two hours per week over five weeks assisting Ms. Banks in a variety of formal and informal activities related to the "Challenge and Change in Society" course. After the first week of observing, Ryerson students were integrated more formally into "Challenge and Change in Society". To ease their transition into this course, Ryerson students were divided into two groups to coincide with the day of their weekly visits.

A Monday group member contacted the course instructor to inquire about using case studies from our "Education Politics and Policy" course as an activity at Maple Heights. The instructor agreed but on the condition that Ms. Banks approve, which she did after reviewing the four case studies. After dividing the class into four groups, with Ryerson students leading each group, Maple Heights students were asked to comment on the cases in relation to their "Challenge and Change in Society" course. Overall, as will be discussed in the reflections section, this activity was well-presented by the Monday group and well-received by Maple Heights students.

The Tuesday group's activity involved taking a cake, referred to as the "World Cake" to one of the "Challenge and Change in Society" classes. The cake was divided into the following geographic regions: North America, Latin America, Europe, Africa, and Asia-Pacific, and the size of each slice of cake represented the per capita gross income of each region. Students were then divided based on the five regions, and the region with the largest slice of cake was Asia and the smallest was Africa. Students representing "regions with small slices of cake" were encouraged to see if they could "trade" with "regions with large slices of cake", thereby increasing their "share" of cake. Immediately, students representing small-slice regions noticed large-slice regions were unwilling to share. To retaliate against this obstacle, one small-slice region "appropriated" a share of cake from a large-slice region to better balance regional incomes.

Reflections

First Reflective Assignment

This assignment involved Ryerson students describing their thoughts and observations related to their half-day orientation at Maple Heights. In particular, students were to compare their visit to Maple Heights to what they thought would be before them, and then to discuss Maple Heights in relation to their own high school experience. Some students found the Principal's responses to their questions a bit surprising because he was so forthright in describing the serious social and economic challenges before Maple Heights's students. Ryerson students commented that they did not realize the degree of poverty and disconnectedness within Maple Heights High School. In some of the first reflective assignments, Ryerson students were surprised at learning from the Principal, that financial difficulties prevent a number of Maple Heights's academically-eligible students from attending university or college. In addition, some Ryerson students were dismayed to learn, from the Principal, some Maple Heights students would like to attend university but had no one in their family to turn to for support, and also that some students felt pressure from their families to seek employment directly after high school. A Ryerson student, who had attended a neighboring high-achieving school, reflected on the perception that only students not bound for university enrol at Maple Heights.

Second Reflective Assignment

Ryerson University students commented on how well their case studies and "world cake" activities were received by students in the "Challenge and Change in Society" course. Interestingly, Monday group members reported being pleased at the level of understanding these Maple Heights students demonstrated regarding the case studies, which focused on complex social issues such as: discrimination, racism, and sexual orientation in school and family settings. Tuesday group members were impressed by the degree of resourcefulness and insight Maple Heights students offered with respect to regional income distribution and social justice issues. Ms. Banks expressed gratitude for both the leadership and team-building skills evident in these Ryerson students and the high level of responsiveness from Maple Heights students. Ms. Banks indicated her interest in using the case studies in future offerings of "Challenge and Change in Society".

Third Reflective Assignment

Ryerson service learning students were required to incorporate cultural and/ or social capital theories as the foundation through which to examine their experiences at Maple Heights. These Ryerson students offered detailed examples of how they came to realize the importance of schools as places that socialize citizens; furthermore, the degree to which one is socialized is dependent on both family and social circumstances. In discussing financial and family issues relating to attending college or university, some Ryerson students reflected that they too faced the same challenges as the Maple Heights students. The Maple Height students learned that what gave these current Ryerson students the drive to apply to university was family encouragement and financial support. In addition, Ryerson students noted that Maple Heights students found the Ryerson orientation session a rewarding and empowering experience. Furthermore, some Maple Height students commented positively to Ryerson students with regard to Ryerson's diverse student population. Ryerson students relayed to the Maple Heights students that many Ryerson students are also first-generation Canadians. As comfort levels grew, Ryerson students reflected that inquiries from Maple Heights students began to focus on university admission and financial requirements.

Ryerson students, in their third reflective assignment, commented that this service learning experience provided different ways to apply course theories hands on, and it gave them the opportunity to interact, learn, and become more familiar with the public school system. Ryerson students also found that service learning enhanced both their perspective on policy in action along with applying certain theories to practice. Students also offered that there was a connection between course content and service learning because the issues students dealt with at Maple Heights were portrayed in course readings and lectures. Ryerson students hoped that these Maple Heights students gained as much as they did from this service learning experience.

Conclusions

This service learning project was organized to enable Ryerson university students to volunteer their time at an urban high school, and to provide students in a Grade 12 course with an opportunity to interact with these students to help demystify university. The importance of establishing good rapport with the host organization at all stages of the service learning project is vital (Ramsdell, 2004). The initial site visit by the course instructor to Maple Heights was worthwhile, and the orientation sessions at Maple Heights and Ryerson University helped to strengthen this connection. As Ramsdell (2004) suggests, it is virtually impossible for the instructor to understand the organization's needs, and thus to prepare student volunteers, without being physically present to witness the surroundings in which the students will be working. During the site visit, the instructor was able ascertain aspects of Maple Heights's student population and the setting within which Ryerson students would volunteer their time.

Ryerson students were required to write three reflective assignments that examined first, their perceptions of Maple Heights High School; second, an activity that their group had led at Maple Heights; and third, analyse their Maple Heights service learning experience, using theories discussed in our "Education Politics and Policy" course. Young et al. (2007) note, the benefits of service learning programs are that they may help to improve academic performance of both high school and university students in terms of boosting their sense of personal and social responsibility. Service-learning may also enhance other skills such as: critical thinking, communication, teamwork, problem solving, and time management. Ryerson students reflected that, in leading the case studies and world cake activities, their teamwork and communication skills were enhanced. A few students commented that they would like to enter the teaching profession, and that the Maple Heights service learning experience "opened their eyes" to the complexities of life in an urban high school. Jagla (2008) refers to this as enhancing the relevance of knowledge from service learning. By actively involving students in the process of constructing their own knowledge, they more readily see how it relates to the real world as opposed to just learning the theoretical concepts in isolation. As Catapano (2006) notes, placing people in real situations helps them to compare what they are learning in the course to what they are experiencing in their service learning project.

Ryerson students viewed their service learning experience as an effective way to connect high school and university students, and some hoped that this would motivate more high school students from underrepresented groups to attend university. In addition, service learning helped to break down some educational barriers because it offered university students a chance to get "real-life" experience in an urban school. Ryerson students were enthusiastic that service learning be incorporated in future offerings of "Education Politics and Policy". The instructor was hoping to include comments from Maple Heights students but was unable to due to tight time constraints related to when this service learning project ended. However,

Ryerson students commented to the instructor that the verbal feedback they received from Maple Height students was very positive regarding this service learning project. The use of reflective assignments helped to ground this service learning project, both in relation to course expectations and interactions between Maple Heights and Ryerson students. Service learning has the potential to allow for "relevant and meaningful academic learning..." (Payne-Jackson, 2005, p. 60).

Yet, we must keep in mind that service learning is still in its infancy. Actual research in this field reflects the fact that service learning has been viewed quite broadly, so developing a theoretical body in this field has been challenging. Part of this problem stems from the absence of a clear theoretical base in terms of how service learning is to be considered; therefore, a number of theoretical perspective may apply. Furthermore, service learning would benefit from more robust studies based on qualitative, quantitative, or mixed methods. On a related note, service-learning researchers should be mindful not to overstate or overgeneralise their findings (Billig and Waterman, 2003).

With the above cautions in mind, some service learning projects have the potential to offer students a glimpse into real-world problems that may build on university or high school courses (Desrochers, 2006: Sterling, 2007). This service learning project enabled Ryerson students to widen their educational learning with practical experience, and it offered Maple Heights students the opportunity to help them demystify university. The instructor also became more aware, from visiting Maple Heights and reading Ryerson students' reflective assignments, of the widening social, cultural, and financial gaps that still disengage significant numbers of marginalize urban students from seeking educational training beyond high school. This study is limited in its ability to generalize results, and it is proposed that further research is needed to substantiate and advance the observations noted here.

References

Billig, S., and Waterman, A. (2003). Studying service learning: Challenges and solutions. In S. Billing and A. Waterman, (Eds.), *Studying service-learning: Innovations in education research methodology* (pp. vii-xiv). Mahwah, NJ: Lawrence Erlbaum Associates, Publishers.

Brown, B., Heaton, P., & Wall, A. (2007). A service-learning elective to promote enhanced understanding in civic, cultural, and social issues and health disparitiesin pharmacy. *American Journal of Pharmaceutical Education*, 71(1), 1-7.

Campus Contact (2003). *Introduction to service learning toolkit. Readings and resources for faculty*. Providence, RI: Campus Compact.

Catapano, S. (2006). Teaching in urban schools: Mentoring pre-service teaches to apply advocacy strategies. *Mentoring & Tutoring: Partnership in Learning*, 14(1), 81-96.

City of Toronto (2009). *Toronto's racial diversity*. Retrieved 03 June 2009 from http://www.toronto.ca/toronto_facts/diverstiy.htm.

Day, D. (2008). Connecting student achievement and personal development: Service learning and academic personal development: Service learning and academic credit. *The International Journal of Learning*, 15(11), 41-50.

Desrochers, C. (2006). Educating preservice teaching for diversity: Perspectives on the possibilities and limitations of service learning. *Journal of Educational Thought*, 40(3), 263-280.

Elson, D., Johns, L., & Petrie, J. (2007). Jumpstart's service-learning initiative: Enhanced outcomes for at-risk children. In S. Gelmon & S. Billig, (Eds.), *Service learning: From passion to objectivity: International and cross-disciplinary perspectives on service-learning research* (pp. 65-88). Charlotte, NC: Information Age Publishing, Inc.

Frazer, L., Raasch, M., Pertzborn, D., & Bradley, F., (2007). The impact of community clients on student learning: The case of a university service-learning course *Journal of Experiential Education*, 29(3), 407-412.

Gupta, J. (2006). A model for interdisciplinary service-learning experience for social change. *Journal of Physical Therapy Education*, 20(3), 55-60.

Hollander, E., Saltmarsh, J., & Zlotkowski, E. (2002). Indicators of engagement. In M. Kenny, L. Simon, K. Kiley-Brabeck & R. Lerner (Eds.), *Learning to serve: Promoting civil society through service learning* (pp. 31-49). Norwell, MA: Kluwer Academic Publishers.

Howard, R. (2006). Bending toward justice: Service-learning and social capital as means to the tipping point. *Mentoring & Tutoring: Partnership in Learning*, 14(1), 5-15.

Jagla, V. (2008). Service–learning prepares teachers to meet the needs of diverse learners. *The International Journal of Learning*, 15(6), 1-7.

Kenny, M., Simon, L., Kiley-Brabeck, K., & Lerner, R. (2002). Promoting civil society through service learning: A view of the issues. In M. Kenny, L. Simon, K. Kiley-Brabeck, & R. Lerner, (Eds.), *Learning to serve: Promoting civil society through service learning* (pp. 1-14). Norwell, MA: Kluwer Academic Publishers.

Lareau, A. (1987). Social class difference in family-school relationships: The importance of cultural capitalism. *Sociology of Education,* 60(2), 73-85.

MacLellan, D. (2008). Diversity and immigrant needs: Examining Toronto through a place-based approach. *Policy Matters*. No. 32, 1-13. Toronto, ON: Centre for Excellence in Research in Immigration and Settlement (CERIS).

Ontario Ministry of Education. (2002). *Course profile: Challenge and change in society. Grade 12 University/College Preparation.* Toronto, ON: Author.

Ontario Ministry of Education (2008). *Secondary school profiles.* Retrieved from http://www.edu.gov.on.ca on 09 June 2009.

Oakes, J. (2005). Keeping track: How schools structure inequality, (2nd ed.). New Haven, CT: Yale University Press.

O'Quin, J. (2003). Serve to learn and learn to serve. *The International Journal of Learning,* 10, 3697-3704.

Payne-Jackson, A. (2005). A model of service learning. *The International Journal of Learning,* 12(10), 55-63.

Pearce, A. (2008). Finding your place in the world of service learning: Is the journey worth the effort? *The International Journal of Learning,* 15(10), 115-121.

Ramsdell, L. (2004). Reciprocity: The heart of service learning. *The International Journal of Learning,* 11, 523-527.

Ryerson University (2008). Ryerson University full-time undergraduate calendar 2008-2009. Toronto, ON: Author.

Ryerson University (2008a). *A toolkit for service learning course design.* Toronto, ON: Faculty of Arts, Ryerson University.

Ryerson University (2008b). *Progress indicators and related statistics for 2008.* Toronto: ON: Author.

Sterling, M. (2007). Service-learning and interior design: A case study. *Journal of Experiential Education,* 20(3), 331-343.

Terry, A. (2005). A K-12 development service-learning typology. *The International Journal of Learning,* 12(9), 321-330.

Toronto District School Board (2009). *Our school 2009-2010.* Toronto, ON: Author.

Webster, N. (2007). Enriching school connection and learning in African American urban youth: The impact of service-learning feasibility in inner-city Philadelphia. In S. Gelman & S. Billing (Eds.), *Service learning: From passion to objectivity: International and cross-disciplinary perspectives on service learning* (pp.159-176). Charlotte, NC: Information Age Publishing.

Young, C., Shinnar, R., Ackerman, R., Carruthers, C., & Young, D. (2007). Implementing and sustaining service-learning at the institutional level. *Journal of Experiential Education,* 29(3), 344-365.

Zlotkowski, E. (2003). Pedagogy and engagement. In Campus Compact (Ed.), *Introduction to service-learning toolkit: Readings and resources for faculty* (pp. 63-77). Providence, RI: Campus Compact Publishers.

Chapter 17

Effective Service-Learning Assessment

Assessment of Service-Learning Outcomes

Examining the Effects of Class Size, Major, Service-Learning Experience, and Sex

Claudia Pragman, Minnesota State University, Minnesota, UNITED STATES

Brenda Flannery, Minnesota State University, Minnesota, UNITED STATES

Abstract: Principles of management is a core course required of all business majors and several non-business majors at Minnesota State University, Mankato. College of Business faculty members have determined that this course is the one where team and leadership skills are assessed. To assess these skills, students participated in a team-based project that served Campus Kitchen @ Minnesota State University, Mankato. The purpose of this project was not only to assess team and leadership skills, but also to assess the development of professional business skills and civic engagement. Campus Kitchens, a national program affiliated with colleges and universities in the United States, recovers surplus food from campus dining services and delivers it to needy community members. For their part, the principles of management students devised projects that supported the infrastructure of Campus Kitchens. Teams of students were required to write a proposal for their project, implement it, and report their results. In addition to the direct assessments (proposal and reports), indirect assessments of learning outcomes were made. Students in two different sections of the course (n = 31 and n = 54) were assessed about their service-learning experience regarding making a connection to the university and the community, participating in a real-world business application, applying problem-solving skills, applying theory to practice, practicing teamwork skills, learning workplace skills, and building professional self-confidence. When collecting this data, the authors requested additional data about the students' class size, college major, prior service-learning experience, and sex. Noting that the results of the assessment did not appear to be uniform, the authors decided to pursue the differences in the achievement of those learning outcomes based on this additional data.

Introduction

Service learning is a pedagogy that allows students to learn by doing. The implementation of service-learning in a curricular setting provides a real and experience-based opportunity for students to become immersed in critical thinking while applying course curricula to a local problem. Godfrey and Grasso (2000) describe service learning as having four components:

1. Students actively participate in organized service experiences that meet actual community needs and that are coordinated in collaboration with the school and community.
2. These experiences are integrated into the students' academic curriculum, and/or structured time is provided for them to think, talk, or write about what they did and saw during their actual service activity.
3. Students have opportunities to use newly acquired skills and knowledge in real-life situations in their own communities.
4. These experiences help to foster the development of a sense of caring for others.

Assessment helps us measure what we try to achieve through our pedagogy. As professors we want to know whether our curricular activities are achieving the outcomes we desire. Unfortunately, professors cannot control all the factors that may affect the achievement of those outcomes. Therefore, service-learning activities need to be robust against uncontrollable factors that might hinder student learning and the achievement of desired outcomes.

In this study we examine the effects of some of those uncontrollable factors—class size, college major, previous service-learning experience, and sex—on outcomes related to civic engagement, application of management theory, and business skills development. To present our findings we will 1) describe the course and the project used to implement service learning; 2) identify the service-learning outcomes we assessed and the factors we were concerned might compromise the achievement of those outcomes;

3) describe the methodology used to collect and analyse the assessment data; and 4) present the results of the analysis, discuss those results, and state the conclusions we reached based on those results.

Principles of Management Course and Campus Kitchens

At our university all business majors (accounting, finance, international business, management, and marketing) and several nonbusiness majors (primarily aviation management, construction management, computer science, economics, and music industry management) are required to take a principles of management course. Students enrol in this junior-level course after being admitted to their college; for nonmanagement majors this course is the single exposure to formal management theory, including theories regarding effective teamwork. For that reason, our business college assesses its core outcomes related to teamwork and leadership in the principles of management course. Therefore, a team project of some kind is required for this course.

The principles of management students involved in this study were required to choose a team project that supported Campus Kitchens. Campus Kitchens, a national program affiliated with colleges and universities, recovers surplus food from campus dining services and delivers it to needy community members (http://www.campuskitchens.org/). Rather than packaging and delivering food, our students planned and implemented projects that raised funds to support the infrastructure of Campus Kitchens.

Student Assessments

In addition to the college's assessment of teamwork and leadership, separate direct and indirect student assessments unique to the Campus Kitchens project were conducted. Direct assessments for each team included a written project proposal, a written final report about the project, and an oral presentation of the final report to the entire class. As an individual direct assessment, students also wrote a reflection paper about their experience with their project and as a team member. These direct assessments of the Campus Kitchens team project were used to determine 46% of a student's semester grade. Thus the project was an integral part of the course and a student's grade.

For the purposes of this study, an indirect capstone assessment about the service-learning project was also conducted. We developed outcomes based on the benefits of service learning purported by Kenworthy-U'Ren (2000). She believed that service learning enabled students to apply classroom concepts and skills, produce a tangible product for use by an actual organization, and learn about community service.

Based on her research, we developed outcomes that were used to determine whether or not the Campus Kitchens service-learning project enabled students to become civically engaged, apply management theory, and develop professional, business-related skills. The following list identifies the statements we used to assess those outcomes. Later in the methodology section, we will explain how the statements from this capstone assessment were used to gather assessment data for our analysis.

1. The project enabled me to connect to the MSU campus community.
2. The project enabled me to connect to the Mankato community.
3. The project provided me with a real-world business application.
4. The project allowed me to apply problem-solving techniques.
5. The project allowed me to apply management theory.
6. The project allowed me to practice teamwork skills.
7. The project allowed me to learn practical workplace skills.
8. The project allowed me to build professional self-confidence.

Factors that May Affect Student Achievement

There were both similarities and differences among our students. Nearly all of our students were the same age, were admitted to their college at the university, and were third or fourth year students. Yet it was after we began our service-learning project that we became more aware—through experience, student comments, and research literature—that the factors of class size, a student's college major, previous service-learning experience, and a student's sex might affect student learning.

Does class size matter? We had two class sizes; a small class of 34 students and a larger class of 57 students. Despite the difference in the sizes of the classes, we managed to keep the number of students per team at 5-7 members. However, this meant that more teams in the larger class were more difficult to manage because they received less individual attention during class time.

Does a student's college major matter? A few of the nonmanagement students commented that the service-learning project was appropriate for management majors, but not for them. McCarthy and Tucker (1999) did not find any significant differences between business and nonbusiness students' attitudes toward service learning. However, Astin et al. (2000) reported that the single most important factor leading to a positive service learning experience was the student's degree of interest in the subject matter. These authors found evidence that service learning should be part of the student's major field. Our course was based in the discipline of management. We wanted to learn whether our nonmanagement or nonbusiness students believed they were getting less benefit from the service-learning project than were the management majors.

Is the experience more valuable if the student has participated in service-learning in other courses? Or does the novelty of the experience wear off and decrease the value of the learning experience? McCarthy and Tucker's study (1999) found that students who had previous experience with service learning were more likely to believe they could make a valuable contribution to a new project. Yet some of our students commented that the project was unfair because it was mandatory and required too much work. We wanted to know whether there were differences in the outcomes based on whether or not the students had previous service-learning experience.

Does the student's sex matter? Previous research has indicated that females are better students, take grades more seriously, and are more caring and willing to be involved in community service (Fitch, 1987; Hayghe, 1991; McCarthy &Tucker, 1999; Wilson, 2007). Yet earlier studies found no significant differences between male and female students concerning community involvement (Allen, 1982; Booth, 1972; Verba & Nie, 1972). Based on these contradictory findings, we wanted to test for differences between our male and female students.

Methodology

The capstone assessment was given as an anonymous electronic survey at the end of the semester. The 85 students involved in this study were undergraduates enrolled in two sections (classes) of a principles of management course taught by the same professor during the same semester. The two classes, a large and a small class, enrolled 54 and 31 students, respectively. (The original data set had 91 students; 57 students in the large class and 34 students in the small class. However, six students were omitted from the study due to missing data.)

Each of the service-learning capstone outcomes was written as a positive statement (see list given in the previous Student Assessments section) and the students were asked to report their level of agreement with each statement using a 7-point Likert scale (1 = strongly disagree, 2 = disagree, 3 = somewhat disagree, 4 = neutral, 5 = somewhat agree, 6 = agree, and 7 = strongly agree). For analysis the mean score for each outcome was calculated. In addition the students were asked to identify their class section (class size), their college major, previous service-learning experience, and sex.

A series of eight, four-factor ANOVAs (analysis of variance) was used to analyse the data. The mean score for an outcome was used as the dependent variable in each ANOVA. Individual ANOVAs were performed because of the high correlation between the mean scores of all the outcomes. The four factors used for each ANOVA were class size, major, previous service-learning experience, and student's sex. The factorial ANOVA allowed us to analyse the differences among the means of the outcomes based upon different levels of the four factors simultaneously (Levine et al., 2008). Table 1 summarizes the factors and their levels.

Table 1: Factors and Levels for Outcomes

Factor (Code)	Level (Code)
Class Size (CLSIZE)	Large
	Small
Major (MAJOR)	Accounting (ACCT)
	Finance (FINA)
	International Business (IBUS)
	Management (MGMT)
	Marketing (MKTG)
	Nonbusiness (NONB)
Previous Service-Learning Experience (PREVSL)	Yes
	No
Sex (SEX)	Male
	Female

This design resulted in a 48 (2 X 6 X 2 X 2) cell ANOVA for each dependent variable (outcome).

Results

Service-Learning Outcomes

The means for each of the service-learning outcomes associated with participation in the Campus Kitchens project were tabulated. The means ranged from a low of 5.39 (establishing a connection to MSU, MSU) to a high of 6.31 (practicing teamwork skills, TEAM). Table 2 reports the mean and standard deviation for each of the outcomes. Based on the 7-point scale, students reported that they somewhat agreed or agreed they accomplished the outcomes.

Table 2: Means and Standard Deviations for Service-Learning Outcomes

Outcome	Mean	Standard Deviation
MSU	5.39*	1.481
MANKATO	5.52	1.278
REALWORLD	5.68	1.424
PROBSOLV	5.82	1.347
APPLY	5.62	1.327
TEAM	6.31	1.102
WRKPLCE	5.77	1.264
SELFCON	5.89	1.069
*$p < .05$.		

The factorial ANOVAs indicated that only one of the service-learning outcomes, connection to MSU (MSU), was statistically significant at the 0.05 level. Therefore, only the connection to MSU outcome was analysed further for this study.

Analysis of Variance for Connection to MSU

The ANOVA results for the connection to MSU outcome are found in Table 3. Proper analysis dictates that significant interactions be interpreted before main effects. Results indicated that a three-way (MAJOR*PREVSL*SEX) and a two-way (PREVSL*SEX) interaction were significant at the 0.05 level, so those interactions were interpreted in that order.

Table 3: Analysis of Variance for Connection to MSU

Source	df	F	p
CLSIZE	1	.518	.475
MAJOR	5	2.169	.072
PREVSL	1	.456	.503
SEX	1	3.341	.074
CLSIZE * MAJOR	4	.810	.525
CLSIZE * PREVSL	1	.113	.738
MAJOR * PREVSL	4	2.319	.070
CLSIZE * MAJOR * PREVSL	1	3.397	.071
CLSIZE * SEX	1	3.178	.081
MAJOR * SEX	4	1.024	.404
CLSIZE * MAJOR * SEX	3	1.872	.146
PREVSL * SEX	1	4.085*	.049
CLSIZE * PREVSL * SEX	1	2.093	.154
MAJOR * PREVSL * SEX	2	4.341*	.018
CLSIZE * MAJOR * PREVSL * SEX	1	2.577	.115
*$p < .05$.			

To enhance the understanding of the connection to MSU data, Table 4 provides the details for each student in our study. Individual students were identified based on the size of the class in which they were enrolled, their college major, whether or not they had previous service-learning experience, and their sex. This classification assigned each of the 85 students to one of the 48 cells. Inspection of the table's data reveals that some cells are empty and some cells have only one student. These unequal cells occurred because students registered for the course themselves rather than being assigned to the course. Assigning students to the course would have allowed the authors to design a study with equal cell sample sizes. A cursory look at the main effects associated with this table would indicate that male management majors, enrolled in the small class, without previous service-learning experience, would have the highest connection to MSU. Further analysis was made to determine whether or not this was the case.

Table 4: Connection to MSU—Means and Sample Size by Student Type

CLSIZE	PREVSL	SEX	MAJOR						TOTAL
			ACCT	FINA	IBUS	MGMT	MKTG	NONB	
Large	Yes	Male		6.00 (1)	4.50 (2)	5.25 (4)			6.00 (2)	5.33 (9)
Large	Yes	Female	4.33 (3)	1.00 (1)		5.00 (2)	6.50 (2)	7.00 (1)	4.89 (9)
Large	No	Male	3.00 (2)	4.33 (3)		6.00 (7)	6.33 (6)	5.17 (6)	5.42 (24)
Large	No	Female	5.25 (4)	6.00 (1)	6.00 (1)	7.00 (1)	5.00 (3)	3.50 (2)	5.17 (12)
Small	Yes	Male	5.00 (1)	6.00 (1)		7.00 (1)	4.67 (3)	7.00 (1)	5.57 (7)
Small	Yes	Female				6.00 (3)		3.00 (1)	5.25 (4)
Small	No	Male	6.50 (2)			6.33 (3)	6.00 (1)	5.25 (4)	5.90 (10)
Small	No	Female	5.00 (3)			6.25 (4)	5.00 (2)	5.00 (1)	5.50 (10)
Large 5.26 (54)	Yes 5.24 (29)	Male 5.52 (50)	4.87 (15)	4.57 (7)	5.00 (3)	5.96 (25)	5.65 (17)	5.17 (18)	5.39 (85)
Small 5.61 (31)	No 5.46 (56)	Female 5.20 (35)							

Note: Means are given for each cell. The numbers in parentheses are cell sample sizes. Empty cells indicate there were no students in that cell.

Major * Prevsl * Sex

The interaction between previous service-learning experience, sex, and major was significant for the connection to MSU outcome. Table 5 provides the means and cell sizes for these factors collapsed across class size.

Table 5: Connection to MSU—Means and Cell Sizes for PREVSL*SEX* MAJOR

PREVSL	SEX	MAJOR	Mean
No	Female	ACCT	5.13 (7)
		FINA	6.00 (1)
		IBUS	6.00 (1)
		MGMT	6.63 (5)
		MKTG	5.00 (5)
		NONB	4.25 (3)
	Male	ACCT	4.75 (4)
		FINA	4.33 (3)
		IBUS	
		MGMT	6.17 (10)
		MKTG	6.17 (7)
		NONB	5.21 (10)
Yes	Female	ACCT	4.33 (3)
		FINA	1.00 (1)
		IBUS	
		MGMT	5.50 (5)
		MKTG	6.50 (2)
		NONB	5.00 (2)
	Male	ACCT	5.00 (1)
		FINA	6.00 (2)
		IBUS	4.50 (2)
		MGMT	6.13 (5)
		MKTG	4.67 (3)
		NONB	6.50 (3)

Note: Means are given for each cell. The numbers in parentheses are cell sample sizes. Empty cells indicate there were no students in that cell.

There were not enough international business majors to compare based on these factors. However, for students without previous service-learning experience, female accounting, finance, and management majors indicated they felt more connected to MSU through the project than did their male counterparts. Female marketing and nonbusiness majors indicated they were less connected to MSU than the male students in those majors.

Female accounting, finance, management, and nonbusiness majors with previous service-learning experience reported being less connected to MSU than did the male students. Female marketing majors with previous service-learning experience stated they felt more connection to MSU than did male marketing majors.

In order to interpret the significance of the interaction, post hoc tests for the majors were conducted. The Games-Howell test was used to perform the post hoc tests because there was evidence that the cell variances were not homogeneous (SPSS, 2006). The post hoc tests revealed that the means for feeling connected to MSU were not statistically significant at the 0.05 level for any of the majors. Therefore, the source of the significance of the interaction could not be traced to any one major. We therefore turned our attention to interpreting the interaction between whether or not the student had previous service-learning experience and the student's sex.

Prevsl * Sex

Female students who had not had a previous service-learning experience reported a mean connection to MSU of 5.32; male students reported a mean of 5.56. For those students with a previous service-learning experience, the means reported were 5.00 and 5.44 for females and males, respectively. The interaction between previous service learning and sex was significant in the original factorial ANOVA, but when pursued as a subset of the MAJOR*PREVSL*SEX interaction, the significance of the interaction did not hold. Neither the PREVSL*SEX interaction, nor the PREVSL and SEX main effects were significant at the 0.05 level.

Discussion

The first outcome, enabling the student to connect to MSU, was the only outcome that appeared to be significantly affected by the factors we studied. Our initial examination of the main effects (refer to Table 4) associated with our study indicated that male management majors, enrolled in the small class, without previous service-learning experience, would have the highest connection to MSU. Our analysis of the data revealed that this was not the case.

Class size had no effect on the achievement of the connection to MSU outcome. None of the interactions involving CLSIZE, nor the main effect CLSIZE, were statistically significant. Therefore, no negative effects from being enrolled in the larger class rather than the smaller class were detected.

Based on the significance of the MAJOR*PREVSL*SEX and PREVSL*SEX interactions, these remaining factors appeared to have an effect on whether or not a student established a connection to MSU. Subsequent analysis hinted that this was due more to a student's major rather than to previous service-learning experience and the student's sex. However, we failed to identify the particular major or majors that were the source of the significance. This failure occurred because some of the cell sample sizes in the ANOVA were too small and the means in those cells did not vary enough to make a difference. We did not have enough students from all the individual majors (ACCT, FINA, IBUS, MGMT, MKTG, NONB) enrolled in the course to detect which major or majors were responsible for the differences (in the cell means) in achieving the outcome. Furthermore, the main effects MAJOR, PREVSL, and SEX were not significant.

For the students in our study, these findings led us to conclude that major, previous service-learning experience, and a student's sex did not have an affect on establishing a connection to MSU. But rather it is the comingling of those factors that has an effect on how well the outcome was achieved. Yet we were unable to determine with statistical significance which combination of major, service-learning experience, and sex increased or decreased a student's ability to establish a connection to MSU.

Conclusions

When analysing our data, we wanted to know if any of the factors we tracked put our students at a disadvantage for achieving any of our service-learning outcomes. None of the means for the service-learning outcomes were disappointingly low because all of the means were greater than 5 on a 7-point scale. Moreover the seven outcomes with the highest means (MANKATO, REALWORLD, PROBSOLV, APPLY, TEAM, WRKPLCE, and SELFCON) were not affected significantly by any of the factors.

These results allowed us to conclude that being in a large class, studying a certain major, having or not having experience with service learning, or being a certain sex did not affect the achievement of most of our desired outcomes, especially those related to developing professional business skills—real world business experience, problem solving, applying management theory, practicing workplace skills, and developing professional self-confidence. Of the two outcomes related to civic engagement, connection to MSU and connection to MANKATO, only the outcome concerning a connection to MSU was affected by the combined factors of major, service-learning experience, and a student's sex.

Unfortunately, these two outcomes related to civic engagement had the lowest means, 5.39 for connection to MSU and 5.52 for connection to MANKATO. This finding concerns us because research indicates that service learning should enhance civic engagement (Kohls, 1996; Kolenko et al., 1996; Papamarcos, 2002, 2005; Steiner and Watson, 2006; Weber and Sleeper, 2003; Wittmer, 2004; Zlotkowski, 1996). However, we must remember that these means were greater than 5, indicating that students did somewhat agree that their Campus Kitchen project contributed to their connection to the campus and local community. Just because the means for these two outcomes were lower than those related to business skills, does not imply that the students failed at civic engagement, but rather that they succeeded more in developing their business skills. Our civic engagement (Campus Kitchens) project was geared heavily toward the development of business skills. Moreover, previous studies did not compare outcomes related to civic engagement to our outcomes related to business skills development.

Yet our results did confirm previous research findings that service learning is more successful when it is related to the students' disciplines (Astin et al., 2000). The Campus Kitchens project was an assignment in a principles of management course required of business and nonbusiness majors. All of these majors required students to study the discipline of management. In our course the Campus Kitchen project was used to apply management theory to the development of civic engagement and business skills. The results of our study indicated that students from a variety of majors were able to link their major to the discipline of management and successfully achieve our service-learning outcomes.

Nevertheless the results for the outcome about connection to MSU remains a concern for us because a student's major came close to affecting this outcome significantly. For example, accounting and finance majors had means less than 5 for this outcome. In the future we would like to analyse data with larger sample sizes (larger cell sizes) to determine if college majors are making a difference. When cell sizes are too small, it takes a large difference in the means to identify the source of the significance. The differences in the means between the majors in our study were not large enough to determine the source of that significance. Future studies with more students enrolled in the individual majors could resolve this shortcoming.

The original purpose of our study was to determine whether or not factors we professors could not control would comprise student learning and negatively affect the achievement of our service-learning outcomes. Based on the analysis of the data in our study, we have concluded that the factors we cannot control—class size, previous service-learning experience, and a student's sex—do not seem to have an effect on our outcomes. Perhaps professors and students would prefer to have smaller class sizes, but our data do not indicate that class size matters. This is a positive finding because we cannot feasibly offer the principles of management course only in small sections of 30 or so students. To meet the demand for this core course, larger sections must be offered. Thus it is reassuring to know that larger class sizes do not compromise learning.

With respect to previous service learning, our results do not confirm previous service-learning experience as a positive factor in achieving our outcomes. This is not consistent with previous research (McCarthy and Tucker, 1999), but it does indicate that for our students, first-time service learning can produce the outcomes we desire. It is possible that our results were affected by the fact that service learning for our students was not a choice: it was a course requirement. For those of our students who had prior experience with service learning, if that previous experience was also a course requirement, it may have mitigated the positive effects from service learning found by other researchers.

We are pleased that there is no evidence that our students' sex affects the achievement of our service-learning outcomes. We professors do not have control over who enrols in our courses. Our results confirm those of earlier studies that found no significant differences between male and female students regarding community involvement (Allen, 1982; Booth, 1972; Verba & Nie, 1972).

But we must remember that the interaction of the factors of major, service-learning, and sex were significant in our study. Therefore, we need to continue to analyse data of this type to confirm that class size, major, previous service-learning experience, and sex as individual factors do not have an effect on achieving the outcomes. This will continue to reassure us that the factors we cannot control are not compromising student learning.

References

Allen, K. (1982, Winter). Americans Volunteer, 1981: A Gallup survey on volunteering. *Voluntary Action Leadership*, 21-33.

Astin, A. W., Vogelgesang, L. J., Ikeda, E. K. & Yee, J. A. (2000). *How service learning affects students*. Los Angeles, CA: Higher Education Research Institute.

Booth, A. (1972, April). Sex and social participation. *American Sociological Review*, 37, 183-192.

Fitch, R. T. (1987). Characteristics and motivations of college students volunteering for community service. *Journal of College Student Personnel*, 28(5), 424-431.

Godfrey, P.C. & Grasso, E.T. (2000). Introduction. In E. Zlotkowski (Series Ed.) & P.C. Godfrey E.T. Grasso (Vol. Eds.), *Working for the common good: Concepts and models for service-earning in management* (pp. 1-9). Washington, D.C.: American Association for Higher Education.

Hayghe, H. V. (1991, February). Volunteers in the U.S.: Who donates the time? *Monthly Labor Review*, 114, 17-23.

Kenworthy-U'Ren, A.L. (2000). Management students as consultants: An strategy for service-learning in management education. In E. Zlotkowski (Series Ed.) & P.C. Godfrey & E.T. Grasso (Vol. Eds.), *Working for the Common Good: Concepts and Models for Service-Learning in Management* (pp. 55-67). Washington, DC: American Association for Higher Education.

Kohls, J. (1996). Student experiences with service learning in a business ethics course. *Journal of Business Ethics,* 15(1), 45-57.

Kolenko, T. A., Porter, G., Wheatley, W., & Colby, M. (1996). A critique of service learning projects in management education: Pedagogical foundations, barriers, and guidelines, *Journal of Business Ethics*, 15(1), 133-142.

Levine, D.M., Stephan, D.F., Krehbiel, T.C., & Berenson, M.L. (2008). *Statistics for managers using Microsoft Excel* (5th ed.). New Jersey: Pearson Prentice Hall.

McCarthy, A.M., & Tucker, M. L. (1999). Student attitudes toward service-learning: implications for implementation. *Journal of Management Education, 23(5), 554-573.*

Papamarcos, S. D. (2002). The "next wave" in service-learning: Integrative, team-based engagements with structural objectives. *Review of Business,* 23(2), 31-38.

___ (2005). Giving traction to management theory: Today's service-learning. *Academy of Management Learning & Education,* 4(3), 325-335.

Project, C. K. Retrieved March 29, 2008 from http://www.campuskitchens.org/whatwedo.php *SPSS Base 15.0 User's Guide* (2006). Chicago: SPSS Inc.

Steiner, S. D. & Watson, M. A. (2006). The service learning component in business education: The values linkage void. *Academy of Management Learning & Education,* 5(4), 422-434.

Verba, S., & Nie, N. (1972).*Participation in America: Political Democracy and Social Equality* New York: Harper & Row.

Weber, P.S. & Sleeper, B. (2003). Enriching student experiences. *Teaching Business Ethics,* 7(4), 417-435.

Wilson, R. (2007, January 26). The new gender divide. *The Chronicle of Higher Education,* A36-A39.

Wittmer, D. P. (2004). Business and community: Integrating service learning in graduate business education. *Journal of Business Ethics,* 51(4), 359-371.

Zlotkowski, E. (1996). Opportunity for all: Linking service-learning and business education. *Journal of Business Ethics,* 15(1), 5-19.

Chapter 18
Student Reflections as a
Service-Learning Assessment

Written Reflection

The Link Between Study Abroad and Service-Learning

Donna L. Cowan, Rachel Faber Machacha, Cheryl Hausafus, and Margaret Torrie

Introduction

An outcome of the 2002 International Partnership for Service-Learning conference held in Prague, Czech Republic, was a challenge made to all the participants to enhance the body of knowledge surrounding reflection as "a critical common denominator" in international experiences and service-learning (L. Albert, personal communication, June 17, 2000). The conference underscored the importance of reflection in the learning process and the urgency to study student reflection upon international and service experiences. As Dewey describes the tie between experience and learning, he calls for "the progressive development of what is already experienced into a fuller and richer and also more organized form" recognizing that through reflection upon previous experiences, more development and learning occur

(Dewey, 1938, p.87). Jacoby describes Hutchings and Wutzdoff's definition of reflection as a way for one to abstract meaning from knowledge and experience. Reflection is the transformative agent from experience to learning (Jacoby and Associates, 1996, p. 286).

Reflection serves as the link between a service-learning experience and its context in a study abroad program and provides a vehicle for gauging student growth. By reflecting on an academic experience abroad into which service is integrated, students have the opportunity to advance their epistemic knowledge as well as develop their reflective judgment capabilities. The focus of this study is to use written reflection to explore the degree to which service learning in a developing-country setting affects student growth represented by levels of reflection.

Study Abroad and Service-Learning Program Design

The "Experience Kenya" study abroad program consists of a five-week immersion experience at a major East African university. Participants are in residence at the university, earning three credits in classes taught by Kenyan scholars. They earn three credits from the home institution, an American public university, by taking a class integrating fieldwork, cultural study, and service.

Student involvement in the "Experience Kenya" program begins on the home campus when they attend informational sessions, undergo an application process, and successfully complete a credit-bearing, pre-departure orientation seminar class. At each juncture, the invitation to serve and learn abroad is made to the students. Students accept an invitation to serve while on study abroad before gaining any firsthand, in-country experience. During the pre-departure orientation, the students are advised of the considerations for living, studying, and working in a developing nation. They learn the academic and ambassadorial expectations placed upon them and how to meet these requirements. Upon completion of the pre-departure orientation seminar, students travel to Kenya to initiate their on-campus and fieldwork classes.

The fieldwork class requires students to keep an analytical and reflective journal throughout the experience. Prior to embarking on fieldwork, students attend briefings by the instructor and local experts to gain epistemic knowledge of what they are about to experience. The briefings are supplemented by required readings. In addition to the briefings and fieldwork, students attend regular meetings with the instructor to maintain an open forum throughout the class and are also required to read the news reported by the major East African print media outlets.

The service-learning component of the fieldwork class is based upon partnerships among the home and host universities as well as service clubs in Kenya and the United States. The program directors cooperate with community liaisons in identifying suitable projects for the program participants and the service-learning portion of their class. The unique feature of service-learning in the program makes the experience different from either academic tourism in which the participants would not become engaged in service in their host community or mission-type volunteer work, in which the projects typically would neither contain an academic component nor be community identified.

Projects identified by the institutional and service club partnerships must also be of the appropriate scope for participants; service learning is one component of their academic experience while abroad. Previous projects that "Experience Kenya" has integrated into service-learning include protecting the environment of a rural primary school through a tree-planting, erosion-control project and providing labor to dig drainage systems and clean the grounds at a street children's rehabilitation center. In addition to the manual labor performed at the center, program participants also planned and supervised recreational activities for the children and helped prepare and serve meals.

Reflective Approach and Journaling Methods

The "Experience Kenya" program meets the requirements O'Neill sets for a reflective classroom (O'Neill, 1999). A reflective classroom is based on the assumptions that it takes place in a realistic setting, there is adequate teacher explanation of the decision-making process, students possess a diversity of opinions, students form opinions of the classroom experience, and the program is context-specific (O'Neill, 1999, p.9). The setting for the "Experience Kenya" classroom is in a university or on a university-sponsored event. Through the syllabus and frequent meetings, instructor explanation of expectations is clearly outlined. "Experience Kenya" is offered campus-wide by a major American public land grant university, so students from a wide range of disciplines and majors take part in the program. The people the students have contact with throughout the program come from diverse social, ethnic, and economic backgrounds, so participants are exposed to diverse opinions and views. Students also have different perceptions of the classroom experience; although they all must be capable scholars to participate, students are interested in different aspects of fieldwork and cultural activities. Finally, the program is context-specific in that while students continually gain knowledge about Kenya through their class work, reading newspapers, and briefings, their encounter with service on the program reinforces much of the information they have received about social concerns in country.

Reflection during service-learning can take place at several levels: alone, with classmates, and with community partners (Eyler, 2001). Reflection can take the form of journals, essays, portfolios, or discussion groups. Chisholm describes journal writing as a process "through which new thinking is derived and change occurs" (Chisholm, 2000, p.11). Blake-Yancy and Weiser describe portfolio reflection as a "well-theorized reflective practice" which is "grounded in a felt experience" (Blake-Yancy and Weiser, 1997, p.9).

Journaling was chosen as a means for reflection for the "Experience Kenya" students. Cole and Knowles describe journaling as "central to both the inquiry and development process" (Cole and Knowles, 2000, p. 56). By viewing writing as "a problem-solving or thinking-through process" the action of journal keeping can be a tool for reflection (Cole and Knowles,2000, p. 49). The students were required to make regular reflective and analytical entries in their journals. The students were able to harness their journal entries for longer papers they wrote to fulfill the academic requirements of their fieldwork experiences. The first journal entry was due prior to departure. A final reflective entry was due two months after return from Kenya.

Levels of Reflection

Written reflection is used in King and Kitchener's (1994) Reflective Judgment Model to determine the level of sophistication at which a student is reflecting. King and Kitchener found that with regard to college students, older students (seniors) scored higher on reflective thinking than freshmen (King and Kitchener, 1994, p. 224). This increase in capability to think reflectively is attributed to key assumptions King and Kitchener make regarding the development of reflective judgment capabilities. These assumptions include: individuals actively interpret and attempt to make sense of what they experience; individual interpretation of events is affected by their epistemic assumptions; people's ways of making meaning develop over time; individuals function within a developmental range of stages; interactions with the environment strongly affect an individual's development; development is stimulated when an individual's experience does not match expectations; and development in reflective thinking occurs within the context of the individual's background, previous educational experiences, and current life situation (King and Kitchener, 1994, pp. 226-9).

King and Kitchener generated a reflective judgment model that would account for their perceived neglect of epistemic assumptions in others' previous models (King and Kitchener, 1994, p. 8). Their model illustrates the critical thinking developmental process of learners that concludes with subjects capable of making reflective judgments. Three overarching categories house the seven stages of reflective thought. The first category, Pre-Reflective Thinking, encompasses three stages: "I know what I have seen;" "If it is in the news it has to be true;" and "When there is evidence that people can give to convince everybody one way or another, then it will be knowledge -- until then, it's just a guess." The second category includes Quasi-Reflective Thinking, stages four and five, which are characterized by uncertainty about facts and reasoning. Reflective Thinking is finally achieved in steps six and seven, when the student is able to reason about the sources of knowledge and judgment (King and Kitchener, 1994, pp.14-15).

Examples of challenges for students in the three categories of reflective thinking illustrate the levels at which students are engaged in reasoning. For students at the Pre-Reflective Thinking level, difficult tasks include using evidence to justify a point of view or recognizing authority as being better-qualified than themselves when making judgments on controversial issues (King and Kitchener, 1994, pp.250-1). Students operating in the category of Quasi-Reflective Thinking are challenged by choosing among competing interpretations or by understanding the importance of evidence in forming opinions (King and Kitchener, 1994, pp. 252-3). Students in the highest category, wherein reflective thinking is achieved, may still grapple with generalizing knowledge beyond the immediate situation or determining which point of view has greater truth value (King and Kitchener, 1994, p. 254.)

The Iowa Service Learning Partnership, a consortium of Iowa colleges and universities promoting service-learning on campus, conducted a study at different private institutions to identify the impact of service-learning upon students' development. Preliminary findings indicated that students' scores increased in the areas of cognitive, civic, personal, and emotional development after engaging in service-learning. Although the Iowa consortium study did not address reflection in those particular areas, it gave direction to this study to note developmental areas students included in their written reflections.

Procedure

Similar to the King and Kitchener study approach, the students on "Experience Kenya" were measured for their level of reflection before and after an experience. In the case of the King and Kitchener (1994) study, the experience was college; in the case of "Experience Kenya" students, it was before departure for and upon returning from the five-week immersion study abroad program. As part of the class work for the compulsory one-credit pre-departure orientation, students prepared their first reflective, analytical journal entry. They were also required to prepare a final reflective piece after completing the program. Research on the pre-departure entries and reflective summaries was conducted in accord with the university human subjects research protocol, including obtaining student permission to release material for research.

The students' first and final entries were examined using textual analysis, and values were assigned to each passage, ranking them in one of the seven levels of reflective thinking devised by King and Kitchener (1994). The rankings were then clustered into the three categories – Pre-Reflective Thinking, Quasi-Reflective Thinking, and Reflective Thinking. Double-blind review of the passages and subsequent comparison of rankings indicated high inter-rater reliability. Using the King and Kitchener (1994) model, student reflective pieces were assigned a level of reflection. Each piece was then reviewed for inclusion of areas of development as described by the Iowa consortium study. Thus, levels of reflection were measured and areas of development were noted.

Collective Case Studies

Student reflective journal entries were interpreted using the collective case study method (Stake, 1995) which includes multiple cases providing insight into an issue through description and comparison (Creswell, 2002). Case study analysis enabled researchers to gauge student development while accommodating for variables of student demographics, including age, gender, major, and previous experience abroad. Moreover, the case study method revealed student thoughts indicating not only the level at which they were reflecting, but also if their reflection contained examples of personal development.

Yin (1994) describes case studies as the preferred strategy when " 'how' or 'why' questions are being posed, when the investigator has little control over the events, and when the focus is on a contemporary phenomenon within some real-life context" (Yin,1994, p.1). Because the focus of the reflection research was on how students reflected via journaling during a new experience in their lives, one which the researchers could not control, the case study method for investigating student reflection during the "Experience Kenya" program is validated by Yin's claim that certain research questions are particularly well-suited to the case study method of investigation (1994).

The following case studies are illustrative of the breadth of responses the 15 participants in "Experience Kenya" gave in both their pre-departure pieces and reflective summaries.

Case Study A- Student #13

This student, a sophomore in the social sciences, was reflecting at a level in the lowest category in the King and Kitchener (1994) reflective development model, Pre-Reflective Thinking. However, the final entry is written at the highest level – Reflective Thinking.

Pre-departure Entry:

> "As of yet, it is still pretty hard to believe that I'm going to Kenya in less than two weeks. I anticipate that before I know it, I'll already be there...This will offer me a unique perspective on how Kenyans view their own culture and help me to have more understanding of cultural differences. Learning about Kenya while in Kenya seems to be the best way to do it.... I am hoping that going to Kenya will broaden my perspectives about education and economics. Being able to see how other students from a different background approach issues will give me a more diverse outlook, apart from my single socioeconomic upbringing. It is always good to have different experiences to draw upon when considering issues."

Final Entry:

> "What truly amazes me about SCANN [service-learning placement] is the way in which the organization operates. A woman who works there drives around Nakuru looking for street children. She visits a place a few times to see that a child is indeed homeless. Then she offers the child food and a place

to go where they can be taken care of. Later, a parent or relative must sign a waiver to allow the child to be raised at SCANN. The amazing thing is that a scenario like this would be considered kidnapping or other predatory behavior in America. It's a shame that the basic actions of finding those in need then helping them have gotten so bogged down in red tape and legal concerns that assisting the homeless in America can take the Government far longer than the system in Nakuru. There may not be as many precautions taken in Nakuru, but it is a credit to the people of SCANN the speed and focus of the assistance given to the children." "The most emotional part of the trip would be when the lady who takes in the children brought in the two children she found that morning. She asked the Kenyan students from Egerton if they knew the mentally handicapped woman who lived on the steps of the Barclay's Bank building. The two little boys, one of whom was wearing only one red galosh, were her sons. It made me extremely sad to look at the little boys and know that their mother couldn't care for them and probably couldn't care for herself either. They didn't understand what was going on and there were just so many factors working against their family that I just felt like crying. It is comforting to know, though, that the boys will have a chance to grow up here with the things they need at SCANN. This organization will give those boys and many others a chance at a normal life. Our visit to SCANN has to be one of the most memorable and emotional parts of the trip that I have experienced."

Characteristic of reflective thinking at lower levels, the pre-departure journal entry discusses how things seem and what the student hopes. Because the student is neither using evidence to support the claims made nor making a personal stand on the issues, it is clearly not reflection on the highest level. In contrast, in the final entry, the student was willing to support views with evidence and take a personal stand on the matter of homelessness in Kenya – all while recognizing that differences in assistance systems were important in the Kenyan context. These indicate reflection at the highest level – Reflective Thinking. In the first passage the student refers to cognitive and personal development anticipated in the experience. In the final passage, the student describes emotional and personal development while using knowledge gained as evidence in reflecting upon the experience. This cognitive development, as well as the civic engagement evident in the final piece, affirms that these areas are being self-identified as a result of participation in and reflection upon service-learning experiences.

Case Study B Student # 12

This student, a junior in family and consumer sciences, was reflecting at a relatively low level prior to departure – only able to make Pre-Reflective Thinking judgments about things seen and heard. However, in the final piece, the student exhibits characteristics of a student at the highest level – Reflective Thinking.

Pre-departure Entry:

"Time is going away from me and soon I'll be in Kenya where time is so trivial. I'm so excited to actually go. I keep on thinking of other things though which make me tiresome. Finals, school papers, friends & men are all on my mind. I'm sure it will seem so unimportant when I experience this 3rd world country.

I need to be getting organized and packed – or at least plan a time slot to do so. The things I plan to experience in Kenya are things about their culture. I'm also excited to see their beautiful (so I've heard) environment. I want to make a lot of friends also. Sometimes I think I should do something constructive that I would love – like joining the Peace Corps – who knows maybe this experience will push me to do it."

Final Entry:

"...A lot of issues in Kenya like health care and poverty really frustrated me at first. But, I came to realize that different parts of the world deal with different issues. All people deal with these issues in a different manner too. I noticed, for example, that in Kenya, the poorest person could be walking down a dirt road and still have the biggest smile on his face. They don't look at the things they don't have, like most of us Americans. Instead, they see more of the things that they do have and they appreciate them to the fullest.

"Living in Kenya has changed and influenced my life tremendously. I'm a lot more easy going and I don't tend to worry near as much about the little things that used to bother me. The biggest example that I can give is how much I used to worry about my weight and how I looked. After being in Kenya, I realized how selfish it was of me to worry about something as petty as my appearance. There are too many people out in the world wondering when and how they are going to get their next meal. I realized that I should appreciate the fact that I can eat and I don't have to worry about me or my family starving. It's kind of strange, too, because I've actually lost weight thinking this way."

In the first entry, the student exhibited Pre-Reflective Thinking, relying on the predeparture details and second-hand information in describing the experience. However, in the final reflective piece, the student is able to integrate the facts presented during the study abroad classes with the opportunity to engage in service-learning. The student touches on the civic area of impact by questioning the desire to serve abroad. The civic engagement area of impact was evident also in the final passage, describing the social conditions and the reaction the student had to them. The student also showed personal and emotional development in the final passage.

Case Study C – Student #15

This student, a senior in engineering, was already reflecting at the Quasi-Reflective level prior to departure, showing that he understood that different points of view exist. In the final piece he exhibited Reflective Thinking by taking a personal stand on the issues he had encountered and supporting his views with evidence gained through his cognitive growth while abroad.

Pre-departure Entry:

"Have extremely high expectations of self and of program experience. Hard to realize that imminent departure is less than two weeks away. Twelve days until all of my priorities and day-to-day routines are rendered irrelevant and I step into a new way of life; the risk that I discover something about myself (or the world) that casts doubt on my perceptions and beliefs, that are the defining factors of who I am, is a risk I am invariably prepared to face. Certainly the repetitious concerns of a Midwestern middle class male Caucasian college student must seem frivolous and somewhat absurd to a young man in Kenya, Africa."

Final Entry:

"When I think about my time in Kenya, the prevailing thought is of the friendships that I made and of the people that I met....Kenya, like America is made up of a variety of ethnicities. Kenya has certain regions noted for their cultural makeup (e.g. the Kikuyu in central Kenya and the Masai in southern Kenya). I mention this faction only because I think Americans have a tendency to view diversity in terms of skin color; although most Kenyans are black, there are approximately 40 different cultures and languages within the country. It was through these exchanges through the eyes of my friends: as a young nation facing political adversity but laden with youth who promise to propel their country past the problems of the past."

"Egerton students made a significant contribution to the growth of my character and the philosophies I use to evaluate certain properties of life. At the time I had little insights into the indelible marks that they and other experiences in Kenya would make on my perception of the world..."

"...During my study abroad I learned that finding work in Kenya is more difficult than finding a job in the U.S. In America, if you are determined and willing, you can get a job. In Kenya, this is not necessarily true. Our view in the U.S. of the unemployed is that these people are lazy and apathetic. In Kenya, however, there is even competition in obtaining simple, low-wage, and remedial work."

"Another amazing part of the Kenya experience was working at SCANN.... Without a doubt, the most gratifying part of the entire study abroad experience was working and playing with these children. Although they had already faced many demanding and heartbreaking obstacles in their short lives, they retained the innocence and hope that characterizes humanity. I realize that it would take a much more committed and long-lived approach to make a significant impact at SCANN, but I think we did create a palpable connection with the children. And although philanthropy is based on helping others in need, I think that we may have benefited from this experience more than the children did. It was truly inspirational."

The student shows progress from Quasi-Reflective Thinking to Reflective Thinking. In the pre-departure reflective piece, the student relies heavily on emotional anticipation of the experience as well as uncertainty. While these characteristics of written reflection indicate the student was at a level higher than his pre-reflective peers prior to departure, a marked increase in the level of reflection as well as content of written reflection is evident in the final piece. Cognitive development is evident in the epistemic knowledge gained about Kenya; it is applied as evidence for the student's opinion. The student also spent a great deal of the final passage reflecting on the aspect of civic engagement, showing that the student had felt an impact from the opportunity to serve. The student also describes a transformation in his personal development, highlighting how his critical view of the world changed as the result of the experience.

Case Study D – Student # 1

This student, a senior in design, remained at the lowest level, Pre-Reflective Thinking, throughout the course of journal entries. While the majority of students exhibited more sophisticated reflection at the end of the program, this student's level of reflection may be attributed to writing skills or misunderstanding the written assignment.

Pre-departure Entry:

"I anticipate that I will see many major experiences during the Experience Kenya trip. I expect to interact w/the students, and the citizens will be a great experience."

"Also, I think that seeing how the Kenyan people live, and work will also be a great experience. I also look forward to seeing the geography and the plant and animal diversity in Kenya. I anticipate that seeing the Kenyan people for the first time will also be a great experience."

"I think that I will come back from this trip with a better attitude and understand people of another culture, race, country, etc."

"I think that I will also be surprised by the vastly different world that the Kenyans live in, how they survive w/out all the high tech gizmos we have here."

Final Entry:

"It has been over a month since our return from Kenya and there isn't a day that goes by without thinking about it."

"When I first returned I thought most about the animals we saw and the U.S. food I wanted to eat. Now I think most about the people we met and saw. They were warm, friendly, and inviting. All of this even though most of them live in extreme poverty."

"Some events scared me, but despite those things I find myself wanting to go back more and more daily. It was a journey of a lifetime that I hope I will be able to experience sometime soon again."

Despite the student's relatively low level of reflection and lack of progress toward developing higher reflective thinking skills, the student still briefly discusses the areas of impact experienced, exhibiting inquiry to feed cognitive development and a heightened civic awareness of those in need. Moreover, the student hints at personal development by overcoming fears of the new situations presented while on study abroad.

Findings

Although student's journal entries contained passages in a wide range of reflective levels, a decisive majority of students showed a general trend to progress to a more sophisticated category of reflective thinking in their final reflective piece. Post-Assessment revealed that nearly three-fourths of the students progressed to the level of Reflective Thinking. In Pre-Assessment, seven students (#1,2,3,4,5,12,13) were at the Pre-Reflective Thinking level; seven (# 6,7,8,9,10,14,15) were at the Quasi-Reflective Thinking level; and one (#11) was at the Reflective Thinking level. Post Assessment results revealed that one student (#1) was at the Pre-Reflective Thinking Level; three (#2,4,5) were at the Quasi-Reflective Thinking level, and 11 (#3,6,7,8,9,10,11,12,13, 14,15) had reached the Reflective Thinking level. No student regressed, and only one had no change but was already at the Reflective Thinking level. Figure 1.

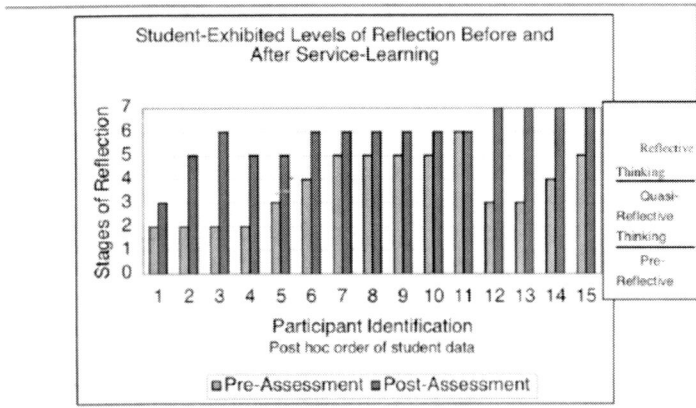

Figure 1: Student-Exhibited Levels of Reflection Before After Service-Learning.

Several factors may have affected the students' level of reflection in the first and final pieces. First, the period of time after the experience when students composed their final reflective piece may not have been optimal for students to recall what they had learned and how their new knowledge affected them. Second, some students may prefer reflecting orally rather than in writing or in an interactive discussion group rather than alone. Finally, students may not have completely understood the request to write reflectively and therefore recounted events rather than introspecting upon their experience.

Discussion

Reflection upon experiential learning has shown its worth as a tool for gauging student development. It was used as an academic component in a five-week, six-credit immersion study abroad program incorporating service-learning into traditional classroom academics. Students from the United States were immersed in a developing country setting and participated in service-learning to meet their academic requirements. Using the King and Kitchener (1994) Reflective Judgment Model levels of reflection to analyze student journals, it was discovered that students usually exhibited higher-level reflective thinking after the program was completed while they reflected at lower levels prior to participating in the program. The decisive majority of students were more able to use evidence and to weave in cognitive knowledge gained to support their thoughts. Moreover, students were more able to probe the complexity of problems presented in the Kenyan setting, recognize different and legitimate approaches to the solution, and take a personal stand on issues they had learned about and experienced. Upon investigating the levels of reflection developed by King and Kitchener (1994) using students' written reflective pieces, it was found that students usually progressed to a more complex level of written reflection, and no student regressed. Simultaneously, students reported their interest in the areas of development, which supports the notion that growth in these areas is recognized by students following a service-learning experience.

The program coordinators and professors created an expansive and instructional reflective classroom environment and required journaling, a method of learning recognized for its reflective benefits. Students were guided throughout the experience and were able to construct new knowledge while broadening their civic involvement. Through reflection, many students readily testified to the value such an experience has had in their lives. In their final reflective summaries, they independently reported an influential impact in the areas of civic, cognitive, emotional, and personal development and social and cultural awareness. Such growth, based on Burner's constructivist theory, illustrates the benefits of linking study abroad and service learning (Bruner, 1990). In the case of the "Experience Kenya" program, reflection in the months following the experience allowed students not only to recall their experience, but also to consider how it changed their outlook on the world.

Implications

Reflection will continue to be an effective method for students to construct knowledge based on their international experiences. This process encourages students to discover principles for themselves. Journaling is one vehicle for this reflection; others such as interviews or focus groups may also be appropriate. Further research by interviewing students and encouraging them to share their experiences may allow for students of greater comfort with oral expression to voice their reflections in a way other than writing. Longitudinal study of participants, reflecting one, five, or ten years after their experience may give insight into how the experience affected a participant's long-term choices. While student-identified areas of development, as a result of service-learning, served to create an expanded picture of student development in this study, the concept needs to be tested and grounded in future research. Furthermore, the educational community may be more able to assess the efficacy of programs by examining students' reflections. Reflection links the experience of service-learning with the opportunity to study abroad, enabling students to learn about themselves and the new world they are experiencing. Dewey sets the standard for the value of experiential learning, describing the educator's role "to arrange for the kind of experiences which, while they do not repel the student, but rather engage his activities are...more than immediately enjoyable since they promote having desirable future experiences" (Dewey, 1938, p.16). The findings in these case studies indicate that written reflection is an effective tool for prolonging and deepening student development in concert with an international developing country service-learning experience.

References

Astin, A.W. & Sax, L. (1998). How undergraduates are affected by service participation. *Journal of College Student Development*. 39(3), 251-263.

Blake-Yancey, K. & Weiser, I. (Eds.). (1997). *Situating portfolios*. Logan, UT: Utah State University Press. Bruner, J. (1990). *Acts of meaning*. Cambridge, MA: Harvard University Press.

Chen, A. & Van Maanen, J. (Eds.). (1999) *The reflective spin: case studies of teachers in higher education transforming action*. Singapore: World Scientific.

Chisholm, L. A. (2000). *Charting a hero's journey*. New York: International Partnership for Service-Learning.

Cole, A. L. & Knowles J. G. (2000). *Researching teaching*. Needham Heights, MA: Allyn & Bacon.

Creswell, J. (2002). *Educational research: planning, conducting, and evaluating quantitative and qualitative Research*. Columbus Ohio: Merrill Prentice Hall.

Dewey, J. (1938). *Experience and education*. Kappa Delta Pi.

Eyler, J. (2001). Creating your reflection map. *New Directions in Higher Education*, no. 114, pp. 35-43.

Eyler, J. & Giles D. E., Jr. (1999). *Where's the learning in service-learning?* San Francisco: Jossey–Bass.

Iowa Service Learning Partnership. *Identifying successes in model service-learning programs across Iowa*.

Jacoby, B., & Associates. 1996. *Service learning in higher education*. San Francisco: Jossey-Bass.

King, P.M., and Kitchener, K.S. (1994). *Developing reflective judgment: understanding and promoting intellectual growth and critical thinking in adolescents and adults*. San Francisco: Jossey-Bass.

O'Neill, M. (1999). In *The reflective spin: case studies of teachers in higher education transforming action*. Ai-Yen Chen, and John Van Maanen, Eds. Singapore: World Scientific. p. 9.

Pascarella, E.T. and Terenzini, P.T. (1991). *How college affects students: findings and insights from twenty years of research*. San Francisco: Jossey-Bass.

Stake, R. E. (1995). *The art of case study research*. Thousand Oaks, CA: Sage Publications.

Yin, R. K. (1994). *Case study research design and methods*. Second Edition. Thousand Oaks, CA: Sage Publications.

Part VII

Examples of Service-Learning across the Disciplines

Overview

Part 7 of the book is made up of 10 different examples of service-learning courses taught across a wide variety of disciplines, including: (1) fashion design, (2) Spanish, (3) math, (4) foreign language, (5) information systems, (6) sociology, (7) science, (8) management, (9) literature, and (10) biology.

Fashion Design

Service Learning

Opportunities for Deep Learning in Fashion Design and Merchandising Education

Karen Videtic, Virginia Commonwealth University, Virginia, USA

Abstract: Service Learning is the new buzz word on college campuses today, and many programs lack strategic course design nor build in a reflection component to ensure or at least attempt to engineer "deep learning" for their participants. The creation of service learning opportunities requires planning, implementation and evaluation of course design, as well as creating community partnerships that can withstand the test of time. This paper will explore the two major service learning opportunities that have been developed for fashion majors, and their impact on the students that have participated. One of the courses has taken place in Guatemala working with indigenous women for the past three years, and attempts to take traditional weaving skills and apply them to contemporary fashion items that can be sold for a "fair labor wage". Students spend time in the classroom learning at their home campus as well as time in Guatemala, working and learning with the Mayan women. The second course was developed around the philanthropic arm of the pediatric oncology unit of the university's medical campus, ASK. Students created the print or surface design for a pajama or loungewear item that would be developed in the following semester. The loungewear items were "port friendly" allowing young patients an alternative to a hospital gown as well as an item of clothing designed specifically to adapt for

receiving chemotherapy without the removal of their clothing. This paper will com-
pare and contrast the planning process, the implementation and the community and
learning outcomes of both of these projects.

Introduction

Service Learning is a growing and pervasive movement on college campuses
throughout the United States and has been integrated into numerous academic programs from art education to social work to business education.
Brown University, Georgetown University and Stanford University started
a consortium to create service learning opportunities for students that address ethics and community service (Andrews, 2007). The *Campus Compact*
originally had a membership of 23 schools in 1985, and today has over 1,000
participating colleges and universities involved in integrating student learning with their respective communities (Andrews, 2007).

Service learning is designed to improve learning for students by coordinating an experiential learning opportunity that serves the student, the university and the community. From the curricular perspective, the benefits of
service learning include a sense of civic responsibility (Scales, Blyth, Berkas,
& Kielsmeier, 2000), cognitive and intellectual development, improvement
of self-concept and tolerance for others, and leadership skills. Cognitive development includes knowledge of specific information, processing of data
and problem solving skills (Smith, 2008).

The student's educational goals are somewhat different. They want to
create an opportunity to learn outside of the classroom walls, and to practice what they have learned in the traditional classroom setting. Students
also want to add to their resume with positive experiences that foster and
highlight their leadership skills, decision making and problem solving abilities. Some students have a sense of community responsibility and feel com-
pelled to "give back". The service learning opportunity provides college
credit and fulfills these needs.

Universities want to be "good neighbors" within their immediate communities and cities where they previously were viewed as large organizations
that bought up land, students and faculty that "took over" towns and neighborhoods, and in general, were not always positively viewed as good local citizens. Universities today realize that their communities are vital partners in
the growth and survival of learning institutions. Working together with service learning programs serves not only students but the communities where
they both reside. The long term effects are significant in the quality of life
for all involved. For example, the Criminal Justice program and its students
at Virginia Commonwealth University work with the local community to
lower crime rates for residents and college students. VCU has been name by
the President of the United States to the *Higher Education Community Ser-*
vice Honor Roll for its outstanding efforts in community engagement.

This paper will review the key components and considerations of the development of a service learning program for fashion design and merchandising students at Virginia Commonwealth University. Those components/considerations are: community partnership, marketing, student preparation, development of action based experiential learning opportunity, student reflection and reporting, and presentation to the community.

Community Partnership

Understanding the importance of developing service learning opportunities among not only the local community but throughout the world, the Department of Fashion Design and Merchandising program at Virginia Commonwealth University created a partnership with a local church based group in Richmond, Virginia in the spring of 2005. The program's overarching goals were to assist Maya women in the remote mountains of Guatemala obtain a fair labor wage for their native handwork. The learning for the fashion students revolved around an existing course, FASH 450 Fashion Line Development, normally taught as a simulation where students research and develop a line of denim jeans for a targeted market in the United States. (A traditional semester course, FASH 450 has 45 contact hours and meets twice a week for one hour and 15 minutes during the fall and spring semesters.) Faculty reviewed the course's learning objectives and determined that they could still be met through a service learning component. A series of steps were developed to organize and implement this program during the summer of 2005, and that process was reviewed, adapted and restructured over the next three years.

In 2007, the Department of Fashion Design and Merchandising developed a relationship with ASK, the philanthropic arm of the Pediatric Oncology Unit on VCU's medical campus. We developed a two semester studio course (six hours weekly for 15 weeks) where design students created the artwork for the fabrication, printed the fabric and create "port friendly" lounge wear for patients from about five years old to 21 years old in the hospital receiving treatment. The project was called *ASK for Comfort.*

Marketing

Once the department was committed to the summer program, the marketing of the "Guatemala Line Development" course was essential to its success. Word of mouth spurned interest, and informational meetings involving key faculty and members of the non-profit organization backing the trip sealed the involvement. Each ensuing year the marketing of the summer program used student testimonials and images from the previous summer. Garments were made available to showcase the student's designs and Maya women's handwork. One year a collection of native Guatemalan textiles and clothing was featured in an exhibition, "Contemporary Daughters of Exchel: Maya Weaving from the Bowdler Textile Collection" at the university's Anderson gallery. There was also a VCU HD TV special (http://www.vcutvhd.vcu.edu/shows/studyabroad/guatemala1.html) developed during the second year complete with a series of videos shot on location and chronicling the students work both in Richmond and Guatemala. This "special" was broadcast not only on campus but locally and regionally. Between eight and twelve students participated in each of the first three years of the program. Considering the other opportunities to study abroad in Italy or intern in New York City, the department was pleased with the student involvement.

Junior and senior design students were briefly told about the assigned *ASK for Comfort* project once they were enrolled in the surface design class. In the fall, it was one of many assignments for the development of fabrication. In the spring semester, the students knew they would be designing children's clothing and they knew the garments were to be worn by children with cancer. Neither of the *ASK for Comfort* courses was marketed as "service learning".

Student Preparation

Student preparation for the Guatemala course included conversational Spanish language skills (although most of the Maya women spoke a native language and not Spanish), Maya culture and customs, cross cultural perspectives such as Geert Hofstede's Four Dimensions of Culture, and of course, the curricular content about fashion product development were covered. The students were to design and source a line of contemporary apparel inspired by the indigenous textiles of the Maya. The items would be made by the women in Guatemala, and sent back to Richmond to be sold at "Alternatives", a boutique owned by the non-profit organization. Students researched their target market/customer to determine who shopped the local "artisan" boutiques and fair labor retailers such as Ten Thousand Villages, and their product requirements with regard to fashion items. Color and trend forecasts were analyzed for their relevance to their customer. Theme and product presentation boards were created and discussed. Technical specification packages were created and sourcing of materials was begun. Marketing and promotion of the apparel line was also addressed concentrating on the marketability of garments made based on fair labor and trade issues. The preparation took place on the Richmond, Virginia campus prior to the excursion to Guatemala. All necessary equipment and supplies were collected and shipped ahead including sewing machines and cutting boards during the second and third years.

Student preparation for the **ASK for Comfort** course included market research with patients, family, nurses and doctors from the medical campus. The faculty led a focus group to understand the needs of the children receiving chemotherapy on site at the ASK clinic. The design students were given a tour of the treatment facilities in the fall semester while working on their fabrication but not in the spring semester (not all students took both classes).

Development of Action based Experiential Learning Opportunity

Probably the most surprising and overwhelming part of the learning experience in the Guatemala course was the actual implementation of the "service" for this economically and socially challenged community. The majority of the students enrolled in the class were middle class and privileged by world standards. Lack of electricity, limited selection of food choices (if any choice at all), bathroom facilities and living conditions were obstacles to be overcome on an individual basis before the fashion design, sewing and the creation of saleable items could be addressed.

Students learned about local weaving and embroidery practices, and met with the women from a local cooperative that they would be working with everyday of the eleven days they would spend in Guatemala. Days were filled with explanations of the student designs to the local women through a translator. Adjustments were made with regard to design and local availability of materials, and actual garments were produced to be sold back in Richmond. Meals were shared and often students would be invited to local homes for lunch and/or dinner. Speakers were a large part of the evening events, and sometimes students went into the city to visit the markets or meet with other study abroad students for meals and entertainment.

The **ASK for Comfort** course was run as a traditional design studio course with students meeting on campus in a departmental sewing studio, and run like the majority of fashion design studios they have already taken. A jury of fashion professionals and the grantee for the funds to do this project selected both the best fabrications and the best designs. Students received dollar awards/scholarships if their fabrication and/or garment were chosen.

Student Reflection and Reporting

Upon their return to Richmond, the **Guatemala** students met for three additional days to finalize their work and make plans for the continuation of the product production. They "costed out" their items and recommended a retail selling price. They were required to write an essay about their experience and were part of a classroom discussion about their learning and what might be considered for the following year's program.

The *ASK for Comfort* students had no reflection component embedded in the course.

275

Presentation to the Community

The final day of the **Guatemala** course, students presented their work they had completed over the past three weeks including presentation boards, specification sheets, and finished garments. They also reflected on their experience with a PowerPoint/Photoshop presentation to the faculty, the departmental chairperson, the School of the Arts and university administration as well as the management of the community non-profit. Many of the students became very emotional when they discussed their relationships with the Maya women they had worked with in Guatemala. Of the 29 students that have participated in this course over the last three years, six have stayed involved either by working for the local non-profit retail store or working with a similar fair trade organization. Four have returned to Guatemala on several occasions to continue their design work.

A fashion show showcasing the **ASK for Comfort** loungewear and the fabrication was held the following September during Pediatric Cancer Month. Several patients (children and young adults) and their siblings were the models to launch this line of clothing which would be given away to each new patient entering the pediatric cancer unit (http://www.vcu.edu/arts/fashion/dept/gallery.shtml). Only two of over twenty students from the fashion design classes attended the fashion show.

Learning Outcomes

Reflecting upon the three year service learning experience in Guatemala, the educational outcomes were much broader and significant than the Department of Fashion could ever have imagined. This part of the paper will examine the learning outcomes for the fashion students and explore what made this Guatemala service learning course so different, and life changing for so many students.

Upon reviewing the literature, in 1976 Gardiner and Howe noted a distinction between passive, surface learning and an "intrinsically motivated process of personalized meaning construction or *deep learning*" (Clare, 2007). They believed that the learning process had to be explored from both the educators and the learner's perspective. Educators tended to be preoccupied with a quantitative approach to learning rather than what is learned and how this knowledge was obtained (qualitative approach) (Clare, 2007). Gardiner and Howe placed emphasis on context and evaluation to promote deep learning, and later Clare promoted "stop and reflect" moments to promote active learning in her research. Reflective journaling is a common component in the literature review of active, deep and action learning articles. The writing assignments tend to create critical examination of the learning environment, the student's involvement and application of new knowledge and theory. Numerous articles noted that teaching has continued to be primarily didactic having students read assigned texts and listen to lectures. (Falzon, 1998; Meihls & Moffatt, 2000) (Reynolds, 1985). It was also noted that students are uncomfortable with public expression of their experiences and often find that reflection is too time consuming with regard to the demands of their time and lifestyle.

Clare concludes in her research with social work students that faculty must go beyond "encouraging dialogue" and developing evaluation processes that encourage critical evaluation. Her students were asked to "incorporate three levels of analysis into their learning summaries: concepts and issues introduced in the lectures, reading and seminars; their understanding about social work –purpose, profession and located activity; and their learning about themselves as beginner practitioners, insights gained and challenges raised for them" (Clare, 2007). Synthesizing personal experience with abstract concepts, lectures, texts and readings is the process that meets Gardiner's criteria for deep learning or personalized learning.

Fiddler and Marienau state that there are four elements of reflection: active participation, an unusual or perplexing situation/event, an examination of one's assumptions in light of the new experience and the integration of new understanding of one's experiences.

Conclusions and Concerns

The conclusions drawn from my involvement in the Service Learning course and my experience with Action Learning has brought me to the assertion that we must create opportunities for students "to learn from the service and community experience rather than learn about them" if we are going to encourage deep learning (Fiddler & Marienau, 2008). Our student's involvement in both courses that served marginalized communities was dramatically different as noted by their personal investment of the outcomes. It should also be noted that the community learning experience brings a unique and personalized set of skills and knowledge based on the individual student's perceptions and experiences. We cannot control the entirety of the learning outcomes nor should we try.

The students that participated in our Guatemala service learning course, first and foremost, examined their lifestyle and their personal sense of comfort and quality of life. Some students marveled at "how happy the women seemed although they lived in poverty". They questioned their own beliefs and values about their career choice to enter what is seen as a superficial field of fashion. They ate new foods, they didn't wear makeup nor blew dried their hair for eleven days. Many became ill from the water and took care of one another, and created new friendships with people they would never have related to previously. What does this mean? The student's inquiry or reflection (both written and discussion) resulted in forming a new understanding of their experience and lead to making "meaning" of the adventure (Fiddler & Marienau, 2008)

Making meaning is not just a personal connection but also includes what students have learned in relation to what they thought they knew or clarification of their assumptions or even the development of new skills. Many merchandising students learned to sew in Guatemala, and they experienced what it was like to be a fashion designer. Some students realized that there were alternatives to a Seventh Avenue career. Many chose to continue their work providing marginalized communities of women the opportunity to obtain a fair labor wage. To quote one student: "the experience taught tolerance, understanding, communication skills...how to be humble and courteous....it opened my eyes to see that not everyone lives the same way that I do....act the same way .... or want the same things.....the class also highlighted marketing skills in a specific way, making the material easier to digest."

As an educator, I believe that my peers (including myself) are too busy checking off a list of competencies and making sure the entire textbook is covered in a 15-week semester. Curriculum must be developed assisting and developing student's capacity to reflect on their experiences. Educators must teach students how to reflect. With the advent of "teaching to the test" most young adults have been discouraged from reflecting and instead have been encouraged to use repetition or superficial learning to achieve maximum test scores.

Service learning and action learning are just two opportunities to access "deep learning" experiences. Action learning adds solving real problems in real time to the learning experience. Journaling, blogs, discussion and critics are useful ways of encouraging reflection and "owning" ones knowledge.

In conclusion, I would like to express, in the words of Reg Revans, what I think is the most important and relevant questions for educators today:

"Most education is concerned with passing on the theories and practices of yesterday...but if today is significantly different from yesterday, and tomorrow is likely to be very different from today, how shall we know what to teach?

References

Andrews, C. P. (2007). Service Learning: Application and Research in Business. *Journal of Education for Business* , p. 19-26.

Anstee, J. L., Harris, S. G., Pruitt, K. D., & Sugar, J. (2008). Service-Learning Projects in an Undergraduate Gerontology Course: A six-Stage Model and Application. *Educational Gerontologoy*, p. 595-609.

Butin, Dan W. (2005). *Service-Learning in Higher Education: Critical Issues and Directions.* Gordonsville, VA: Palgrave Macmillian.

Clare, B. (2007). Promoting Deep Learning: A Teaching, Learning and Assessment Endeavour. *Social Work Education* , p. 433-446.

Driscoll, A., Holland, B., Glemon, S., & Kerrigan, S. (1996). An Assessment Mode for Service-Learning: comprehensive Case Studies of Impact on FAculty, Students, Community and Institution. *Michigan oJournal of Community Service Learning* , 66-71.

Falzon, C. (1998). *Foucault and Social Dealogue.* London: Routledge.

Fiddler, M., & Marienau, C. (2008). Developing Habits of Reflection for Leaningful Learning. *New Directions for Adult and Continuing Education*, 75-85.

Meihls, D., & Moffatt, K. (2000). Construcing social work identity based on the reflexive self. *British Journal of Sockial Work*, 339-448.

Reynolds, B. (1985). Learning and Teaching in the Pratice of Social Work. *National Association of Social Workers*.

Scales, P. C., Blyth, D. A., Berkas, T. H., & Kielsmeier, J. C. (2000). The Effects of Service Learning on Middle School Students' Social Responsibility and Academic Success. *Journal of Early Adolescence*, 332-358.

Smith, M. C. (2008). Does Service Learning Promote Adult Development? Theoretical Persepctives and Directions for Research. *New Direction for Adult and Continuing Education*, p. 5-15.

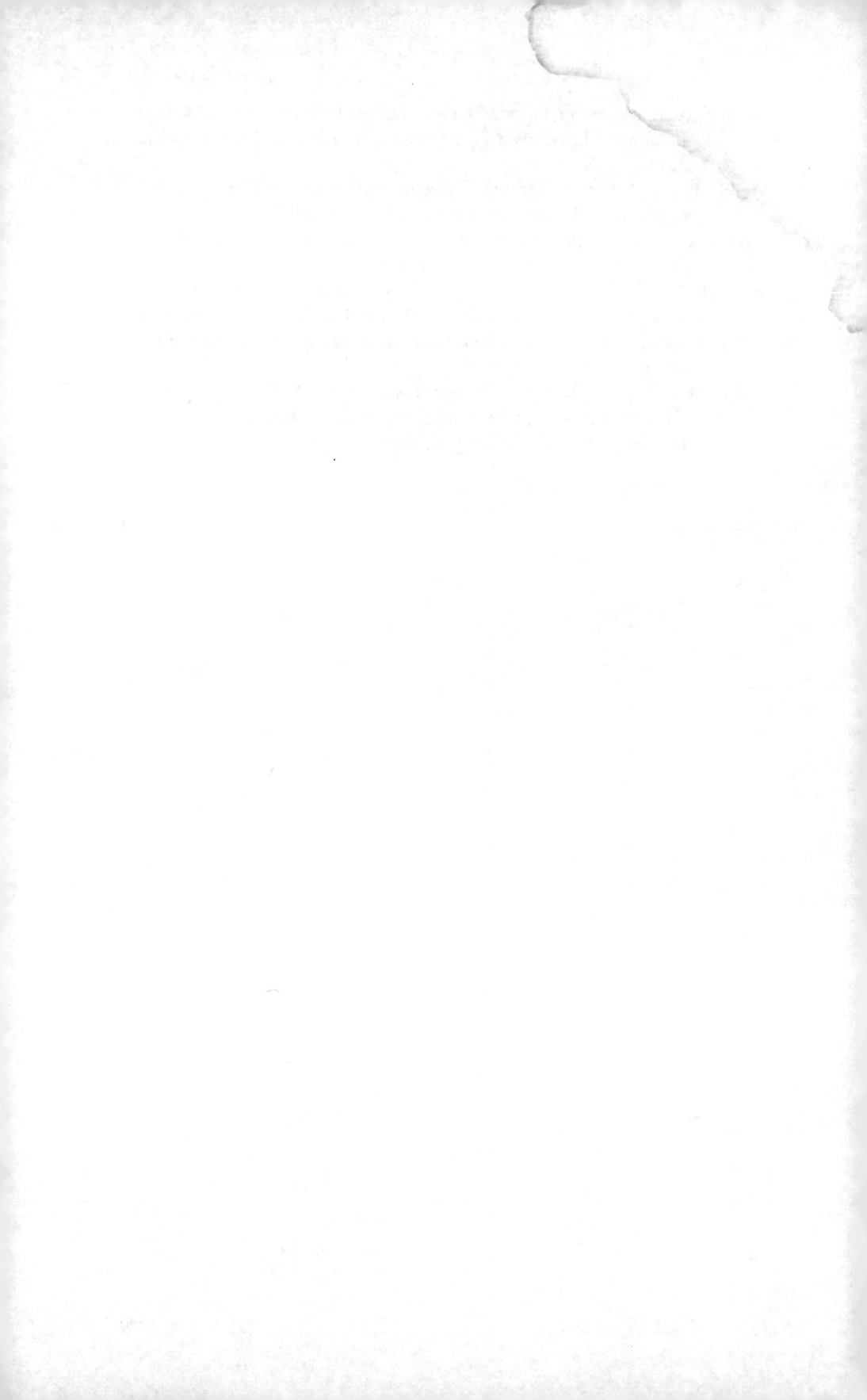

Community as Classroom

Service-Learning in the Foreign Language Classroom

Allison D. Krogstad, Ph.D.

As educators, we have a tendency to complain about students' apathy and lack of involvement in what goes on around them in their university, community, and world. We expect them to sit in class, learn, and then go out and change the world. However, traditionally, the goal of education has been to make changes in individuals, not in society (Slimbach 101). While focusing on the individual students and their abilities, goals, and potential, we teach them *about* society, but perhaps we have forgotten to teach *how* to exist and interact within that society. If they are not prepared through their education to take part in such interaction, society will not get a passing grade.

Much of the basis of such interaction is communication, and the basis of human communication is language. Therefore, societal interaction, well-being, and potential lies in our ability to communicate through language--thus the tie between society and language. In our language classes, then, we must teach the value of civic engagement, and the most valuable way to do this is through service-learning. In teaching Spanish in the United States, using service-learning can be an invaluable tool to connecting and engaging our students with the Hispanic community.

Why service-learning?

Service-learning shares many characteristics with language learning. First of all, it combines skills and knowledge with civic responsibility (Zlotkowski 85). Likewise, learning a language is a skill as well as a means to engage others in society and communicate with them in a culturally responsible manner. Service-learning is an interaction between people and making a connection to other people. This is also the purpose of language (Mullaney 54). Service-learning is experiential as well as academic, and classroom language learning is an academic endeavor with the objective of creating students who both can and want to use their language in real-life experience. Due to these similarities, it seems quite obvious that service-learning and language learning could and should be used in conjunction to create more knowledgeable and responsible language learners.

In regard to language acquisition, there is no doubt that speaking with native speakers in "real-life" situations, getting to know them, exchanging ideas with them, and helping them while they help you is one of the most effective ways to learn and practice a language. In a "natural environment", "the focus is on the content of the communication rather than the form" (Mullaney 52-53). So, while in class students may be focusing on the intricacies of correctly forming the preterite tense, in a service-learning situation, they will focus on getting their past tense point across. There is a "need for building a relationship between what is taught in the classroom and what is utilized in the real world" (Hale 10). Using class and service-learning together, students will learn the technical as well as the practical and personal.

Also, through service-learning, not only will students be using their language, they will be using it within a cultural context--something that is next to impossible to recreate in the classroom. Students will learn to comprehend the "depth and complexity" of culture and will "understand more realistically the nature of human institutions, behavior, and culture" (Berry, "Experiential..." 326). In addition, personal interactions bring about patience, humility, and interdependence (Hale 13)--valuable characteristics to have when interacting in a culture and language other than one's own and, again, difficult to duplicate in class. Service-learning has the "capacity to further international and intercultural literacy, knowledge, and sensitivity" (Berry, "Service-Learning..." 311). In my opinion, this is the most important goal of language learning. I teach language and its use so that students will be able to enter the world, communicate, and interact in a mature, responsible, and fulfilling manner. After learning Spanish, students can communicate through language with about 350 million more people, who belong to distinctive cultures, than before they learned the language. This fact alone demands that we also teach cultural sensitivity and that we give students the opportunity to experience the culture--not just the language.

How to incorporate service-learning into the language classroom

The most basic characteristic of service-learning in the language classroom should be that it is seen as an imperative part of the learning process. It should be a course (if not a curricular) objective and a part of class content. It is not just an extra, not just something to do for fun if there is time in the semester. "If service is an add-on that is not designed to advance the objectives of a course or does not help students learn course content, it degrades the academic integrity of the course" (Enos and Troppe 61) and the effectiveness of the service experience. In deciding how to incorporate the service, one should consider the language level of the students, previous experience, time constraints, location issues, class content, the community to be contacted, etc.

Next, there should always be pre-departure preparation. This could include discussion, readings, research, reflection on expectations, language preparation, or a guest speaker from the community to be served. If students are not prepared for their experience, they will not fully be able to gain what you want them to gain. "Students venturing into communities perceive those things that they are mentally prepared to see" (Cone and Harris 48). Also, if there are certain issues that will impact their experience, prepare them to deal with them. For example, if race is going to be an issue, confront that issue before they go. The instructor "should intentionally and systematically confront the fact that students' values may be different from those of the communities where they are placed" (Berry, "Service-Learning..." 313). If they are not prepared to deal with the situation, they may come away feeling only uncomfortable, and the learning opportunity will have been lost.

When properly prepared, students can then "venture" into the experience. The service-learning sites should be chosen for their ability to provide students with personal contact with the individuals representing the target culture and target language. Doing tasks such as filing for a non-profit organization, for example, is a nice thing to do, but it in no way meets language and culture objectives, nor does it engage the student in understanding and appreciating the lives of others. "We must work *with*, rather than for, others" (Green 19). Students and those they interact with must all see that they are learning and benefiting from each other. For example, one of my students tutored two Guatemalan children and their mother, and, in addition to allowing the student to practice her Spanish, the mother taught her how to cook some Guatemalan dishes. All involved had something to learn and something to give. "The activity [should] change both the recipient and the provider of the service" (Learn and Serve). This sense of "mutuality" (Berry, "Service-learning in..." 311) will keep students from getting a sort of paternalistic view of what they are doing. We do not want them leaving the experience simply thinking, "What a good person I am. I helped someone in need." They must think, "Wow, I really got to know that person and to understand them. Maybe I should work with people like her more often." As

Margot Kennard says, "Students move beyond paternalistic service when they develop a sense of care and connection to those community members they are serving" (46). Thus, students need personal contact.

After the experiences, students should take part in personal reflection. Students should think and write about the experience (in the target language), answering some questions posed by the teacher and also freely writing their thoughts. With the teacher partially directing the reflection, the students will be more likely to focus on what the teacher wants them to get out of the experience, think about it, and internalize it. There should be a certain amount of freedom of reflection, also. If they were to write a weekly journal and be free to say whatever they wanted, the teacher could identify problems that may be keeping the student from learning (Cone and Harris 51). Also, with some freedom, a student might discover something wonderful that the instructor had not anticipated.

If the entire class or a small group of students have taken part in the same experience, they can also reflect as a group--sharing ideas, observations, reactions, etc. Even if they have not all gone to the same site, there are certain things that they can share with each other and learn from each other.

Another important aspect to incorporating service-learning into the language classroom is that the experience must be repeated. One time for a few hours does not give the student the variety of contact needed nor the depth of understanding that can be gained by repeated visits, repeated reflections, and continuing personal connections. As Learn and Serve Clearinghouse website states:

Learning occurs through a cycle of action and reflection as students work with others through a process of applying what they are learning to community problems and, at the same time, reflecting upon their experience as they seek to achieve real objectives for the community and deeper understanding and skills for themselves.

At the end, there should be some sort of evaluation of the experience by the student, the teacher, and the site supervisor. Depending on the activity, it may also be appropriate to have the "recipients" of the service also evaluate the experience and the student.

A specific plan for Intermediate or Advanced Spanish

Intermediate Spanish (specifically second semester of second year college-level language) is an ideal time to incorporate service-learning. At that level, though by no means fluent, students have a survival ability in Spanish, so they can have some meaningful language practice and communicate somewhat effectively. Also, after intermediate language, a lot of students tend to disappear from language study. They have perhaps taken Spanish to fulfill a college requirement but do not wish to continue to get a minor or a major. Therefore, if we can give them a personal connection to the Hispanic community, they will be getting something they will be missing out on by not continuing to the major or minor level and studying abroad. Also, I hope that with the personal connection, they will be inspired to continue their studies of language, study abroad, and earn a minor or major in Spanish. (The plan described below could be used in Advanced Spanish as well.)

For this experience, it is recommended that students spend at least 15 hours during the semester doing service-learning and write at least 5 reflection papers. The sites may include such things as doing immigration paperwork with individuals wanting to bring their families to the U.S., tutoring children whose first language is Spanish, working at day care centers that serve mostly Hispanic families, working with employment agencies and health clinics, helping with tax forms, and a variety of other experiences which will vary depending on your college or university's location and resources.

The following are the 5 possible reflection activities for before, during, and after the experience (to be written in Spanish):

1. Pre-departure activity: Information about the agency or organization you will be working with (where it is, what it does, who it serves, etc.), why you want to serve there, and what you expect to get out of the experience.
2. Reflection on your first service experience (how did you feel beforehand or when you arrived, was it what you expected, what did you do, who did you meet, etc.)
3. Reflection on the needs of the people your agency serves (what are their greatest needs, how is the agency serving them, what more seems to be needed, etc.)
4. Research about Latinos in the U.S. and reflection about how those with whom you are working fit into the national situation.
5. After the experiences are completed: Reflection on the experience as a whole (what have you gained from the experience, was it worthwhile, what or who will you most remember, how has your understanding of language and/or culture changed, etc.)

If this is to be an optional experience, I suggest that the students who do not participate in service be given an alternative assignment. For instance, ask each student to research a different Spanish-speaking country, and write 5 papers discussing topics that would be helpful for getting to know the country's needs and potential for growth, such as economy, politics, human rights, demographics, social classes, environmental issues, etc. These topics should be matched to the cultural topics in the course text if possible. Later in the semester, while service students must be representatives for their organizations, research students will be representatives for their countries.

At the end of the semester, as a part of their final evaluation, students should give a presentation. However, it is recommended that it not be a traditional, stand-in-front-of-the-class-while-everyone-else-falls-asleep type of presentation. One way to avoid typical presentation problems is to make it an interactive, community government simulation in which the class acts as community leaders who have funds to allocate to worthy organizations.

Service option students must then be advocates for their agencies. Students who did the research option take part in a meeting of the "United Hispanic Nations", in which funds will also be allocated. Here is how it works:

Day 1: In small groups, students create questions to ask others about their agencies or countries. (Service option students make questions for other service option students and research students for other research students.) The goal of the questions will be to determine who has the most need and the most potential for growth if given some money. The instructor helps the groups and gives them guidance in regard to the type of questions to be asked and how to ask them.

Day 2: Each small group gets to ask other groups their questions, taking note of the answers given. Each individual is also given an opportunity to give a planned report about their agency (or country), discussing anything that might not have been covered by the questions. (This provides students with the opportunity to demonstrate both planned and spontaneous speech.) (If the class is very large, this may take more than one day.)

Day 3: In small groups, students discuss the value of each organization and its potential ability to use community funds. (The research option students discuss the countries, their needs, and their potential use of the funds.) Each group presents its opinions on how much each organization (or country) should get and why. The class then comes to a consensus.

The purpose of this exercise is, first, to evaluate speaking ability. The different speech tasks (from discussion to formal presentation) allow the teacher to see a variety of examples of oral ability. Secondly, this exercise makes the students think beyond themselves one more time. They must, metaphorically, stand beside those with whom they worked one last time, support the work of their agency, and personally advocate for them. Even those students who did not do the service option will gain some sense of service and community involvement as they advocate for their countries and listen to the experiences of others. And, hopefully, all will realize, through their personal involvement, concern, work, and willingness to take a risk and do something they have not done before with people they have not interacted with before, that everyone in this world is connected and we should make the most of that connection.

Student reactions

The following are the reactions of several students to the experiences described above.

Student #1, who worked with individuals to fill out immigration paperwork: "When I began, I was really scared. I didn't know much about immigrants and their way of life. I am from Iowa, from a place with little diversity. This experience has taught me more about other cultures in only month than in all of my years in school."

Student #2: "Service-learning has been a big part of my life. It's a great way to learn Spanish and volunteer. Last year, I volunteered at HER [Hispanic Education Resources] in Des Moines. While I was there, I helped fill out tax forms and met a lot of neat people. I have also translated for Jefferson Elementary School in Pella [Iowa], and this year, I am studying abroad in Spain...I am still doing service-learning over here. I am volunteering at a disability home where the people are physically and mentally disabled. I help them with vocabulary, math, computer skills, etc. I am helping at an Animal Shelter, too. My life feels more complete while I am helping others and I am practicing my Spanish."

Student #3, who tutored 2 Guatemalan children and their mother: "As I walked away from this service-learning experience, I gathered more than I had ever anticipated. The personal interaction and using my language skills to help others was very powerful. The relationships I built with the children were amazing, and my last day working with them brought a very emotional goodbye from not only myself and the two of them, but also from their mother and father. I realized what a difference I had made, and reading the letters from their teachers was touching in that the children talked about me as if I were a superstar. The experience I had as a result of working with this family outnumber any possibilities within the classroom. I had the opportunity to attend Sunday mass, work directly with a Spanish-speaking Sister of the church, learn a thing or two in the kitchen, and experience a different and yet not-so-different way of life. It is challenging to sum up this four month experience because it is something that students must encounter for themselves. My experience with service-learning gave me an immeasurable amount of joy as I developed my language skills through helping others."

I think that these reactions sum up the purpose of service-learning in the languages. #1: You can do a lot more, linguistically and culturally, in a lot less time. #2: It inspires students to continue serving their community and the world in the future. #3: It gives students a personal connection to other people, and to the target culture and language, that produces a sense of joy. It is seldom that you find a student who gets profound joy out of studying verbs in class. However, if you get them out of classroom, into contact with real people, they will find joy in using those verbs to make a connection, communicate, and serve.

References

Berry, Howard A. "Experiential Education: The Neglected Dimension of International/Intercultural Studies." *Combining Service and Learning, A Resource Book for Community and Public Service* Volume 1. Raleigh, NC: National Society for Internships and Experiential Education, 1990. 324-332.

---. "Service-Learning in International and Intercultural Settings." *Combining Service and Learning, A Resource Book for Community and Public Service* Volume 1. Raleigh, NC: National Society for Internships and Experiential Education, 1990. 311-313.

Boyle, J. Patrick and Denise M. Overfield. "Community-Based Language Learning: Integrating Language and Service." *Construyendo Puentes (Building Bridges): Concepts and Models for Service-learning in Spanish.* Ed. Josef Hellebrandt and Lucía T. Varona. Washington, D.C.: American Association for Higher Education, 1999. 137-147.

Cone, Dick and Susan Harris. "Service-Learning Practice: Developing a Theoretical Framework." *Introduction to Service-Learning Toolkit: Readings and Resources for Faculty.* Providence, RI: Campus Contact/Brown University, 2000. 43-55.

Enos, Sandra L. and Marie L. Troppe. "Service-Learning in the Curriculum." *Introduction to Service-learning Toolkit: Readings and Resources for Faculty.* Providence, Rhode Island: Campus Contact/Brown University, 2000. 61-72.

Furco, Andrew. "Service-Learning: A Balanced Approach to Experiential Education." *Introduction to Service-Learning Toolkit: Readings and Resources for Faculty.* Providence, Rhode Island: Campus Contact/Brown University, 2000. 9-13.

Giles, Dwight E., Jr. and Janet Eyler. "The Theoretical Roots of Service-Learning in John Dewey: Toward a Theory of Service-Learning." *Michigan Journal of Community Service-learning* 1 (Fall 1994): 77-85.

Green, Ann E. "'But You Aren't White:' Racial Perceptions and Service-Learning." *Michigan Journal of Community Service-learning* 8 (Fall 2001): 18-26.

Hale, Aileen. "Service-Learning and Spanish: A Missing Link." *Construyendo Puentes (Building Bridges): Concepts and Models for Service-Learning in Spanish.* Ed. Josef Hellebrandt and Lucía T. Varona. Washington, D.C.: American Association for Higher Education, 1999. 9-31.

Kennard, Margot. "Stories and Reflections on Learning to Care." *Trying the Ties that Bind: Essays on Service-Learning and Moral Life of Faculty.* Ed. David D. Cooper. Lansing: The Fetzer Institute, 2000. 45-62.

Kuh, George D., Katie Branch Douglas, Jon P. Lund, and Jackie Ramin-Gyurnek. *Student Learning Outside the Classroom: Transcending Artificial Boundaries*. Washington, D.C.: The George Washington University, 1994.

Learn and Serve Clearinghouse. 10/9/07.www.servicelearning.org/what_is_servicelearning/service-learning_is/index.php.

Mullaney, Jeanne. "Service-Learning and Language-Acquisition Theory and Practice." *Construyendo Puentes (Building Bridges): Concepts and Models for Service Learning in Spanish*. Ed. Josef Hellebrandt and Lucía T. Varona. Washington, DC: American Association for Higher Education, 1999. 49-60.

Slimbach, Richard. "Connecting Head, Heart, and Hands: Developing Intercultural Service Competence." *Journey to Service-Learning: Experiences from Independent Liberal Arts Colleges and Universities*. Ed. Stephen G. Pelletier. Washington D.C.: Council of Independent Colleges, 1996.

Stewart, Greig M. "Learning Styles as a Filter for Developing Service-Learning Interventions." *Introduction to Service-Learning Toolkit: Readings and Resources for Faculty*. Providence, Rhode Island: Campus Contact/Brown University, 2000. 35-41.

Zlotkowski, Edward. "Pedagogy and Engagement." *Introduction to Service-Learning Toolkit: Readings and Resources for Faculty*. Providence, Rhode Island: Campus Contact/Brown University, 2000. 79-93.

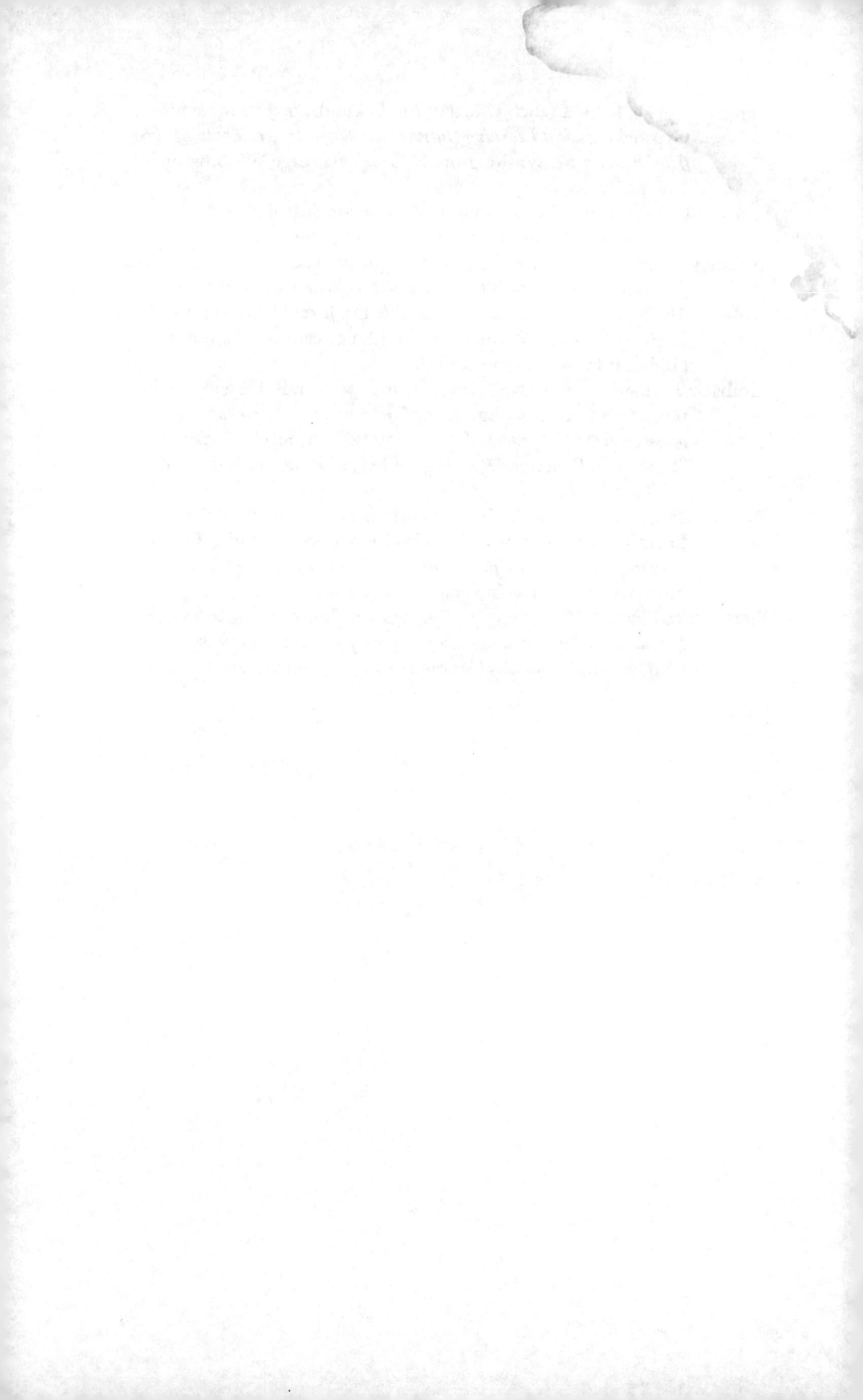

Service-Learning and Math Anxiety

An Effective Pedagogy

Bridget Connor, MD, UNITED STATES

Abstract: This study involved 18 participants enrolled in a college math methods class. Tooke and Lindstrom (1998) findings suggested that a math methods course would reduce math anxiety. For this study, Suinn's (2004) Mathematics Anxiety Rating Scale of Adults (MARS) was administered the second week and the last week of the math method course. A Service-Learning pedagogy was used as a major vehicle for the delivery of this course. Pre-intern reflections of their Service- Learning experiences are in keeping with benefits identified by other research (Anderson, Swick and Yff, J., 2001; Hart, S.; King, J. R.(2007); Swick, 1999).

Introduction

Math anxiety is a very real concern. Math anxiety has limited students desire to continue in math courses and avoid careers that have math related components (Metie, Frank, and Croft, 2007; Scarpello, G. 2007). Metie, Frank, and Croft wrote that one of the biggest challenges for teachers is supporting students in overcoming their fear of mathematics.

Service-Learning is an effective pedagogy that has been used at all levels of education. This study examined math anxiety in pre-interns enrolled in a math methods course. Service-Learning was used as one of the major pedagogy for the course.

Brief Review of the Literature

Service-Learning Design

What is Service-Learning? It is a pedagogy that can be used at all levels of education. It meets a recognized need and renders a service while meeting course objective/s. A business student who completes a tax return for a non-English speaking person and a nurse intern who monitors the health of a nursing-home patient of low socioeconomic status are examples of Service-Learning projects.

Maryland was the first in the United States to require 75 hours of Service-Learning as a graduation requirement for high-school students. This decision was received with mixed results. Some welcomed the idea of required Service-Learning hours; others thought it was not the purview of schools to required service. When challenged by parents, the Maryland courts upheld the decisions to require Service-Learning hours. The courts noted that as long as it was part of the learning objectives of course content, schools had the right to implement the service-learning requirement.

Do teachers know enough about Service-Learning to implement good programs? This is a teacher preparatory question as well. Do professors know enough about Service-Learning to teach it?

Well designed Service-Learning projects involve several key elements. Three of those key elements are listed here. The first key element is to decide the Service-Learning level of involvement. Root, Anderson, Callahan, Duckenfield, Hill, Pickeral, and Wade (1997) identified three levels of involvement or participation.

The first level is exposure. Typically a teacher in K-16 will develop a project in conjunction with course objectives, and students are expected to participate in that project. Thus, the students are exposed to the concept of service-learning through their active participation and reflection on their experiences.

Teachers, if they are to implement a service-learning component in their classroom, need to be aware of service-learning as pedagogy, the second level. Teacher preparation programs are realizing the importance of including the theory of service-learning as an important pedagogy and introducing best practices for Service-Learning experiences.

The third level is to actually create and implement a meaningful service-learning project that relates realistically to course objectives. The third step is realized as teachers create, sometimes in conjunction with their students, a meaningful service-learning project. Exposure and participation typically come before creation and implementation of service-learning designs. Pedagogy can be introduced before, during or after participation in service-learning projects.

A second key element is that Service-Learning meets a community need. The existing partnership at one of the elementary schools provided us with the opportunity to plan a service-learning project within a course framework, Math Methods. In this case, the elementary school requested assistance in math, geometry in particular.

A third key element of Service-Learning is reflection. Root, Anderson, Callahan, Duckenfield, Hill, Pickeral, and Wade (1997) stated "For students to benefit from service-learning, they must engage in structured reflection on their experiences" (p.13).

Service-Learning Benefits

Positive reports of Service-Learning have encouraged professors to use this as a pedagogical strategy. Eyler and Giles (1999) have researched and identified some of the student benefits of service-learning engagements:

greater motivation towards course involvement

deeper understanding of course content

general improved learning

enhanced critical thinking and problem-solving

reflective judgment

social responsibility

Similar findings are supported by Anderson, Swick, and Yff, J., (2001), Hart, and King (2007) and Nelson and Eckstein (2008). While most research identifies the benefits of Service-Learning, it is important to note that not all research findings are found to be as beneficial (McClam, Diambra, Burton, Fuss and Fudge, 2008).

Service-Learning pedagogy is a constructivist approach. Elkind (2003) briefly describes three epistemologies: the empiricist, one who learns basically by mime; the nativist, one who is born knowing; and the constructivist, one in which the learner is the architect of his or her own knowledge. In the constructivist approach each person is responsible for constructing knowledge through engagement. Bordrova (2003) explained the importance of the constructivist approach in the learning process. She identified educational authors such as Montessori and Vygotsky as constructivist theorist. She further described Vygotsky's approach to be co-constructive, since one learns with others. Jennings and Caulfield (2003) stated "the brain works best with experimental learning principles, meaning that students are deeply engaged in active interaction with the topic" (p. 47). When students are involved and interested, they work harder. Again they emphasized, "Learning is contextual; that is, content and skills are learned in the context of need and use. Lessons that are provided in the context of a real problem take root in the student's brain because that's how the brain works" (p. 48).

Math Concerns

Prichard(1995) outlined the efforts of The National Council of Teachers of Mathematics (NCTM) to educate all students towards mathematics literacy. He mentioned the difficulties in the affective area. Attending to math anxiety or the affective domain for some students is necessary, if they are to attain mathematics literacy. Prichard wrote "Mathematics anxiety which historically has been a persistent delimiter for successful mathematics experiences, may increase initially for some students as they are exposed to less algorithms and more conceptually based courses". Tobias' Math clinic (1991) has been successful in eliminating some of those anxieties by challenging the concept that math anxiety is innate. Although some research (Casey, Nuttall & Pezaris, 1997) have found some gender differences in processing math (spatial skills - which may have more to do with learning styles, personality types and experience), Tobias wrote, "All people have some math anxiety, but it disables women and minorities more than others. There is a cure, but it involves changing learners' and teachers' attitudes at the same time"(p.91). Her research with 600 undergraduates demonstrated that most average students can do advanced math and that they did not need a "mathematical mind". Working with students in her clinic, she found that for some of the students, the sources of math anxiety were particularly related to emotional impact on students from poor instruction, such as parents or teachers embarrassing youngsters. Jackson and Leffingwell's (1992) study found only 7% of their participants (T = 157) had positive math experiences. Some areas that they isolated as having influenced students in negative and long-lasting ways are hostile instructor behavior, gender bias, insensitive or uncaring instructors, angry behavior of instructor, unrealistic expectations, poor instruction and difficulty of material. Fiore (1999) described two case studies in which students had long lasting effects of math anxiety due to poor instruction. He wrote, "Evidence suggests that math anxiety results more from the way the subject matter is presented than from the subject matter itself" (p.403).

Tooke and Lindstrom (1998) administered the Mathematics Anxiety Rating Scale of Adults (MARS). They postulated whether a math content class or math methods class might make a difference in reducing math anxiety in college students preparing to be teachers. The classes were being delivered in traditional and newly revised manner. "The study produced no evidence that mathematics anxiety of pre-service elementary students is significantly affected by completing a semester of mathematics for teachers, regardless of it being taught in the traditional manner or in the nontraditional manner. This study did produce evidence that students' mathematics anxiety may be reduced by completing a mathematics methodology course" (p. 137).

Method

College pre-interns participated in a Service-Learning experience. Service-Learning pedagogy was used as a major vehicle for the delivery of this math methods course. The Service-Learning experience included planning and teaching lessons in geometry at the request of a local elementary school. The elementary school also requested, as part of their Service-Learning experience, that the pre-interns work with young students in building math skills. Pre-interns received instruction on best practices of Service-Learning during the math methods class as well as assistance in planning for lessons and skill building. It was hoped that Service-Learning would be used as a tool to increase pre-interns knowledge of elementary math by focusing on the young elementary students' needs.

Pre-interns kept a journal throughout the course. They were given a set of prepared questions. They also wrote freely. Prepared questions were related to professional skills such as: What worked well in classroom management in the lesson that you presented? What transition techniques did you use to facilitate student learning? Diversity issues were expected to be examined through questions such as: What have you done to ensure gender equity? Do you consider yourself to be a suitable teacher candidate in meeting multi-ethnic needs? Students were also expected to review an educational theory and highlight the practical implications of service-learning to this theory. Other professional developmental questions were asked as well, such as: Having these semester experiences thus far, do you feel it is your responsibility to make a difference in the lives of children? Reflections were collected and reviewed mid-term and at the end of the semester.

College pre-interns were given the option to complete the Suinn's Mathematics Anxiety Rating Scale of Adults (MARS) as a pre and post survey. Eighteen females completed both pre and post. MARS was administered the second week of the math methods course and the last week of the course.

A pre-survey was also given to find the best time for the Service-Learning experience. Pre-interns in this study spent an average of 17.36 hours weekly in work, 20.45 hours weekly in class including lab, and 22.72 hours weekly of study time, a total of 60.53 hours weekly for work, class and study. In addition, several pre-interns attended to family needs such as their children. The major part of pre-intern lesson planning was outside of class. Because of time issues, however, part of the math methods' lab time was used for service-learning. Pre-interns meet at the local elementary school as agreed upon by the elementary teacher involved. During a three time period they taught, tutored and reflected on experience.

As part of their initial visit, pre-interns gave a pre-geometry test to the elementary students. Pre-interns received regular input as how to proceed in lesson planning and tutoring. The elementary teacher regularly gave feedback to pre-interns and prepared her students to say goodbye at the end of the Service-Learning experience. Pre-interns as well planned their goodbyes.

Results

Math anxiety, as measured on the MARS, at the beginning of the course for the math methods pre-interns was high. Eighteen participants' mean average was 219. Suinn studies indicated that college students of humanities had a mean high of 196.46. Suinn reported similar standard deviations as found in this study.

T-tests for Paired Samples

Variable	Number of Pairs	Mean	SD	SE of Mean
PreMARS	18	218.7222	54.971	12.957
PostMARS		189.0556	51.022	12.026

The mean difference from the beginning of the class to the end of the semester was a difference of 29 points. The difference in the mean score is of significant value (.003).

Paired Differences

Mean	SD	SE of Mean	t-value	df	2-tail Sig
29.6667	37.020	8.726	3.40	17	.003

Pre-intern Reflective Statements are Reported below

Initial reflections are in keeping with Sloan, Daane, and Giesen, J. (2002), Tobias' (1991) and Jackson and Leffingwell's (1992) findings that experiences can influence attitudes towards math.

The following are some of the pre-interns math experiences as recorded in their journal just prior to Service-Learning.

"In high school my math teacher kicked me out".

"My experience of math is horrible, I gave up in third grade when my teacher got really frustrated at me for not understanding it".

"In 9th grade my teacher was excellent but in 10th grade, the teacher had no concept of teaching math and I hated the class".

"I remember going in front of the class [writing] on the blackboard and getting the math problem wrong"

"I remember we would play math races and games and I'd always take longer to process the answer, therefore letting my team down".

Service-Learning Reflection on Math Teaching

"Working in the schools and one-on-one with the children has helped me a lot. I loved teaching the children and have them learn new material because of us. The children developed a love for math because of us teaching them!"

Another wrote, *"Getting the chance to interact with the students"* has changed her to have a positive attitude towards math.

"I think knowing how to break down the material and having practice teaching of the lesson, as well as watching other teachers through observations has influenced my view of math".

When asked if her views towards math are the same or different one student wrote, "I was a little scared about teaching math because I never really liked math, but now I feel more comfortable and prepared, I think I will enjoy teaching math in the future".

Another student also indicated that she now has a more positive view; she wrote, *"preparing for the lesson and carrying it out was a great experience".*

All students indicated a positive change towards math except one who already had a very positive attitude. While other ideas were mentioned as helpful such as examples presented in class, all students indicated in one way or another that the experience of the service-learning project made a positive difference.

Student Responses in Teaching Practice

Similar to the benefits described by Eyler and Giles (1999), Joiner (2000) and McClam, Diambra, Burton, Fuss, and Fudge, D. L. (2008) such as career and professional development, and academic advances, so too, the Math Methods pre-interns reported in their journals. The following are excerpts from their reflection:

"During my service learning experience I found that I was using theories taught in class to teach my students. I received experience that was very valuable to my course work"

"...When it was my group's turn to come up with a lesson plan, I took into consideration how my students learn".

"My experience ... has renewed my desire to be a teacher; my desire is to make a difference in at least one child's life, more if possible".

"When comparing the pre-assessment and post-assessment tests given to the two students... that I worked with, the test scores of both boys were raised significantly on the posttest. I believe the experience has increased the confidence level of the children in the class.

"Throughout this experience, service-learning has taught me three positive values: leadership, citizenship, and personal responsibility... and prepared me to be a better person all around. Not only has service learning helped me, it has allowed me to help many students... and make a difference in their lives..."

Moral Development

Pre-intern reflections were related to care and justice concerns. Piaget (1932/1997) and Kohlberg (1958 and 1976) outlined the different stages of moral development. Both researchers identified an occurrence within the stages. This event or occurrence described by Piaget and Kohlberg indicated that point in which a person would move from one stage or level to the next in his/her journey of moral development. The process is as follows: a new concept or perspective is presented; a person's balance or equilibrium is offset; moral convictions are challenged (disequilibrium) with new prospects which are assimilated and finally accommodated or rejected. When one's moral equilibrium is offset, the researchers noted that the possibility for moral development is present. In this case, the new concept or differing view is the catalyst for moral growth. While seemingly simple this is a very challenging process. Treasured beliefs are very difficult to change. Moral development has been explained in various ways but it is clear that when one's equilibrium is offset the possibility for development is present.

In the seminal work of Gilligan (1985/1993) moral development is explained in terms of care. Perspective taking is indicative that a person can view others in their own uniqueness. When one can perceive the other, he/she moves from an egocentric perspective to a capacity that allows for the inclusion of others. Perspective taking is essential if one is to care for another. Similarly, Liddell, Halpin and Halpin (1992) stated

> The ethic of care is characterized by subjectiveness, intuition, and responsiveness. One who demonstrate an ethic of care responds to people in a way that ensures that the least harm will be done and that no one will be left alone. There is an assumption of connectedness and attachment and an understanding that everyone is different and may have a different reality. Decisions are contextual and relative to a particular situation (p. 326).

While the following statements do not indicate stage growth or permanent change, they are surprising and interesting to note in regard to knowledge of self and care of others.

"Who has not heard stories or seen newscasts about all the fighting that is done among African American youth? ... Put all of these influences together with the phrase "Baltimore city school", and perhaps my apprehension can be understood, if not justified. I feel much better now, after several visits. I fully realize that these students are just children, although I could not help but feel a little nervous.... My previous exposure to African Americans has not been positive, but I am willing to learn. [This school experience] has given me the opportunity to do just that".

"During our introduction to the school, the principal informed us that the school population was 99.9% African-American. It made me wonder how I would feel if I were the only white person in the classroom, or even in the entire school. As I worked with my team during the whole-class lessons, I realized that kids are kids, and math is math. My concern that there might be a problem or that I would feel out of place was unfounded. You can not be 110% sure of how you will react in a certain situation until you have lived it".

"My experience at [this school] has taught me a lot about diversity. I have never worked in a school before that is mostly African American. I didn't know what to expect when I first started. I was afraid of feeling really left out and unwanted. Luckily, it has been going great so far. I don't feel left out or unwanted at all. I feel very accepted by both the children and the teachers. .... My goal as a teacher will be to make my entire class feel included and loved".

"*I must admit even though I feel comfortable around people of different ethnic backgrounds I was a little uncomfortable the first day at [this school]. We were definitely in the minority and now I know how people of other races must feel when they are in the same position. This has enlightened me...*"

"*I come from a rural community and the students at [this school] come from an urban area. It was a real eye opener for me to see the different life styles of these students*".

"*Most of us did admit though, that our first experience with diversity made us feel uncomfortable. Although, by having this experience it has made us grow*".

These responses indicate pre-interns are aware of their discomfort level and that an experience and reflections on that experience can change their views.

In addition, other comments linked service-learning and the area of care which is identified as one of the moral development processes (Gilligan, 1985).

"*...I was surprised that I was shocked because I did not actually think that the entire... class would not be able to pass [last year] assessment.... I find it very discouraging and disheartening that some children can be at such low levels. ...This makes me want to make an even greater difference as a future educator than before*".

"*I had always known there was a community out there that needed my help and support, but I just didn't know how to reach them. Now, after service learning I can say that I have the emotional capacity and the physical drive to get out and help those in need*".

"*My service-learning experience at [this school] has increased my interpersonal skills and has given me an understanding of people with a background different from my own. This situation was the first time that I was in the minority and it had a tremendous impact on me, enabling me to empathize with minorities*".

"*While working with low income students at [this school], I found myself gasping at my lack of socio-economical understanding and sensitivity. I had thought myself to be sensitive to these issues, but through my experience I found that I need to be more aware of my own personal stereotypes. I developed a sense of responsibility to the children I was working with*".

"*I found an awakened desire within myself to work with children from a low economical stratum. I found myself questioning my preconceived notions about class and status*".

Conclusions

MARS scale for measuring math anxiety showed a significant difference from pre to post test in this sample. This is encouraging. It supports the research of Tooke and Lindstrom (1998) who stated that math methods course would decrease math anxiety.

Attitudes towards math changed as described by pre-interns because of their Service-Learning experiences. Journal writing indicated that pre-interns were aware of professional and personal growth.

Kinsley (1997) wrote, "Service learning is a way to help our young people grow individually and as members of society."...What it means to live as a truly compassionate and caring human being."

One semester is only a brief interlude in a person's life. The quality statements of pre-interns do express a personal challenge and a thought change in the area of tolerance and care towards others. These are essentially the concerns of morality.

This study does not directly relate service-learning and the reduction of math anxiety. Its findings support that a math methods course can reduce math anxiety and pre-interns anecdotal remarks indicate that their Service-Learning experience has influenced their attitude towards math as well as helped them grow personally and professionally.

Further study in this area would be of benefit if a direct cause and effect of Service-Learning and reduction in math anxiety could be established.

References

Anderson, J. , Swick, K. J., & Yff, J. (2001) *Service-learning in teacher education: Enhancing the growth of new teachers, their students, and communities*. New York: AACTE Publications.

Bordrova, E.(2003). Vygotsky and Montessori: One dream, two visions. *Montessori Life*,15(1), 30-33.

Casey, M. B., Nuttall, R. L., and Pezaris, E. (1997). Mediators of gender differences in mathematics college entrance test scores: A comparison of spatial skills with internalized beliefs and anxieties. *Developmental Psychology*, 33(4), 669-680.

Elkind, D. (2003). Montessori and constructivism. *Montessori Life*, 15 (1), 26-29.

Eyler J., Giles, D. E. Jr. (1999). *Where's the Learning in Service-Learning?* San Francisco. CA: Jossey-Bass Publishers.

Fiore, G. (1999). Math-abused students: Are we prepared to teach them? *Mathematics Teacher*, 92 (5), 403- 407.

Gilligan, C. (1985/1993). *In a Different Voice: Psychological Theory and Women's Development*. Cambridge, MA: Harvard University Press.

Hart, S.; King, J. R.(2007). Service learning and literacy tutoring: Academic impact on pre-service teachers. *Teaching and Teacher Education: An International Journal of Research and Studies,* 23(4), 323-338.

Jackson, C. D., Leffingwell, J. R. (1999). The role of instructors in creating math anxiety in students from kindergarten through college. *Mathematics Teacher*, 92 (7), 583-587.

Jennings, W., Caulfield, J. (2003). Inciting learning in action. *Principal Leadership*, 3 (9), 45-49.

Joiner, L.L. (2000). Learning to serve: Community service meets curriculum objectives. *American School Board*,187 (11)32-36.

Kinsley, C. W. (Oct.,1997). *Bulletin*. TX: Delta Kappa Gamma Society International.

Kohlberg, L. (1958). *Moral Development*. Unpublished doctoral dissertation, University of Chicago, Chicago, Ill.

Kohlberg, L. (1976). Moral stages and moralization: The cognitive-developmental approach. In T. Lickona (Ed.), *Moral development and behavior: Theory, Research, and Social Issues* (pp. 31-53). New York: Holt, Rinehart, and Winston.

Liddell, D. L., Halpin, G., & Halpin, W. G. (1992). The measure of moral orientation: Measuring the ethics of care and justice. *Journal of College Student Development*, 33, 325-330.

Metie, N.: Frank, H. & Croft, P. (2007). Can't do maths—Understanding students' maths anxiety. Teaching Mathematics and Its Application: An International Journal in the IMA, 26(2), 79-81.

McClam, T.; Diambra, J.;Burton, B.;Fuss, A.;Fudge, D. L. (2008). An analysis of a Service-Learning project: Students' expectations, concerns, and reflections. *Journal of Experiential Education*, 30(3), 236-249.

Nelson, J. A.; Eckstein, D. (2008). A Service-Learning model for At-Risk adolescents. *Education and Treatment of Children*, 31(2) 223-237.

Piaget, J., (1932/1997). *The Moral Judgment of the Child*. (translated by M. Gabain). New York: Free Press Paperbacks.

Prichard, G. R., (1995). The NCTM standards and community colleges: Opportunities and challenges. *Community College Review*, 23 (1), 23-33.

Root S., Anderson J, Callahan P., Duckenfield M., Hill D., Pickeral T., & Wade R.(1997). Service-learning in teacher education: A handbook. Washington DC: Learn and Serve America Program.

Scarpello, G. (2007). Helping students get past math anxiety. Techniques: Connecting Education and Careere, 83 (1), 34-35.

Sloan, T., Daane, C. J., and Giesen, J. (2002). Mathematics anxiety and learning styles: What is the relationship in elementary preservice teachers?. *School Science & Mathematics*, 102, 84-88.

Swick, K.J., (1999). "Service learning helps future teachers strengthen caring perspectives". *The Clearing House* (Sept/Oct).

Taylor J., Mohr , J.(2001). Mathematics for math anxious students studying at a distance. *Journal of Developmental Education*, 25 (1), 30-37.

Tobias, S. (1991). Math anxiety. *College Teaching*, 39 (3), 91-91.

Tooke, D., Lindstrom, L. (1998). Effectiveness of a mathematics methods course in reducing math anxiety of pre-service elementary teachers. *School Science & Mathematics*, 98 (3), 136-140.

Foreign Language

Teaching a Foreign Language in a Service Learning Context

A Case Study

Dosinda Garcia-Alvite, Denison University, United States of America

Abstract: Meaningful learning of a foreign language is heightened when the student has to put new knowledge to use immediately, such as in a service-learning context. This essay summarizes and analyzes ways in which learning of the Spanish language and Hispanic culture became effective and permanent when third-year college students worked with migrant Hispanic children in elementary and high schools. I pay special attention to different models derived from this class' experiences for building cross-cultural understanding.

The tradition of service learning is very rich in models and in thinkers who have paved the way for its contemporary resurgence; people like Jane Addams, John Dewey, Dorothy Day and more recently, Paulo Freire and Robert Sigmon provide varied histories and theoretical approaches to the field. During the last few decades, academia in the U.S. has shown a growth of interest in service learning, which may be related to three criticisms that have been made of the higher (or post-secondary) education system: lack of curricular relevance, lack of faculty commitment to teaching, and lack of institutional (and faculty) responsiveness to the larger public (Kezar & Rhoads 150). However, the enrichment service learning provides goes beyond responding to criticisms. Service learning has been found to be very useful in several aspects of education, such as enhancing conceptual and theoretical understanding, factual learning, cognitive skill development, valuing education, and developing tolerance and appreciation of diversity (Butin1679). Other demonstrated benefits are a sense of social responsibility, a sense of personal efficacy, and development of community and civic engagement skills (Krain194). These advantages are more or less evident depending on the perspective from which service learning is put to practice. Dan W. Butin distinguishes four main conceptualizations of the theory and practice of service learning: technical, cultural, political and structuralist (1674-5).

The analysis I present here of a Spanish language and culture class that was designed to include a service learning component is influenced by Matthew Krain's approach to it, which uses multiple theoretical perspectives. According to Krain, a service learning course allows students to learn and apply course concepts in the real world when it incorporates experiential learning by responding to a need in a community. Service learning differs from community service in that the former involves the interdependent linkages between coursework and volunteer activity. Thus coursework is informed by student action, and action is informed by, and occurs within the context of, the academic study of relevant topics. To be a successful pedagogical tool, the service activity must be directly linked to the course and its objectives, and must be carefully interwoven into the learning process set out in the course. Service learning allows students to move beyond textbook examples and participate in actual cases (191). Following these guidelines, the course Spanish 323 "Hispanic Culture through Service Learning in Central Ohio/Licking County," was designed to be an inquiry into the nature of the Hispanic community through the topic of culture. The class combined seminar discussions on the changing character of the Hispanic community presently residing in the U.S. with two-hour service visits in the community for the purpose of tutoring Hispanic school children in Licking county. The course integrated the goals of both a service-learning course and an intermediate level Hispanic culture course.[1] Therefore, the objectives were formulated as follows:

- Strengthen students' speaking, writing, listening and reading skills in the Spanish languages.

- Gain an understanding of the Hispanic community presently residing in the U.S. by interacting with the Latino community of Licking county.

- Analyze the present issues of concern for the Hispanic communities in the U.S. and their historical origins through readings, discussions, community service experience, in-class speakers and films.

1.The institution where this class was put to practice is Denison University, a small private liberal arts college (2200 students), with a strong record of commitment to the surrounding community. The college's Service Learning Center supported the class' development with manpower and logistics. Although service learning is recognized and highly valued among the University faculty, its purposes and goals are quite unknown to a large number of students.

- Develop responsiveness to other communities and strengthening willingness to engage in community service.

Implementation and Typical Problems of a Foreign Culture/Language Class in a Service Learning Context

The learning process in this class was structured around three axes, i. e. dialogue between community members and service providers, seamless learning and collaborative learning. These defining characteristics and goals were frequently challenged, making evident the complexity of bringing service learning to an academic context, and, specifically, to the less common mix of Spanish and service learning. Some of the behavioral trends observed in the implementation of this Spanish 323 class have been identified previously by specialists who worked in various academic fields, while other problems that arose were concretely related to the development of Spanish language and culture skills in a service-learning environment.

As Bickford and Reynolds point out, one of the biggest challenges of working in a service-learning environment is that students typically ask, How can we help these people? How can I solve these people's problems in the period of time I am taking this class? instead of the deeper and more difficult question, Why are conditions this way? (230). To facilitate a reflective process that would lead to posing and analyzing this bigger question, I requested that students keep journals of their reactions and experiences and try to go beyond description of their activities, in order to be able to reflect on and structure their service learning experience. Students were also asked to consider, to analyze, and to examine the reasons why they were taking the class and doing service learning. In addition, seminar discussions were organized as a combination of reading and writing activities on historical and critical issues, and viewing of documentaries and performances related to different aspects of Hispanic culture, with a focus on Hispanics in the U.S. The challenge of this ambitious approach was to balance discipline-related content with readings that raised critical consciousness or performances that were a manifestation of activism and a desire for social change.[2] One successful example was the use of the video *Border Brujo* by the Mexican-American performer Guillermo Gómez Peña, which poses questions about ethnic and cultural hybridization in a world increasingly dominated by globalization. The video establishes connections between the possible perceptions U.S. language students may have about Hispanics and the different reactions they may provoke upon contact with this population, leading to animated discussions about the Mexico-USA border and processes of "othering."

2. Please see "Principles of Good Practice for Integrating Service with Academic Study" by Jeffrey Howard for a comprehensive list of different aspects that should be combined in a class of this type.

A main concern in implementing this class was the idea of equal participation, in which community members (mainly teachers and Hispanic students) and campus service providers (college students and myself) engaged jointly and democratically in identifying needs and how such needs were to be met. After initial phone contacts we had the principals and school counselors visit our class at the beginning of the semester to meet with the college students and explain their needs and expectations. Later on, communication with teachers was maintained, through e-mail and regular mail. Thus, reciprocity was really important and was achieved, creating a sense of mutual responsibility and respect among all the individuals participating (Kezar 160). Another important aspect of the conception of the class was related to Dewey's philosophy of continuity, or "seamless learning." As Kezar notes, "Seamless learning suggests that separate learning departments and divisions are viewed as interconnected" (162). This meant that continuity and persistent linking between service learning and classroom learning as well as previous personal and academic learning were addressed and explored. Denison students commented frequently on how their vision of the education system was enriched beyond their own childhood-youth experience by their current projects with students from economic, social and racial backgrounds very different from their own. Finally, a further emphasis of the class was collaborative learning. According to Ehrlich, privatization and atomization of learning can tend toward conformity and stagnation (494). In this course, my role as a faculty member went from facilitator, director and classroom manager to coach, resource person and organizer. Student interest was the starting point for the education process. Daily student-led discussions on the service learning experience and the academic materials were considered necessary means to achieve active engagement. The development of interpersonal skills by practicing attentive and empathic listening, preparing questions for the group, leading discussions, accepting divergent opinions, compromising, and showing the ability to change one's mind was an important element of personal interaction that enhanced productive team work.

Although the three main theoretical objectives of the class were kept in focus through regular reflective and analytical work, there were still some problems concerning specific aspects of experiential learning. The points of contention that question the immediate efficacy of service learning correspond to those already pointed out by Krain and Nurse. Following these authors' guidelines, I will comment on the difficulties that were particularly salient in this class and the approaches that were tried to address them.

Problem 1: Service Learning Might Encourage Reliance on Anecdotal Evidence.

In several occasions, in class discussions about economic and social positions of Hispanics in American society, students substituted their own conclusions for investigative reports with unexpected ease, limiting the depth and scope of the analysis that was necessary. In order to ensure that experiential learning complemented, rather than replaced, systematic analysis, every effort was made to integrate the course curriculum with the students' community experiences. This helped facilitate an instructor- and student –moderated experiential-intellectual dialogue in the classroom. During seminar discussions, students drew from course concepts and other students' experiences, as well as from their own personal experiences, to make or question generalizations about Hispanics in the U.S. Discussions fomented critical perspectives that broke down stereotypes and recognized the complexity and diversity of the real world.

Problem 2: Service Learning Might Reinforce Negative Stereotypes.

As Krain and Nurse express, in some instances service learning may reinforce negative stereotypes about oppressed groups, in this case, recent immigrants. Sometimes students encountered Hispanics who did, in fact, mirror society's image of them. However, one of the most common problems students found in working with Hispanics was how to deal with difference. It was a challenge for some college students to establish relationships with some elementary level children and with the broader educational community-teachers, principals, secretaries, etc. Sometimes students had to challenge their own preconceptions about difference in ways they had not explored before in their contacts with Hispanics (i.e. urban versus rural environments, upper and middle class backgrounds versus low income households, good public schools versus underperforming ones). To address this problem I specifically stressed the richness and diverse histories of Hispanic groups in the USA at the beginning of the semester, as well as including readings on race, class, gender and ethnicity throughout the course. Practical exercises in cross cultural understanding were common, such as the analysis of personal appearance, the study of different cultural values given to personal space or the importance of racial and ethnic social groups and individuals.

Problem 3: Service Learning Might Promote Voluntarism as THE Solution.

Closely related to the first problem examined above, as students established close and fulfilling relationships with the Hispanic youth they tutored, in the face of problems some Hispanic children had with the school system, their patience and willingness to search for a long-term solution waned. Some students became uncomfortable or upset with the difficulties of effecting rapid changes in the structures within which they were working and expressed the desire to create new groups and organizations of volunteers that could overcome structural problems. To expand their perspectives on the short term solution they were proposing, it was necessary to remind them that community volunteering usually involves a more sporadic and temporary time commitment than the regular weekly meetings they themselves had committed to for four months, facilitated by the university's links and responsibilities to the community over decades. The relationship between the university and public schools in the area has a long-standing tradition, and we hope to continue the project through the coming years. Although the class was quite popular among students and a good number of them were willing to do volunteer work at the end of the semester and to continue their tutoring activities, the critical analysis and academic learning that took place during the course are irreplaceable as they provide a richer understanding beyond mere volunteerism.

Problem 4: Service Learning Is Often Imposed on a Captive Target Population.

We were fortunate to be contacted by two nearby public schools that requested any type of help that we might offer, and later we contacted two others that had similar characteristics, and were serving similar populations: lower to middle income rural students, of whom a small percentage were children of migrant workers who find jobs in egg farms and apple orchards in surrounding areas, and who usually stay in the area for periods of time that range from six to nine months a year. The fact that the public schools expressed a need and desire for the college students' collaboration greatly facilitated our establishing a presence within the community. The Latino students' families we helped were contacted in writing, through letters written in Spanish (since many of them are recently arrived immigrants and have only developed survival English language skills) that explained the project and offered contact numbers and the names of persons who could also provide help if needed. All families and students chose to participate fully in the project. When contacted later at the end of the semester to hold a gathering of all the students from Denison and the elementary and high school students as an end-of-semester project, they expressed their satisfaction and the hope that it would continue to be offered in following semesters.

Apart from these problems, which arise in teaching any class with a service-learning component, there are some very specific challenges a service learning approach can bring to a Hispanic language and culture class. The majority of the difficulties observed were related to content development and advancement of Spanish language skills. Because the class was devised for students to learn holistically, the lack of emphasis in any one single area was perceived on occasion as a general, rather than in-depth, approach to Hispanic topics and language abilities.

Problem 1: Students might improve their Spanish speaking skills only slightly.

Although college students take this class at their third year of foreign language preparation, in both minor and major tracks, and their language skills are well advanced, one of the obstacles in conceiving the class as a Spanish class is that students have to use English to a certain degree with the children they tutor. This gives college students the impression that they are not making progress in their linguistic skills in Spanish. However, writing two journal entries of 500 words or more each week in Spanish, participating in three one-hour class discussions per week and twenty-minute biweekly office meetings with me in the target language, as well as using Spanish in everyday situations with the students they were helping, offered very realistic uses of the Spanish language. Additionally, their interactions with public school students provided unexpected, unstructured demands on their communicative abilities, which enriched their linguistic and thematic knowledge. The final essays that close the portfolios they kept during the semester, in fact, reflect a high level command of the Spanish language. They showed the students' ability to communicate effectively in different contexts: academic, professional, educational and colloquial.

Problem 2: Students might experience difficulties connecting academic enrichment with field experience.

As previously noted, class discussions were furthered through journal writing activities designed to help students link their experiences in the public schools with different aspects of Hispanic culture in the U.S. that were addressed in the academic setting. Sometimes, however, students displayed impatience, for example, at connecting historical facts with currently relevant situations or when we crossed beyond familiar religious and ethnic boundaries. These difficulties were discussed during the semester through persistent references to and analysis of these topics in readings, documentaries, films, and other materials. In order to emphasize the importance of academic learning, a final reflection and evaluation exercise at the end of the semester was required. Students had to reread their journal entries up to that point and reflect using an agreed-upon structure on how their service learning experiences related to the issues studied, and how their perceptions, views, and education had evolved in the course of the semester. An additional means of deepening students' reflections was through peer editing, both in content and language, of two journal entries during the semester. Lastly, participants wrote a letter to future students of the course with recommendations on how to approach the class, drawing on the knowledge and experience that they, themselves, had acquired by the end of the semester.

Problem 3: Students can feel frustrated with academic assessment of course work.

This is a frequent problem that derives from the fact that students had emotional reactions toward their experiences in the community, the students, or the personnel at the schools they worked at. These reactions of anger, pity, elation, contempt, and so on required an added effort from the instructor to manage students' attitudes processing and encourage them to continue their work. Additionally, the expression of these emotions put pressure on the equilibrium between personal and group priorities, as well as between academic and service learning. Negative feelings and/or reactions to experiences become even more complex when they can affect the way students' accomplishments in the course are measured. Detachment from the issues at hand to achieve an objective analysis of the subjective experience was extremely difficult. At the end of the semester, key criteria in student work were clarity, persuasiveness, analysis of a variety of issues and students' efforts to deal with problems, to confront and scrutinize issues as they arose. Basically, it was the students' written, verbal and active commitment to understand and negotiate difference that was constantly emphasized in the class because it is through these reflective activities that students will learn their own degree of complicity in the social structures that reproduce the present system.

Effects on Student Learning

At the moment, there is a need to develop specific learning assessments in the class since this type of course is in its developmental stages. Class evaluations, however, can be considered to offer an approximate appraisal of the class. In general, students feel enlightened and challenged in both the affective and the cognitive levels. The combination of a foreign culture and language class with a service learning component is transformative at the personal and social levels according to some student comments: "This course is really helpful in understanding Hispanic culture, as we spent time hands on with Mexican students. It is a totally different type of class unlike any others I have ever taken, but also one of the more beneficial. It is personally challenging, but well worth it." And, "This was a great course that offered me the opportunity to explore my interest in education without being an education major. I enjoyed my service learning and this course and experience will enrich my graduate work." Other students commented, "I liked going out into the community and helping the Mexican students. I think we made a big difference this semester in their lives." "The time spent outside the classroom with the kids was the highlight of the class." "I feel that a course like this is very important and I feel it should be offered every year. I have taken three years of Spanish at Denison, and although this is not the most intellectually challenging course, it is the most important one I have taken. My time with my student in the classroom opened my eyes to Hispanic culture more than any reading ever could, and would strongly recommend this class to any Spanish major or minor, in fact, I feel that a class working with the local Hispanic community should be required for majors and minors."

In the light of these comments, several conclusions can be drawn in connection to the value and impact service learning classes have on student learning. As pointed out by many specialists (Flower, Boyte, Gregory among others), it can be observed that students appreciate on one side the immediacy of the experience, and on the other they value the commitment, the engagement in social issues. The approach to learning that facilitates direct contact with school children, teachers, administrators and parents enables college students to establish connections among different fields through interdisciplinary observations. Additionally, at the affective level, students' confidence and self-awareness grows exponentially.

In a parallel way, as Jones and Abes point out, the meaning of responsible citizenship is increasingly complex (149), but the service learning in this class makes it possible for college students to go beyond a "tourist" attitude in their analysis of the Hispanic community. Furthermore, they not only seek solutions to a social problem, but at the same time, they are changing the status quo, both in the educational system and in our hegemonic society. This is because they take an active role, rather than looking for a comfortable, safely removed position in the learning process.

As for the problems the class raised, although there is a strong tendency to look for the differences that separate the private college student from the Hispanic immigrant student, it is precisely the reflection college students do in their journals, in class discussions and in their comments during office meetings that help them to analyze, understand and become better citizens by working out these differences.

To conclude, by linking student learning and faculty teaching to community concerns through service learning courses such as this one, an institution like Denison University is able to address broader community, state, and regional needs and challenges, offering the students an opportunity to consider their roles as community members and citizens in a democratic society. Now, it can only be hoped that Denison students will establish a relationship between the achievement of critical awareness and the ability to take effective action for social change.

References

Addams, Jane. *Democracy and Social Ethics*. Cambridge: Belknap Press of Harvard University Press, 1964.

Antonio, Anthony Lising, Helen S. Astin, and Christine M. Cress Tables. "Community Service in Higher Education: A Look at the Nation's Faculty." *The Review of Higher Education* 23.4 (2000): 373-97.

Bickford, Donna M., and Nedra Reynolds. "Activism and Service-Learning: Reframing Volunteerism As Acts of Dissent." *Pedagogy* 2.2 (2002): 229-52.

Boyte, Harry C. "A Different Kind of Politics: John Dewey and the Meaning of Citizenship in the 21st Century." *The Good Society* 12.2 (2003): 1-15.

Flower, Linda. "Intercultural Inquiry and the Transformation of Service." *College English* 65.2 (2002): 181-201.

Butin, Dan W. "Of What Use Is It? Multiple Conceptualizations of Service Learning Within Education." *Teachers College Record* 105.9 (2003): 1674-92.

Dewey, John. *Democracy and Education*. New York: Simon and Schuster, 1997. Ehrlich, Thomas. "Reinventing John Dewey's 'Pedagogy as a University Discipline.'" *The Elementary School Journal* 98.5 (1998): 489-509.

Freire, Paulo. *Pedagogy of the Oppressed*. New York: Continuum, 1994.

Gregory, Marshall. "Curriculum, Pedagogy, and Teacherly Ethos." *Pedagogy* 1.1 (2001): 69-89.

Howard, Jeffrey. "Community Service Learning in the Curriculum." *Praxis I: A Faculty Casebook on Community Service Learning.* Ann Arbor: OCSL, 1993. 3-12.

Jones Susan R., and Elisa S. Abes. "Enduring Influences of Service-Learning on College Students' Identity Development." *Journal of College Student Development* 45.2 (2004): 149-166.

Kezar, Adrianna and Robert A. Rhoads. "The Dynamic Tensions of Service Learning in Higher Education: A Philosophical Perspective." *The Journal of Higher Education* 72.2 (2001): 148-171.

Krain, Matthew and Anne M. Nurse. "Teaching Human Rights through Service Learning." *Human Rights Quarterly* 26.1 (2004): 189-207.

Sigmon, Robert. *Linking Service with Learning: A Report from CIC.* Washington, D.C.: Council of Independent Colleges, 1994.

Tsui, Lisa. "Faculty Attitudes and the Development of Students' Critical Thinking.'" *The Journal of General Education* 50.1 (2001): 1-28.

About the Author

Dosinda Garcia-Alvite is an Associate Professor of Spanish at Denison University. She has taught several service learning courses that combined foreign language and cultures learning with service to the community. Her research interests and publications focus on: critical consciousness pedagogy, border studies, cross-cultural identities and bilingualism in the areas of both Mexico-USA and Africa-Spain.

Information Systems

An Information Systems Service Learning Experience

Karen Videtic, University of Southern Indiana, Indiana, USA

Abstract: A student often views his academic career as multiple time-blocks with specific starting and ending dates. During each block of time, the student concentrates on discrete subjects and views them as unrelated to any which preceded or which will follow. Few courses enunciate the contiguity and entwinement of courses better than one focused on service learning projects. Organizations for which the project is designed, within and/or outside the university community, benefit by the product created by the students. The students, in turn, gain valuable experience working with "real world" needs for bona fide organizations that will implement the product(s) developed. The students acquire experience, knowledge, confidence in their ability to function in a business environment, and a sense of accomplishment and pride in a job successfully completed. This paper focuses on strategies developed, instructional issues, lessons learned, and byproduct bonuses realized from having facilitated a service learning course. It is a descriptive exhortation of an undergraduate Information Systems (IS) course at a medium-sized university located in Midwest USA. The course is not a capstone course, and the only absolute common background for all participating students is coursework or equivalent experience in Excel and Access.

Introduction

A student often views his academic career as multiple time-blocks with specific starting and ending dates. During each block of time, the student concentrates on discrete subjects and views them as unrelated to any which preceded or which will follow. Few courses enunciate the contiguity and entwinement of courses better than one focused on service learning projects. Organizations for which the project is designed, within and/or outside the university community, benefit by the product created by the students. The students, in turn, gain valuable experience working with "real world" needs for bona fide organizations that will implement the product(s) developed. The students acquire experience, knowledge, confidence in their ability to function in a business environment, and a sense of accomplishment and pride in a job successfully completed.

This paper focuses on strategies developed, instructional issues, lessons learned, and byproduct bonuses realized from having facilitated a service learning course. It is a descriptive exhortation of an undergraduate Information Systems (IS) course at a medium-sized university located in Midwest USA. The course is not a capstone course, and the only absolute common background for all participating students is coursework or equivalent experience in Excel and Access.

What is Service Learning

Service learning has been described as an educational strategy that gives students hands-on experience working as volunteers (Jordan and Orwig 2010), combining classroom instruction with reflection and meaningful service to the community (___ March 25 2010). This teaching method provides students an opportunity to use their classroom theory to help others and in the process to strengthen their understanding of subject material. It is like a bridge connecting education with the outside world, breathing life and clarity into any subject and better preparing students for life after college. (___ March 2 2010).

Skilton, Forsyth, and White(2008) refer to service learning as real-life projects and note that the complexity of the project usually is high, especially compared to academic assignments. They further note that the project mission and resources may not be fully defined; projects often have many elements with ambiguous relationships between them; projects occur inside the workplace and often within and between functions and firms, creating layers of political considerations that further complicate action; roles and work can be ambiguous and contested; and there may be intense pressure to make deadlines.

Kiltz (2010) contrasts service learning with community Service, volunteerism, field education, and internship programs. She distinguishes service learning from other approaches by intent to benefit both provider and service recipient equally, as well as intent to ensure equal focus on both service and learning. She states that "for students, service learning is an opportunity to enrich and apply classroom knowledge to real world problems; to explore different careers and develop occupational skills; and to develop civic literacy and a concern for social problems, which leads to a sense of social responsibility and commitment to public service. For many community and government organizations, students involved in service-learning augment service delivery, meet crucial human needs, and use applied research techniques to identify and solve community problems."

Course and Student Profile

This service learning course is a 300-level Information Systems course. The prerequisite is a microcomputer applications course required of most Business majors. The 200-level prerequisite devotes about half of the semester to Excel and half to Access. All students, therefore, are expected to possess adequate skills in Excel and Access.

Students who register for the course are primarily CIS majors; however, students from other majors do register. The typical class population is approximately one half graduating seniors (exhibiting the traditional illness known as "senioritis" as well as the more productive, though time-robbing activity, of job-hunting), although a few sophomores and juniors also register for the course.

The senior-level CIS students will have completed or be currently enrolled in, among other things, Business Communications, Management Information Systems, two semesters of Accounting, two semesters of a programming language, and most likely a semester of at least one additional programming language. Other students who enroll in the course typically have a random selection of completed courses, which does not include programming.

As may be deduced, the difference in student backgrounds presents a challenge. Since most of the students are CIS majors, the professor typically evaluates the background of the CIS students first and divides the students into fairly balanced teams. The remaining students' academic backgrounds are then evaluated and each student is assigned to a team where he/she can contribute significantly and can learn new skills. For example, a student with an acceptable grade in Business Communication could certainly contribute by writing proposals and reports. That same student could learn basic web page design and publication by watching and assisting team members. It is, admittedly, a delicate juggling act to put together workable, productive teams.

Course Design and Strategies

For this course, clients are solicited by the professor from within or from outside the University community, prior to the start of each semester. Occasionally a student may also request that a project be developed for a particular organization, usually one with personal significance to the student; for instance, a business owned by the student's family. During the initial offerings of the course, clients were solicited by the professor from personal contacts, a board of advisors, and references from various sources. After the first few semesters, most of the clients were chosen from requests by businesses for students to assist in projects.

During the selection process, potential clients are provided an explanation of the course and are alerted that projects are for a semester's duration and will be terminated at the end of the semester regardless of the stage of completion. (Clients occasionally procrastinate in supplying needed information to students and then expect completion after the semester is ended.) Although a team approach is typically used, potential clients are advised that an individual or a team could be assigned to a project depending on its scope and nature. Since this is not a capstone course in which students are expected to have completed almost all of their undergraduate class work, potential clients are also made aware that students will be assigned to projects which will stretch the student's current abilities. (The student with the least knowledge of Excel may be assigned a project requiring Excel, and one who has not designed a web page may be assigned web design, etc.)

Once a potential client has expressed an interest in participating in the service learning environment, various types of appropriate projects are discussed and the potential client proposes a project. Most of the projects initially proposed were stand-alone, while a few were part of a larger project being implemented by the organization. Initially, most of the projects were web site development. After a few semesters the emphasis shifted to database design and decision support systems. After a potential client suggests a project, the professor and the client must thoroughly discuss the scope of the project and the expectations of both the client and the professor. The professor must be confident that the proposed project is viable for a semester's work and that the skills required for project completion are within the grasp of the students taking the course yet sufficiently challenging to create a learning environment. Again, since this is not a capstone course, it is imperative that expectations are realistic. Client, student, and professor responsibilities are also discussed.

The first day of class students are required to complete a questionnaire designed to assess strengths and weaknesses (or at least to determine exposure) in the use of Access, Excel, and Visual Basic, in web design, in written communication and oral presentations, and in team work. Written communication sophistication is also evaluated via the first assignment. Since students will be interacting with clients as software developers, it is important that they consider what is and is not ethical behavior; thus, their first assignment is to research and write a paper on ethics as it relates to software development and to the Internet. While they research and write, it befalls the professor to solve the puzzle of appropriate matches of individual students, teams, and clients.

In partial explanation of the course, students are made aware that the professor is a facilitator; there are few class lectures and no exams. Each student is required to independently master whatever hurtle looms between him and satisfactory completion of the project for the client. To assist, the professor's collection of books and reference materials is made available to students; the professor helps locate appropriate resource personnel whenever needed; the professor provides protocol guidance in University matters; etc.

The primary focus of the course, particularly from a student standpoint, is developing a software application. Students choose the appropriate development tool(s) (a programming language, a database, a spreadsheet, etc.), share project management functions (systems analysis and design, time-line development, human relations issues, etc.), divide responsibilities (programming, meeting with the client(s), writing documentation, etc.), and overall, coordinate the project(s).

Instructional Issues

One of the first classroom issues encountered is attendance. Should students be required to assemble at a particular time on specific days? To comply with university regulations, the answer to that may be "yes". Realistically, if students are taking responsibility for their project, are meeting with clients and team members, and are making adequate progress toward completion, it should not matter where or when they meet. In this particular course, the professor imposes deadlines for each phase of project development and requires that each team (or individual in the rare instance when only one student is assigned to a project) meet with the professor and present both a written and an oral report of progress to date. One part of the written report is a group evaluation of the team's progress and ability to work together. Another part is private peer evaluations of each team member's contribution. The private peer evaluations are seen only by the professor whereas the group evaluation is compiled by the team.

Associated with classroom attendance is new knowledge acquisition. Since one of the goals of this particular service learning course is for students to expand their knowledge base, how can the professor assess whether the goal is being achieved? Expansion of knowledge base for this course is not so clear cut or uniform as may be the case for many other courses. The professor for this course has individualized this objective for each student. After several semesters of facilitating the course, check sheets have been developed for the most common areas in which students need to (and do) expand their knowledge base. After evaluation of each student's transcript, appropriate check sheets are distributed to each individual. Throughout the semester the professor meets with students individually to review progress and at the end of the semester the check sheet is, hopefully, completed.

Individual contribution (or lack thereof) to the team's objective is, not surprisingly, a recurring cause of student irritation and team conflict. When team members are unable to resolve issues, conflict management becomes an instructional issue. All teams are not equal. Some seem to lack the ability to resolve ANY problems and turn to the professor for multiple resolutions. Others wait until there is no viable solution and no possibility of restoring a meaningful working relationship and then ask for a resolution.

Interaction with clients can likewise pose an instructional issue. The client will explain the nature of the project, usually in very general terms. The students must then ask probing questions to determine the scope and project design requirements. Even senior-level students are often intimidated by the challenge of interacting with a professional in this manner. Thus, students sometimes leave meetings with the client still unsure of their task or with misconceptions of the task. It may be well into the development phase before either the students or the client recognize or acknowledge the problem and seek the intervention of the professor.

Instructional issues, then, for this service learning course are not confined to a classroom or to a specific subject matter. They are varied and dynamic, involving not only students but also clients. The professor, as facilitator, is challenged to stay abreast of multiple teams and projects and to be proactive in offering solutions.

Lessons Learned

Overall the experiences of this service learning course have been positive. However, there were also a few problematic areas. Following are a few problems encountered and the resolution implemented.

There will always been instances when a team member drops the course. The impact of the loss of a team member varies. At the beginning of the course there may be opportunity to reassign a student to a different team. For example, if one team had four members and one dropped, and another team had five members; a student could be reassigned so that both of the remaining teams would consist of four members. Later in the semester that solution may be inappropriate. Thus, as in a business, the remaining group members must complete the project. Depending on the contribution of the exiting team member, the solution could have a dramatic effect on the project outcome.

A related issue is encountered when a team member is ill for an extended period of time or on multiple occasions and is unable to contribute at an appropriate level. Absence due to illness is a challenge for all organizations. Unfortunately, the solution is the same: the remaining group members must fill in and complete the project. The service learning course is no exception.

Avoidable absences and/or irresponsibility are much more serious issues. When a team member fails to fulfill his/her responsibilities to the point that the rest of the group is incensed, in this service learning course the team is allowed to fire the non-productive member. That member is then in a group with team members fired by other groups and/or the professor who, not surprisingly, refuses to be productive. In most instances, a fired team member is unsuccessful in completing the requirements for the course.

Problematic issues do not always reside with the team, however. In a couple of instances, a client has failed to respond to emails or voice mail and/or has repeatedly missed appointments with students after the project is well underway. This, of course, causes a delay in productivity unrelated to student ability or effort. In these cases the professor became the client and the students completed the project. The project, however, was not delivered to the client at the end of the semester.

In a very limited number of cases, a client has made requests/demands that were either unreasonable, unethical, or beyond the scope of the course, even after the professor's initial screening and after an agreement had supposedly been reached regarding the client's project. Students, eager to please, sometimes yield to such requests without informing the professor. Sometimes students tactfully refuse and the situation dissipates. Occasionally the professor handles the situation and either the client rescinds the request or the project is terminated.

Students are assigned to clients, and as the software developer, should satisfy the client. But even though students are strongly encouraged to complete projects, there are occasions when a group fails and a project is still incomplete at the end of the semester. In one instance the client worked for the university and had a student worker who completed the project. In another instance the client graciously accepted the situation, and to his credit, was willing to pursue another project the following semester. And in one instance, the professor, because of the nature of the project, completed it as a service to the university.

Byproduct Bonuses

The service learning experience often becomes a partnership between the client and the professor as they encourage student learning. In some cases, the client/student relationship was such that the client began to groom the student during the service learning semester and hired the student full time upon graduation, which in some instances is a full two or more years after the service learning experience.

In the service learning course students are often required to learn and implement concepts that will be encountered in future courses, thus preparing them to better comprehend the relevance and impact when an entire course is devoted to the subject. It also emphasizes that courses are not intended to be discrete, stand alone units of knowledge but rather integrated, intertwined pieces of knowledge that comprise a whole.

Some projects undertaken align with the American Association of Collegiate Schools of Business' (AACSB) exhortations to integrate courses and provide opportunities for cross-discipline instruction. One such project that proved especially viable to cross-discipline integration was the development of a DSS for small businesses considering adoption of a cafeteria plan benefits package, and more specifically, a Flexible Spending Account (FSA) plan. A comparison by size of organization study had shown that only 5% of employers with less than 50 employees had adopted a FSA plan, whereas over 75% of large-sized businesses offered a FSA plan. One reason for the low adoption rate by small-sized businesses, according to research, was their inaccessibility to means and/or methods of estimating the cost-benefit for employers and employees (Giovetti 1996; Rhim and Kim 1997). In response to this drawback, the service learning students developed a DSS.

The software application embodied two models by which an employer could estimate cost benefits and tax savings for an employer and employees from FSA plan adoption. Both models, showing employer as well as employee benefits, were supported by the software application, thus providing a clear projection of where benefits would be realized. The DSS provided summary data for all employees as well as benefits by individual employee. It allowed an employer to input regulatory data (federal, state, and county tax rates), employee data (salary, number of tax deductions claimed, residence, etc.), and employer data (taxes, retirement contributions, administration costs, etc.), and to determine whether the benefits would exceed costs by adopting a FSA plan. In addition, the software application provided an estimate of realized/foregone benefits to a regional economy and identified several managerial implications.

The students working on the project gained valuable insight about a cafeteria plan, a FSA, and cafeteria plan significance to a business and employees. Understanding the math models was another significant step for the students and an opportunity for cross-discipline cooperation. A professor from finance and another from accounting explained the ramifications of the cafeteria plan on tax savings and human resource management as well as the intricacies of the math models.

Once the students grasped the accounting/taxation, finance, math and HR aspects of the project, system development work could finally be undertaken. That, as noted by multiple students, was the only part of the process they had expected to encounter in the service learning course. The necessity of incorporating subject matter from other courses was somehow unanticipated. But alas, as the application was completed, the usual program documentation along with a user manual was required. And for that phase of the project, a professor from business communication was consulted.

Conclusion

Service learning projects, although a challenge to facilitate, can provide valuable experiences for students. The course does not need to be a capstone course to benefit student learning, but the projects must be well chosen to ensure that the scope of the project and the skills required are within the time and ability range of the course and the students. Instructional issues involve a wide range of circumstances beyond those encountered in a typical class room setting. Students learn many valuable lessons beyond the skills required for software development. Cross-discipline curriculum integration is often complex but the student benefits are multi-faceted. Students themselves note the necessity of integrating knowledge from a variety of subjects in addition to Excel, Access, and/or programming, to produce an acceptable software package, thus providing a bridge among disciplines. Taking all of this into consideration, and reflecting on the challenges, benefits, achievements, and accolades from clients and students, the service learning course is successful in achieving the desired goals and objectives.

References

_____. "Educators Embrace Service-Learning as a Strategy for Improving Learning." *Business Wire* (March 25, 2010).

_____. "An Adventure in Service-Learning." *Business Wire* (March 2, 2010).

Giovetti, Alfred C. "Champion Controller bridges the gap," *Accounting Technology* (April 1996), 12-16.

Jordan, Mark and Bob Orwig. "Service Learning: Informing the Science & Art of Leadership." *Nonprofit World* 28:2, (March/April 2010) 10-12.

Kiltz, Linda. "Service-Learning Through Colleges and Universities, Part I," *The Public Manager* (Summer 2010), 17-21.

Rhim, Jong C. and Kwang Kim. "Adoption of a Cafeteria Plan: Tax-Created Positive-Sum Opportunity," *Journal of Accounting and Finance Research* (Summer 1997), 69-76.

Skilton, Paul F., David Forsyth, and Otis J. White. "Interdependence and Integration Learning in Student Project Teams: Do Team Project Assignments Achieve What We Want Them To?", *Journal of Marketing Education*, (2008), 30; 57-65.

Sociology

Statistics Don't Bleed

Teaching Sociology of Terrorism and Genocide through Multimedia Technologies and Service Learning

Michael W. Smith, Ph.D., Department of Sociology, Saint Anselm College, USA

Abstract:The teaching of terrorism and genocide by sociologists is grounded in the theoretical study of historical circumstances influencing social forces and social structure; of individual and collective memories and behavior leading to social movements; of social groups; of group dynamics and group identity; of conflicts of ideology, of ethnicity, religion and social class; and of the motivations and sources for terrorism and genocide. (Smith 2003; MacDougall and Elder 2003; Abowitz 2002). In teaching an undergraduate course in the sociology of terrorism and genocide, this paper examines and evaluates the use of multimedia technologies (internet, <u>BlackBoard</u> and films) and service learning. The use of these different teaching approaches personalized these incomprehensible events to students in ways that are difficult to convey through traditional texts and lecture format. The use of the internet sites exposed students to not only primary and secondary documents, but also to oral histories and visual sociology of the terrorism and genocide. Visual images through films and the internet are susceptible to a wide range of interpretations and provide the students with socio-historical "connection to lives in process and a fuller range of contextual details". (Valdez and Halley 1999:287). From a socio-historical perspective, this paper evaluates six films on terrorism and genocide. As cultural products of American *society, the socio-historical context and content of these films become an important source for understanding cultural ideas, beliefs, norms, myths, stereotypes, and values of that population in that time period. (Dowd 1999:330). The technology of Black-Board was used to not only manage the course, but to encourage and facilitate on-line venues for students' discussions of these incomprehensible events. Finally, all students were required to volunteer 20 hours at a refugee center in Manchester, New Hampshire. This service learning experience provided students with educational benefits what at the same time provided invaluable assistance to the refugee population. This paper includes with the students' assessment evaluates the use of multimedia, technology, the internet and service learning in this course.*

We owe respect to the living; to the dead we owe only development and teaching of a course on the truth. *Sociology of Terrorism and Genocide* at Saint —Voltaire. *Oeuvres* Vol. I, p. 15n Anselm College (Manchester, New Hampshire, U.S.A.) in the Spring semesters of 2002 and 2004. This article discusses and evaluates the use of the At 8:45 a.m. on September 11, 2001, American multimedia technologies and service learning in Airlines Flight 11 from Boston, Massachusetts teaching this course in the Spring 2004. struck Tower 1 of the New York City's World Trade Center. Eighteen minutes later, United Airlines The Pedagogy of Teaching Terrorism Flight 175, flying again from Boston, struck Tower **and Genocide** 2. Later that morning, a third hijacked plane crashed into the Pentagon Building in Washington, D.C. and Arthur Koestler's phrase, "Statistics don't bleed..." a fourth plane crashed in a field in Pennsylvania. creates a subtext to teaching terrorism and genocide This tragic event, along with this author's because students cannot understand the context of experiences living and teaching throughout the these horrific political crimes and the dire human Middle East and Europe from 1981-1992,[1] led to the consequences merely by a body count. Therefore, the role of the sociologist in teaching about terrorism and genocide is not just in teaching about these tragic historical events, but rather in assisting students in understanding what these past events mean for today's culture.

Freeman (1995:221-222) contends that "genocidal social engineering has a long history" by noting that

... The Assyrians celebrated their killings. Modern culture, in the face of genocide is weak, vacillating, collaborationist, shocked, and ineffectually humanitarian. The historical-sociological study reveals important structural and motivational similarities throughout the millennia of social change.

Thus, the sociology of terrorism and genocide is a story of continuity and differences and is grounded in the theoretical study of historical circumstances influencing social forces and social structure; of individual and collective memories and behavior leading to social movements; of social groups

---

1. person was frequently searched or detained, whether it be at border crossings, train stations, military installations or while 1 The nature and extent of terrorism in Europe and the Middle driving through London (during the IRA's 1982 bombings), East during this time period was profound and deadly. U.S. Israel, Lebanon, and southeastern Turkey which was under Military installations were always on alert. My automobile and/or martial law and the home of the Kurdish PKK.

and group dynamics; of race, ethnicity, religion and social class; of the motivations and ideologies for terrorism and genocide; and of the political responses to terrorism and genocide. (Smith 2003; MacDougall and Elder 2003; Abowitz 2002; Dabag 1995.).

This article examines and evaluates the use of multimedia technologies (Internet, BlackBoard and films) and service learning in teaching an undergraduate course in the sociology of terrorism and genocide. The use of these different teaching approaches personalized these incomprehensible events to students in ways that are difficult to convey through traditional texts and lecture format.

BlackBoard and the Internet

BlackBoard's virtual classroom features a "comprehensive array of work tools" giving students access to course documents, course assignments, grades, discussion groups, e-mail, and even exam-taking (Carter 2002:11). In this course, BlackBoard was utilized to give students access to terrorism and genocide websites, to create interactive writing assignments, and to encourage student participation in discussion groups.

Appendix "A" identifies the author's BlackBoard course document that identifies numerous Internet web sites on terrorism (domestic and international), genocide (Armenian, Holocaust, Cambodian, Bosnia, and Rwandan), democide, Islam, and war tribunals (military and international). Each web site has a short description of its contents and/or source. Because some students are "high tech – low touch," this instructor and several students tutored the class on evaluating selected we bsites on the Armenian, Holocaust, and Bosnian genocides.

Besides assigning students to review internet sources or to read specific articles related to terrorism and genocide, interactive written assignments through the Internet were utilized. For instance, students were instructed to go to the "Center for Holocaust & Genocide Studies" (http://www.chgs.umn.edu) and then to go to the site's "Virtual Museum of Holocaust and Genocide Art" to access Fritz Hirshenberg's "The Holocaust Series: Sur-Rational Paintings."[2]

Students were then required to view all twenty of his paintings and then to select two paintings to write about how these paintings both elated to the Holocaust and to the broader concept of genocide. Students did very well in

---

2. In 1938, Fritz Hirschberger was arrested bv the Gestapo and deported to Poland as an undesirable Polish, Jewish alien. There, he fought in the Polish Army against the invading Nazis, but was later captured by the Soviet Secret Police (NKVD) and sentenced to 20 years in a slave labor camp for his membership in the militant right wing Zionist organization the Betar. In 1941, he was released from the labor camps and rejoined the Polish Army, participating in the invasion of Italy. After the war, he continued his art education in London before coming to the United States and working with artist teaching at New Yorlk City's New School.

connecting race, state power, obedience to authority and the failure to respond by religious and international bodies from these paintings to today's events.

The final use of <u>BlackBoard</u> was to have the class and students interact in discussions through the use of discussion groups. During the course of the semester, a question was posted by this instructor after Wednesday evenings class. Each student was required to post their response by a set time on Friday. They were then required to read their classmates' responses and to respond to at least one of their classmates' responses by a set time on Sunday. On Monday and Tuesday, each student was required to respond back to all classmates that responded to their initial response to the instructor's Wednesday evening question.[3] The following five questions were posted:

React to the following statement: "President George W. Bush's reasons/justifications for invading Irag were all lies and this has resulted the deaths of over 500 America soldiers and countless innocent Iraquis.

React to the following statement by Robin Morgan: "...organized religion has always been about power, and thus has always been political."

A "Time Machine" takes you to Berlin, Germany and as you get your bearings you discover that it is January 30, 1932, just one year before Adolf *Statistics Don't Bleed* Hitler will be appointed Chancellor of Germany. You know what the future will hold and as you enter a Beerhaus, you bump into him as he is leaving. Do you follow Adolph Hitler and kill him? Why or why not?

The movie we saw Wednesday night, "Pretty Village Pretty Flame", was based on a true event during the Serban-Bosnian War. Milan [Serbia] and Halil [Bosnian Muslim] were friends since childhood, yet this war destroyed their country and their lives. How does this movie relate to terrorism and genocide? Were you surprised to find the Bosnian Muslims negatively portrayed or was this just the retribution by the victims of war.

We have examined the Armenian, the Holocaust, Cambodian, Rwandan, and Bosnian genocides. After the Holocaust, the international community said: "Never Again!!" ... yet genocide and other crimes by governments against civilian populations continue while the international community repeatedly fails to respond. What role should or can the United Nations play in reducing the likelihood of future genocide or should this role be assumed by the United States?

3.Except for the posting of each question, this instructor intentionally did not participate in the discussions in order not to influence the student interactions or to cause an individual respondent any embarrassment by the instructor's public comments. This instructor read all comments and would have spoken privately to any student whose responses were inappropriate. There was a general discussion on the Wednesday evening class after the posting that generated exceptional further interaction amongst the students on the question topic.

While the responses by the students to each of these five questions were thoughtful, the interactions between the students were respectful, but at times contentious. For example, Question 1 divided those students who supported the Iraqi invasion with those who were vehemently against President Bush's decision and reasons for going to war. Question 3 divided those students into groups that would kill Hitler to save the lives of those victims of the Holocaust with those students who would not kill Hitler on moral/religious grounds or because such an act would change the course of history as they knew it. Question 5 made students not only consider the future role of the United Nations and the United States as it relates to future genocide, but whether either body has the moral and/or legal standing, and even courage, to combat international and terrorism and genocide. Not surprisingly, a significant number of students took an isolationist view toward United States intervention, despite conceding the past history of the ineffectual response of the United Nations and others in the international community toward international and terrorism and genocide.

At the end of the semester, students were asked to "rate the value of the discussion on BlackBoard" on a 1-10 scale (#10 being the highest rating). The class mean score was 7.17.

Teaching Terrorism and Genocide through Films

Sociologists have used films to explore a variety of social issues and problems. (Baker-Sperry, et al. 1999, gender; Valdez and Halley 1999, Mexican-Americans; Dawson 1995, American lesbians in the 1920s; Dressel 1990, social problems; Hannon and Maruallo 1988, war; Getz 1981, ideology and sex roles). Other sociologists have written more generally about the sociology of film and art. (Tudor 1975; Huaco 1967).

Visual sociologists use films to study the visual cultural artifacts and social construction of a given society. (Bowes 2002; Becker 1995; Chaplin 1994; Harper 1988). As cultural products of American society, the socio-historical context and content of films become an important source for understanding cultural ideas, beliefs, norms, myths, stereotypes, and values of that population in that time period. (Dowd 1999:330).

For students, visual images carry surplus, are susceptible to a wide range of interpretations and provide the students with socio-historical "connection to lives in process and a fuller range of contextual details". (Valdez and Halley 1999:287). Moreover, the use of films in teaching an undergraduate course on terrorism and genocide personalized these incomprehensible events to students in ways that are difficult to convey through lectures and texts.

The following are seven films that were shown during the Spring 2004 semester. An overview is presented of each film as well as how each film connected to various sociological concepts and theories. Additionally, each film was evaluated on a 1-10 scale ("10" being the highest score by students in three categories: bias, cinematic/artistic quality, and relationship of film to course content. A mean score is reported for each category. Student comments are also reported for each category.

"9/11"

This 2001 film is the "accidental documentary" made by French brothers and filmmakers, Gedeon and Jules Naudet. They were making a film documentary about a young New York City firefighter during his 9-month probationary period. On September 11, 2001 at 8:46 a.m., Jules Naudet was filming as Battalion Chief Joseph Pfeiffer and 13 other firefighters were investigating an odor of gas, when the first plane flew overhead and into Tower 1 of the World Trade Center. What transpires is the only known footage of the struggle of the firefighters in Tower 1 as they try to figure our what to do in the mass chaos and confusion, while the rest of the world looked on, helplessly.

The other story of this film was that of the courageous firefighters who unconditionally gave their lives on what may be characterized as a "suicide mission" to save those still in Tower 1. From a sociology of occupations perspective, the filmmakers captured the "brotherhood" of firefighters; the extreme of Mead's (1934:119) socialization process leading to "generalized other".

Student ratings for this film were the following: bias = 2.92; cinematic/artistic quality = 8.97; and relationship of film to course content = 9.63. Written comments on the film emphasized how the raw emotion and reactions by the firefighters and those persons at "ground zero" personally effected them as citizens of the United States. For them, September 11, 2001 is a defining event for their generation, as was the assassination of John F. Kennedy and Martin Luther King for their parents' generation.

Applying the symbolic interactionist perspective to the targets on 9/11, many students identified the World Trade Center as the symbol of globalization and capitalism, the Pentagon as the symbol of United States military might, and the White House as United States power and imperialism. Several students commented that for others in world community, the destruction was that of an avenging angel.

"9-11 Saudi Eyes"

This 2002 film with English subtitles was directed by Bader Ben Hirsi and was the first documentary to examine 9/11 from what the filmmakers characterize as:

a broad cross-section of Saudis—parents and neighbors of the accused hijackers, editors of Arab News and Asharq al Awasat, political and military analysts, a psychologist and others—give their perceptions of events and issues involving September 11th. Interviews provide background on the insight into the lives and minds of the alleged hijackers, the recruitment practices of al Qaeda, the co-opting of jihad for militant political ends, Osama bin Laden's cult of personality, the Israeli/Palestinian conflict, and frustration over U.S. foreign policy.

This film has been characterized by some reviewers as the Saudi Arabian government's "official position" on the reasons, causes and responses to September 11th. Through the use of long interviews with academicians, government officials, and members of the families of the accused hijackers, this film does cast an interesting and important perspective on this event. Among those interviewed were: Huwaida Halabi (writer), Dr. Waheed Hamza (Professor of Political Science), Nana Al Segga (businesswoman), Dr. Samira Al Ghamdi (psychologist), Dr. Ali Saad Al Moussa (Professor of Political Science), Omar Al Zobidy (Editor of Asharq Al Awasat), Faheed Shakir Al Abdali (retired headmaster), Dr. Mahmoud Shakir (teacher), Saeed Assiri (neighbor of accused hijacker Ahmed Nehm), Muhammad Al Shehri Al Segelli (father of accused hijackers of Wa 'il and Waleed). By providing students with the background into the lives and minds of the alleged hijackers, the recruitment practices of al Qaeda and the co-opting of jihad for militant political ends, this film facilitated the analysis of revolutionary social and religious movements and of what religious, economic, historical and cultural factors attracted these Saudis to join and/or support the ranks of al Qaeda.

Student ratings for this film were the following: bias = 7.00; cinematic/artistic quality = 7.56; and relationship of film to course content = 10.00.

For most students in the course, this was truly the first time that that they saw and heard academic and government officials Saudis explain to them not only why the events of September 11th occurred, but that that this event was justified because of United States imperialism and our country's relationship with Israel. Many students wrote with anger toward the Saudis (whom they thought were "friends" of the United States), others thought that the Saudis responded in this matter out of fear that they may be the next target of terrorists. Students also commented on the relationship between terrorism and Islamic radicalism, noting that many of the 9/11 terrorists appeared to come from "good" homes, yet were somehow drawn to become involved in this terrorist act.

"Triumph des Willens" ("Triumph of the Will")

"Fraulein Riefenstahl, you have to have more self-confidence. You can and you will do this project." It sounded almost like an order.
(Riefenstahl 1992:158)

Adolf Hilter ordered Leni Riefenstahl, an "obscure" actress whose only directorial credit was *Das blaue Licht* (*Blue Light*), to direct this 1934 film as a pictorial record of the Sixth Nazi Congress at Nuremberg. This film is considered to be the most controversial propaganda film on Nazi Germany and Riefenstahl's "skill as a filmmaker is a evident in the production as her homage to Hitler." (Giesen 2003:23).

This film opens with a title card reminding the viewer that September 5, 1934 is 20 years after the outbreak of WWI, 16 years after Germany's woes and travails began (Treaty of Versailles and Weimar Republic) and just 19 months since Germany's rebirth.

The first visual is Hitler descending by plane through the clouds to Nuremberg as a Christ-like figure, the savior and Fuhrer ("Leader") of Germany. Speeches by Hitler (as well as Goebbels, Goering, Streicher, Himmler and Hess) are visually orchestrated to create a mystical, primitive union between the dictator and these followers.

Student ratings for this film were the following: bias = 9.04; cinematic/artistic quality = 5.82; and relationship of film to course content = 8.17.

Student written comments emphasized how the film both promoted Adolph Hitler's "cult of personality" and, through the use propaganda and nationalistic symbols to demonize Jews and other groups in Germany, led to both the obedience to and admiration of Hitler.

Through this film, students came to better understand the connections between social forces, reactionary social movements (National Socialism) and the cult of personality (Adolph Hitler). From a symbolic interactionists perspective, the cultural artifacts on display in this film function to strengthen societal support and allegiance to the *Volk*.

"Opening the Gates of Hell: American Liberators of the Nazi Concentration Camps"

This 1992 film is quite graphic with original 1945 film footage of the Allied Forces liberating Nazi concentration camps U.S. military veterans, who were among the first troops to enter the Nazi concentration camps, are interviewed and they relate their memories of emaciated prisoners, victims of "medical experiments" and sexual cruelty, gas chambers, mass graves, and their own bulldozing of a mountain of bodies into pits at Bergen-Belsen.

Among students, this film elicited the most profound emotional responses of horror and disbelief. Some students left the class speechless and others reported that they could not sleep that evening.

Student ratings for this film were the following: bias = 5.27; cinematic/artistic quality = 6.74; and relationship of film to course content = 9.79. Student written comments emphasized the graphic nature of the film as well as how the liberation of concentration camps still effect the lives of the liberators, the U.S. soldiers.

While this film provided irrefutable evidence to the Nuremburg Tribunal of what occurred, the unprecedented nature of the atrocities complicated the prosecution's task of convicting Nazis under the existing law and, specifically, to convict them of genocide. (Douglas 1995). This led to class discussions about the sociology of law and the social construction of new definitions by the United Nations relating to crimes against humanity and genocide.

"The Road to Palestine"

The "Road to Palestine" is Part II of the 1993 award-winning film series, "Beirut to Bosnia: Muslims and the West." The *London Independent's* correspondent Robert Fisk examines the displacement of Palestinians by Zionist immigrants and Jewish refugees in Israel. This film focuses on the militant Islamic group Hamas, the effects of Israeli rule in occupied Gaza, and the attitudes of

Statistics Don't Bleed

Zionist settlers and Palestinian holdouts on the outskirts of Jerusalem.

The viewing of this controversial film series, with its strong message of Western complicity with Israel, enhanced the students' understanding how the sociological concepts of individual and collective memory (Coser 1992) strengthens collective behavior and leads to religious and ethnic conflict. (Kifner 2000; Grossman 1998; Al-Batrawi and Rabbani 1991).

Student ratings for this film were the following: bias = 6.40; cinematic/artistic quality = 8.05; and relationship of film to course content = 9.45. The written comments by the students emphasized how the film demonstrated how the past and present conflict between Israel and the Palestinians is related to their history and geography. Many students wrote that that they had never before been exposed to the film's Pro-Palestinian and Anti-U.S.A.

"Lepa Sela Lepo Gore" ("Pretty Village, Pretty Flame")

What's the name of the village?

Who gives a shit!

We set a place on fire, and we don't even know its name. We are killing each other for a fistful of ashes...

They say that war brings out the best and worst in man. What is the best?

Director Srdjan Dragojevic's provacative and disturbing 1996 film, with explosions of pyrotechnics and rock music, is based on an incident that happened in the first winter (1992) of the war in Bosnia. Two best friends in the ethnically diverse Bosnia, Halil (Nikola Pejakovic), a Muslim, and Milan (Drajan Bjelogrlic), a Serb, played as children by the Marshall Tito's decaying "Brotherhood and Unity Tunnel" and later were partners in an auto repair business. But, now in 1992 they are on opposing sides of the Bosnian-Serbian War, their friendship tattered and in ruins.

As Milan lies badly injured alongside wounded Serbs and Muslims in the same hospital as Halil, he recalls the events that brought him there. Ironically, Halil's flashbacks take us to that same tunnel where now he and his Serbian soldiers are pinned down by Bosnian soldiers led by Halil.

Dragojevic's character development of the Serbian soldiers, and their reasons for fighting this brutal and insane war are exposed through the hollowness and fragility of their "Communist" or "Greater Serbia" ideals. These

Serbians burned down houses of their Muslim neighbors and marched the surviving Muslim fathers and sons to "work camps."

Student ratings for this film were the following: bias = 6.19; cinematic/artistic quality = 8.31; and relationship of film to course content = 9.27. Student written comments emphasized the chaos and sadness of war and of how religious/ethnic group identification and hatred triumphed over the friendship of Milan and Halil.

In the class after this film, this instructor utilized

C. Wright Mills' (1959) concept of the "sociological imagination" to trace the historical, ideological, structural and social changes that have taken place in Yugoslavia from WW II to present. Through this analysis, students understood how the 1980 death of Marshall Josip Broz Tito and the fall of the Soviet Union led to the rise of nationalistic Serbian President Slobodan, decimating ethnic relations in Bosnia-Hercegovina, and resulting in Milosevic's "ethnic cleansing" campaign.

"A Good Man in Hell"

This 2002 film was produced by the United States Holocaust Memorial Museum's Committee on Conscience. While this film did show the aftermath of the Rwandan genocide that took place between April and June, 1994, it was primarily an interview with General RomŽo Dallaire, the Commander of United Nations Assistance Mission in Rwanda.

General Dallaire warned the United Nations in 1993 and in the early months of 1994 that Hutu rebel forces were going overthrow the Rwandan government and "cleanse" the country of the Tutsi population. No intervention was taken by the United Nations (or the United States and other Western countries who had similar warnings) and, in April 1994, the United Nations ordered General Dallaire to stand-down as the now government-backed Hutu rebel forces massacred an estimated 800,000 Tutsis.

In his initial conversation with *Nightline's* Ted Koppel, General RomŽo Dallaire declares:

The ones I hold accountable for not understanding and not rising above self-interest to a level of humanity where every human counts and we're all the same are: the British, the French, and the Americans. Self-interest, political posturing, image dominated their decision processes in regard to Rwanda"

... Are all humans human or some more human than others? ....They [the West] came in to evacuate the white men and the odd Rwandan who was politically well suited to what they want. As an example the French evacuated the bulk of the president's family who were not necessarily the nicest people on earth. And so all the expatriates within five days picked up what they had, left the Rwandans who had served them for years, decades, who raised their kids, left them to be slaughtered behind and went back to Brussels and Paris and all these other places.

The Rwandan genocide forced General Dallaire to question the depth of his belief in moral values, in ethical and in humanity. He states:

You just can't walk through all that blood and all that gore and all that sound. You can't just walk by a woman who has just given birth beside the road in the pouring rain with thousands of people walking by her and she picks up her child and she tries to arrange herself, stands up, takes three steps, falls down, and dies. Who takes care of the kid? Everybody is under terrible duress. You can't walk away from that.

... there is no conceivable way of actually being able to walk away from the immensity of what it is. You can't imagine the smell, the sounds of dogs eating humans throughout the night howling by the hundreds, of seeing children living amongst the corpses of their families because there's nowhere else to go and there's no orphanage and nobody could pick them up at the time, of watching women who are being moved to safety and all of a sudden a sniper just shoot her head off and say that you can come back from that.

Student ratings for this film were the following: bias = 3.61; cinematic/artistic quality = 7.70; and relationship of film to course content = 9.79. The students' written comments demonstrated they were emotionally moved by General Dallaire's interview and that the students understood the moral and ethical dilemma he faced as the Commander of United Nations Assistance Mission in Rwanda. This film complemented the final discussion group Question 5 that they were assigned to answer during the week between next class.

Teaching Terrorism and Genocide through Service Learning

Deeply influenced by philosopher/educator John Dewey (1938) and sociologist C. Wright Mills (1963), service learning at colleges and universities is characterized by the merging of service to one's community and an experiential emphasis to pedagogy (Alt & Medrich, 1994).[4] The Saint Anselm College Model for Service Learning (www.anselm.edu/volunteer/sl/model.htm). emphasizes the "rigorous integration of academic content" with the service learning experience.

---

4. The Commission on National and Community Service has defined service learning as a method under which students learn and develop through active participation in thoughtfully organized service experiences that meet actual community needs and that are coordinated in collaboration with the school and community; that is integrated into the into the students' academic curriculum or provides structured time for the student to think, talk or write about what the student did and saw during the actual service activity; that provides students with opportunities to use newly acquired skills and knowledge in real-life situations in their own communities; and that enhances what is taught in school by extending student learning beyond the classroom and into the community and helps to foster the development of a sense of caring for others. [National and Community Service Act of 1990].

In the Fall of 2003, this instructor began to explore the possibility of including a service learning component in the Spring 2004 semester course in the sociology of terrorism and genocide. While service learning has been incorporated in teaching about justice in Peace Studies courses (Weigert and Crews 1999), this instructor was seeking to find a service learning project that would be related to terrorism and genocide and where students would have personal contact with a persons who had, themselves, experienced the events of terrorism and/or genocide.

In the Fall of 2003, the College's Meelia Center began offering ESL classes in the City of Manchester under the State of New Hampshire's *English for New Americans* ("ENA") program[5] in the City of Manchester. These 113 ESL students were from some 32 countries, to include Sudan, Rwanda, Bosnia, Serbia, Columbia, China, Russia, Cuba, and Haiti. Most of these students were refugees who had fled their country to avoid terrorism and/or genocide.

After discussions with the Director of the Meelia Center, this instructor decided that if the students in this course were to make a significant contribution to the ENA program and to be able to fully share with one another their experiences, then service learning must be a mandatory component of the course.

Students were notified in December 2003, that there would be a mandatory service learning component to course, that they would be required to volunteer 20 hours over the semester in teaching ESL and volunteering in other related activities, participate in a pre-training forum, and keep a detailed journal of their volunteering. Students were also required to write a paper discussing the following: 1) how this service learning experience benefited them personally; 2) how, and if, this service learning experience contributed to the academic content of the course and the student's better understanding of terrorism and genocide.

Traditionally, service learning at Saint Anselm College has been an option to a research paper in course, not a requirement in a course. Although students were given notice a month before the course started of the requirement of the mandatory service learning component, a number of the students were resistance to the mandatory requirement. This resistance can be attributed to the fact that 46% (n=14) of the students had never elected to do service learning in other courses. Moreover, the demographics of the class (all white male and females with middle-to-upper class, suburban

---

5. In the Fall of 2002, the State of New Hampshire's Office of Refugee Settlement created a new ESL program, The English for New Americans ("ENA")" to assist new immigrants in assimilating, securing employment and assisting in the education of their own children. When funding was stopped in the Spring of 2003, Saint Anselm College was approached by the Office of Refugee Settlement to restart and manage the ENA and manage in the City of Manchester through the College's Meelia Center (formerly the Center for Volunteers). The first ESL classes began in the Fall of 2003.

backgrounds), suggests that there may have been apprehension among some students in servicing this diverse ESL population, and especially in taking on the responsibility of teaching them English.

To address this resistance, students were required to attend a pre-training forum that focused in on the ESL population and at the beginning of each Wednesday night class there was an open discussion about their service learning experience the previous week. This instructor also devoted a 2-hour class on the socio-political and historical context of migration and immigration, from his perspective not only as a sociologist, but also as a practicing immigration lawyer who represents aliens in political asylum and deportation proceedings. At the end of the semester, students were asked to rate the value of the weekly service learning reflections and the class on migration and immigration on a 1-10 scale (#10 being the highest rating). The class mean score was 8.1.

The success of this approach to reduce resistance is evidenced by the following comments from two student papers:

... The service learning requirement was something I had no interest in. In fact, I almost considered dropping the course because of it. My belief was that service learning should never be mandatory as it loses its point when it is not optional and I also saw no connection to class material. Now that I have participated in the program for an entire semester my view has changed dramatically. The ESL program is an exceptional one for what it does for its clients as well as what it gives to the people who work or volunteer in it. ... Being around people from all over the world has shown me that the way we view the world is not the right way ... Everyday we sit here and do nothing while thousands die around the world from things that could be prevented.

... I did not want to participate in service learning at all, however actually doing it, I would not have had it any other way. ... Some of the individuals grew up in Communist Russia, or Cuba, countries torn by war and genocide like Bosnia and certain countries in Africa, or places torn by drug wars full of murder and kidnappings like Columbia. I don't think I can comprehend the excitement and happiness that these students have now being a free person in the United States of America... The experiences I had will last a lifetime.

(Editorial comment: This student volunteered **34 hours!**)

Evaluation and Assessment: The participation by this class of 30 students was exceptional. During the course of the semester, the students volunteered a total of 668 hours, an average of 21.3 hours per student. Sixteen students volunteered more than the required 20 hours and three students volunteered more than 30 hours. This commitment and participation contributed greatly to the success of the ESL program.

A "Volunteer Evaluation" was administered by the Director of the ESL program to 28 students. Students were asked: *How would you rate your experience with the refugees?* Twenty-four students (88%) rated the experience "Very Positive" and the remaining four students (12%) rated the experience

"Positive." The Director also evaluated each student in 14 categories[6] giving a score of 1 to 5 (#5 being the highest rating) for each category and a perfect score overall would be 70. The mean evaluation score for the class was 68.57.

Students reported both in a questionnaire and in their papers about the benefits they derived from their service learning experiences. The common benefit themes in the student questionaire responses were that they developed a better understanding and appreciation of the immigrant's culture, the struggles the immigrants faced in their home countries and the challenges that these new immigrants face in the United States.

A nursing student in her paper wrote that service learning experience helped her to learn the "true meaning of democracy, tolerance, compassion and benevolence." She noted, that before this course, she worked in the emergency room of a hospital where it was not uncommon for an immigrant to be unable to pay for the services they were seeking. Before she "grumbled" about the resources this person was taking away United States citizens. Now, she reports that she is "treating these people with the respect they deserve for having survived such inhumane circumstances."

A sociology major wrote about why she was so committed to this service learning volunteering:

Students from Rwanda, regal, tall and beautiful, smiled graciously at each class. During the ethnic "conflict" between the ancient tribes of the Hutus and Tutsis of Rwanda in 1994, 800,000 people suffered from the acts of genocide. How did they survive, I pondered, as I am engaging in conversation with them? Each student presents themselves behind decorum and civility, yet I am aware that they have all witnessed poverty, war, death, suffering, and despair. Yet, they come each week, after strenuous work days with the filth of machines upon their hands, aches in their backs, and a myriad of obstacles waiting them at home> And so, I, too, come each week.

Students reported both in a questionnaire and in their papers about the benefits the immigrants received from through their service learning volunteering. The common themes in the questionaire were that the immigrants benefited from the students teaching them English and by assisting and encouraging these new immigrants to learn about American culture. A student echoed these two themes in her paper:

... (The students) helped the ESL students far more in a cultural sense than in learning the language. The volunteers did help with grammar and speech, but I think the main benefit offered from them was showing the ESL students that there are Americans who care about them, that want to help them, and see them achieve. In addition, they were able to ask the students about their lives and discuss the similarities and differences of the cultures.

6.The categories included personal growth and development, attitude, communications skills, teamwork, initiative, motivation, punctuality, attendance, understanding mission, understanding needs of clients and contribution to clients and the mission.

The final question to be answered is whether a student's volunteering in this ESL program contributed to a better understanding of terrorism and genocide. Each student was asked to rate on a 1-10 scale (#10 being the highest score) "the value of your service learning experience in better understanding the academic content in this course." The class mean score was 8.13. The following excepts from student papers are further evidence of the connection of the students service learning experiences to their study of terrorism and genocide:

...It's chilling to know that everything that we have been reading about the Bosnian war, all of the sick and twisted ways that the Serbians were going about and killing their fellow neighbors had actually happened to these adult parents who stood right before me. I just cannot believe what they must have gone through physically and emotionally ... Izet told me about one woman who comes and silently watches as her son is tutored every Sunday. I was surprised to learn that she had actually been able to speak English fluently before the war broke out, but during the war she had been taken to a prisoner camp where she had been severely beaten, raped and god knows what else was done to her. And from then on, she refused to speak any English at all, almost as a way of somehow blocking the memories from that time...

... The refugee family that I visited with had been here for three weeks. Abokt (the wife) and Tet (the husband) had two boys, ages two and four. They were from the Dinka tribe in Sudan, which is the largest tribe in Southern Sudan. Fighting started up between their tribe and the Nuer tribe and they fled to a refugee camp. They were in a refugee camp for four years before they were told they could come to the United States. Before theyu got to the camp they had experienced the killing of their neighbors by the government, and also had seen religious terrorism committed by the Muslim terrorism groups that exist in the Sudan.

... Reading about terrorism and genocide in a textbook is very different from meeting and interacting with a refugee who has experienced what you read in the textbook.. Although the refugees, who did mention the persecutions in their counties, did not go into personal experiences they had suffered through, they did share stories about leaving their homes, professions and countries. It was never said, but it was certainly understood, these refugees left their lives in danger.

... Miroslav maintained his Yugoslavian nationalism, refusing to acknowledge the country as divided regions.

Statistics Don't Bleed

As an ethnic Serb, I wondered what part he played in the The films provided the students with a socio mass murder of Bosnian Muslims during the historical connection to these terrorism and genocide Yugoslavian war in the early 1990's. Surely, I prayed, events. This visual imagery personalized these he didn't believe Milosevic's propaganda. horrific and incomprehensible events to students in ways that would have been impossible to convey Conclusions through lectures and texts. Teaching the sociology of terrorism and geno- cide, But, the service learning component was the most through the use of multiple pedagogues, rewarding experience for these students. The person- alized these horrific and incomprehensible students were not only able to connect this service events for students in ways that are difficult to learning experience to the academic content of this convey through traditional texts and lecture format. terrorism and genocide course, but many students

The use of BlackBoard internet resources gave the had the unique oppor- tunity to speak with the victims students the opportunity and initiative to more fully (and maybe even perpetrators) of terrorism and understand the depth and complexity of terrorism genocide, to tell their stories and to re- flect upon the and genocide. The BlackBoard discussion horrific and incom- prehensible experiences of these questions allowed the students to freely interact in a New Americans. No textbook can deliver this non-threaten- ing environment and to confront, experience! question, and support one an- other's views on a Armed with this new knowledge, understanding specific topic. This interaction had a spill-over and appreciation of our New Amer- icans, it is this effect on class participation --- the students wanted author profound hope that these students will to continue these discussions when we met for the become their advocates and join with others in the following class. international community to campaign against terrorism and genocide.

References

Abowitz, Deborah A. 2002. "Bringing the Sociological into the Discussion: Teaching the Sociology of Genocide and the Holocaust." *Teaching Sociology*. 30:26-38.

Al-Batrawi, Khaled and Mouin Rabbani. 1991. "Break Up of families: A Case Study in Creeping Transfer." *Race and Class. 32(4):35-44.*

Alt M. N. & E. A. Medrich E. A. (1994). "Student Outcomes from Particip- ation in Community Service." (Report prepared for the U.S. De- partment of Education, Office of Research) Berkeley, CA: MPR Associates.

Baker-Sperry, Lori, Autumn Behringer, and Liz Grauerholz. 1999 "Bringing Gender to L Life in the Classroom: Recommended Videos That Teach About Gender" Teaching *Sociology* 27:193-207.

Becker, Howard. 1995. "Visual Sociology: Documentary Photography and Photojournalism: It's Almost All a Matter of Context." Visual So- ciology 10(1-2) 5-14.

Carter, Kim. 2002. "Let's Meet Online: Collaboration Tools." *Technology and Learning*. 22:8:10-12.

Chalk, Frank and Kirt Jonassohn. 1990. *The History of and Sociology of Geno- cide.* .New Haven, CT: Yale University Press.

Chaplin, Elizabeth. 1994. *Sociology and Visual Representation*. London: Routledge.

Coser, Lewis. 1992. "The Revival of the Sociology of Culture: The Case of
Collective Memory." *Sociological Forum*. 7(2): 365-373.

Dabag, Mihran. 2002. "The Realm of Perspectives: Some Reflections on an
Interdisciplinary Approach to Genocide Studies." *International
Journal of Contemporary Sociology*. 39:177-197.

Dawson, D. 1995. "20 something". *Lesbian News*. Jan:40-42.

Douglas, Lawrence. 1995. "Film as Witness: Screening 'Nazi Concentration
Camps' before the Nuremberg Tribunal." *Yale Law University
Journal*. Nov.449-481

Dowd, James J. 1999. "Waiting for Louis Prima: On the Possibility of a Sociology of Film." *Teaching Sociology*. 27:226-230. Freeman, Michael
1995. "Genocide, Civilization and Modernity." *British Journal of
Sociology*. 46:207-223.

Getz, Greg. 1981. "Films Transmission of Ideology through Film: The
Rhetoric of Sex Roles." *Society for the Study of Social Problems
(SSSP)*.

Giesen, Ralf. 2003. "Triumph of the Will: The Odd Case of Lieni Riefenstahl." *Nazi Propaganda Films: A History and Filmography*. . Jefferson, N.C.: MacFarland & Co. pp. 18-34.

Hannon, James T. & Sam Marullo. 1988. "Education for Survival: Using
Films to Teach War as a Social Problem." *Teaching Sociology*
16:245-255.

Harper, Douglas. 1988."Visual Sociology: Expanding the Sociological
View." *The American Sociologist Review*. 19(1)54-70.

Huaco, George. 1967. *The Sociology of Film Art*. New York, NY: Basic
Books.

Mead, George Herbet. 1934. *Mind, Self and Society*. Chicago: University of
Chicago Press.

MacDougall, John and Morten Elder (eds.) 2003. *The Sociology of Peace, War
and Social Conflict:: A Curriculum Guide*. Washington DC: American Sociological Association.

Mills, C. Wright. 1959. *The Sociological Imagination*. New York, N.Y: Oxford University Press.

National and Community Service Act of 1990. Public Law 101-610, as
amended.

Riefenstahl, Leni. 1992. *A Memoir*. New York, NY: St. Martin's Press.

Smith, Michael. 2003. "Sociology of Terrorism and Genocide." *The Soci-
ology of Peace, War and Social Conflict: A Curriculum Guide*.
MacDougall, John and Morten Elder (co-editors). Washington
DC: American Sociological Association.

Tudor, Andrew. 1975. *Image and Influence: Studies in the Sociology of Film*.
New York, NY: St. Martin's Press.

Valdez , Avelardo and Jeffrey A. Halley. 1999. "Teaching Mexican American Experiences Through Film: Private Issues and Public Problems." *Teaching Sociology.* 27:286-295.

Weigert, Kathlen Maas and Robin Crews. 1999, Teaching for Justice: Concepts and Models for Service-Learning in Peace Studies. Washington, D.C.:American Association for Higher Education.

Statistics Don't Bleed

Appendix "A" BlackBoard Websites

Democide University of Hawaii - Democide is the murder of any person or people by a government, including genocide, politicide, and mass murder. http://www.hawaii.edu/powerkills/

Genocide - Armenian Armenian National Institute ... Organization dedicated to the study, research, and affirmation of the Armenian Genocide by the Turks during World War I. http://www.armenian-genocide.org/

University of Michigan -- Three Fact Sheets on Armenia, Karabagh, and the Armenian Genocide. Bibliographies on the Armenian Genocide. http://www.umd.umich.edu/dept/armenian/facts

HyeEtch: Armenian Genocide -Compilation of articles & book excerpts, including academic overview and eyewitness accounts. http://www.hyeetch.nareg.com.au/genocide

Scholars Debate Motives for Armenian Genocide -http://www.gomidas.org/forum/af2gen.htm

Armenian Genocide - Provides articles, fact sheets, and photographs depicting the atrocious crimes committed against the Armenians in 1915 by Ottoman killers. http://www.hr-action.org/armenia

April 24, 1915-2001 86th Anniversary of Armenian Genocide This website is dedicated to the memory of the victims of the First Genocide of the 20th Century, carried out by Ottoman Turks against it's Armenian Christian population in period from 1890 to 1920. More than 1,500,000 lives were starved to death or killed. http://www.15levels.com/24.April

Genocide – Cambodian Cambodian Genocide Program -- Yale University's study of the Cambodian genocide between 1975 and 1979, in which at least 1.7 million people (20% of the entire population) lost their lives. http://www.yale.edu/cg

The Dith Pran Holocaust Awareness Project, Inc. --- Founded by Dith Pran, whose war time story was portrayed in the movie, The Killing Fields, it aims to educate American students about the Cambodian genocide. Goals, information, news, and links. http://www.dithpran.org

The Documentation Center of Cambodia

Non-profit international non-governmental organization by Yale University's Cambodian Genocide Program to facilitate training and field research in Cambodia. http://www.bigpond.com.kh/users/dccam.genocide

Genocide – Rwandan

Frontline: The Triumph of Evil A report on the Rwanda genocide and how the United Nations and the West ignored warning of the 1994 Rwanda genocide and turned its back on the victims. www.pbs.org/wgbh/pages/frontline/shows/evil/
    Frontline Valentina's Nightmare – Personal account of Rwandan genocide. www.pbs.org/wgbh/pages/frontline/shows/rwanda/
    Rwanda Genocide: What The U.S. Knew. www.rnw.nl/hotspots/html/us010823.htm
    Yale Genocide Studies Program: Rwandan Genocide Project: www.yale.edu/gsp/rwanda/
    Report on Inquiry of United Nations In Rwanda: http://www.ess.uwe.ac.uk/genocide/Rwanda.htm
    International Criminal Tribunal for Rwanda Official Site of International Criminal Tribunal for Rwanda www.ictr.org/
    The Rwandan Prosecution of Genocide Foreign Prosecutions www.hrw.org/reports/1999/rwanda/
    Is the Prosecution Fair? www.rudyfoto.com/RwandaPage.html

Holocaust

Center for Holocaust & Genocide Studies - Academic endeavor designed to assist in the development of Holocaust and genocide education. http://www.chgs.umn.edu
    United States Holocaust Memorial Museum - Reconstructing the history of the Holocaust through multiple media. http://www.ushmm.org/
    Fortunoff Video Archive for Holocaust Testimonies - Collection of thousands of videotaped interviews with witnesses and survivors of the Holocaust. http://www.library.yale.edu/testimonies/
    Jan Karski: A Hero of the Holocaust - Writings of the Polish underground agent who brought some of the first news of Hitler's extermination policy to the West in 1942. http://remember.org/karski/karski.html

Holocaust History Project

http://www.holocaust-history.org/ Voice Vision: Holocaust Survivor Oral Histories - Transcripts of interviews with over 150 survivors.
    http://holocaust.umd.umich.edu/ Holocaust Timeline -comprehensive chronology with text and photos.

http://www.historyplace.com/worldwar2/holocaust/timeline.html Jewish Virtual Library: The Holocaust - Collection of articles and original documents pertaining to all aspects of the Holocaust.

http://www.us-israel.org/jsource/holo.html Holocaust Assets - Historical study of U.S. and Allied efforts to recover and restore gold and other assets stolen or hidden by Germany during World War II. From the U. S. Department of State.

http://www.state.gov/www/regions/eur/holocausthp.html

Islam & Terrorism

How Islam and Politics Mixed - Saad Mehio

http://www.nytimes.com/2001/12/02/opinion/02MEHI.html?today-sheadlines

Thomas Friedman – Religious Totalitarianism, an internationally acclaimed author of eighteen novels, John LeCarre is also an astute political observer. In an exclusive essay published in the November 19, 2001 issue of The Nation, LeCarre insists that the US's current war on terrorism, rather than vanquishing the terrorist threat, is in fact likely to increase it.

http://www.nytimes.com/2001/11/27/opinion/27FRIE.html?todaysheadlines=&pagewanted=print
http://www.thenation.com/doc.mhtml?i=20011119&s=lecarre

Terrorism – Domestic United States

The Nation 9/11 - Articles, links, activist info, media resources, section on Islam and remarks on what patriotism is and ought to be.

http://www.thenation.com/special/wtc/index.mhtml FindLaw – 9/11 Resources

http://news.findlaw.com/legalnews/us/terrorism/index.html US v. Zacarias Moussaoui (Dec. 2001) Indictment Alleging Suspect Involved In Sept. 11 Conspiracy [PDF]

http://news.findlaw.com/hdocs/docs/terrorism/moussaoui1201.pdf

USA v. Jack Reimer, a/k/a Jakob Reimer http://caselaw.lp.findlaw.com/data2/circs/2nd/026286p.pdf

National Commission on Terrorism Attacks upon the United States

Prepared Statements and Submitted Testimony On What Military and Diplomatic Efforts Were Undertaken Prior To Sept. 11, 2001 By The United States Against Terrorism, In General, As Well As al Qaeda And The Taliban [PDF Files]

Staff Statements: Military Report: http://news.findlaw.com/hdocs/docs/911rpt/32304mltryrpt.pdf

Diplomacy Report: http://news.findlaw.com/hdocs/docs/911rpt/32304d-plmcyrpt.pdf

Intelligence Policy: http://news.findlaw.com/hdocs/docs/911rpt/32404-intel.pdf

National Policy Coordination: http://news.findlaw.com/hdocs/docs/911rpt/32404npc.pdf

Submitted Testimony: Secretary of State Donald Rumsfeld: http://news.findlaw.com/hdocs/docs/911rpt/rums32304stmnt.pdf Former

Secretary of State William Cohen: http://news.findlaw.com/hdocs/docs/911rpt/cohen32304stmnt.pdf

Secretary of State Colin Powell: http://news.findlaw.com/hdocs/docs/911rpt/powell32304stmnt.pdf Former

Secretary of State Madeline Albright: http://news.findlaw.com/hdocs/docs/911rpt/albright32304stmnt.pdf

Terrorism – International Suspect Calls Malaysia a Staging Area for Terror Attacks --- An operative of Al Qaeda provided new evidence to show that the Southeast Asian nation was a major staging area for the Sept. 11 terror attacks.: http://www.nytimes.com/2002/01/31/national/31INQU-.html?todaysheadlines

War Tribunals – Military MARCI HAMILTON | Liberals1 Hypocrisy Over Military Tribunals: Why The Liberals Who Fought For Discretion During The Clinton Administration Should Continue To Do So Now
Statistics Don't Bleed
Cardozo law professor Marci Hamilton offers a new perspective on the controversy over the Bush Administration's use of military tribunals. http://writ.news.findlaw.com/hamilton/20011206.html

Laying Down The Law

Lawyers To Consider Stand On Military Tribunals

The American Bar Association's policy-making body is exploring a proposal to back President Bush's order authorizing military tribunal also in the U.S.-led war on terror if steps are taken to ensure fairness. http://news.find-law.com/politics/s/20020130/lawyersdc.html

MICHAEL DORF | What Is An "Unlawful Combatant," And Why It Matters: The Status Of Detained Al Qaeda And Taliban Fighters

Columbia Law School Vice Dean and professor Michael Dorf clarifies the legal status of the al Qaeda and Taliban detainees at Guantanamo Bay. http://writ.news.findlaw.com/dorf/20020123.html

JOHN DEAN | Military Tribunals: A Long And Mostly Honorable History

Former counsel to the President John Dean discusses the historical use of military tribunals. Drawing his examples from the Mexican-American War, the Civil War, and FDR's Presidency, http://writ.news.findlaw.com/dean/20011207.html

War Tribunals - International Prosecutor v. Slobodan Milosevic et al. (Oct. 29, 2001) Second Amended Indictment By Int'l War Crimes Tribunal [PDF]: http://news.findlaw.com/cnn/docs/icty/milosevic2amdin-dict102-901.pdf

ACHIEVING JUSTICE BEFORE THE INTERNATIONAL WAR CRIMES TRIBUNAL: CHALLENGES FOR THE DEFENSE COUNSEL MARK S. ELLIS* http://www.law.duke.edu/journals/djcil/art-icles/djcil7p519.htm

JOANNE MARINER | Milosevic, NATO And The Serbs: Whose Trial, Whose Crimes?

Human rights attorney Joanne Mariner discusses Slobodan Milosevic's defense in his ongoing war crimes trial at The Hague. http://writ.news.find-law.com/mariner/20020218.html

Prosecutor v. Slobodan Milosevic et al. (Oct. 29, 2001) Second Amended Indictment By Int'l War Crimes Tribunal [PDF] http://news.findlaw.com/cnn/docs/icty/milosevic2amdindict102901.pdf

MICHAEL DORF | Can One Nation Arrest The Foreign Minister Of Another? The World Court Says No

Columbia Law School Vice Dean and professor Michael Dorf discusses animportant recent ruling by the International Court of Justice. http://writ.news.findlaw.com/dorf/20020220.html

Integration of Service-learning into Elementary Science Teaching Methods Courses

Byoung Sug Kim, Roosevelt University, IL, USA

Abstract: It has been a challenging task for science educators to help preservice teachers conceptualize inquiry-based teaching methods (Henning & King, 2005). However, service-learning programs present alternative strategies that provide pre-service teachers with meaningful contexts to deepen their learning experiences (Oates & Leavitt, 2003). The purpose of this research was to explore the impact of service-learning experiences on preservice teachers' learning. In the school community, science fairs become one of the struggles that high-need elementary students are faced with, especially those who do not get support from home. To meet the needs of the community, the author provided service-learning experiences in science teaching methods courses. The author examined four different contexts of service-learning. In the first setting, six undergraduate students visited an elementary school during an after-school program and helped 14 high-need elementary students complete their science fair projects. The second setting was a reverse science fair, in which 20 graduate students presented authentic and exciting science experiments to elementary students and their parents. Similar to the second setting, in the third setting 10 undergraduate students visited an elementary school and presented their science fair projects to middle school students. In the last setting, five graduate students helped ESL second graders complete their science fair projects during regular class time and the school hosted a family night for the science fair. The author's field observation and students' re-

flective journals indicated that service-learning experiences in all four different contexts helped them understand teaching science through scientific inquiry better and increased their confidence in teaching science. In addition, some considerations were identified.

Introduction

Scientific literacy is a desired outcome of science education, and it involves a broad and functional understanding of science for scientifically informed adults (DeBoer, 2000). Inquiry is considered an essential aspect of science education reform efforts by virtue of its connection with scientific literacy (American Association for the Advancement of Science [AAAS], 1993; National Research Council [NRC], 1996). The *National Science Education Standards* (NRC, 1996) categorize inquiry in two ways: as content that students should learn and as an instructional strategy. Therefore, preservice elementary teachers should possess the ability to both do scientific inquiry and implement inquiry-based science lessons. Inquiry-based instruction is generally viewed as following the process of scientific inquiry, in which students are engaged in generating a question, conducting an investigation, and drawing a conclusion from the collected data.

However, the literature shows that preservice teachers are resistant to accepting and implementing inquiry-based instruction (Henning & King, 2005). This may be because preservice teachers' learning experiences during their previous school years have firmly shaped their traditional teaching models (e.g., expository teaching). Moreover, these models are often inconsistent with teaching science as inquiry. In addition, it is well known that preservice elementary teachers do not have self-confidence in their ability to teach science (Fulp, 2002) and are often afraid to teach science because of a lack of science content knowledge (Davis, Petish, & Smithey, 2006) or a lack of adequate understanding of inquiry-based science (Windschitl, 2004).

As such, preservice teacher education should provide preservice teachers with substantial opportunities to improve their abilities to do scientific inquiry, their understanding of science content, and their understanding of inquiry-based instruction. From an elementary science teaching methods course, it is expected that preservice teachers would enhance their knowledge of scientific inquiry and knowledge of how to teach science as inquiry. However, teaching science is a highly complex cognitive activity in applying knowledge from multiple domains. Translating that knowledge into teaching practice is another challenge (Crawford, 2007; Zembal-Saul, Blumenfeld, & Krajcik, 2000). Adequate pedagogical knowledge of teaching does not necessarily reflect their real teaching practice. Therefore, science teaching methods courses should incorporate teaching practices into which elementary preservice teachers translate knowledge of inquiry, science content, and teaching methods. Teaching experiences would help them become familiar with teaching science and improve their self-confidence in their ability to teach science.

The author advocated inquiry-based teaching approaches in an elementary science teaching methods course and incorporated peer teaching practice. Although peer teaching practice was effective in enhancing elementary preservice teachers' ability to implement inquiry-based science lessons, it appeared they need more authentic teaching experience in which they can interact with real students. As a result, the author integrated service-learning into an elementary science methods course in order to more enhance preservice teachers' ability to teach elementary students with inquiry-based instruction and improve their confidence in teaching science.

In teacher education, service-learning programs present alternative strategies that provide preservice teachers with meaningful contexts to deepen their learning experiences (Oates & Leavitt, 2003). Bringle and Hatcher (1996) define service-learning as "credit-bearing educational experience in which students participate in an organized service activity that meets identified community needs and reflect on course content with a broader appreciation of the discipline and an enhanced sense of civic responsibility." Notably, service-learning is distinct from community service, which students often provide as volunteers. When community service incorporates explicit learning experience, it can become service-learning. For example, if preservice teachers tutor elementary students in an after-school program as volunteers, it can be considered community service. However, if they also analyze their teaching and students' learning and make suggestions for better teaching strategies by reflecting on the content of their teaching methods course, this can become service-learning. From this service-learning experience, preservice teachers can improve their understanding of teaching and learning while providing the community with a better quality of teaching.

The identified community needs also affected the author's integration of service-learning into an elementary science methods course. In the public school community of Chicago, teachers and students expressed a need of external support for planning science fairs. The primary purpose of a science fair is to encourage students to take a more active interest in the study of science by conducting and publicly presenting their independent science projects. A science fair is considered one of the best ways to develop students' abilities to do inquiry and a positive attitude toward science (Czerniak, 1996). However, there are some obstacles in achieving the purpose of science fairs in elementary schools. From the author's field experience with science teachers and students, these obstacles are three-fold. First, it is not feasible for one teacher to advise all individuals' science fair projects since each student needs long-term assistance to complete their science fair project. Therefore, the goal of a science fair is not likely to apply to academically struggling students who need more support than high-achieving students. Second, since one science teacher cannot guide all students in detail, students inevitably need extra help from home (e.g., guidance in designing and conducting an experiment, making graphs, printing materials out, etc). However, some students do not have access to an enriched learning environment at home and cannot get a great deal of help from their family. Third, although some students may have a creative and interesting project, they may have to abandon their interest if the project requires specific materials that they cannot afford.

To support the school community's need and assist preservice teachers' science education, the author incorporated different types of service-learning activities into an elementary science methods course. Since carrying out the experience of a science fair project requires an adequate ability to follow scientific methods, the author believed that the experience of helping elementary students' science fair projects or conducting their own science fair projects would reinforce preservice teachers' knowledge of scientific inquiry. In addition, the author predicted that interacting with students doing scientific inquiry would help preservice teachers become familiar with inquiry-based instruction as well as improve preservice teachers' self-confidence in teaching science as inquiry.

To reiterate, the purpose of the present study was to explore the impact of service-learning on preservice teachers' learning. The author examined preservice teachers' self-evaluation on what they learned from their involvement in service-learning activities. Although the author predicted that such service-learning experiences could help preservice teachers enhance their ability to implement inquiry-based science lessons and improve their confidence to teach science, they might have different interpretations of their service-learning experiences. Preservice teachers' self-evaluation would bring an insight into what outcomes we can expect from service-learning.

Methods

Context of the Study

Over the past three years, the author provided four different service-learning activities as part of an elementary science teaching methods course: An after-school program at a local public school, a reverse science fair at a local university as well as a fair at the public school site, and finally, an in-class service-learning project. Except for the in-class service-learning project, the activities were provided in collaboration with an urban public school in Chicago. The school was an urban K-8 school with middle socio-economic status. Demographically, the school was an equal mix of Black, Hispanic, and White students and 48% of the students came from low-income families (Illinois State Board of Education, 2007). The other elementary school where the in-class service-learning project took place was located in a suburban area outside of Chicago. Hispanic students made up 62% of the student body, followed by White (19%) and Black students (14%) (Illinois

State Board of Education, 2007). Seventy-three percent of the students came from low-income families. In addition, 41 preservice teachers (16 undergraduates and 25 graduates) participated in the study. They were ethnically diverse, primarily female (88%), and enrolled in the elementary education program at Roosevelt University.

After-school program: As shown in Table 1, six undergraduate students from an elementary science teaching methods course participated in this service-learning activity. To help high-need elementary students complete their science fair projects, a local public school science teacher and the author ran an after-school program. The science teacher invited 14 fifth and sixth grade students who needed more support for their science fair projects to the after-school program. During the program, the undergraduate students in the elementary science teaching methods course visited the school five times every other Tuesday to help the elementary students design and conduct science projects. Each undergraduate student guided a group of two or three elementary students during an hour long meeting. All project supplies were provided to the elementary students from the service-learning grant given by the university. At the end of the semester, all elementary students, their parents, and the science teacher were invited to a science fair that took place in the evening at the university. Eighteen graduate students from another science methods course also joined the science fair as judges.

Table 1: Summary of Four Different Service-learning Activities

Service-learning Activity	After-school Program	Reverse Science Fair at the University	Reverse Science Fair at the Site	In-class Service-learning Project
University participants	6 undegraduates	20 graduates	10 undergraduates	5 graduates
School participants	14 fifth and sixth graders	Over 100 fifth through eighth graders and parents	20 seventh graders	15 second graders
Main activity	Helping elementary students complete their science fair projects	Presenting science fair projects to elementary students and parents at the university	Presenting science fair projects to middle school students at the site	Helping elementary students complete their science fair projects

Reverse science fair at the university: Twenty graduate students who were enrolled in an elementary science methods course participated in this service-learning activity. Unlike undergraduate students, most of the graduate students were working full-time and took the course as part-time students in the evening. Since most of them had work schedules, the after-school program was not appropriate for graduate students. Therefore, the author adopted a reverse science fair activity (Rose et al., 2004) to take place on a Saturday afternoon, in which graduate students prepared science fair projects and presented them to invited elementary students and their families.

In the middle of the semester, graduate students were asked to generate science projects in relation to the concept of photosynthesis and respiration. The author intentionally provided a specific topic to reduce preservice teachers' workload in choosing a topic, and more importantly, to reinforce the scientific concept of photosynthesis and other relevant concepts (e.g., respiration, combustion, ecosystem, cell structure, etc). Under the author's supervision, the preservice teachers designed an experiment around specific research questions they had generated. At the end of the semester, the preservice teachers ran a three-hour science fair in which they presented their experiments to more than 100 elementary students and their parents. When presenting their projects, the preservice teachers engaged students in a simple hands-on investigation.

Reverse science fair at the site: When the reverse science fair took place at the university, there were logistical issues (e.g., space availability, parking, etc). Therefore, the author decided to hold a reverse science fair at an elementary school. Over the course of the semester, 10 undergraduate students prepared individual science fair projects about photosynthesis and respiration. At the end of the semester, an hour-long reverse science fair took place in a middle school classroom after school with 20 seventh graders. Groups of four seventh graders moved around each undergraduate student's presentation every ten minutes so that each undergraduate student had a chance to present their projects five times to different groups of seventh graders.

In-class service-learning: Five graduate students from an elementary science methods course participated in an in-class service-learning activity. As a course requirement, graduate students needed to complete 25 field observation hours. The author placed all five graduate students in a second grade classroom at a primarily Hispanic elementary school, in which the classroom's students were exclusively English Language Learners. In the middle of the semester, graduate students completed their field observation requirement for four consecutive full Thursdays. The difference of this field observation from regular observation was that the graduate students helped the second graders complete their science projects during their field observation. Since the science unit was on insects, caterpillars of monarch butterflies were provided to allow students to observe the life cycle of butterflies. The graduate students encouraged second graders to generate questions about caterpillars and find answers to their questions based on their observations. A science class lasted for two hours during each field observation day. Each graduate student guided a group of three students in their science fair projects. After the field observation was over, the classroom teacher hosted a family night in which second graders presented their projects on caterpillars and butterflies to their families, other teachers, and the graduate students.

Data Collection and Analysis

Preservice teachers were asked to complete their service-learning portfolio by including a title page, the purpose of service-learning, personal goals, and reflective journals on what they learned from their service-learning experience. In particular, preservice teachers' reflective journals were the main data source in determining how they evaluated their service-learning experience. In addition, the author's classroom discussion notes and field observation notes were used to corroborate the author's interpretation of preservice teachers' reflective journals. Whenever the author had a classroom discussion with preservice teachers about their reflection on service-learning activities, he took a brief note and wrote his reflection right after the class. Finally, when preservice teachers participated in service-learning activities, the author made observations on how they interacted with students, and these observations were then used in a performance-based assessment. Preservice teachers' responses and the author's observation notes were summarized. Summaries were then compared and contrasted across service-learning activities to obtain patterns that had logical consistency within the collected data.

Results

The data analysis of preservice teachers' reflective journals indicated that the majority of the preservice teachers viewed service-learning as a beneficial experience. Only two out of 41 mentioned a concern about not having enough preparation time.

When the preservice teachers were asked what they learned from their service-learning experience, their responses included various learning outcomes (e.g., about students, about scientific inquiry, about pedagogical knowledge, etc). However, it was evident that 73% of the preservice teachers, regardless of the type of service-learning, stated that they improved their self-confidence in teaching science. As predicted, many of the preservice teachers were afraid of teaching science, but the service-learning experience helped ameliorate such fear. Sample responses are as follows:

> "I have never been a good science student throughout my academic career...barely squeaked out a C in science...However, I really do like science. I am truly interested in how things work and would love to learn along with my students and explore their questions, as well as my own." (CJ, F07)

> "My confidence in teaching science was very low. I thought there would be no way I could teach science...Doing this science fair, actually showed me that I could teach science if I needed to. I was excited to see the students interested in my experiment and seeing them being part of it by having them test things out...I am happy that we had this science fair to show me that I could teach science..." (FM, F08)

As seen in words from the above quotations such as "explore their questions" and "having them test things out," the preservice teachers' confidence stemmed from the success of interacting with students by doing science, which was the main point of inquiry-based instruction. In other words, they realized that engaging students in doing science worked well in teaching science.

Another main response was about the appreciation of inquiry-based teaching. Fifty-four percent of the preservice teachers found that inquiry-based instruction was more helpful in keeping students active and interested than traditional teaching styles. The preservice teachers stated that:

> "This challenges my prior conceptions that in order to be truly scholarly, teaching must be all lecture and reading text books. Anytime kids are able to learn and have fun, you can actually stretch their minds to accept more ideas and embrace concepts than forcing them to read paragraphs of information they will only memorize and then forget." (CJ, Fo8)

> "Even though they were only 2nd graders, my group came up with some great questions...always excited to find the answers through observing. They were very excited about the whole unit because it was not just the teacher sitting and lecturing in front of them at the board, they took part in their learning process and were allowed to research and study anything they wondered about insects." (AA, So9)

Finally, 43% of the preservice teachers who participated in the reverse science fair and the in-class service-learning project mentioned an increase in their content knowledge. These three service-learning activities were similar in their specific content focus (e.g., photosynthesis and insects). One stated that:

> "I recently learned about photosynthesis in a science lab prior to taking this course but again it was a situation that I learned for the moment and never really retained the information to use at a later date. This experience helped to improve my science content knowledge because we asked the "real question" things that we wanted to know... I think that photosynthesis is a complex concept to teach students but this experience broke the complex terms into simpler terms...this experience will allow me to re-teach it in my own classroom." (KH, Fo8)

The data analysis of classroom discussion revealed that the preservice teachers were anxious about service-learning activities during the first and second weeks. The anxiety came from a lack of confidence in interacting with students and in doing inquiry. The common question was "How are we going to do that?" They often informed the author that they were unsure of how a service-learning activity was going to turn out and felt nervous because they thought they would not have enough information to keep students interested. As weeks passed, however, the classroom discussion centered on how to prepare experiments for students and how to help elementary students improve. When the service-learning activity was over, classroom discussion was filled with words of appreciation such as "thank you," "nice job," and "great experience," which indicated that the preservice teachers enjoyed and appreciated their service-learning experience.

Conclusions and Discussion

Effective teacher education programs usually help preservice teachers analyze their teaching practice and reflect on their teaching with field experiences (Darling-Hammond & Bransford, 2005). The present results indicate that service-learning experiences can be an effective teaching strategy used to enhance preservice teachers' self-confidence in science teaching methodology as well as to highlight the benefits of using inquiry-based teaching and learning in the classroom.

In the author's elementary science teaching methods courses, the preservice teachers had the opportunity to present an inquiry-based science lesson as a peer teaching practice. Although peer teaching was helpful, the preservice teachers learned more from interacting with real elementary students in their service-learning experience. Arguably, one may see little difference between the impact of service-learning activities in the present study and the impact of regular field experiences. Graduate students at Roosevelt University are required to complete 25 field observation hours, which includes classroom observation and teaching an entire lesson. From the author's observation notes it was evident that preservice teachers had more interaction with students and received more appreciation from students and parents in service-learning activities than their regular field experience. The author assumed that it was because the goals of the service-learning activity were to meet the community needs: namely, supporting what elementary students needed, and to involve preservice teachers in teaching science as inquiry. In short, the service-learning activities can be a better strategy than regular field placement experiences in helping preservice teachers become familiar with teaching science in the context of doing inquiry and thus improve their self-confidence in teaching science as inquiry.

The present results also indicate that when preservice teachers are involved in science fair projects on a specific topic (e.g., photosynthesis and insects), they are also more likely to enhance their confidence in science content knowledge. Although science fair projects can be a great vehicle to improve students' content knowledge, such projects are often carried out without exploring a science concept (Chinn & Malhotra, 2002). Following scientific methods can enhance students' abilities to do scientific inquiry, but does not necessarily guarantee their improvement of a scientific concept embedded in inquiry activities if the purpose of inquiry is to solve some technical problem (e.g., the egg drop activity). From the present results, however, the author can conclude that science fair projects within a particular context of science content can be an alternative to improve preservice teachers' science content knowledge by guiding them to generate and test their explanations about a targeted science concept.

Finally, classroom discussion notes indicate that the clear purposes and learning outcomes of service-learning appear to be the motivation to help preservice teachers overcome the challenges of service-learning. In the beginning, the preservice teachers generally showed some anxiety about the service-learning requirement. However, such anxiety eventually diminished

353

and turned to excitement and confidence at the end. It appears to be critical to provide an orientation for preservice teachers to share expected outcomes of service-learning and to help them set their individual goals (Oates & Leavitt, 2003).

When integrating a servcie-learning project into a teaching methods course, an instructor should consider two issues. First, a service-learning activity should not be optional, but rather a required assignment that is assessed as part of a student's final grade. When the author first offered a service-learning activity, some preservice teachers were not willing to participate, because they thought it was an extra assignment. As a result, the author explicitly includes service-learning as a required assignment in the syllabus and thus far, little resistance has been identified. Second, incorporating service-learning into a teaching methods course results in a reduction of other course content and activities to be due within an usual time limit. Based on preservice teachers' abilites and needs, an instructor needs to be careful in replacing existing course content and activities with a service-learning activity.

Acknowledgement

Thanks to Joyce Jung Eun Kim who reviewed this paper and provided critical points. Additional thanks to Alexis Storch who reviewed the final draft of this paper.

References

American Association for the Advancement of Science. (1993). Benchmarks for science literacy, Project 2061. New York: Oxford University Press.

Bringle, R. C., & Hatcher, J. A. (1996). Implementing service learning in higher education. Journal of Higher Education, 67(2), 221-240.

Chinn, C., & Malhotra, B. (2002). Epistemologically authentic inquiry in schools: A theoretical framework for evaluating inquiry tasks. Science Education, 86(2), 175-218.

Crawford, B. (2007). Learning to teach science as inquiry in the rough and tumble of practice. Journal of Research in Science Teaching, 44(4), 613–642.

Czerniak, C. M. (1996). Predictors of success in a district science fair competition: An exploratory study. School Science and Mathematics, 96(1), 21-27.

Darling-Hammond, L., & Bransford, J. (2005). Preparing teachers for a changing world: What teachers should learn and be able to do. San Francisco, CA: Jossey-Bass.

Davis, E. A. (2006). Preservice elementary teachers' critique of instructional materials for science. Science Education, 90(2), 348 – 375.

Davis, E. A., Petish, D., & Smithey, J. (2006). Challenges new science teachers face. Review of Educational Research, 76(4), 607-651.

DeBoer, G. E. (2000). Scientific literacy: Another look at its historical and contemporary meanings and its relationship to science education reform. Journal of Research in Science Teaching, 37(6), 582-601.

Fulp, S. L. (2002). Status of elementary school science teaching. Retrieved from www.horizon-research.com

Henning, M. B. & King, K. P. (2005). Implementing STS in the elementary classroom: From university courses to elementary classroom. Bulletin of Science, Technology, and Society, 25(3), 1-6.

Illinois State Board of Education (2007). Illinois School Report Card. [Online]. Available: http://www.isbe.state.il.us/research/htmls/report_card.htm

National Research Council. (1996). National science education standards. Washington, DC: National Academic Press.

Oates, K. K., & Leavitt, L. H. (2003). Service-learning and learning communities: Tools for integration and assessment. Washington, DC: Association of American Colleges and Universities.

Rose, J., Zardetto-Smith, A., Mu, K., & Demetrikopoulos, M. K. (2004). Reverse Your Science Fair with Educational Partnerships. Science Scope, 27(6), 16-19

Windschitl, M. (2004). Folk theories of 'inquiry': How preservice teachers reproduce the discourse and practices of an atheoretical scientific method. Journal of Research in Science Teaching, 41(5), 481–512.

Zembal-Saul, C., Blumenfeld, P., & Krajcik, J. (2000). Influence of guided cycles of planning, teaching and reflection on prospective elementary teachers' science content representations. Journal of Research in Science Teaching, 37(4), 318–339.

Service-Learning in an Introduction to Management Course

Dr. Audrey Cohen

Abstract: Service-learning allows students to integrate academic study and reflective work with service to the community. This pedagogy is particularly appropriate for the study of management. The paper provides a model for incorporating service learning into an introductory management course. It provides a syllabus, lists learning goals, suggests project guidelines, discusses classroom challenges, and presents examples of community projects. Management faculty in other countries can customize this "real-world" learning to their own cultural and institutional settings.

Background

The U. S. philosopher John Dewey believed that the aim of education is to serve democracy [Field, 2003]. He felt that schools have an obligation to help the community to solve its problems. Dewey also believed that students learn best when they are actively engaged in the learning process in a self-directed and meaningful way. As a result, he felt that both students and society would benefit from enhanced interaction with each other.

In recent years Dewey's ideas have been used to support the development of service learning in the U. S. In 1990 the U. S. Congress passed the National and Community Service Act that authorized demonstration grants to colleges and universities. In 1993 the U. S. Congress passed the National and Community Trust Act that created the Corporation for National and Community Service. Since then the Corporation has funded institutions of higher education through Learn and Serve America.

The legislation defines the goals of Learn and Serve:

> ... service learning combines meaningful service in the community with a formal educational curriculum and structured time for participants to reflect on their service and educational experience. Service Learning stands in contrast to traditional volunteering or community service, which generally does not include reflection or links to any organized curriculum.

(http://learnandserve.org/research/slhe.html)

A growing body of research shows that service learning benefits students and the community in a variety of ways. McCarthy, Tucker and Dean [2002] cited research showing that service learning contributes to: academic and personal development; theory application; skill application; the creation of community in the classroom, school, and community; and civic responsibility. Eyler, Giles, Stenson and Gray [2001] compiled a guide to research findings from 1993-2002 about the impact of service learning on students, faculty, institutions of higher education and communities. Their compendium showed that service learning had a positive effect on: students' personal outcomes, social outcomes, learning outcomes, and graduation rates; faculty satisfaction with student learning; enhanced institutional relations with its community; and increased community host satisfaction.

Faculty in different disciplines will need to consider how best to introduce service learning into their curricula so that the service component contributes to student learning and community improvement. In this regard, the study of management is particularly well suited for service learning. After all, a common definition of management is "the process of working with and through others to achieve organizational objectives in a changing environment" [Kreitner, 2001]. What better place for students to learn how to work with and through others to achieve a common goal than on a real project with real stakeholders. In service learning activities, students can try out management concepts while attempting to help a community organization. The balance of this paper discusses issues for management educators to consider if they want to enhance an Introduction to Management course with a service-learning component.

The Introduction to Management Course

Typical "Introduction to Management" textbooks help students understand what management is and what managers do. These books highlight the importance of planning, organizing, leading and controlling people so that organizational goals are achieved effectively and efficiently [Kreitner, 2001; Lewis, Goodman and Fandt, 2001; Williams, 2003]. Management faculty devote many classroom hours to teaching these textbook concepts. Some faculty also apply the concepts to case studies and to current business situations as described in newspaper and magazine articles. However, adding a service-learning component allows students in an Introduction to Management course to actually work with each other and with the community to realize a common goal. In doing so, students experience the challenges and satisfactions of being managers. As both individual students and groups of students grapple with real issues, they have the opportunity to experience first hand what management is and what managers do. Students frequently return to the classroom looking for advice on how to accomplish their goals more effectively and efficiently. They are motivated to reflect on their experience. Such is the true aim of the course.

Faculty who want to try this approach should think through the role of service learning in the syllabus. They should be clear about the goals and guidelines for the service-learning module. The paper will lead interested faculty through a set of considerations. It will provide specific examples of service-learning projects, discuss classroom challenges and raise several ancillary issues. It concludes by suggesting that faculty in other settings will want to customize this approach to their own distinctive educational cultures.

Syllabus

Exhibit 1 shows the sections of the syllabus devoted to service-learning.

Topics from the text that are most helpful for the service-learning projects are introduced first. Classroom discussion focuses on how the textbook concepts can help the groups manage their projects most effectively and efficiently. Early in the semester groups are required to meet in the classroom during "group work" to discuss issues with each other and with me. Once group projects are approved, students can use the group time for meetings and activities in the community. Groups are urged to keep attendance records to document participation.

Service-Learning Goals and Guidelines

On the first day of the semester, students are introduced to the notion of service-learning. They are told that they will have an opportunity to experience management by planning, implementing and evaluating a service-learning project. They receive a handout with the following goals and guidelines. Each group will:

develop a mission statement acceptable to the College, to me, and to a community host; set qualitative and quantitative objectives; develop a strategy; implement it; and provide a self-assessment of the project and the process.

work with me and College administrators to satisfy College liability requirements.

locate a suitable host institution and form a working relationship with an appropriate person at that institution.

- learn why it is important to clarify each partner's role and responsibilities and each group member's role and responsibilities.
- obtain external validation -in the form of an evaluation -from the host institution.

reflect on the management process (communication, negotiation, problem-solving, decision-making, resource management, etc.) and the management product (the outcome) in a well documented, written report.

present their findings to the class in an oral presentation.

After reviewing these guidelines, I ask students to suggest which populations they may want to serve. Some students identify community groups such as elementary or high school students, the homeless, the ill or the elderly. Other students want to help their classmates or other college students. We discuss in class what kinds of projects could be developed for each target population and what institutions in New York City might be appropriate hosts. Students subsequently form groups based on common interests. From this point on, students are part of self-managed teams charged with "managing" a real project to benefit a specific community organization.

In the next several classes students are introduced – via lecture and text – to the concepts of mission, objectives and strategy. Each student writes a mission statement for the College and we compare these statements with the published version. Each student is asked to locate a mission statement and list of objectives from a corporate annual report.

Following these exercises, each service-learning group develops a mission statement, defines quantifiable and qualitative objectives, and develops a strategy for realizing its own mission. Each group must locate and contact a host institution that will serve as a collaborative partner. The students and the partner must agree on the mission and strategy and work out a plan for implementation and evaluation. Students work with the host institution over the semester to actually carry out their activity. At the end of the semester students assess their work. The host institution must also provide evaluation and external validation.

Classroom Challenges

Service learning presents many challenges for the instructor. Chief among them are suitability of projects, loss of control, dysfunctional groups and methods of assessment.

Students often have overly ambitious ideas of what they can accomplish in a semester. For example, one group wanted to sponsor a fundraiser where neighborhood retail stores would donate goods for a raffle. They envisioned renting a hall and charging friends and family a steep entrance fee. They stayed committed to this project even though it seemed unworkable. Only after they were unable to find donors and a hall were they willing to modify their plans.

College liability concerns make other projects unsuitable. One group wanted to sponsor a fundraising dance in a local bar. Since many classmates are below the legal drinking age in New York, we could not sponsor this event. Another group wanted to plan a day's outing for children from homeless shelters. In that case, we needed assurance that the homeless shelter would assume liability for any accident. Students are often frustrated when they confront real constraints, but meeting those constraints helps students learn about the real world.

Unlike the traditional classroom where the teacher is in control of the classroom, in service learning the teacher gives much of the control to students. They must create the mission statement and define objectives. They must find a host institution and establish a rapport with a sponsor. They must find the resources to implement the project. They must assume responsibility to complete the project on time, with adequate quality, and at or under budget. Most especially, they must learn how to work together to achieve their goals. At any stage, the process can break down or develop problems. Although students must provide a series of reports to keep the teacher informed, nevertheless the teacher does not know the inner workings of each group. Teachers must themselves be comfortable delegating.

Groups can be dysfunctional in many ways. Members can fail to agree and fail to cooperate. Members can drop out and refuse to do their share of the work. Members can be bossy and take charge or they can be silent and refuse to contribute. They can procrastinate. They can be disrespectful of each other. Cultural and language differences may hamper communication. Much of the teacher's work is helping students learn how to work with each other so that they can move forward with the tasks. Management professors can use these situations as they develop as live case studies to discuss negotiation, communication, time management and other management concepts.

As discussed above, students have a chance to learn management processes and to accomplish a management project in their service-learning activities. Assessment, therefore, should cover both process and product. It is the teacher's responsibility to make these two learning goals clear from the outset.

Having two learning goals means that several measures of performance are necessary. To model performance by objectives, students should develop a checklist of performance measures at the beginning of the semester. Measures of process might include reports on the group's ability to communicate regularly (with each other, with the teacher, and with the host sponsor), the ability to negotiate over tasks and deadlines, and the ability to keep group members motivated. Measures of product include handing in reports on time and achieving group objectives.

Many different people can assess service-learning projects. Group members can assess each other and/or they can assess themselves. The host institution can assess the group. So can the teacher. Frequently these measures will yield different results. Deciding who will do the assessment can itself provide material for a useful classroom discussion.

The class can also discuss the frequency of assessment. Too much assess-ment can be counterproductive and take time away from the project. Too little assessment may allow students to slack off and under-perform.

Examples of Service Learning Projects

Students have initiated and completed various types of service projects.

Students raised money for a college scholarship. A relative of one student died in the attack on the World Trade Center. My student proposed raising funds for a scholarship fund set up in memory of his deceased uncle. Seven traditional aged classmates (ages 18-22) decided to host a fundraising dinner party at the College. About 50 relatives, friends, and co-workers attended. My student introduced his widowed aunt and other relatives, and spoke about the need to have hope and courage. The evening was very emotional. Financially, the group contributed over $1300 to the Scholarship Fund.

Students sponsored a children's party at a New York hospital. The students in this group were working adults. Their mission was "to bring joy and a smile to the faces of handicapped and abused children." Their strategy was to work with the director of volunteers at a New York Hospital to host a party for children aged 4-8. They carried this out in April 20, 2002. In their final report they analyzed their group experience in terms of management concepts: organization, leadership, communication, social responsibility, negotiation, decision-making, motivation, financial account-ability, time management, and evaluation. The hospital provided a letter of appreciation.

Students managed a soup kitchen. This group wanted to learn how to manage a soup kitchen for the homeless. They volunteered at the soup kit-chen several times to learn how to organize and allocate tasks – from prepar-ing and delivering meals to greeting and interacting with clients – and how to manage their own time and resources. At the end of the semester they as-sumed responsibility for managing the soup kitchen for one day.

Students presented a career forum. This group wanted to help their classmates prepare for job interviews. They brought several human resource professionals to campus to address the student body. They also assembled and distributed a useful information packet. They advertised the event through flyers, newspaper articles and word-of-mouth. Students who atten-ded rated the presentations on an evaluation form.

Ancillary Learning

In addition to learning what management is and what managers do, service learning has the potential to help students develop as persons. They can learn that they are capable of helping others and that the effort matters. They can learn to respect people with needs and institutions designed to serve those people. They can learn that a well-functioning group can accomplish more than an individual. They can learn that groups need a lot of attention and that management requires spending a lot of time listening to, and talking with, others. They can learn that management is not as simple as it seems or necessarily straightforward or guaranteed to succeed. Hopefully they learn that working together can be effective and fun and rewarding.

Implications for the Future

Each faculty member should consider how best to advance the use of this pedagogy on his campus. Think how you can demonstrate that service learning contributes to your institution's mission and goals. Create a proposal to catch the attention of your academic dean and departmental chair since their support can help facilitate your work. Be sure to customize service learning to your particular institutional culture and the educational culture of your country. For example, settings where "town" and "gown" frictions exist will create special barriers. Contact faculty who are already using this methodology to exchange best practices. International conferences and special issues of management journals are other helpful resources.

References

Eyler, Janet, S., Giles, Dwight E., Stenson, Christine M. and Gray, Charlene J., "At a Glance: What We Know about The Effects of Service-Learning on College Students, Faculty, Institutions and Communities, 1993 – 2000: Third Edition as presented at the Campus Compact National Summit, Providence, R.I., November, 2002

Field, Richard, "John Dewey: 1859 – 1952." The Internet Encyclopedia of Philosophy. Retrieved on February 7, 2003 from http://www.utm.edu/research/iep/d/dewey.htm

Godfrey, Paul C. and Grasso, Edward T., Eds. *Working for the Common Good: Concepts and Models for Service Learning in Management.* (2000). Washington, D.C.: American Association for Higher Education.

Kreitner, Robert. *Management, 8th edition.* (2001). New York: Houghton Mifflin. Lewis, Pamela S., Goodman, Stephen H., and Fandt, Patricia M. *Management.* (2001). Cincinnati, Ohio: South-Western.

McCarthy, Anne M., Tucker, Mary L., and Dean, Kathy Lund. "Service-Learning: Creating Community" in Wankel, Charles and DeFillippi, Robert, Editors, *Rethinking Management Education for the 21st Century.* (2002). Greenwich, CT: Information

Rand, (1999). "Combining Service and Learning in Higher Education" as re-
    trieved on February 28, 2003 from http://learnandserve.org/re-
    search/slhe.html
Wankel, Charles and DeFillippi. *Rethinking Management Education for the
    21st Century*. (2002). Greenwich, CT: Information Age Publishing.
    Williams, Chuck. *Management*. (2003). Mason, Ohio: South-
    Western.

Exhibit 1

Relevant Sections of the Introduction to Management Syllabus

Objectives

This course will help students understand what management is and what
managers do. Students will learn the importance of planning, organizing,
leading and controlling people so that organizational goals are achieved effectively and efficiently. To reinforce the text, students will work in groups
and apply these concepts and processes. Each group will plan and implement a service-learning project with a host institution. The host institution
will help assess the outcome. Students will reflect on their work in oral and
written presentations.

Student responsibilities

Groups of students will design and manage service-learning projects. Each
group will develop a mission statement, a list of objectives, and a strategy
to achieve its mission and objectives. Each group will implement its project
and provide a self-assessment. Each student will participate in the group's
oral presentation to classmates and each group will hand in a written report
with an evaluation by an outside group. The ability to work together to
achieve the group goal is an important part of this course.

Class	Topics for discussion	Assignments Due
1	Introduction. What is service learning?	
2	Mission, Objectives and Strategy	
3	Discussion of service learning projects	
4	Social and ethical responsibilities. How will your group project contribute to community welfare?	
5	Formation of service learning groups	Membership / Topics
6	Communication. How will you insure adequate communication in your group?	
7	Group work	Draft one: Mission and Objectives
8	Planning and project planning. How do limited resources impact your group project?	
9	Group work	Draft one: Strategy and Gantt Chart
10	Motivating job performance. How do you keep group members motivated?	
11	TEST 1	
12	Group work	Revisions of drafts
13	Group dynamics and teamwork. How do you promote teamwork?	
14	Group work	
15	Decision-making and problem solving. How are decisions made in your group?	
16	Group work	Progress report due
17	Influence processes and leadership. Does your group have a leader?	
18	Change, conflict and negotiation. How does your group resolve conflict?	
19	Group work	
20	Human resource management. What are appropriate measures of performance for your group?	
21	Group work	Progress report due
22	International management	
23	Group work	
24	Organizations. What culture has developed in your group?	
25	Strategic management	
26	TEST 2	
27	Group presentations	Reports / evaluations
28	Group presentations	Reports / evaluations

Literature

Boys and Men Reading Shakespeare's 1 Henry 4

Using Service-Learning Strategies to Accommodate Male Learners and to Disseminate Male-Positive Literacy

Dennis S. Gouws, Springfield College, Massachusetts, USA

Abstract: Literacy scholars such as Ralph Fletcher and Thomas Newkirk have suggested perceptive ways to understand masculine cultures and to enable boys' and men's literacy. Service-learning strategies could usefully augment this male-positive scholarly work in praxis: these strategies promote active, participatory learning; they encourage reflection on the learning process; they enable this learning to take place in real-life situations; they assume that learning often occurs in a broader context than the traditional classroom; and they promote caring for others. Approaching boys' and men's education with this kind of respect for their diverse learning circumstances could productively involve boys, men, and their teachers in practical male-positive learning; moreover, participating in this kind of service learning could help disseminate strategies for male-positive literacy. Shakespeare's 1 Henry 4 offers challenging but fruitful occasions to accommodate male readers; this play also affords educators opportunities to encourage male-positive literacy in praxis. In addition to dramatizing the coming-of-age of Prince Hal, 1 Henry 4 contains dynamic and vital events that lend themselves to the types of male-friendly writing (for example, sports journalism, creative nonfiction, horror, graphic novels, and comic books) discussed by Fletcher and Newkirk. This paper discusses qualitative research into the process and the outcomes of a male-positive service-learning project given in my senior-year college-level Shakespeare class. Students worked with me to develop male-positive service-learning strategies with the goal of both engaging boys and men (from these students' own communities) with 1 Henry 4 and encouraging male-positive literacy.

Studies concerning male literacy are topical and timely. Data from the United States, for example, suggest that boys and men are not benefitting sufficiently from their education. They are more likely than girls or women to be diagnosed as having learning disabilities or behavioral problems, to fail, or to drop out of school.[1] More boys will graduate being unable to read proficiently.[2] In addition, men are increasingly underrepresented in higher education: Peg Tyre notes that, "[i]n 2005, ... 57.2 percent of the undergraduates enrolled in American colleges and universities were women," that "[f]or the first time in history, women are better educated," that "[a]t present, 33 percent of women between twenty-five and twenty-nine years of age hold a four-year degree compared to 26 percent of men" (Trouble 32). A 2008 American Association of University Women report on girls' performance in education notes that women have earned more bachelor degrees than men since 1982 and that women earned fifty-eight percent of all the bachelor degrees conferred in 2005-2006.[3] Failing any significant male-attentive intervention, this trend of men being underrepresented in higher-education degree programs is projected to continue for the next ten years. A 2009 report from the U. S. Department of Education predicts that 593,000 women will be awarded associate's degrees, and only 319,000 will be awarded to men; that 1,078,000 women will be awarded bachelor's degrees, and only 743,000 will be awarded to men; that 480,000 master's degrees will be awarded to women, and only 293,000 will be awarded to men; and that 50,000 doctor's degrees will be awarded to women, and only 41,000 will be awarded to men.[4] These data suggest that our education system is not supporting boys and men, often with tragic consequences: suicide attempts and completion rates among secondary and tertiary age boys and men in the United States far outstrip those of girls and women.[5] This serious neglect of males in education pervades much of the industrial world according to Tyre's research, and a new concern about masculinities and men's literacy is increasingly apparent in popular and academic forums ranging from websites and

---

1. See my "Enabling Men in Literature: Teaching Male-Positive Masculinities in a College English Class" 148-158 for a summary of how boys and men are poorly served by educational institutions in the United States. Megan Rosenfeld discusses diagnoses of learning and behavioral problems in school boys (A1); See "Boys in School" Understanding and Raising Boys for information on boys' failure and drop-out rates.

2. David von Drehle discusses important issues influencing the literacy proficiency of high-school boys.

3. See Corbett et al. 55 and 62.

4. These data are tabulated in W. J. Hussar and T. M. Bailey on 14-15.

5. See Rosenfeld, Joe Manthey, and "Boys in School" for data on suicides in this demographic.

publications to colloquia and conferences where participants are exploring alternatives to education methods informed primarily by gynocentric assumptions (Trouble 33).[6]

One effective male-attentive intervention into current educational practice I have explored involves adopting male-oriented approaches to learning and literacy within a framework of the male-positive, a concept which encourages a celebratory, ongoing dialogue about masculinities. Deriving from the work of the male feminist, Michael Flood, my initial definition of male positive was "to celebrate masculinities, to be pro-gay, and to be pro women."[7] A subsequent conversation with Tom Golden on a paper I wrote on this topic afforded me an interesting insight: he observed

> The one tiny nitpick of your paper that I wanted to mention was the idea of male positive being linked to pro-gay and pro-female. While I am all for being pro-gay and pro-female I just don't see it as a necessity to tag on to being male positive. We should be male-positive without any restrictions. We surely wouldn't say that in order to be female positive that we have to be pro-male nor would we tell Blacks that in order to be pro-Black they needed to be

---

6. A useful web resource for popular debates on these issues is Misandry Review [www.misandryreview.com]. Gar Kellom and Miles Groth's Engaging College Men offers much useful practical information on male-attentive education. Recent public forums for discussing these issue include the Boys and Boys Crisis, held in Washington D. C. on July 13-14, 2007, and in 2008 through 2009 New York University's Department of Comparative Literature's "Man Enough" colloquium on masculinity. In May, 2009, The Steinhardt School of Culture, Education and Human Development, along with the Wagner Graduate School of Public Service hosted a breakfast symposium on "The Future of Men" and responses to their declining representation in higher education. The Oxford English Dictionary defines gynocentric as "Centered on, dominated by, or concerned exclusively with women; taking a female or a feminist point of view."

7. In my essay cited above, I explained the evolution of the concept at that stage: "My definition derives from Michael Flood's, given in XY magazine:
To be male-positive is to be affirming of men and optimistic about men; to believe that men can change; to support every man's efforts at positive change. To be male-positive is to build close relations and supportive alliances among men. It is to acknowledge men's many acts of compassion and kindness. To be male-positive is to resist feeling hopeless about men and writing men off, and to reject the idea that men are somehow intrinsically bad, oppressive or sexist.
Flood adds that being male positive also means being 'gay affirmative' and 'pro-feminist.' While I agree with the spirit of Flood's definition, I differ from it in two important ways. First, I substitute the term 'pro-women' for 'pro-feminist' for two reasons: because doing so avoids the male-marginalizing gynocentric freight evident in much feminist criticism (as I discuss below) and because the term I use is more inclusive—noting support for women regardless of their credos. The vast majority of my women and men students do not identify as feminists. Second, I leave the choice of whether to change, or how to change positively, up to men and their allies. Supporters of male-positive masculinities should consider their responsible role in their families, communities, and societies: they should be willing to negotiate with diverse groups—such as feminists or members of various men's movements (be their agendas mythopoetic or pro-feminist)—to find common ground to create a better society for all" (148n4). With hindsight, I see how I unconsciously made this definition contingent on factors not intrinsic to boys, men, and their respective identities.

pro-Asian. We wouldn't say that in order to be pro Buick you had to be pro Chrysler or pro Cadillac. So my bias would be to simply be pro-male just on its own with no contingents. No strings attached.

This assertion that we "should be male-positive without any restrictions" made me realize the extent to which I had internalized both what I call a please-and-placate mentality concerning men's interaction with women and the impression that men were somehow automatically responsible for the well-being of all people. This mentality exemplifies one contemporary variation of a traditional chivalric, sexist concept of men as compulsive pleasers of women and compulsory providers, and I believe that we men must resist it. This restrictive, pathological construction of masculinities inherent in this way of thinking does not benefit boys and men. So, informed by Tom's remarks, I suggest that being male positive involves supporting different masculinities and boys' and men's attempts to live meaningful, fulfilling lives. Male-accommodating education strategies are central to enabling those attempts, and as recent scholarship indicates, boys' and men's literacy is a crucial area for male-positive intervention—a situation even acknowledged by gynocentric researchers.[8]

What might male-positive literacy involve? A challenging but accommodating, often-embodied approach to reading and writing about a broader variety of texts than those usually studied in an academic environment.[9] Recent research undertaken by Susannah Smith, Michael Smith and Jeffrey D. Wilhelm finds that boys and men are successful readers when they can draw on their experience as readers of what Susannah Smith calls, "their masculine interest area and hobbies" (12). Smith and Wilhelm, however, argue that competence in boys "literate life outside school" might not transfer to traditional academic reading unless they feel supported and can see the point of the text and lessons; they conclude that boys "rejected school literacy although they did not seem to reject literate activity itself," that boys did so "because of the ways students encounter literate activity in school" (455, 460-61). Michael Kehler and Chris Greig argue that male literacy can best be understood if one were to "broaden the definition of literacy practice to include that of the socially literate self" which means an embodied understanding of their experience as male readers of themselves, others, and literary texts (352). In other words, if boys and men were to correlate strategies used to maintain their social proficiency with those for reading and understanding traditional academic texts, they could achieve more as readers and as confident students. Male-positive literacy, therefore, intervenes and provides alternatives to persistent stereotypical and negative discursive constructions and representations of boys and men—what Kehler

---

8. In my above-mentioned paper I note that although their agendas are primarily gynocentric, Gill (110-111, 115), Lingard (46-49), and Mills (69-70) accept that boys need help with literacy and with modeling of positive male behavior in academic environments.

9. See Gouws 151-154 for a more detailed discussion of male-positive literacy.

and Greig call "familiar stories of old in which boy meets book, boy rejects book, boy finds car, boy becomes a mechanic" (365). In this familiar narrative, the boy becomes a mechanic by default, by failing to achieve academically, rather than by choice. Male-positive literacy would enable him to make an informed choice for a dignified and meaningful life—and that choice would include the option of becoming a mechanic, an academic, or whatever else he chooses, while feeling confident and competent at embodied literacy.

Service-learning strategies could effectively encourage men to draw on their lived, embodied male literacy to succeed with conventional academic literacy. Service learning is "a teaching and learning strategy that integrates meaningful community service with instruction and reflection to enrich the learning experience, teach civic responsibility, and strengthen communities" (Seifer and Connors 4). In practice it might consist, for example, of a biology major college student applying his or her academic knowledge to teach members of a community how to sustain a community garden while he or she learns about the culture of that community. Service learning encourages mutual, thoughtful learning for both provider and client while serving the latter and his or her community. Its efficacy, effects, and agenda have been the subject of some debate. Opponents denigrate it as ineffective anti-liberal-education time wasting; proponents laud it as an effective tool for social-justice empowerment and civic education. John W. Eby voices the opinion of those who question the efficacy of service learning, noting that some in the academy, "talk of McService, service bites, quick fix service, happy meal community service, or service in a box" and argues that an inevitable lack of participant training and complementary course objectives could result in the "potential to do actual harm" (2, 5). A liberal-education advocate, James V. Schall, criticizes what he sees as service learning's anti-individualist approach: he argues that unlike "social justice" which "seeks to remove justice from the soul and relocate it in the relationships that constitute the polity," a liberal education should "mean that we, each in our individual souls, are free to learn what is to be learned" and consequently have "the capacity to rule ourselves so that we are free to direct our fears or pleasures or interests in such a way that we can really see what is there" (46-47). In a similar vein, John B. Egger argues that "wrapping a veneer of learning over community service conceals the promotion of a particular social agenda"—"a socialist communitarian philosophy"—and "wastes students' valuable time and other resources"; it also "seeks to exploit young students' natural sympathy for the less fortunate" and by "attempting to substitute emotions for reason, [...] contravenes the purpose of liberal education"—which he argues is "civility" and "a work ethic [...] befitting a student: reading, thinking, and writing"—"while chipping away at students' respect for social order" (183, 191, 194).

Although she acknowledges that faculty members are reluctant to incorporate service learning into their courses because it takes away time from teaching content, Amy Strage, however, claims that students who participate in service-learning generally earn higher grades than their nonparticipating classmates.[10] David Palmer and Christina Standerfer advocate for a kind of "participatory education" whose assignments "share attributes with the service-learning model"; they argue that it appropriately addresses a new reality where "the university reshapes itself in service to the private sector" and where the "deep sense of detachment from life" resulting from liberal education is no longer effective (123,122). Jon F. Schamber and Sandra L. Mahoney similarly see service learning's social and civic agenda as serving "the New Academy" and "[o]ne of the primary purposes of liberal education for twenty-first century" (75).[11] Proponents of service learning argue that it usefully contests, or realistically modifies, liberal education pedagogy the better to serve contemporary society. Whether it does so effectively, ineffectively, or even adversely, has yet to be determined conclusively.[12]

Whatever the nature its impact, service learning can deftly support male-positive literacy in ways that satisfy both liberal-education and social-justice advocates. Reflection, which involves incorporating what one has understood into one's experience, is central to effective learning for both camps.[13] Reading is an individual act, criticism a communal one. Reading is affective and effective: students of literature engage with texts in personal ways that more than merely confirm the operation of social mechanisms

---

10. Strage cites three "major reasons" for faculty reluctance to participate in service learning: first, "the time and effort required of them to establish the necessary partnerships, to modify their courses, and to monitor and assess students' service"; second, "the concern that time spent addressing the service-learning requirements of the course—both in class and out of class—detracts from coverage of 'core' material and might leave students under-prepared for subsequent coursework"; and three, "the uncertainty about the depth and breadth of academic advantages service-learning provides within and beyond the isolated course within which it is embedded" (260).

11. Schamberger and Mahoney offer a useful review of the literature on service learning on 76-80. See also Strage 257-258.

12. Michelle E. Schmidt et al. argue for the benefits to both parties involved in the "reciprocal relationship" central to service learning in mentoring programs (206). Tricia McClam et al. found that student in their study valued "having hands-on experience, gaining knowledge, translating theory into practice, and developing skills" (245). They concluded that "students exposed to well-planned experiential learning activities overcome initial concerns, develop professional confidence, and demonstrate learning at an advanced level when confronted by real and meaningful workplace challenges" (247). Robert F. Kronick's initial research finds that while students who have participated in service learning "may get involved in their community and may serve on a board," their service-learning experience "doesn't change their career plans" (303). Mary Prentice examines some significant conflicting results of service learning (136-137). John T. King incisively and usefully discusses how service learning has been "vulnerable to criticisms that it exacerbates both power differentials and prejudice (123).

13. In his examination of the major theories informing reflection, Russell R. Rogers asserts that, "[u]litmately, the intent of reflection is to integrate the understanding gained into one's experience in order to enable better choices or actions in the future as well as enhance one's overall effectiveness" (41). This agenda would surely accommodate excellent liberal-arts and service-learning education.

and forces operating in a work of literature; criticism requires, in addition, consistent reflective reasoning. Writing about literature involves the kind of reflection that satisfies the goals of the liberal arts education described by Schall and Egger. Encouraging a boy or a man to read and reflect, in the context of an embodied literacy, might accommodate his effective and comfortable participation in a community of readers or scholars. In addition, the community oriented teaching and learning strategies promoted by proponents of participatory education for contemporary liberal education are a necessary part of the kind of reflection needed to educate service-providers about boys' and men's literacy needs and to promote male-positive learning communities. Reading and reflecting enable the service-provider and the client to learn from each other's response to texts. Using service-learning strategies in this reflective, cooperative venture could promote male-positive literacy in three ways. First, doing so could help make reading more male friendly. Service providers could research the client's embodied extracurricular and curricular literacy experiences and incorporate insights from those experiences into their service-learning activities. (Having the clients complete interest inventories would adroitly provide this information.[14]) Thomas Newkirk argues that "literacy instruction" should not define itself as contrary to those "forms of narrative pleasure that can be experienced in a culture" (171,172). Male-positive literacy development might require a broadening of those acceptable "school-sanctioned narratives" in which "[b]ooks trump magazines; print trumps the visual; the serious trumps the humorous; fiction trumps nonfiction" (171). Michael Smith and Jeffrey D. Wilhelm argue that successful male literacy involves allowing boys and men to "employ literacy in contexts where they could demonstrate competence" and experience flow (458). Flow, Mihály Csíkszentmihályi's term for the state "in which people are so involved in an activity that nothing else seems to matter" and in which they attain "optimal experience: a sense that one's skills are adequate to cope with the challenges at hand, in a goal-directed, rule-bound action system that provides clear clues as to how well one is performing" is a useful measure of the kind of cross-discipline and diverse-skill attainment central to curricular and extracurricular embodied men's literacy, whether it involves sporting, socializing, or researching (4, 71). Emphasizing service-learning's respect for the client's culture and its sensitivity to provider-paternalism might help educators "[open] up the literacy curriculum to make it more appealing to boys" and change the pervasive "construction of literacy as feminized" (Newkirk 169, 170).

---

14. In her useful essay on employing them in service-learning-type situations, Marya Grande defines interest inventories as "questionnaires or surveys of student interests that include closed and open-ended questions whose answers will allow the surveyor to learn more about the interests of the surveyee" (56). One of the teachers who had used these inventories praises them for giving "more information about the student in settings outside the classroom"—a useful strategy for learning more about the wide circle of men's extracurricular literacy (62).

Second, using these service-learning strategies could help one investigate the extent to which boys and men need social justice in education, whether they need appropriate teaching methods and environments (perhaps even single-sex classrooms) to enable them to attain excellent literacy.[15] Calls for male-positive education are often poorly recieved. Tyre offers an important insight into the narrow, hostile reception often encountered by education advocates for males:

> Working to address the underachievement of boys is not part of an antifem-inist agenda. And we need to stop acting as if it were. For too long, any dis-cussion of the new gender gap has become quickly mired in a reactive and un-sophisticated kind of gender politics. We need to change the terms of the de-bate [....] we need to give boys strong, positive, and coherent messages about how to become productive, useful members of society. (285)

What she argues for is gender equity, which assures both boys and girls of appropriate academic support (286).[16] Social justice in education for boys and men requires gender equity. Service-providers' shared or published re-flections could effectively disseminate strategies for accommodating male learners in their quest for gender equity and provide practical instances of male-positive literacy in practice.

A third way in which using service-learning strategies could promote male-positive literacy is by fostering the creation of male-positive literacy groups or communities in which boys or men could communally experience flow. Ralph Fletcher describes how educators were successfully able "to cre-ate an environment where boys are truly engaged to learn" (142). Further-more, Fletcher argues, these environments, that include a "skateboard ex-hibition, a fifth-grade classroom, and a Boys Writing Club," can help us "better nurture and support our struggling [male] writers," and they could lead to the creation of male-literacy communities (Fletcher 149, 166). Char-acteristics of this environment include cooperative dialogue among the par-ticipants, much activity—doing rather than just talking, playfulness and a sense of fun, choices of subject matter and activities, and strong mentoring (149). Smith and Wilhelm note that by employing the kind of male-positive literacy discussed above, the young men in their study managed "to display

---

15. See Tyre 201-224 and Christina Hoff Sommers 170-178 for cogent, differing views on single-sex schooling.

16. To illustrate her distinction between gender equity and gender equality, Tyre quotes from a report issued by the state of Maine's Task Force on Gender Equity in Educa-tion:

Gender equity is often confused with gender equality. Achieving gender equality in schools requires that we provide the same resources and opportunities to all stu-dents regardless of their gender. This is a relatively simple task in comparison to creating gender equity in our education system. Gender equity goes beyond the ex-pectations for gender equality. Gender equity ensures that boys and girls are given the necessary supports to achieve the same standards of excellence. Equity acknow-ledges that boys and girls may need different supports to achieve these outcomes. (qtd. In Tyre 286)

and develop competence and an identity as an insider of a community of practice"—exemplifying a male-positive literacy group or community (458). Because service learning flexibly serves different communities, because it genuinely encourages reflection on the part of provider and client, it potentially addresses the often unformulated, or ignored, needs of men as a literacy community. It is likely, therefore, that a service-learning experience would usefully accommodate male learners and their particular learning habits and empower providers to disseminate male-positive literacy.

Why would reading Shakespeare, and particularly 1 Henry 4, in the context of a male-positive literacy study be useful? Doing so provides two important opportunities: first, to address those negative impressions male learners might have about Shakespeare—bad feelings about Shakespeare which often result from ineffective teaching in high school—and second, to test the three ways in which a service-learning project might promote male-positive literacy. Because Prince Hal's challenging, contested progress to manhood is central to Shakespeare's 1 Henry 4, the play lends itself well to male-positive literacy. The costs and benefits of becoming a man are dramatized in an action-packed, fun-to-watch play; we learn about the gambits and consequences inherent the prince's different ways of "doing boy" (Kehler and Greig 358).[17] The dramatic action obviously encourages one to understand the play as a performance, which in turn enables educators and students to "embrace a broader definition of writing" about the play, one that might "include drawing, talking, and even gesticulating" (Fletcher 97). Along the same lines, the sympathetic, often humorous characters and the events that befall them—partying, practical joking, contesting, battling—encourage reflection and analysis through male-friendly genres of writing, such as "[s]ports writing, [s]ports commentary, [c]reative [n]onfiction, [f]antasy, [s]cience fiction, [m]ovie or TV scripts, [h]orror, [g]raphic novels, [and] [c]omic books" (Fletcher 135-136).

The service-learning project was given to a junior-and-senior-level Shakespeare class of eleven men and eight women, all but one of whom (a mature student) were in their early twenties.[18] It required students to find

---

17. Bruce R. Smith's Shakespeare and Masculinity offers a useful introduction to Renaissance male culture and its ideals. Robin Headlam Wells'introduction and first chapter of Shakespeare on Masculinity astutely examine the tension between chivalric and humanistic masculine ideals central to Elizabethan culture and dramatized in Shakespeare's plays. See, also, Richard C McCoy and Eugene M. Waith for information on Elizabethan masculine ideals. Useful critical readings of Prince Hal's development can be found in Jonas A. Barish, A. C. Bradley, Gerhard H. Cox, William B. Hunter, C. W. R. D. Moseley, and M. M. Reese (312-317). Chapter four of Barbara Hodgdon's edition of the play contains fascinating excerpts from and comments on texts that describe the education of a renaissance prince for kingship.

18. The research undertaken for this service-learning project was funded by a service-learning fellowship granted to me at Springfield College in the 2008-2009 academic year. I would like to thank the students in my Shakespeare class at the College for permitting me to quote from their work in this paper. All of the student and client names in this paper are pseudonyms.

ways to encourage a male from their self-chosen and self-defined community—many chose a student from our college—to experience male-positive literacy by discussing with him 1 Henry 4, which we were studying with two other plays from the Henriad, Richard 2 and 2 Henry 4.[19] We methodically examined the evolution of Prince Hal throughout 1 Henry 4, evaluating closely his thoughts and actions concerning his feelings about Falstaff (most notably in 2.5 and 5.4), Hotspur (in 3.2 and 5.4), and King Henry (in 3.2 and 5.1.). The project lasted for seven weeks and required the student service-providers to meet regularly with their clients and to record in writing their and their clients' learning experiences based on a continuous reflection model, designed to analyze their situation before during and after reflection, compiled by Carrie Williams Howe.[20] I set aside class time for class-reflection, both class discussion and peer dialogue, so the student service-providers could share their experiences, and we could offer encouragement and suggest useful resources. (The students also had access to relevant articles and book chapters on service learning and male literacy listed in the references section of this paper.) Although most were college students; the clients included Tyler, Delaney Brennan's fourteen-year-old nephew; Liam, Whitney Hay's fourteen-year-old student; and Ray, Shannon Doorman's fifty-one-year-old uncle. The service-providing students learned much from this experience as did some of their clients. Addressing a pervasive dislike for Shakespeare the students learned much about its causes and offered suggestions for changing how his plays are studied. Also, in their critical reflections on their service-learning experience, some participants experienced a productive defamiliarization of how they perceived the system of assumptions, beliefs, and practices that inform education in praxis, an experience which involves "choos[ing] to attending to those perspectives that challenge their current understandings," resulting in their calling

---

19. Having students choose clients from their communities expediently mitigates the time-consuming need "to establish the necessary community partnerships" acknowledged by Strage (260). Theresa M. Judge argues that much profitable service learning can take place on campus.

20. Howe graphically represented these three phases as thirds of a continuous experiential circle in her presentation. Students were encourage to use as reflection prompts the questions associated with each phase:
   Pre-Service Reflection/Preparation: What biases are we bringing? What academic topics do we think relate? What challenges might arise? What are we worried about? How much experience do we have? What skills do we possess or need to learn? During-Service Reflection: What is our gut reaction and why? How is this connecting to our class? What are we learning about ourselves and our abilities? What is surprising us? What critical incidents are sticking with us? Post-Service Reflection: What impact have we made? What have we learned about ourselves, about the academic topic, about the community, about the social issue? Were our assumptions valid? Does this change where we go from here? What would we do differently next time?

for gender equity (King 125).[21] Remarkably, some participants were able to experience flow in their male-positive "community of practice"—a certain indicator of service-learning success in this context.

Teaching Shakespeare to the boys and men in the study required the students to address pervasive negative feelings about the Bard of Avon and his plays. Four of these students noted that their clients attributed their dislike of Shakespeare to their experience with one play: Romeo and Juliet. Philip Frye typically describes the challenging situation that he and other novice service-providers faced when dealing with the feminization of literacy and its consequences exemplified by the clients' response to Romeo and Juliet: "Patrick hated the play and called it a 'really old chick-flick.' Since this is the only bit of Shakespeare that Patrick had experienced, he believes that everything written by Shakespeare is too emotional and boring. Add this to the fact that I have never taught at any level, and the perfect storm of education was created." Both providers and clients had reservations about Shakespeare based on their experience with this play. Hank Scorpio acknowledges that his service-learning experience was colored by his own introduction to Shakespeare: "My freshman year we read Romeo and Juliet and this turned me off almost entirely to everything we read in high school." Brad Poirier notes that his client, Kevin, a twenty-two-year-old carpenter, was first introduced to the play in the eighth grade: "He failed even to turn the title-page of Romeo and Juliet. He refused to read the play, and received a zero on the assignment. [...] 'I'm not reading that sappy bull-shit.' [...] When I asked what he thought Shakespeare wrote about, he said, 'sappy love stories.' I immediately knew I needed to change that preconceived notion he had of Shakespeare." He, like all of the other providers, tried to change these negative notions by incorporating interests from their clients' culture and traditionally male-friendly topics into their discussions of 1 Henry 4.

Max Flanders, Harrison Reisweber, and Miles Tee successfully drew on extracurricular male literacy—in this case, their shared knowledge of American football—when discussing the play. Flanders's client, Lesnick, enthusiastically embraced the idea that Prince Hal, like a "star football player," showed "intensity, aggressiveness, instincts, motivation, accountability, and was a leader." Reisweber's client, Nemo, "compared Falstaff to a lazy reserve player that did not pull his weight on the team." Like Annakin Jones (who used movies, graphic novels, and video), Tee incorporated multimedia in his project: "The [Seinfeld] TV episode [in which a character does not read a required book because it is not about sports] hooked my subject into thinking about what he likes to read and write about [....] The object of the [football] video game was to get the subject to remember characters' qualities." In addition to football, Tee used the movie, Saving Private Ryan, product-

---

21.King observes that when defamiliarization takes place, "new information, situations, and perspectives are not simply assimilated into students' existing belief systems but serve to disrupt those systems in such a way that they themselves become the subject of critical examination" (136).

ively: he first asked his client, Ben, to consider "which 'soldier' he would rather have on his side"; they then applied lessons learned from the film and the television episode to understanding character and plot in the play. John Stamos used a similar strategy: his high-school-aged clients, John and Christopher, watched the movie, My Private Idaho, which is loosely based on 1 Henry 4, then compared meaningful scenes from the movie to quotations from the play. Stamos concludes that the boys were not only able to discuss the quotations in light of the movie—"to make Shakespearean connections"—but also "social connections" to their own lives. The fact that male learners respond positively to this broader understanding of literacy is succinctly demonstrated by Tyler's prior experience with Romeo and Juliet: according to Brennan, "[t]he only positive memories he has of this unit was creating a play bill and reading the fight scene between Mercutio and Tybalt." Some students suggested that high-school students study 1 Henry 4 as well as Romeo and Juliet. All agreed that broadening the circle of acceptable texts to encourage male-positive literacy could successfully engage boys and men with Shakespeare.

Most participants discovered that male-positive literacy works for boys and men; some, however, wrote about their new insights into how boys and men were adversely constructed in and poorly treated by the educational system, how they needed social-justice in education. Christopher Romin's reflections on his experience lead him to a similar position as Tyre's notion of gender equity: he observed that this service-learning assignment "was enlightening as it was scary. Having been a product of the same [educational] institutions being researched in this paper, I never thought how narrow-minded our culture truly is. While I don't agree with the idea that females get too much attention, I do feel that males do not get enough." Reisweber experienced a sense of partnership with his client and a productive defamiliarization concerning his education:

> I realized that instead of this being an assignment for class, I viewed these meetings as conversations between two friends [....] The time and effort put into this project was all well worth it for me at the end because I have learned a great deal from my partner, and I'm sure he has learned from me [....] This project says something about the community I worked with. It shows that even at the end of senior year, you can still learn something valuable [....] If more students can make an effort to better their education with a project like this, it benefits the student body and the teachers that administer the material.

Reisweber seems to have discovered the potential power of communal learning for men; moreover, he recognizes the positively disruptive implications for changing how men might benefit from a service-learning influenced learning environment.

Amir Hassan, an Egyptian American, worked with Elias, a Palestinian client; their experience of Middle-East and gender politics richly informed their discussion of the play, affording them new insights into similarities between political and gender-based entitlement. Their debate concerning Falstaff's attitude to honor resulted in Elias's assertion that, "Falstaff's love of life is founded by greed whereas the suicide bombers love/hate for life is motivated by deep compassion for their people's suffering." I Henry 4 became more than a history play; it became their history play. Moreover, Amir learned how hostile some women can be to male social justice from his exchange concerning his service-learning project with a dismissive colleague. After mentioning that "women still get paid less than men and are still suffering," she "angrily" asked, "[h]ow can you say that boys are being screwed by the education system?" In addition to her confusion of gender equity and gender equality, she enacted what Amir calls a "toxic ideology [...] very similar to one Elias and I know very well; the ideology the Israelis have towards the Palestinians is parallel to the ideology women have of men. The fact that a group of people have once suffered does not give that group of people the right to make others suffer. Israel uses the Holocaust and anti-Semitism, and Feminists use sexism and inequality." Amir's and Elias's service-learning project successfully resulted not only in their being able to relate events from I Henry 4 to their sociopolitical identities and circumstances, but also to how education impacts on their gendered identities as men. Shakespeare is, indeed, still our contemporary.

Several service-providers reported that they and their clients experienced a reasonable degree of competence during this short service-learning project. Anakin Jones, for example, notes that "this experiment brought literacy in men to my attention. Teaching Matt, I received a hands-on perspective of the issue. I love movies, comic books, and videogames as well. I tend to learn visually and physically rather than by reading and regurgitating facts. Learning through interaction, I feel in my niche." Alan Smithers' collaboration with Nick, his client, a person with dyslexia, and Nick's roommates, Jon and Bobby, resulted in the establishment of an ad hoc male-positive literacy group of men who, in their own ways, experienced competence and flow. Both Alan's collaboration with these men and his written account of it is often playful, often insightful. This project enabled a male-positive workshop of the kind Fletcher mentions; with partners cooperating, doing, and playing under Alan's mentorship. The culmination of the project was a performance of an excerpt from 5.4 of I Henry 4 (with Nick as Hal) in the residence suite shared by the roommates:

> We clear some space in the common area. I let everyone know that I will read the italicized directions. We begin the scene when Hotspur confronts Hal. The giggling begins right away when Jon stumbles over his opening lines. Hotspur enters the scene and says to Hal: 'If I mistake not, thou art Harry Monmouth." Instead, Jon says, "thou art Harry Monmouth." I think that Nick is immediately energized by two things. One, Nick knows he is performing in a loose atmosphere. Also I get the feeling that Nick thinks he can outdo Jon in reading and acting their respective parts [....] They each stutter over their lines, but Nick remains confident. Although reading Shakespeare aloud is a challenge for many, Nick does his best to remain in character, using voice inflection and hand gestures [....] A spontaneous incident happens when I read the direction that notes Hotspur and Hal fight. Before I can enter the scene as Falstaff, Nick and Jon drop their scripts and begin to wrestle [....] I raise my voice to remind Nick and Jon that Hal wins the fight. Jon then rolls over and allows Nick to pin him. Nick then jumps to his feet, fists raised in the air, and shouts a victorious, 'Yeah!'

Although much fun was had by all, much learning occurred as well: Alan notes, "Not only did [Nick] want to perform as well as possible when we acted the scene, but he was genuinely interested in the events and characters that preceded our scene. [...] Even if he knows he can't be the best, he still wants the spotlight. This is not an ideal trait for the real acting world. Still I catered to Nick's personality to get him interested in 1 Henry 4." All of the men studied their parts to make the performance worthwhile. By using their knowledge of how to "do boy"—to wrestle in this instance—these friends were able to display masculine competence and to attain flow; moreover, they, like the other service providers and clients in this study, learned how much Shakespeare has to offer their experience of the world.

Given its limited time frame, this service-learning project succeeded remarkably well: the students, their clients, and I successfully used service-learning strategies to accommodate male learners and to disseminate male-positive literacy in our respective communities. As a result of their addressing some boys' and men's dislike of Shakespeare, these participants codified possible reasons for it and suggested ways to change how the plays are studied. Moreover, many participants understood how prejudices about men inform our society and its education system. Most notably, some students successfully experienced flow in their community of male learners. I noticed, however, one critical challenge: some students claimed that theirs was a successful service-learning experience but provided no compelling supporting evidence to substantiate their claim. Sarah L. Ash and Patti H Clayton note that it is "not enough to rely on students' testimonials and self-reports to assess the quality of their learning and the meeting of learning objectives" (138). These authors recommend that students adopt "a rigorous reflection framework," that emphasizes "description," "analysis," and an "articulation of learning outcomes" to encourage the productive assessment of their service-learning project (140). Perhaps having the service-providing students and their clients create on-line dialogue journals, accessible to all class members would help; these journals could encourage mutual learning and the "model[ing]" of literacy skills for the client "in an informal setting" and might more clearly demonstrate the effectiveness of the service learning project (Grande 57). I look forward to using the insights I gained from service-learning scholars, service providers, and clients in my next male-positive literacy project.

References

Ash, Sarah L. and Patti H. Clayton. "The Articulated Learning: An Approach to Guided Reflection and Assessment." Innovative Higher Education 29.2 (Winter 2004): 137-154.

Barish, Jonas A. "The Turning Away of Prince Hal." Shakespeare Studies 1 (1965): 9-17.

Bradley, A. C. "The Rejection of Falstaff." Bradley, A. C. Oxford Lectures on Poetry London: Macmillan, 1909. 245-75.

Connor-Greene, Patricia. "Problem-Based Service Learning: The Evolution of a Team Project." Teaching of Psychology 29.3 (2002): 193-197.

Corbett, Christianne, Catherine Hall, and Andresse St. Rose. Where the Girls Are: The Facts about Gender Equity in Education Washington D.C.: AAUW Education Foundation, May 2008.

Cox, Gerhard H. "'Like a Prince Indeed': Hal's Triumph of Honor in 1 Henry IV." Bergeron, David M. Ed. Pageantry in the Shakespearean Theater Athens: University of Georgia Press, 1985. 130-149.

Csíkszentmihályi, Mihály. Flow: The Psychology of Optimal Experience. New York: Harper & Rowe, 1990.

Dubinsky, James. "The Role of Relfection in Service Learning." Business Communication Quarterly 69.3 (2006): 306-311.

Eby, John W. "Why Service-Learning Is Bad." March 1998. 25 June 2009 <http://www.messiah.edu/external_programs/agape/servicelearning/articles/wrongsvc.pdf.>.

Egger, John B. "No Service to Learning: 'Service-Learning' Reappraised." Academic Questions 21 (2008): 183-194.

Fletcher, Ralph. Boy Writers: Reclaiming Their Voices. Portland, Maine: Stenhouse Publishers, 2006.

Flood, Michael. "Three Principles for Men." XY January 28, 2008. <http://www.xyonline.net/3princip.shtml>.

Gill, Zoe. "Boys: Getting It Right: The 'New" Disadvantaged or 'Disadvantage' Redefined?" The Australian Educational Researcher 32.2 (2005): 105-124.

Golden, Tom. The Definition of Male-Positive. Dennis Gouws. 28 November 2008.

Gouws, Dennis S. "Enabling Men in Literature: Teaching Male-Positive Masculinities in a College English Class." The International Journal of Learning 15.7 (2008): 147-157.

Grande, Marya. "Using Dialogue Journals and Interest Inventories with Classroom Volunteers." TEACHING Exceptional Children 41.2 (2008): 56-63.

Howe, Carrie Williams. "Enhancing Critical Reflection in Service-Learning and Experiential Education." University of Connecticut, West Hartford, 19 March 2009.

Hunter, William B. Jr. "Prince Hal, His Struggle Toward Moral Perfection." South Atlantic Quarterly January 1951: 86-95.

Hussar, W.J., and T. M. Bailey. Projections of Education Statistics to 2018 (NCES 2009-062). Washington, DC: National Center for Education Statistics, Institute of Education Sciences, U.S. Department of Education, 2009.

Judge, Therese M. "Service Learning on Campus." Business Communication Quarterly 69.2 (2006): 189-192.

Kehler, Michael and Chris Greig. "Reading Masculinities: Exploring the Socially Literate Practices of High School Young Men." International Journal of Inclusive Education 9.4 (2005): 351-370.

Kellom, Gar and Miles Groth. Eds. *Engaging College Men: What Works and Why*. Harriman, TN: Men's Studies Press, 2010.

King, John T. "Service-Learning as a Site for Critical Pedagogy: A Case of Collaboration, Caring, and Defamiliarization Across Borders." Journal of Experiential Education 26.3 (2004): 121-137.

Kronick, Robert F. "Service-Learning and the University Student." College Student Journal 41.2 (2007): 296-304.

Lingard, Bob. "Where to in Gender Policy in Education after Recuperative Masculinity Politics?" International Journal of Inclusive Education 7.1 (2003): 33-56.

Manthey, Joe. "Boys and Education." True Equality 20 July 2009 <http://www.trueequality.com/booklet/#BoysandEducation>.

McClam, Tricia, Joel F. Diambra, Bobbie Burton, Angie Fuss, and Daniel L. Fudge. "An Analysis of a Service-Learning Project: Students' Expectations, Concerns, and Reflections." Journal of Experiential Education 30.3 (2008): 236-249.

McCoy, Richard C. The Rites of Knighthood: The Literature and Politics of Elizabethan Chivalry. Berkeley: University of California Press, 1989.

Mills, Martin. "'Shaping the Boys' Agenda: The Backlash Blockbusters." International Journal of Inclusive Education 7.1 (2003): 57-73. *Misandry Review*. <http://www.misandryreview.com>.

Moseley, C. W. R. D. Shakespeare's History Plays: Richard II to Henry V, the Making of a King. New York: Penguin, 1991.

Newkirk, Thomas. Misreading Masculinity: Boys, Literacy, and Popular Culture. Portsmouth, NH: Heinemann, 2002.

Palmer, David L. and Christina Standerfer. "Employing Civic Participation in College Teaching Designs." College Teaching 52.4 (Fall 2004): 122-127.

Prentice, Mary. "Service Learning and Civic Engagement." Academic Questions 20.2 (2007): 135-145.

Reese, M. M. The Cease of Majesty: A Study of Shakespeare's History Plays. London: Edward Arnold Ltd, 1961.

Rogers, Russell R. "Reflection in Higher Education: A Concept Analysis." Innovative Higher Education 26.1 (2001): 37-57.

Rosenfeld, Megan. "Reexamining the Plight of Young Males." Washington Post 26 March 1998: A1.

Schall, James V. "Liberal Education and 'Social Justice'." Liberal Education 92.4 (Fall 2006): 44-47.

Schamber, Jon F. and Sandra L. Mahoney. "The Development of Political Awareness and Social Justice Citizenship Through Community-Based Learning in a First-Year General Education Seminar." The Journal of General Education 57.2 (2008): 75-99.

Schmidt, Michelle E., Jaime L. Marks, and Lindsay Derrico. "What a Difference Mentoring Makes: Service Learning and Engagement for College Students." Mentoring and Tutoring 12.2 (2004): 205-217.

Seifer, S. D. and Connors, K. Eds. Faculty Toolkit for Service-Learning in Higher Education. Scotts Valley, CA: National Service-Learning Clearinghouse, 2007.

Shakespeare, William. The First Part of King Henry the Fourth. Ed. Barara Hodgdon. Boston & New York: Bedford Books, 1997.

Smith, Bruce R. Shakespeare and Masculinity. Oxford: Oxford University Press, 2000.

Smith, Michael and Jeffrey D. Wilhelm. "'I just like being good at it': The Importance of Compentence in the Literate Lives of Young Men." Journal of Adolescent & Adult Litracy 47.6 (2004): 454-481.

Smith, Susannah. "The Non-Fiction Reading Habits of Young Successful Boy Readers: Forming Connections between Masculinity and Reading." Literacy (2004): 10-16.

Sommers, Christina Hoff. The War Against Boys: How Misguided Feminism is Harming Our Young Men. New York: Touchstone, 2000.

Strage, Amy. "Long-Term Academic Benefits of Service-Learning: When and Where Do They Manifest Themselves?" College Student Journal 38.2 (2004): 257-262.

Tyre, Peg. The Trouble with Boys: A Surprising Report Card on Our Sons, Their Problems at School, and What Parents and Educators Must Do. New York: Crown Publishers, 2008.

Understanding Raising Boys. PBS Parents. 20 July 2009 <http://www.pbs.org/parents/raisingboys/helpingboys.html>.

von Drehle, David. "The Myth about Boys." 26 July 2007. Time 20 July 2009 <http://www.time.com/time/magazine/article/0,9171,1647452,00.html>.

Waith, Eugene M. The Herculean Hero in Marlowe, Chapman, Shakespeare, and Dryden. New York: Columbia University Press, 1962.

Wells, Carole V. and Chisty Grabert. "Service-Learning and Mentoring: Effective Pedagogical Strategies." College Student Journal 38.4 (2004): 673-679.

Wells, Robin Headlam. Shakespeare on Masculinity. Cambridge: Cambridge University Press, 2000.

Biology

Authentic Learning as a Mechanism for Learner Centredness

Steven Newmaster, University of Guelph, Canada

Eric Dwyer and Hilary Landorf

Abstract: Learner centredness places a student at the centre of their education, engaging them in a cognitive learning experience. In biology, we often use 'hands-on' projects where a student works within an ecosystem or directly with an organism. We hypothesize that 'Authentic Learning' directly engages the student through intrinsic inquiry where a student takes ownership in the products of their education, if they are applied to the benefit of others in socially conscientious ways. This moves the student from extrinsic inquiry to an internally motivated learning mechanism. We tested our hypothesis within three different classes of 40 students over a period of two years. Academically embedded Service Learning projects were used to provide students with authentic and non-authentic ways to explore their education. A biometric analysis indicates that Authentic Learning may be a mechanism for increasing learner centredness. Although Authentic Learning is well adapted to biology curriculum, this mechanism may be appropriate in many other disciplines.

Introduction

Perhaps the most rewarding experience for a teacher at any level of education is the moment of intellectual enlightenment as evidenced by a student's expression and excitement. We relate this event to that of turning on a light bulb because it is literally an instantaneous event that does not go unnoticed by student or the teacher. This coincides with the goals of life long learning and student centered learning. We often phrase this as "putting the student in the drivers seat", which intrinsically engages students in their education as explorers on a life long journey. However, the pursuit of learner centredness in the education system is not a simple task.

Learner centredness can place a student at the centre of their education, engaging them in a cognitive learning experience. Like ours, many institutions are determined to put the learner at the centre of all it does, recognizing that research and teaching are intimately linked, and that learning is a life-long commitment (University of Guelph Mission Statement). In biology, we often use 'hands-on' projects where a student works directly with an organism or within an ecosystem. Leaner-centeredness begins with a paradigm shift from teaching content to student learning, from a focus on the instructor to that of the learner, and from an institutional mission of providing instruction to one of producing a life-long love of learning (Barr and Tagg 1995).

The roots of learner centredness are found in constructivism. That is, knowledge is constructed in a social inquiry context where the student or learner is an active participant in the construction, renovation and demolition of knowledge as they make sense of the world in which they live (Jonassen 1991). To the constructivists, the development of an instructional activity includes two parts: the identification of a problem and providing the students with the resources to solve the problem (Bednar et al. 1992). The student develops a variety of salient skills including the ability to analyze problems and metacognitive skills (e.g., self-management, self monitoring, and self evaluation) (Palincsar and Brown 1984; Glasgow 1997; Hannafin et al. 1997). The learning community or community of inquiry is a fundamental principal to learner centredness because it engages open sharing of intellect and critical evaluations among the students (Wells 1999; Brush and Saye 2001). There is a rich body of literature on the applications and models of student centred learning (Bandura 1982; McCombs and Whisler 1997; Grant 2003; Slunt and Giancarlo 2004) including great advancements in technology (Hannafin and Land 1997; Edwards and Sutton 1991; Scott et al. 1997; Pederson and Liu 2003). Kolb's (1984) book on experiential learning also provides a firm foundation in concrete experiences, observation and reflection and active experimentation or "hands-on" experiences (Boud et al. 1991). Meyers and Jones (1993) have equated this with active learning, which promotes effective and critical thinking (Cameron 2003). More recently, active experimentation has developed into complex computer models that immerse the student in micro-worlds within interactive multimedia (Hannafin 1997). A critical body of evidence is mounting, which supports the claim that student-centered learning (SCL) promotes the development of higher-order skills such as critical thinking and problem solving (Savery and Duffy 1995; Alper et al. 1996; Gallagher and Stepien 1996; Barab and Landa 1997). However, there are difficulties associated with developing and supporting student-centered learning curriculum such as the need for significant resources and specialized skill sets for both the teacher and the students.

The promise of student-centred education is to make learning a more active process; the impediment consists of several challenging issues. SCL requires significant resources (i.e., instructor time) to develop and deliver. Although there have been successful applications in large classes (Scott et al. 1997) most of the student to teacher ratios are quite small (<20:1 at Univ. of Guelph including teaching assistants). As a professor who embraces SCL, I spend the entire class and many outside classroom hours with the students guiding, supporting and inspiring the active learning process. Albeit very rewarding, it is also very intellectually and energy consuming. Another problem is that the structure of SCL is not appreciated by a small population percentage of the students. The projects or activities used to promote SCL often do not provide enough organized structure to adequately guide students, resulting in student disorientation and frustration (Hannafin et al. 1999; Brush and Saye 2000). Many students want more guidance, particularly those in the early years of post secondary education. However, surveys have shown that a significant majority of students have responded positively to the independence goal of SCL (Edwards and Sutton 1991). The students who excel in SCL possess an additional set of skills than those needed in the traditional teacher-centered education system; these are metacognitive skills such as self-management, monitoring, and evaluation (Brown 1981; Palincsar and Brown 1984; Palincsar 1986; Brown et al. 1989; Glasgow 1997; McCombs and Whisler 1997). In the traditional system, the teacher is responsible for identifying problems, establishing goals and objectives and ultimately the path to solutions for students. Students succeed at the assigned task by following a paved pathway for success with predefined objectives (Bednar et al. 1992). In SCL, the student is required to set meaningful goals for solving a problem and assume more responsibility for meeting and understanding the value of those goals, including self monitoring the effectiveness of their goals (Palincsar and Brown 1984; Palincsar 1986; Hannafin et al. 1994). If a student is not an effective self-manager they may find themselves overwhelmed by the scale of the project, which encompasses the ability to identify what types of information are important, where to find this information and how to analyze the information with respect to solving the problem (Glasgow 1997; McCombs and Whisler 1997; Brush and Saye 2000, 2001). Teaching methods such as modeling, scaffolding and coaching have been developed to address a variety of these challenges in SCL (Brush and Saye 2000, 2001; Darabi 2005). Central to SCL is the support of the student community in which a team of students of varying skills work together to solve problems (Darabi 2005). Ideally, students recognize their strengths and weaknesses and succeed through the collective strength of the team.

The teacher must provide the proper training and experience in cooperative and collaborative skills (Johnson and Johnson 1991). However, there are some students who do not appreciate the community approach presenting further challenges to SCL. These are not trivial problems for either the student or the teacher. In fact we have a responsibility to develop SCL skills in those students who are the most challenged by them. Recently, there have been many developments in the SCL literature, which provide a cadre of tools rooted in pedagogical theory, skills and technology that will assist the teacher in developing student centred learners (Brush and Saye 2000, 2001). Perhaps the most critical impediment to SCL is self-motivation.

One of the assumptions of SCL is that the student is actively engaged in the learning process, which is different from tradition where the teacher engages the student. Renzulli et al. (2004) states if you "challenge students to solve everyday problems in meaningful contexts, then the learning will take care of itself." Students who are intrinsically motivated will set personal goals and launch into the exploration of a problem and will actively seek and engage the skills and solutions (Collins et al. 1991). Several researchers have discussed the need to promote intrinsic motivation by creating learning environments in which students embrace the problems because they are intrinsically related to interesting and coherent goals (Lepper and Greene 1979; Malone 1981; Levin 1982). This is in contrast to the traditional extrinsic reason, such as achieving high grades or external gratification. Although the products of education play an important role in creating authentic learning, students learn principally from the cognitive, affective and motivational processes involved (Renzulli et al. 2004). Research on the mechanisms that intrinsically engage SCL have not been investigated quantitatively. Several researchers have suggested that students learn best when engaged in authentic, integrated, and personally meaningful experiences (Collins et al. 1989; Collins et al. 1991; Kennedy and Tipps 1997; Trichenor and Jewell 2001). However, there is a lack of quantitative classroom research to support this claim. Our definition of 'authentic learning' is limited to environments in which the student is intrinsically motivated to solve a problem or tackle a project. Students will embrace a problem when they choose to 'stake a claim' in their education. Taking ownership of ones property or the products of ones labour is rooted in human nature. The University of Guelph has traditionally offered several SCL courses in which students are involved in hands-on projects in both the field and lab. These projects are designed by the professors and appreciated by the students. However, we have recently developed several projects where the student projects are related to some authentic applied question in the community or result in products of which the students take ownership, such as authorship in a publication. The students of these projects are very enthusiastic and recognize the difference between authentic or real life projects and projects for marks, which are discarded at the end of a course. We hypothesize that authentic learning directly engages the student through intrinsic inquiry where a student takes ownership in the products of their education, if they are applied to the benefit of others in socially conscientious ways. This moves the student from extrinsic inquiry to an internally motivated learning mechanism. The purpose of this study was to investigate the influence of authentic learning environments on SCL in contrast with traditional extrinsically motivated learning environments in several biology classes at the University of Guelph.

Project Design

Our research design included surveys of 490 students within three courses over two years. The courses included: BOT 3710 "Classification and Morphology of Seed Plants" (2003-2005; 116 students); BOT 2030 "Plants in the Ontario Landscape" (2003-2005; 132 students) and BOT 2050 "Plant Ecology" (2003-2004; 242 students). The dependent variables were the responses to a questionnaire in which the response scale ranged from 1(weak) to 10 (strong) (Table 1). The independent variable was the presence/absence of an authentic mechanism in each project. We controlled for variation in several co-variables that we measured: gender (male, female), year (2003, 2004), course (BOT 3710, BOT 2030, BOT 2050), student grades and whether the projects were conducted individually or in groups. We used MANOVA to analyze the dependent variables by the presence/absence of the fixed factor (authentic mechanism). As in a "blind" design, the students were not aware of the experimental approach and we did not mention either the SCL pedagogy or the idea of an authentic mechanism. All assumptions for the MANOVA were evaluated and satisfied. We also used a univariate ANOVA to evaluate the differences in time (quantified from student journals) that students spent on projects in the presence or absence of an authentic mechanism, and the time the professor spent supervising students outside of normal class time. The student questionnaires also included the qualitative personal comments of students of which the prevalent themes in the student responses are presented in our discussion.

The students completed two projects in each course; the first was a student centered project without an authentic mechanism and the second project included the authentic mechanism. The students were asked to keep a journal of time spent on completing various tasks for all projects in the course. These journals were collected by the instructor and the total hours per project was tallied for each student and used as a co-variable in our analyses. The projects for each of the courses are briefly defined below:

BOT 3710 "Classification and Morphology of Seed Plants" – Students were asked to complete two projects in which they had to build a taxonomic key for a group of plants. In the first week we taught the students several types of keys. Project one required the students to make a key for a group of plants assigned to them. The project required them to utilize their knowledge of plant characters and apply the key building skills they acquired during the first week. Project two required the students to make a key for a group of plants that they chose. The students could choose plants that were of interest to them (e.g., if they loved orchids), or plants of some geographic area that was special to them (e.g., plants in their family's woodlot), or a group of plants with a practical application to a community (e.g., vets or farmers - plants poisonous to livestock), or a project related to their summer work (e.g., plants in a local garden centre or provincial park). The students had a personal connection and interest in these projects and took pride in the applications of their efforts to society-at-large. This was in fact the authentic mechanism in the project, which made provision for the students to decide on a project that was of interest to them as well as being useful to others, which spanned beyond the calendar boundaries of the course.

BOT 2030 "Plants in the Ontario Landscape" – Students were asked to collect plants and write a taxonomic monograph on the species they collected including references to the botanical literature on their respective plants. In the first project we chose two plants in the local flora for each student to work on. In the second project, students were asked to submit monographs to the "Flora Ontario" project, which will be considered for publication in a series of county floras within the Province. This was a real submission that had potential for publication and was previously arranged with the Flora's editorial committee. The students had the opportunity to choose species in any county in Ontario. Most of the students chose plants from a county that had special interest to them such as their home, a cottage, a special geographical feature or their place of employment. The authentic mechanism was the ability to choose plants and a county that was of value to them and the possibility that their work may be published and be of value to others.

BOT 2050 "Plant Ecology" – Students were asked to work in groups on a field ecology project within a local wetland. In project one, we assigned groups of students to work together on various wetland projects in the field. Upon completion of the fieldwork, the students compiled and then analyzed their results and gave a presentation to the class at the end of the course. Project two involved a local developer and a concerned community group who presented an ecological problem that could not be resolved to the satisfaction of all the stakeholders in this local community. The students were asked to design projects that would critically evaluate the problem, collect data and present their results including management recommendations in a formal community event, which included all the concerned stakeholders. Students were told that one or a combination of their recommendations would be used to solve this ecological problem. The authentic mechanism was the action of each team of students working together and presenting a solution to an actual ecological problem in local community.

Results/Discussion

Our results indicate that 'Authentic Learning' engages the student through intrinsic inquiry where a student takes ownership in the products of their education. This moves the student from extrinsic inquiry to an internally motivated learning mechanism. Our results are supported by 490 student surveys from three different courses over two years. We considered the co-variation attributed to gender, year, course, student grades and solo versus group projects. All ten of the survey questions had significantly ($p < 0.05$) higher ranks for projects with the authentic mechanism when compared to similar projects without the authentic mechanism (Figure 1). These higher ranks reflect the students' agreement (i.e., 1 = weak to 10 = strong) with inquiries and statements about their projects (Table 1). Although we did not test for difference among the questions, there appears to be little difference among the means and standard deviations (Figure 1). The inquiries and statements explored the students' interest, engagement, self-involve-ment, metacognition, intellectual stimulation, sense of ownership and ac-complishment with respect to their own projects (Table 1). A quantitative analysis of the students' and professor's time indicated that students spent significantly ($p < 0.05$) more time working on projects with the authentic mechanism. There was no significant difference ($p > 0.05$) in the amount of time spent by the professor working with the students on projects with or without the authentic mechanism.

There are several different uses of the term authentic learning in the published literature. Our definition of 'authentic learning' is limited to en-vironments in which the student is intrinsically motivated to solve a prob-lem or tackle a project. Students will embrace a problem when they choose to 'stake a claim' in their education. However, our definition could be ex-panded to include research in reference to 'authentic evaluation/assessment' (Wiggins 1989; Graue 1993; Klenowski 1995; Stiggins 1999; Shepard 2000; Pedderson and Williams 2004). Theories on learning developed by the as-sociationist and behavioral scientists have formed the basis for a solid paradigm in the 20th century that has influenced how we assess students today. The conventional measurement of learning through objective tests is a logical practice, which has formed our present educational system (Ped-derson and Williams 2004). Wiggins (1989) proposed that assessment should be more authentic focusing on how well students perform within the context of their activities. These ideas became the precursors to 'per-formance assessments', which focuses on how students perform the tasks rather than objective tests (Shepard and Bliem 1995). Authentic assessment is innovative in that it helps students develop metacognitive awareness and moves the student's preoccupation with tests and grades to a focus on long-term goals. Research suggests that learners become increasingly compliant in their thinking when conventional measurements of learning are used (McCaslin and Good 1992; Roth and Roychoudhury 1993). Learners tend to view the learning task as meeting the expectations of the course syllabus rather than pursuing personal understanding, which is reinforced by their success (e.g., good grades), perpetuating what some University students refer to as "playing the grades game". However, there is substantial evidence to support the claim that students are more interested in their own learning performance than in the grades they receive on tests (Bloom et al. 1981; Klenowski 1995; Stiggins 1997; Biddulph and Adey 2004). Some researchers have stated that in a stimulating environment, assessment may be of little importance to students because they take for granted that grading is inev-itable and they will do what is necessary to make good grades (Pedderson and Williams 2004; Bolin et al. 2005). A stimulating environment has been defined as one where students are engaged in authentic, integrated, and per-sonally meaningful experiences (Kennedy and Tipps 1997; Trichenor and Jewell 2001).

Recently, research in educational technology has shown that students can be engaged in "authentic learning" using computer-enhanced learning environments, which is predicated on a similar hypothesis to our study

(Hannafin et al. 1994; Brush and Saye 2001; Pedersen and Williams 2004). Hannafin and Land (1997) advocate the idea of technology-enhanced student-centered learning environments. These computer-based environments are just tools or alternatives to direct instruction; they represent an alternative approach based on fundamentally different learning goals (Brush and Saye 2000). Attempts to situate cognition in authentic learning computer models have become widespread since its conception in the late 1980's (Salomon 1979; Brown et al. 1989; Cognition and Technology Group at Vanderbilt 1991, 1992; Hannafin et al. 1994). These systems are not designed to simply to instruct but rather they cultivate understanding and insight (Hannafin et al. 1997). As with our authentic projects, these computer learning environments immerse individuals in authentic learning experiences where the discovery of knowledge and skills are realistically embedded (Brush and Saye 2001). Real-life situations and phenomena can be simulated in the computer model, which provides a similar learning environment to our authentic projects (Volman 2005). In our study, students commented that learning was more concrete and meaningful because more personal connections were made among ideas, contexts and perspectives. These comments resonate with Wilensky's (1991) basic assumptions underlying authentic learning computer models which state that learning is more tangible and meaningful as more personal connections are made among ideas, contexts and perspectives. Supporting research suggests that understanding is facilitated when derived from this type of rich, authentic, hands-on experience (Perkins 1991; APA 1992; National Science Teachers' Association 1993; Linn and Muilenburg 1996).

Many of the students in our study commented that they felt as if they were part of a team working toward a common goal, which they had a personal interest in. The learning community is central to achieving student centred learning (Darabi 2005). Some teams do not harmonize and they cannot be forced into an active learning community. However, we suggest that an active learning community can be fostered by the authentic environment in which the students share experiences in developing skills in order to solve problems. The strengths and weakness in these skills become apparent to the team members and they support each other as they work toward a solution or the completion of a task. The team forms an bond as they struggle to solve the problem and share the celebration of their success. The teacher presents an authentic environment and inspires the team of teaching assistants, technicians, graduate students and undergraduate students to identify the problem and work toward a solution. This conceptual model could take place in the field, lab, and classroom or in a virtual computer setting. Students explore problems and search for solutions that often integrate disciplines that have traditionally been studied in isolation. Our students also commented that their education felt more 'real' to them, and they often connected this reality with a team approach. The identity of reality with a community approach has been referred to as a "community of inquiry or practice" (Wells 1999). A community of inquiry or practice refers to a learning environment in which the participants actively communicate and engage in the skills involved in the expertise of solving problems (Collins et al. 1991). We found that personal investment and the mutual dependency of the team membersleads to a sense of ownership, which underpins the foundations of an apprenticeship.

The authentic mechanism we have proposed is rooted in what is perhaps the most ancient form of teaching - apprenticeship. Teaching and learning has transcended thousands of years through apprenticeship. It is a natural way to learn as evidenced through our own family's ability to teach us how to walk, talk, cook, eat and ride a bike. Apprenticeship was and still is the vehicle for transmitting the knowledge required for expert practice in fields from carpentry to painting, medicine and law. However, in many schools and academia, apprenticeship has largely been replaced by formal schooling with the exception of post-secondary graduate education, co-op placements and internships. We agree with John Dewey's (1933, 1938) statement that educational institutions are settings in which students should receive life-apprenticeships. At the University of Guelph, students in our biology courses gain an understanding for a particular ecosystem or organism when they spend time interacting with an organism or within that organism's environment. Students build and alter their understanding through everyday interactions with their environments while the goal of education, in effect, is to provide a stimulating environment to support the student's natural desire to learn (Piaget 1952; Hannafin et al. 1997). A model of instruction that goes back to apprenticeship but incorporates elements of schooling is "cognitive apprenticeship" (Collins et al. 1989). Cognitive apprenticeship strives to intrinsically motivate students, engaging them in student centred learning, which is directly related to our authentic mechanism hypothesis (Darabi 2005; Collins et al. 1991). As with an apprenticeship, we encourage a reversal of roles in our courses; the students are now in the driver's seat and the teachers provide guidance, tools, examples and inspiration. This is similar to Palinscar and Brown's (1984) 'reciprocal teaching', where the student and teacher took turns leading a dialogue on various aspects of the reading assignment, which was effective in raising students' scores on reading comprehension tests in elementary schools. An apprenticeship requires an individual to take charge of their education, which stimulates intrinsic inquiry. However, intrinsic inquiry is also stimulated by another component of apprenticeship: it is authentic or real.

Authenticity could be considered a basic mechanism in the most ancient pedagogy. Constructivists such as Piaget (1952) and Vygotsky (1978) have shown us that knowledge is not fixed or external; it is constructed by those who seek an understanding through experience. Social cognitivists have studied the relationship between context (including social) and knowledge or understanding (Belmont 1989; Brown et al. 1989; Jonassen 1991; Lave and Wenger 1991; Young and McNeese 1995). This research has shown the inextricable relationship between knowledge, and the contexts in which it derives meaning (Perkins and Salomon 1989). Knowledge isolated from context is perceived to be of little productive value (Whitehead 1929). Our emphasis on a contextually rich, authentic experience is directly supported by these perspectives. The contextually rich learning environment is considered authentic because it encourages participation in realistic activities. Knowledge anchored in relevant contexts enables learners to explore as a scientist to reveal why, when, and how knowledge is used (Cognition and Technology Group at Vanderbilt 1992). This is an internally-mediated process and is founded on cognitive and psychological research such as metacognition and perceived self-efficacy (Salomon 1986), information-processing theory (Gagné 1985), short-term memory capacity (Miller 1956; Klatzky 1975), depth of processing (Craik and Lockhart 1972; Craik and Tulving 1975), elaboration (Anderson and Reder 1979), meaningfulness (Mayer 1984; 1989), and schemata (Anderson et al. 1978). The psychological and constructivist-situated perspectives are supported by our authentic learning contexts, which facilitates student-centeredness. The premise for many contemporary student-centered learning environments emphasizes concrete experiences that serve as catalysts for constructing individual meaning (Hannafin et al. 1997). We have shown that the authenticity of the learning environment is critical to achieving student centred learning. Vygotsky (1978) refers to this authentic learning environment as the "zone of proximal development", which is where the student interacts in ways not possible when independent of the environment (Belmont 1989; Salomon et al. 1989). At the University of Guelph, our students acknowledged that the authentic mechanism increased their awareness of the knowledge construction process. Evolving an understanding of the learning process has been termed 'reflexivity' (Cunningham 1987), which encourages students to reproduce thought processes intentionally without explicit external prompting (Scardamalia et al. 1989). This is one of the goals of student-centered learning.

A University education should enable independent learning, not simply knowledge transmission. Bloom's taxonomy (Bloom 1956) classifies educational objectives into three domains: cognitive, affective, and psychomotor. Traditionally, educators have spent the majority of their time teaching students what they must know, rather than encouraging students to ask why they must know it. Research on neglecting effective outcomes has shown that it actually reduces learning and retention (Ringness 1975; Thompson and Mintzes 2002; Williams 2003). By reducing the focus on the facts and encouraging students explore the uncertainty of knowledge, we will be instilling the habits of scientific inquiry. Scientists explore in various ways in order to build knowledge and understanding. Is this not how we should be teaching our students who are aspiring to be scientists? Scientists emphasize that objects or concepts under study should be experienced rather than being told about them. The student centred experience enables the learner to remodel and revise ongoing theories in a manner that makes sense to them. If learners spend time immersed in a problem they will encounter intricacies and subtleties that are of interest, enabling them to explore and progress from just knowing to understanding (Papert, 1993; Bolin et al 2005). We need to develop educational interactions and experiences that best engage students in the philosophy of self-reliant learning.

Conclusion

We suggest that authentic learning experiences will directly engage students through intrinsic inquiry where a student takes ownership in the products of their education. The authentic mechanism may be effective in engaging student centred learning objectives, which have been historically difficult to implement. Current computer assisted learning environments may integrate authentic learning mechanisms in order to enhance the effectiveness of these learning models. This authentic learning mechanism has been implemented in a variety of academic institutions. Glendinning (2005) gives several successful and creative examples for high schools. There are also examples of authentic learning projects in museums (Metz 2005), which could be used in both elementary and secondary schools. Our local Royal Botanical Garden, in Hamilton Ontario has an authentic learning program where elementary students learn about wetland ecology by actively taking part in a restoration project. These experiences can provide meaningful knowledge for students and sometimes shape their life-long goals. In addition, the authentic learning mechanism will produce a future generation of individuals of critical thinkers who will make better decisions in all aspects of their lives, which in turn will eventually benefit society and humanity as a whole.

Acknowledgments

This research was supported by the Department of Integrative Biology and College of Biological Sciences at the University of Guelph. We would like to acknowledge Candice Newmaster and Aron Fazekas for thier editorial support and Trevor Holmes from Teaching Support Services who provided intellectual stimuli and critical background literature for our research. Finally we would like to thank all of the students who participated in this study and provided many comments within our surveys.

Table 1: Questions and Statements from the Course Surveys

1	*Was this project interesting?*
2	*Did you feel engaged in the project?*
3	*Was the experience beneficial to you?*
4	*Was the topic important to you?*
5	*Was the approach important to you?*
6	*I am learning about how to learn*
7	*The course challenged you intellectually*
8	*You were interested in learning the course material*
9	*Made a significant contribution to your overall personal learning objectives*
10	*Have you become more competent in this area due to this project?*

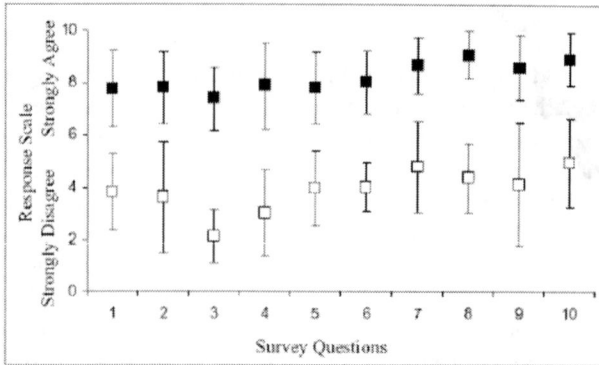

Figure 1: Response of 490 Students to a Survey of 10 Questions Listed in Table 1. Note that the Dark Boxes Represent the Response Mean and SD for Surveys with the Authentic Mechanism and that the White Boxes are the Response Means and SD without the Authentic Mechanism

References

Alper, L., Fendel, D., Fraser, S., and Resek, D. 1996. Problem-based mathematics: Not just for the college-bound. Educational Leadership. 53(8): 18–21.

Anderson, J.R., and Reder, L.M. 1979. An elaborate processing explanation of depth of processing. In L.S. Cermak and F.I.M. Crake (Eds.), Levels of Processing in Human Memory. Hillsdale, NJ. Lawrence Erlbaum Associates.

Anderson, R., Spiro, R., and Anderson, M. 1978. Schemata as scaffolding for the representation of connected discourse. American Educational Research Journal. 15: 433–440.

APA. 1992. Learner-Centered Psychological Principles: Guidelines for School Redesign and Reform. (2nd ed.). Washington, DC. American Psychological Association.

Bandura, A. 1982. Self-efficacy mechanism in human agency. American Psychologist. 37: 122–147.

Barab, S., and Landa, A. 1997. Designing effective interdisciplinary anchors. Educational Leadership. 54(6): 52–55.

Barr, R., and Tagg, J. 1995. From teaching to learning: a paradigm for undergraduate education. Change. 27(6): 13–25.

Bednar, A., Cunningham, D., Duffy, T., and Perry, J. 1992. Theory into practice: How do we link? In T. Duffy and D. Jonassen (Eds.), Constructivism and the technology of instruction: A conversation. Hillsdale, NJ. Lawrence Erlbaum Associates.

Belmont, J. 1989. Cognitive strategies and strategic learning. American Psychologist. 37: 117-121.

Biddulph M., and Adey, K. 2004. Pupil Perceptions of effective teaching and subject relevance in history and geography at Key Stage 3. Research in Education. 71: 1–8.

Bloom, B.S. (Ed.). 1956. Taxonomy of educational objectives: The classification of educational goals. New York. McKay.

Bloom, B.S., Madaus, G.F., and Hastings, J.T. 1981. Evaluation to improve learning. New York. McGraw-Hill.

Bolin, A.U., Khramtsova, I., and Saarnio, D. 2005. Using Student Journals to Stimulate Authentic Learning: Balancing Bloom's Cognitive and Affective Domains. Teaching of Psychology. 32(3): 154–159.

Boud, D., Cohen, R., and Walker, D. 1991. Using Expereince for Learning. The Society for Research into Higher Education. SRHE and Open University Press Bristol, PA.

Brown, A. 1981. Metacognition: The development of selective attention strategies for learning from texts. In M.L. Kamil (Ed.), Directions in reading: research and instruction. Washington, DC. The National Reading Conference.

Brown, J.S., Collins, A., and Duguid, P. 1989. Situated Cognition and the Culture of Learning. Educational Researcher. 18(1): 32–42.

Brush, T., and Saye, J. 2000. Implementation and Evaluation of a Student-Centered Learning Unit: A Case Study. Educational Technology, Research and Development. 48(3): 79–100.

Brush, T., and Saye, J. 2001. The Use of Embedded Scaffolds with Hypermedia-Supported Student-Centered Learning. Journal of Educational Multimedia and Hypermedia. 10(4): 333–356.

Cameron, B.J. 2003. Active Learning. Society for teaching Learning and Higher education. STHLE Green Guide No. 2. Halifax, Nova Scotia.

Cognition and Technology Group at Vanderbilt. 1991. Technology and the design of generative learning environments. Educational Technology. 31(5):34–40.

Cognition and Technology Group at Vanderbilt. 1992. Emerging technologies, ISD, and learning environments: Critical perspectives. Educational Technology Research and Development. 40(1): 65–80.

Collins, A., Brown, J.S., and Newman, S. 1989. Cognitive apprenticeship: Teaching the crafts of reading, writing, and mathematics, In L.B. Resnick (Ed.), Knowing, Learning and Instruction (pp. 453–494). Hillsdale, NJ. Lawrence Erlbaum Associates.

Collins, A., Brown, J.S., and Holum, A. 1991. Cognitive apprenticeship: making thinking visible. American Educator 15(3): 1–18.

Craik, F.I.M., and Lockhart, R.S. 1972. Levels of processing: A framework for memory research. Journal of Verbal Learning and Verbal Behavior. 11: 671–684.

Craik, F.I.M., and Tulving, E. 1975. Depth of processing and the retention of words in episodic memory. Journal of Experimental Psychology: General. 104: 268–294.

Cunningham, D.J. 1987. Outline of an education semiotic. The American Journal of Semiotics. 5(2): 201–216.

Darabi, A.A. 2005. Application of Cognitive Apprenticeship Model to a Graduate Course in Performance System Analysis: A Case Study. Educational Technology, Research and Development. 53(1): 49–61.

Dewey, J. 1933. How We Think. Boston. Heath.

Dewey, J. 1938. Experience and Education. New York. Collier Macmillan.

Edwards, R., and Sutton, A. 1991. A practical approach to student-centred learning. British Journal of Educational Technology. 23 (1): 4–20.

Gagné, R. 1985. The Conditions of Learning (4th ed.). New York. Holt, Rhinehart, and Winston.

Gallagher, S.A., and Stepien, W.J. 1996. Content acquisition in problem-based learning: Depth verses breadth in American Studies. Journal for the Education of the Gifted. 19(3): 257–275.

Glasgow, N. 1997. New curriculum for new times: A guide to student-centered, problem-based learning. Thousand Oaks, CA. Corwin.

Glendinning, M. 2005. Digging Into History: Authentic Learning through Archeology. The History Teacher. 38(2): 209–223.

Grant, M.M. 2003. Finding Your Place in a Student-Centered Classroom as a Teacher-Facilitator. The Agricultural Education Magazine. 76(2): 18–19.

Graue, M.E. 1993. Integrating theory and practice through instructional assessment. Educational Assessment. 1(4): 283–309.

Hannafin, M., Hall, C., Land, S., and Hill, J. 1994. Learning in open-ended environments: Assumptions, methods, and implications. Educational Technology 34: 48–55.

Hannafin, M., Hill, J., and Land, S. 1997. Student-centered learning and interactive multimedia: Status, issues, and implication. Contemporary Education. 68(2): 94–99.

Hannafin, M., and Land, S. 1997. The Foundations and assumptions of technology-enhanced student-centered learning environments. Instructional Science. 25: 167–202.

Hannifin, M., Land, S., and Oliver, K. 1999. Open learning environments: Foundations, methods, and models. In C. Reigeluth (Ed.), Insturctional design theories and models (Vol. II). Mahway, NJ. Erlbaum.

Johnson, D.W., and Johnson, R.T. 1991. Learning together and alone. Englewood Cliffs, NJ. Prentice Hall.

Jonassen, D. 1991. Objectivism versus constructivism: Do we need a new philosophical paradigm? Educational Technology Research and Development. 39: 5–14.

Kennedy, L. M., and Tipps, S. 1997. Guiding childrens' learning of mathematics, 8th ed. Belmont, CA. Wadsworth.

Klatzky, R. 1975. Human Memory: Structures and Processes. San Francisco. Freeman.

Klenowski, V. 1995. Student self-evaluation processes in student-centered teaching and learning contexts of Australia and England. Assessment in Education: Principles, Policy, and Practice. 2(2): 145–163.

Kolb, D. 1984. Experiential learning—experience as the source of learning and development. Prentice-Hall, NJ.

Lave, J., and Wenger, E. 1991. Situated Learning. Legitimate Peripheral Participation. New York. Cambridge.

Lepper, M.R., and Greene, D. 1979. The Hidden Costs of Reward. Hillsdale, NJ. Lawrence Erlbaum Associates.

Levin, J.A. 1982. Microcomputer Communication Networks for Education. The Quarterly Newsletter of the Laboratory of Comparative Human Cognition. 4(2): 2-13.

Linn, M., and Muilenburg, L. 1996. Creating lifelong science learners: What models form a firm foundation? Educational Researcher. 25(5): 18–24.

Malone, T. 1981. Toward a Theory of Intrinsically Motivating Instruction. Cognitive Science. 4: 333–369.

Mayer, R.E. 1984. Aids to text comprehension. Educational Psychologist. 19: 30–42.

Mayer, R.E. 1989. Models for understanding. Review of Educational Research. 59: 43–64.

McCaslin, M., and Good, T. 1992. Compliant cognition: The misalliance of management and instructional goals in current school reform. Educational Researcher. 21(3): 4–17.

McCombs, B., and Whisler, J.S. 1997. The learner-centered classroom and school: Strategies for increasing student motivation and achievement. San Francisco. Jossey-Bass.

Meyers, C., and Jones, T.B. 1993. Promoting active learning: Strategies for the college class-room. San Fancisco. Jossey-Bass.

Metz, D. 2005. Field Based Learning in Science: Animating a museum experience. Teaching Education. 16(2): 165–173.

Miller, G. 1956. Information and memory. Scientific American. 8: 28–32.

National Science Teachers' Association. 1993. NSTA Standards for Science Teacher Preparation: A NSTA Position Statement. Washington, DC. National Science Teachers'Association.

Palincsar, A.S., 1986. Metacognitive strategy instruction. Exceptional Children. 53(2): 118–124.

Palincsar, A.S., and Brown, A.L. 1984. Reciprocal Teaching of Comprehension-fostering and Monitoring Activities. Cognition and Instruction. 1:117–175.

Papert, S. 1993. Mindstorms. New York. Basic Books, Inc.

Pederson, S., and Liu, M. 2003. Teachers' Beliefs about Issues in the Implementation of a Student-Centered Learning Environment. Educational Technology, Research and Development. 51(2): 57–76.

Pedersen, S., and Williams, D. 2004. A Comparison of Assessment Practices and Their Effects on Learning and Motivation in a Student-Centered Learning Environment. Journal of Educational Multimedia and Hypermedia. 13(3): 283–306.

Perkins, D. 1991. Technology meets constructivism: Do they make a marriage? Educational Technology. 31(5): 18–23.

Perkins, D., and Salomon, G. 1989. Are cognitive skills context-bound? Educational Researcher. 18(1): 16–25.

Piaget, J. 1952. The Origins of Intelligence in Children. New York. International University Press.

Renzulli, J.S., Gentry, M., and Reis, S.M. 2004. A Time and a Place for Authentic Learning. Educational Leadership. 62(1): 73–77.

Ringness, T.A. 1975. The affective domain in education. Boston. Little Brown.

Roth, W.M., and Roychoudhury, A. 1993. The development of science process skills in authentic contexts. Journal in Research in Science Teaching. 30(2): 127–152.

Salomon, G. 1979. Interaction of Media, Cognition, and Learning. San Francisco. Jossey-Bass.

Salomon, G. 1986. Information technologies: What you see is not (always) what you get. Educational Psychologist. 20: 207–216.

Salomon, G., Globerson, T. and Guterman, E. 1989. The computer as a zone of proximal development: Internalizing reading-related metacognitions from a reading partner. Journal of Educational Psychology. 81(4): 620–627.

Savery, J.R., and Duffy, T.M. 1995. Problem-based learning: An instructional model and its constructivist framework. Educational Technology. 35(5): 31–38.

Scardamalia, M., Bereiter, C., McLean, R., Swallow, J., and Woodruff, E. 1989. Computer supported intentional learning environments. Journal of Educational Computing Research. 5: 51–68.

Scott, J., Buchanan, J., and Haigh, N. 1997. Reflections on student-centered learning in a large class setting. British Journal of Educational Technology. 28(1): 19–30.

Shepard, L.A. 2000. The role of assessment in a learning culture. Educational Researcher. 29(7): 4–14.

Shepard, L.A., and Bliem, C.L. 1995. Parents' thinking about standardized tests and performance assessments. Educational Researcher. 24: 25–32

Slunt, K.M., and Giancarlo, L.C. 2004. Student-Centered Learning: A Comparison of Two Different Methods of Instruction. Journal of Chemical Education. 81(7): 985–988.

Stiggens, R.J. 1997. Student-centered classroom assessment. Upper Saddle River, NJ. Merrill.

Stiggins, R.J. 1999. Assessment, student confidence, and school success. Phi Delta Kappan. 81(3): 191–198.

Thompson, T.L., and Mintzes, J.J. 2002. Cognitive structure and the affective domain: On knowing and feeling in biology. International Journal of Science Education. 24: 645–660.

Tichenor, M.S., and Jewell, M.J. 2001. Using E-Mail to Write about Math. The Educational Forum. 65: 300–308.

Volman, M. 2005. A variety of roles for a new type of teacher in Educational technology and the teaching profession. Teaching and Teacher Education. 21: 15–31.

Vygotsky, L. 1978. Mind in Society: The Development of Higher Psychological Processes. Cambridge, MA. Harvard University Press.

Wells, G. 1999. Dialogic Inquiry. Towards a sociocultural practice and theory of education. Cambridge. Cambridge University Press.

Whitehead, A.N. 1929. The Aims of Education. New York. MacMillan.

Wiggins, G. 1989. A true test: Toward more authentic and equitable assessment. Phi Delta Kappan. 70: 703–713.

Wilensky, U. 1991. Abstract meditations on the implications for mathematics education, In I. Harel and S. Papert (Eds.), Constructionism. Norwood, NJ. Ablex Publishing Corporation.

Williams, L. 2003. Including the affective domain. Teaching Elementary Physical Education. 14: 2–5.

Younge, M., and McNeese, M. 1995. A situated cognition approach to problem solving. In J. Flach, P. Hancock and K. Vicente (Eds.), The Ecology of Human-Machine Systems. Hillsdale, NJ. Lawrence Erlbaum Associates.

CPSIA information can be obtained at www.ICGtesting.com
Printed in the USA
LVOW071708240412

278951LV00004B/16/P